INFANT AND CHILD
IN THE CULTURE OF TODAY

INFANT AND CHILD
IN THE CULTURE OF TODAY

The Guidance of Development in Home and Nursery School

Arnold Gesell, M.D.
Former Director, Yale Clinic of Child Development

Frances L. Ilg, M.D.
Director Emeritus, Gesell Institute of Child Development

Louise Bates Ames, Ph.D.
Codirector, Gesell Institute of Child Development

In collaboration with
Janet Learned Rodell, Ph.D.
Former Principal, Gesell Guidance Nursery School

REVISED EDITION

JASON ARONSON INC.
Northvale, New Jersey
London

THE MASTER WORK SERIES

First softcover edition 1995

Library of Congress Cataloging-in-Publication Data

Gesell, Arnold, 1880–1961.
    Infant and child in the culture of today : the guidance of
development in home and nursery school / by Arnold Gesell, Frances
L. Ilg, and Louise Bates Ames, in collaboration with Janet Learned
Rodell.
      p.   cm.
    Originally published: New York ; London : Harper & Brothers,
1943. With new introd.
    Includes bibliographical references (p.) and index.
    ISBN 1-56821-567-3
    1. Child psychology. 2. Infant psychology. 3. Child development.
4. Child psychology. I. Ilg, Frances Lillian, 1902-1981. II. Ames,
Louise Bates. III. Rodell, Janet Learned. IV. Title.
BF721.G49   1995
155.4 – dc20
                                     95-17202

Manufactured in the United States of America. Jason Aronson Inc. offers books and cassettes. For information and catalog write to Jason Aronson Inc., 230 Livingston Street, Northvale, New Jersey 07647.

CONTENTS

PART THREE   THE GUIDANCE OF GROWTH

PART FOUR   THE NURSERY SCHOOL

PREFACE TO THE NEW EDITION

Except for the Gesell norms of child development, it seems quite possible that *Infant and Child in the Culture of Today*, first published by Harper in 1943, has been our most important and influential contribution.

One of the strongest supporters of the then, as now, much attacked position that "environmental factors modulate and inflect but *do not determine behavior*," this book maintains that every child is an individual, an individual whose behavior is to a very large extent biologically determined.

It was Dr. Frances L. Ilg who introduced the notion that not only was every person an individual but also every age level as well had its own individuality. That is, a three-year-old is not merely older, larger, and more capable than a two-year-old but in many ways has a quite different kind of individuality.

She, and we, offered the thesis that ages of equilibrium tend to alternate with ages of disequilibrium, inwardized ages with ages of outwardized behavior. This way of thinking has led to the expectation that the often calm and well equilibrated behavior of the two-year-old, for instance, frequently gives way as time progresses to the often obstinate, contrary, and oppositional behavior characteristic of the two-and-a-half-year-old. And so on, for other pairs of ages.

In fact, our own book and this theory has led to the phrase "the terrible twos," so commonly used by parents who may never have read our books. (We ourselves do not designate any age as "terrible," and actually it is closer to two-and-a-half than to two that easygoing and comfortable behavior turns difficult.)

Though the child's individuality, and most especially a discussion of everyday home behaviors such as eating, sleeping, and elimination had been covered in brief in a single chapter of a just-earlier book, *The First Five Years of Life*, published by Dr. Gesell and staff in 1940, that book still, like earlier books, dealt primarily with the infant's and child's response to the by then well-known Gesell Development Test situations. *Infant and Child* was the first of our books to focus on the kinds of home behavior of primary interest to parents.

Partly in order to emphasize that the often rather striking and even startling changes in behavior from one age to the immediately following age were not simply an individual or one-time thing, in this book we covered the entire period from birth to five years.

The wide public acceptance of this book, and the fact that preliminary research was already demonstrating that similar changes in individuality or personality seemed to be continuing in the ages following five, led us to write two more books: *The Child from Five to Ten* and *Youth: The Years from Ten to Sixteen.*

Though to us changes in behavior from year to year seemed quite as interesting as the specific behaviors that might be expected at any one given age, it turned out that not all parents agreed. Many made it known to us that all they wanted to know about at any given time was what to expect at their child's own exact age—not what had happened the year before or what might be expected to happen the following year.

And so was born our subsequent series, *Your One-Year-Old, Your Two-Year-Old, Your Three-Year-Old*, and so on, books that described only one year at a time.

Nevertheless, these books did not entirely satisfy an audience that, like us, was interested in an entire sweep of behavior. This group included students and child specialists as well as those parents who perhaps took a more long range point of view.

Infant and Child also included what we considered valuable information, provided by Janet Learned, Director of our Nursery School, as to kinds of behavior that could be expected of nursery school children at different ages as well as advice useful to individuals who run nursery schools and/or day care centers.

Twenty-five years after the original publication of *Infant and Child*, we published a revised edition. Information provided in this revision about the actual behavior of children at the various ages is not markedly different from that in the first edition. However, an entire age level—three-and-a-half years—not included originally, was added.

Also, since some considered Dr. Gesell's admittedly rather elegant style of writing a bit overelegant for modern readers, this style was somewhat modified. All material about nursery school behavior and techniques, additionally, was grouped as a separate section at the end of the book instead of being included in each age chapter.

Out of deference to the original senior author, Arnold Gesell, Dr. Ilg preferred to keep her original treatment of such practical functions as eating, sleeping, and elimination in his original somewhat theoretical style, rather than give specific practical advice to parents as to how to deal with these functions.

On the whole, this 1974 version of our 1943 book differed more in format than in context from the original version.

Since it was in *Infant and Child* that we presented for the first time the notion that ages of the child's life as well as individuals themselves each had their own uniqueness or personality—a concept now taken for granted by most people who deal with children—we are gratified that the present publisher, Jason Aronson, is giving us the opportunity of keeping this material in print.

Louise Bates Ames, Ph.D.
Co-founder, Gesell Institute

PREFACE TO THE REVISED EDITION

Thirty years have slipped by since the publication of the original edition of *Infant and Child in the Culture of Today,* and 300,000 copies have been distributed. For the past ten years or more we have felt the impact of new cultural forces and have felt that our book should be revised. We hoped that some younger member of our staff would perhaps redo the entire study and bring it up to date. This possibility has not materialized.

It is you, the public, who have now inspired us to undertake the revision ourselves. Our fairly stable yearly sales were suddenly doubled from 1970 to 1971. This was, we conjecture, an expression of an increased interest of people in general in infancy and the early years. As we reviewed our original edition we found that much of the material appeared to be still valid, since the unfolding patterns of behavior remain the same as in generations past. It is the way the environment responds to these growth patterns that changes from generation to generation.

"Gesell and Ilg's *Infant and Child in the Culture of Today* remains a useful book for parents. Its descriptions of behavior at the changing ages are still valid. But in places its language is old-fashioned, almost quaint," commented a recent critic. This long-overdue revision will, therefore, retain its descriptions of behavior, which we, too, believe still to be valid, and we shall attempt to remedy any quaintness of phrase.

All in all, children today do seem to be the same children we have always known. Their behavior develops and unfolds in the same predictable, patterned pathways it has always followed. Only the grownups seem to change, and they, happily, seem to be changing for the better in their increased concern, their more sympathetic and understanding approach to those children they love. We shall discuss some of the more important of these changes.

It will be evident from the detailed character of the contents that this book could have been written only as a cooperative undertaking. It is the outgrowth of many years of practical experience with normal, near normal, and problem children. The experience was correlated with a systematic program of research under the auspices of the Clinic of Child Development of the School of Medicine, Yale University. The original edition of this book was completed while the authors were still at Yale. At the time of Dr. Gesell's retirement from Yale in 1950, the other three authors founded the Gesell Institute of Child Development in his honor. Work on this revised edition has been carried out at the Gesell Institute.

In preparation for the writing of this book, infants and young children were studied with parental cooperation in their homes, at Well Baby Conferences, and in our Guidance Nursery.

The children studied came from homes of varying socioeconomic status in New England. A special group of fourteen Swedish infants was intensively studied by Dr. Ilg in 1936–37 while she was in residence in Stockholm. The children have in general been above an average level of intelligence. The parents of all these children have assisted us with a high order of cooperation. We have learned much from them as well as from the children.

Dr. Catherine S. Amatruda, Assistant Professor of Child Development, read the original manuscript in part and gave us the benefit of valuable criticism. Dr. Amatruda coauthored a volume on *Developmental Diagnosis: Normal and Abnormal Child Development*, published by Paul B. Hoeber, Inc. The J. B. Lippincott Company has kindly permitted certain references to an earlier publication by Gesell and Ilg entitled *Feeding Behavior of Infants: A Pediatric Approach to the Mental Hygiene of Early Life*. The present volume is in many ways a further development of these earlier studies.

We are most fundamentally indebted to the Rockefeller Foundation, which over a period of years gave generous long-range support to the systematic investigations that underlie the present work. Extremely timely support of the Carnegie Corporation of New York made completion of the earlier edition possible.

In our original preface, we emphasized the need of an adequate philosophy of child development to shape our social planning and our practices in home and school. The concept of democracy, we feel, can embrace all aspects of everyday life. The changes we have observed in the past thirty years are the result of democracy at work. It may be bumbling and uncertain at times, but like the growth of the individual child, it is ever moving forward.

The concept of growth has much in common with the ideology of democracy. In both Part Two and Part Four we have documented in concrete detail the growth characteristics of the early years, at home and at school, with special reference to the factors of maturity that must determine our whole outlook upon the nature and needs of the individual child. These growth characteristics are so fundamental that not even the most modern culture can supersede them. A culture is refined through a discriminating recognition of these characteristics. The relationship between a child and his culture should be highly reciprocal.

This new edition of our book is more a reorganization than a compilation of entirely new material. Part One includes the greatest changes, revealing our own growth in concepts of the cycles of development and the expressions of individuality. It also includes a rather detailed discussion of the many cultural changes which both underlie and influence our treatment of our children and our ways of thinking about them.

In Part Two the age level of three and a half has been added to the other ages as a special and very important nodal age. Parents looking for specific help and information about their child's behavior may wish to consult Part Two first and then return to the more theoretical material provided in Part One.

With the increase of society's interest in the life of the young child in group situations, we have felt the need to gather all of our nursery school material, originally included in the several appropriate age chapters, into a separate section, and have presented it as Part Four of this book. Even though we do not recommend formal nursery schools until three years of age, we have included our previous experiences with eighteen-monthers, two-, and two-and-a-half-year-olds, to show not only what the child is like at these early important ages but also why he may not yet be ready for a formalized group experience. Anyone planning for a two-to-two-and-a-half-year-old group might think twice after reading our descriptions.

The effectiveness of our first edition is suggested by the fact that today the difficult, extreme characteristics of the typical two-and-a-half-year-old as described by us have now become immortalized in the everyday expression "the terrible twos," and that four-year-olds are customarily characterized as "out of bounds" by others as well as ourselves. The basic thesis of this book—that behavior changes with age in a patterned, predictable manner—is now well accepted by most experienced parents and others who deal professionally with preschoolers.

The new mother or father has much to learn, many interesting and important things about child behavior that he will need to discover if he or she is to be an effective parent. We hope that this revision, like our original edition, can help in this discovery.

It is also our hope that parents of today may find as much information and support in this revised edition as those many earlier parents both in this country and abroad who have assured us, of its original, "Your book has helped so very much. Now I know that my child is normal."

Frances L. Ilg, M.D.
Louise Bates Ames, Ph.D.

New Haven, Connecticut
December, 1972

GROWTH AND CULTURE

A SALUTE TO THE LATE ARNOLD GESELL

It is with a certain nostalgia that we, the living authors, embark on the revision of this book. Way back in the early forties, it suffered a number of abortive beginnings. But in time we came to know it was a healthy and growing fetus eventually demanding to be born. The birth pangs were many and real, but somehow the four authors were able to surmount their differences. In the end each author was allowed to include his or her own special experience and research findings. But without Dr. Gesell's guiding concept that "behavior grows and is patterned" we could not have completed the study.

These early chapters in Part One remind us who are left how fortunate was our lot. Dr. Gesell gave meaning and purpose to everything we thought and did. He brought forth from our minds ideas we didn't even know were there. He taught us constantly through his wisdom and encouraged a reexamination of the simple day-to-day happenings in the life of the child.

We would wish to let much of the material in these early chapters stand as a tribute to him. He was a master both of thought and of bookmaking. He saw the whole as an artist does, and what he wrote thirty years ago still has strong relevance. We wish to comment on some of his statements and to show how pertinent they are even for today.

Dr. Gesell speaks of the child as being "never ready until the nervous system is ready." He then elaborates this concept through the example of the development of eyes and hands in the infant's successive age responses to a few test objects. We accept these manifestations of growth in infancy as expressions of the laws of nature. We watch growth unfold in infancy with supportive and patient interest.

But as soon as the child shows more response to teaching in the preschool and kindergarten years, we are often not content to wait until his nervous system is ready. We all too often follow our own conception of whatever we think the child should be doing at a certain chronological age. We forget that a child's nervous system speaks through his maturational age, which can be evident to us if we will just take the time to look. If our research on school readiness is revealing that 50 percent of our children are unable to come up to expectation, then we are demanding far too much from many children's nervous systems. The lifetime work of Jean Piaget substantiates our own findings. Piaget warns us that no matter how fast the pace of a child may be, all children must pass through the same phases of understanding. Skipping or reversing those phases poses a risk to the child's development.

Dr. Gesell emphasizes that later chapters of this book will reduce the generalities offered in the earliest chapters "to concrete formulations, and will show how the culture, embodied in parent and teacher, must meet the limitations of immaturity." In this context, by immaturity he seemed to mean merely youngness. As we now use the term, we tend to mean *young for one's age*. We do not use the word in a derogatory way, and we emphasize that even if a child is one or two months or, at later ages, one or two years behind maturational expectancy, we should meet him with a belief in where he is, and should provide an environment to which he can respond comfortably and in which he can be allowed to grow at his own rate.

These are only a few of the thoughts generated by Dr. Gesell that stand even more strongly today than thirty years ago. We wish to take this opportunity to salute our mentor, Arnold Gesell, in gratitude for all the work accomplished with him, and for the release of the many ideas that have kept us functioning and will hopefully continue to keep us functioning for some time to come, as an institute bearing his name.

F. L. I.

L. B. A.

CHAPTER 1

HOW THE MIND GROWS

Mind Manifests Itself

"Mind manifests itself" was one of Dr. Gesell's favorite sayings. He meant that almost anything an infant or child does is an example of his mind in action. Though psychologists today talk a lot about "cognitive behavior" and seem to equate this with things the young individual thinks of or says, much more than verbal behavior is actually involved.

Virtually anything the baby or preschooler does is an example of his mind in action. Mental growth, like physical growth, is a patterning process because the mind is essentially the sum total of a growing multitude of behavior patterns. A behavior pattern is simply a movement or action that has a more or less definite form. An eye blinks, a hand grasps an object, a head turns—these are examples of behavior patterns in which a part of the body reacts to some stimulus.

Or the whole body can react, as in sitting, standing, creeping, and walking. These, too, are behavior patterns. A baby lying in his crib follows a dangling toy with his eyes: eye following is a behavior pattern. He extends his arms and then closes in on the dangling toy

---

Readers interested in finding out exactly what the infant or child may do, and in the more practical aspects of child behavior, may wish to turn directly to Part Two of this book, and then perhaps return to the more theoretical material in Part One later on.

with both hands, seizes it, puts it to his mouth: that is a more complex behavior pattern, one which shows that the baby's mind is indeed growing, changing and elaborating its forms of behavior with increasing maturity.

The subject matter of this book is the sum of all behavior patterns observable at any given age. What parents or others concerned with child behavior need to know is how basic behavior patterns—whether the behavior is merely something basic such as eating, sleeping, or elimination, or is an expression of more complicated interpersonal behavior such as reaction to mother or father or others—change with age. One needs to know what can be expected at all the different age levels, from birth on.

Behavior has form or shape just as physical things have shape. For practical purposes we need not make a sharp distinction between physical patterns and behavior patterns—between body and behavior. The baby is a unitary organism, and from the beginning he grows as a single unit. His body grows in a patterned, predictable way just as his mind grows. Even in the embryonic period, months before birth, living materials of this organism order themselves into patterned structures.

In due time impulses will pass through nerve fibers into muscle fibers to bring about movements. Even these earliest movements will have a certain degree of pattern. The growing mind consists of countless patterns of behavior made possible by the progressive organization of the nervous system.

All growth, whether physical or mental, implies organization. Consider, for example, the early growth of eyes and hands. It is of particular interest because it plays an extremely important part in the mental life of infant and child. The eyes are so important that nature hastens to fashion them as early as the fifth week of the prenatal period.

Shortly after birth, the infant looks at objects long before he can touch them. Looking is an active response. It is not mere sensory impression; it requires motor control. The baby must hold his eyes in position or move them from point to point in order to see. This control is accomplished through twelve tiny muscles (six for each eye), which are attached to the eyeball and the eye socket. They are so tiny that they weigh only a fraction of an ounce. All twelve of them would easily go into a thimble, but they are among the most indispensable muscles in the baby's entire body. With them he fixates his visual attention; with them he scans his surroundings; with them he inspects an object which he holds in his hands.

Vision is so fundamental in the growth of the mind that the baby takes hold of the physical world with his eyes long before he takes hold with his hands. Merely looking at objects is one aspect of the mind in action. The eyes assume the lead in the patterning of behavior. But the infant cannot achieve full acquaintance with things through his eyes alone. He must touch them with his hands as well; feel their impact in his palm; and move his fingers over their surfaces and edges. He must move his hands to manipulate, just as he must move his eyes to inspect. The nerve cells that determine and direct his hand movements are located in the spinal cord and the brain.

The growth of the mind is profoundly and inseparably bound up with the growth of the nervous system. This growth begins even in fetal life. Five months before the baby is born all the nerve cells he will ever possess have already been formed, and many of them are prepared to function in an orderly way. At this time the fetus makes movements of arms and legs so vigorous that they can be seen and felt through the mother's abdominal wall (quickening); the eyelids can wink; the eyeballs can roll; the hands can clasp; the mouth can open and close; the throat can swallow; the chest makes rhythmic movements in preparation for the event of birth, when the breath of postnatal life will rush into the lungs. All child development is like that; it proceeds with reference to the future. When the time comes, the child is normally ready for what he may need to do at that time. *And he is never ready until his nervous system is ready.*

How does the mind grow? It grows *like* the nervous system; it grows *with* the nervous system. Growth is a patterning process. It produces patterned changes in the nerve cells; it produces corresponding changes in patterns of behavior.

The baby has a psychology even during the earliest months, when he cannot as yet balance his head on his shoulders. But this ability, too, is just around the corner.

It may as well be pointed out here that no one taught the baby his progressive series of eye-hand behaviors. He scarcely taught himself. He comes into his increasing powers primarily through intrinsic growth forces which change the inmost architecture of his nervous system. Of course, he needs an environment in which to deploy his powers, and a favorable environment ensures a favorable realization of his growth potentialities. But it must be kept in mind that *environmental factors support, inflect, and modify but they do not generate the progressions of development.* The sequences, the progressions come from within the organism.

The mind, so far as we can fathom it by direct observation, is an expression of the organization of protoplasm, manifested in visible patterns of behavior. The growth of the child's mind is not altogether unlike the growth of a plant. Of itself it brings forth its tokens; it follows inborn sequence.

The World of Things

Grown adults take time and space for granted; not so the growing baby. The infant is not a scientist, yet he must master the very first principles on which all physical science is based. His mind is constantly taking first steps into the physical universe from the moment of birth. He has to acquire an appreciation of spatial *here* and *there* and temporal *now* and *then* by the gradual process of development. Perceptions are complicated behavior patterns based on reactions to things. He is not born with full-fledged perceptions; *they grow.* They grow with experience, and with the advancing maturity of his sensory, motor, and correlating nerve cells.

It has been picturesquely suggested that to the newborn baby the world is a "big, blooming, buzzing confusion." The accuracy of this characterization may be questioned. Most probably, the young baby at first senses the visible world in fugitive and fluctuating blotches against a neutral background. Sounds may likewise be heard as shreds of wavering distinctness against a neutral background of silence or of continuous undertone. Doubtless he feels the pressure of his six- or seven-pound weight as he lies on his back. Perhaps this island of pressure sensation is at the very core of his vague and intermittent sense of self. He also feels from time to time the vigorous movements that he makes with mouth, arms, and legs. Doubtless he has delightful moments of subjectivity at the end of a repleting meal, and he has episodes of distress from hunger or cold. Such experiences in association with strivings impart vividness to the early mental life of the baby, even though the outer world is still almost without form.

It remains formless until he can give it shape with experience gained through his eyes and hands. He must first "learn" the art of wakefulness, and then he must "learn" to fasten his eyes on this object and that, and to unfasten them, too. He soon gives selective regard to the human face. He probably senses it as a pleasant bobbing blotch, suspended but not localized in space, interesting but undefined. He is still quite unsophisticated as to time and space, quite undiscriminating as to present and past, near and far. His present experiences are so discontinuous that it can scarcely be said that he lives in the present; for there is no present if there is no past or future.

Perceptions of time and space values are so complex that it will literally take the child years to perfect them. Just as his time experiences are at first discontinuous, so his appreciations of space are at first discontinuous: he senses merely the immediate space in which he is immersed; he does not sense its context. He is unaware of distance and depth. For him the visible world is a flat screen or a kaleidoscopic succession of flat screens. Not until he is about nine months old does he begin to probe into the beyond and the beneath. Slowly the relationship of container and contained dawns upon him. At that time he begins to thrust his fist intentfully into the hollow of an empty (or full!) cup. At that time also he "discovers" the third dimension. Immediate space loses its flatness; it takes on the perspectives of depth, hollow, solid. Through ceaseless manipulation of objects he penetrates further into the topography and the solid geometry of space—the relationship of *in* and *out, on* and *under, in front of, behind, beside.* Through his tireless locomotion, creeping, walking, and running, he builds up a sense of *here* and *over there,* of *near* and *far,* of *wall* and *corner,* of *indoors* and *outdoors.* He masters these elements of domestic geography through muscular experience. The sheer processes of development thrust him deeper into the manifold sectors of space.

The young child comprehends *under the bed* before he comprehends *under the chair;* and he is no longer a young child when he comprehends underness in the abstract. At first the relationships are concrete and specific, not general. Only by slow degrees does he master such place and position words as "up," "down," "where," "go away," "wall," "corner," "across the room," "across the street."

The sense of time undergoes the same gradualness of development. When a child is eighteen months old he begins to grasp the meaning of "now." Not until he is two years old or older does he comprehend "soon." He is learning to "wait." There is little use in telling younger children to wait, in order to delay their reactions. But after the age of two, many children can and do delay when you say, "Pretty soon." This shows, incidentally, that the appreciation of time and time words is dependent on motor capacity and motor self-control. The three-year-old begins to use the significant word "when," the temporal equivalent of the word "where." His sense of time has so matured that he uses the word itself, saying, "Is it time for orange juice?" He also uses the word "today." He understands when you say "not today." Somewhat later he uses the word "tomorrow." "Yesterday" comes later still. When he says "last night" he usually means anything that happened the previous day or even earlier. Time words, such as "morning," "after," "Tuesday," "week," "two o'clock," "year," emerge in the child's speech as he matures. They come in a more or less lawful developmental sequence. They are used in concrete situations long before they are used as abstract notions. At first they are applied on the correct occasions, but without accuracy. There is much dramatic pretense of telling time from a toy wrist watch at four years of age; but a child may be six years old before he can make a discriminating verbal distinction between morning and afternoon. Concepts of time (duration) are more difficult developmentally than concepts of space (size). The four-year-old, for example, is conscious that he is "bigger" than the three-year-old. Later he realizes also that he is "older."

The ability to perceive numbers shows the same slow advance as the sense of time. A six-month-old child is single-minded when he plays with a block. A nine-month-old child can hold and bring together two blocks and give attention to a third. At one year he manipulates several cubes one by one in a serial manner which is the motor rudiment of counting. At two years he distinguishes between one and many. At three years he has a fair command of "two" and is beginning to understand the simple word "both." At four years he can count three objects, pointing correctly. At five years he counts to ten, pointing correctly. He recites numbers in a series before he uses them intelligently.

At four years he can name at least one color, usually red. At five years he "knows" his colors. He names red, yellow, blue, green. Color is somewhat less advanced than texture. The varied adjectives that describe textures are acquired earlier: hard, soft, sticky, rough, gooshy, crumbly, smooth, etc. While he is a preschool child his vocabulary grows in a rather ordinary manner, keeping pace with the maturity of his experience. The child has to learn the meaning of words, by the same slow growth processes that pattern his perceptions of things.

Words also are things—peculiar things. Whether spoken, written, printed, or communicated by mouth, phone, or radio, they are both realities and symbols of realities. They are the expressions of desires and the tools of thought. Many young children believe that they think with their mouths, and there is a grain of truth in this confusion of thought with voice.

Time, space, number, form, texture, color, and causality—these are the chief elements in the world of things in which the child must find himself. We have shown that he acquires his command of these elements by slow degrees, first through his muscles of manipulation and locomotion, through eyes, hands, and feet. In this motor experience he lays the foundation for his later judgments and concepts. He does not even count to three until he has learned to pick up and release objects one by one with eyes and fingers. Mastery of form, likewise, comes through motor explorations and exploitations.

In the rearing and guidance of young children there is a tendency to rely too much on the supposed magic of words. Sometimes the adult thinks, naïvely, that if the word is uttered loudly enough and often enough it will finally penetrate. Words do not penetrate. They only register. And what they register in the child's mind is often grotesquely different from what they were intended to convey. Words, however, have genuine power in the guidance of children when they are skillfully used and adapted to the contents and the tempo of the child's mind. In chapters that follow we shall point out the kind of speech that the nursery school child and the prenursery child can comprehend—words that register and bring about response and release.

In the present chapter we have indicated the basis and nature of these immaturities. The mind is a growing multiplicity of reaction patterns that mirror the physical world in which the child is reared. It grows not unlike a plant.

Can We Speed Up Behavior?

Much time and scientific endeavor in the past twenty years have been devoted to efforts to improve or speed up infant behavior. However, so far no one has demonstrated that we can speed up any behavior substantially by things we do for and with the infant or child. Piaget goes so far as to call the question—Can we speed up behavior by early intervention?—*the American question.* His answer to this question, like our own, is that one cannot substantially speed up behavior or substantially influence the orderly development of behavior by self-conscious efforts.*

---

* We might mention here that, contrary to rumor, there is no basic disagreement between the Piaget and Gesell points of view. Both emphasize that behavior develops in a highly patterned, predictable way, influenced but not determined by environ-

Certainly parents in their homes should be as responsive as possible to their child or children. They should of course provide as warm, rich, and stimulating an environment as possible. But this should be done in the hope of helping every child to develop fully his basic, inherited potentials. It should not be done with a self-conscious emphasis on his so-called *cognitive development,* or in the false hope that one can substantially either speed up his development or make him more intelligent than nature originally intended.

Obviously the baby or child will find it difficult to look at things if there is little to see, to grasp if there is nothing to grasp, to respond socially if there are no social overtures. Parents should, and at least in many homes do, pay a good deal of attention to the new baby. They do, and should, see to it that he has things to look at, touch, handle, play with, respond to. When they do this they permit their baby to express the many abilities that he has or is developing.

But even without elaborate environmental stimulation, the well-endowed infant is *all* energy and enthusiasm and readiness to try the new. With merely the sights and sounds and objects and people in an ordinary comfortable and unself-conscious household, he finds plenty to respond to, hour after hour and day after day. His life is *all* discovery. And as he matures, little by little, in his inevitable ordinary way, every day if not every hour brings new adventures.

No research so far available has demonstrated that extra and special stimulation either increases the baby's inborn intelligence or speeds up the various stages of behavior. Much enthusiastic research is now being carried on in an effort to do both these things, and should it succeed we would be the first to applaud.

However, Dr. Peter H. Wolff of Harvard states clearly, and we agree, that "there is no evidence that any scientifically designed infant machines available today are superior to ordinary toys or household items as means for discovering the environment. There is no evidence

---

mental factors. The basic difference between the two is that Piaget primarily emphasizes cognitive development or thinking. Gesell maintained that "Mind manifests itself" and that nearly everything the boy or girl does gives a clue as to what is going on in his mind.

that systematic teaching by current methods will accelerate the infant's or young child's intellectual development significantly; no evidence that acceleration in the acquisition of specific sensorimotor skills augments the child's ultimate intellectual attainment."

So far as we know, enriching the child's environment and providing him with the fullest opportunities possible permits him to express himself at his very best, but it does not make him "better" or smarter or speedier than he was born to be.

Organism and Environment

All of this means that environment influences behavior but it does not determine behavior. As Dr. Gesell has phrased it, "The individual comes into his racial (and ancestral) inheritance through the processes of *maturation*. He comes into his social inheritance through processes of *acculturation*. The two processes operate and interact in close conjunction. Growth is a unifying concept which resolves the dualism of heredity and environment."

In other words, basic potential in every area is pretty much laid down genetically. But how the child uses his potential, what he turns out to be, is at all times, and obviously, influenced by what the environment provides.

This present volume describes chiefly what the growing child is like at different stages in his development, but on most pages of this book you will see him coming into contact with his environment. Main emphasis is given to the child, however, because until we know what the growing child himself is like, we are not in a position to evaluate the effect of environmental factors. If we did not know that the three-and-a-half-year-old tended to be a creature who fumbles and falls, totters and trembles, quite characteristically has trouble with his speech, hearing, and vision, finds himself commonly in emotional entanglement with his parents, we would be all too quick to think that something in the environment had caused some particular three-and-a-half-year-old to behave the way he does.

Understanding of normal age changes helps us to determine which things about the child's behavior, good or bad, have been caused by something somebody did to him, and which are simply expressions of normal behavior growth.

CHAPTER 2

THE CYCLE OF CHILD DEVELOPMENT

Some three billion years ago a fiery mass was probably hurled from the sun. Ever since, this mass, which is now our earthly home, has been revolving around its parent sun and has been spinning on its own soft axle. Year in, year out, day in, day out.

About a billion years ago the first simple forms of animal life appeared in the waters that bathed the earth. A million years ago, a dawn man walked upon the breast of the earth. A few thousand years ago the descendants of this ancient man began to name the seasons of the yearly cycle and the hours of the daily cycle. Only yesterday did man achieve an insight into his racial ancestry and the origins of his own life cycle.

This life cycle is vastly more complex than the orbits of earth and sun; but like the heavenly bodies, the human life cycle is governed by natural law. In surety and precision, the laws of development are comparable to those of gravitation.

Stages and Ages

The life cycle of a child begins with the fertilization of an egg cell. This almost microscopic particle undergoes prodigious developmental transformations. It becomes in swiftly moving sequence a living, palpitating embryo, a fetus, a neonate, an infant, a toddler, a preschool child, a schoolchild, an adolescent, an adult. In a biological sense the life cycle is already nearing completion when the individual is mature enough to produce germinal cells competent to perpetuate the species.

Psychological maturity, however, in a modern culture is a more advanced condition. It might be defined as a stage of personal maturity which is competent to undertake the responsibility of parenthood. This kind of maturity is long in the making. In a more primitive epoch, infants became adults early. Civilization prolongs the period of "infancy" and is itself dependent upon such prolongation.

Development takes time. It is a continuous process. Beginning with conception (the fertilization of the egg cell), it proceeds stage by stage in orderly sequence. Each stage represents a degree or level of maturity in the cycle of development. A stage is simply a passing moment, while development, like time, keeps marching on. This does not, however, prevent us from selecting significant moments in the developmental cycle to mark progressions toward maturity.

This is one reason why it has become a cultural custom to celebrate birthdays. Each anniversary marks one more revolution around the sun, but it also marks a higher level of maturity. It takes time to mature. We express the amount of time consumed by age. Age differences figure to an extraordinary degree in social practices and legislation. This is the scientific as well as cultural sanction for defining maturity stages in terms of calendar ages.

We recognize, of course, that the factor of individuality is so strong that no two children are exactly alike at a given age. But individual variations cling closely to a central trend because the sequences and ground plan of human growth are relatively stable characteristics. Study of hundreds of normal infants and young children has enabled us to ascertain the average age trends of behavior development. We think of behavior in terms of age, and we think of age in terms of behavior. For any selected age it is possible to sketch a portrait that delineates the behavior characteristics typical of the age. A series of such maturity portraits is presented in the behavior profiles of Chapters 8 to 20.

For the convenience of the reader, thirteen age levels are represented in these profiles, namely: four, sixteen, twenty-eight, forty weeks; twelve, fifteen, eighteen months; two, two and a half, three, three and a half, four, five years. The developmental changes that take place in the first five years are so swift and variegated that they cannot be taken in at a single glance.

The rate of child development in the first year is so fast that five age intervals are necessary to do justice to the psychological patterns and needs of the infant. In the second year the transformations are so great, and from a cultural standpoint so important, that special consideration is given to the ages of fifteen months and eighteen months. In the third and fourth years the intermediate ages of thirty months and forty-two months prove to be so significant that they need separate discussion.

This does not mean that development proceeds in a staircase manner or by installments. It is always fluent and continuous. The stage-by-stage treatment helps us to make comparisons of adjacent levels and to get a sense of the developmental flow. Without norms of maturity we cannot see the relativities in the patterns of growth. The cycle of child development eludes us unless we manage to envisage the bewildering pageantry of behavior in terms of stages and ages.

The organization of behavior begins long before birth, and the general direction of this organization is from head to foot, from proximal to distal segments. Lips and tongue lead, ears and eye muscles follow, then neck, shoulders, arms, hands, fingers, trunk, legs, feet.

In describing behavior, four fields are distinguished: (1) *motor behavior* (posture, locomotion, prehension, and postural sets); (2) *adaptive behavior* (capacity to perceive significant elements in a situation, and to use present and past experience to adapt to new situations); (3) *language behavior* (all forms of communications and comprehension by gestures, sounds, words); (4) *personal-social behavior* (personal reactions to other persons and to the social culture). Characteristic behavior in these four fields will be outlined in the behavior profiles that follow.

The first five years in the cycle of child development are the most fundamental and the most formative for the simple but sufficient reason that they come first. Their influence upon the years that follow is incalculable. The trends and sequences of this fundamental development may be summed up tersely:

In the *first quarter* of the *first year* the infant, having weathered the hazards of the neonatal period, gains control of his twelve oculomotor muscles.

In the *second quarter* (sixteen to twenty-eight weeks) he gains command of the muscles that support his head and move his arms. He reaches out for things.

In the *third quarter* (twenty-eight to forty weeks) he gains command of his trunk and hands. He sits. He grasps, transfers, and manipulates objects.

In the *fourth quarter* (forty to fifty-two weeks) he extends command to his legs and feet, to his forefingers and thumbs. He pokes and plucks.

By the end of the *second year* he walks and runs; articulates words and phrases; acquires bowel and bladder control; attains a rudimentary sense of personal identity and of personal possession.

At *three years* he speaks in sentences, using words as tools of thought; he shows a positive propensity to understand his environment and to comply with cultural demands. He is no longer a mere infant.

At *four years* he asks innumerable questions, perceives analogies, and displays an active tendency to conceptualize and generalize. He is nearly self-dependent in routines of home life.

At *five* he is well matured in motor control. He hops and skips. He talks without infantile articulation. He can narrate a long tale. He prefers associative play. He feels socialized pride in clothes and accomplishment. He is a self-assured, conforming citizen in his small world.

Interweaving and the Cycles of Development

Information that we can give you, as well as your own common sense and observations, tells you that as the child matures his abilities increase. He moves, inexorably, from simple, immature kinds of responses to the more complex.

Only a few decades ago it was believed by the child specialist that this development took place in what one might describe as a straight-line manner—from the simple to the complex, without complication. Recent research reveals, however, that development proceeds in a more complicated way than had been originally thought.

Overall, if all goes well, it does proceed from the simple to the complex, but there are interesting complications—complications that are useful for parents as well as psychologists and pediatricians to understand.

We have observed that in any growing behavior there are paired but opposed types of response that occur alternately, now one and now the other in repeated alternation, until the behavior has reached its final or complete stage. In practical everyday living, one of these two opposed types of response is likely to be thought of as immature or less desirable; the other, as mature and more desirable. Instead of the immature type of response dropping out with increasing age, it seems that the type of response alternates repeatedly between less and more mature.

However, this is not simply a matter of an infant going back to exactly the same earlier type of immature behavior, but rather it is as though the path of development spirals upward from left to right (but always upward), stressing now the less mature and now the more mature side of the spiral.

This principle of development is perhaps most clearly expressed in the first year of life as the infant develops the ability to crawl, to creep, to stand, and to walk. We have identified twenty-two stages that the normal infant customarily goes through as he lies on his stomach, or prone. We note that, first, arms and legs are flexed; at a later stage they are extended; at a still later stage they are again flexed; still later they are again extended; and so on repeatedly until the infant stands and walks erect.

The most conspicuous alternations in prone behavior are the alternations of predominant flexion and extension of arms and legs. However, other things that alternate are adduction and abduction of arms and legs, and alternation of bilateral and unilateral movements. All these complex forces are working together to determine what posture or progression the infant will achieve as he lies on his stomach in the first year of life.

Because the adult as a rule places no special value judgment on either flexed or extended posturing, or on bilaterality or unilaterality, it is relatively easy for him to observe these alternations calmly, even though with interest. For the most part, people do not believe that the infant assumes these postures because of something that somebody has done, or in response to other environmental stimuli.

As the child grows older, and the kinds of behavior that characterize the succeeding age levels may be, and usually are, considered as good or bad by the culture, it becomes more difficult to see the child's behavior as coming from within and occurring in response to internal growth stimuli, and easier to consider that somebody has *caused* it.

Thus when the two strands of behavior that are interweaving are not merely flexion and extension, or bilaterality and unilaterality, or any other somewhat objective forces, but are instead tendencies toward equilibrium and disequilibrium of response, it is difficult for most parents to remain objective. It is natural for them to seek an environmental explanation of behavior. Their "good" child is suddenly "bad"; their obedient child is disobedient; their child who was getting along so nicely with and in the world around him is suddenly experiencing great difficulties. It is easy and natural to blame somebody or something for these changes for the worse.

Nevertheless, the marked similarity from child to child in behavior changes with age has led us to believe that internal forces of what we may call *reciprocal interweaving* (repeated alternation of opposing or contradictory forces) may play a vital part in an area as big and general as the total way a child responds to the world around him.

We have observed that a child's behavior at any given age seems to consist of more than the sum of things he is able to do. Behavior at any age seems almost to have an individuality of its own, reflecting the stage of growth that the child has reached. There are ages that in the majority of children seem to be characterized by a general equilibrium, an easy adaptation to environmental factors and to the demands of daily living.

Other ages are just the opposite and seem characterized by a general disequilibrium. At such ages all areas of living may be affected and the child may have trouble with eating, sleeping, responding to other people, and behaving in an acceptable manner. Figure 1 gives a simplified notion of the ages that, in general, are characterized by equilibrium and those that, in general, are characterized by disequilibrium, as the child matures. It will be noted that the alternations of times of equilibrium and disequilibrium tend to slow down as the child grows older. The fastest changes in behavior occur in the first year of life or even before that, in fetal life.

That we can describe calmly the fact that the child goes through "good" and "bad" stages, stages of equilibrium and disequilibrium, should not be interpreted to mean that we recommend permissive handling on the part of the parent. *We do not say or imply that just because an undesirable behavior is characteristic and common you should sit idly by and not do anything about it.* In our experience, if a parent knows that some disturbing behavior is characteristic of some given age and thus, hopefully, merely temporary, his or her handling of that behavior tends to be calmer than if it is believed that the behavior has been caused by something the parents did, or is a sign that something has gone wrong with the child.

Of course, you preach and punish and use your best wiles and efforts to get your boy or girl to behave in the manner you prefer. You do not sit with hands folded and tell yourself, "It's just a stage." But you may be able to calm your fears that you have erred or that something is dreadfully wrong with your child if you *can* tell yourself, "It's just a stage."

Now, although we have found it helpful to characterize alternating stages of maturing behavior as equilibrated or disequilibrated, many, many other forces appear to be at work. The swings from equilibrium to disequilibrium are by no means as simple as they may sound. They in no way involve *merely* a back-and-forth movement of alternating stages. We have defined six separate stages in each of five cycles that span the time from birth to sixteen years of age. But even we ourselves were not able to define these stages until we had completed our study of the years from five to ten and could look back on what went before.

One look at Figure 2, Sequence of Stages, almost staggers the imagination as we see in what an orderly way the growth process unfolds, with the repetition of cycles occurring at ever-increasing intervals. Duration of the first cycle is 0.7 years; of the third, 3 years; of the fifth, 6 years. As will be noted, stages of equilibrium (Stages 1, 3, 5) may be expressed in smooth, consolidated behavior (Stage 1), in rounded, well-balanced behavior (Stage 3), or in vigorous, expansive behavior (Stage 5). In like manner, the disequilibrium stages may be expressed through breakup behavior (Stage 2), through inwardizing (Stage 4), or through neurotic, troubled behavior (Stage 6). (That first month, the neonatal period, is indeed a precarious one, with many throwbacks into fetal behavior. A very close relationship between mother and child is necessary to carry the neonate safely through this rough period of Stage 6.)

As Figure 1 shows, this rather complex sequence of stages thus includes a stage which we describe as smooth, consolidated, well-equilibrated; a following stage of breakup or disequilibrium; a succeeding stage when behavior is rounded and well balanced; then an inwardized stage of disequilibrium; then a vigorous, expansive stage; then a somewhat neurotic, inwardized, troubled stage; and then finally once again good equilibrium. The full sequence appears to occur in rather full form five times from birth to sixteen years of age.

That a sequence of stages so complex could appear so clearly, and so repeatedly, supports our basic contention that behavior is indeed

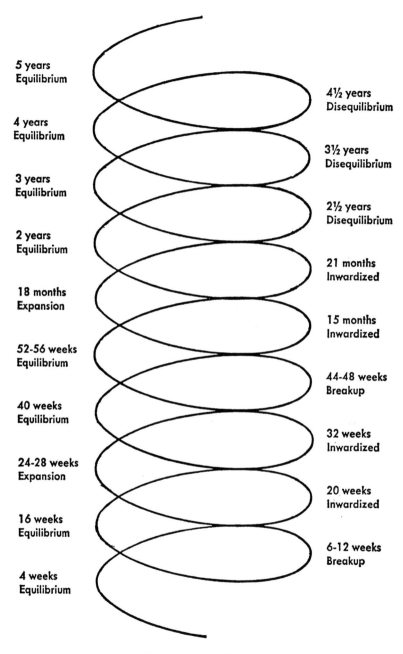

Figure 1 Reciprocal interweaving.

a function of structure and does develop in almost as predictable and patterned a way as the body itself.

The Uses and Misuses of Age Norms

Nature abhors identities. Variation is the rule. No two children are exactly alike and it has been said, perhaps with too much intellectual gravity, that there is no such thing as an average child. This has led some skeptics to suggest that age norms are misleading. Why should we set up such norms when not even brothers and sisters grow up in precisely the same way? We shall attempt to answer this question, for the reader has already observed that this volume is built around the concepts of age and maturity.

In the present stage of our scientific culture it would be very awkward to abandon the notion and the fact of age in any treatise on child development. The human life cycle is inextricably bound up with the factors of agedness and of aging. Duration and development are inseparable, metaphysically and also from the incontrovertible standpoint of common sense.

What is almost the first question we ask of ourselves when we are introduced to a baby or to a child? We ask, "How old is he?" If the mother is very proud of his accomplishments she has already told us in advance. In a general way, we know what to expect of a given age; and we feel better acquainted with a child when we learn how old he is. There is something strangely mysterious about a foundling whose age is unknown. If a foundling is to be adopted in early infancy, it is extremely important to adjudge his chronological age by whatever age norms are available.

We celebrate the birthdays of a growing child not because the earth has made another revolution, but because the child is progressing toward maturity.

Feet and inches tell us how tall a child is; pounds and ounces how heavy. In somewhat the same way norms of behavior development tell us how mature he is. *Age norms are not set up as absolute*

Figure 2
Sequence of Stages

Cycles	Stage 1 Equilibrium	Stage 2 Disequilib.	Stage 3 Equilibrium	Stage 4 Disequilib.	Stage 5 Equilibrium	Stage 6 Disequilib.	Stage 1 Equilibrium	Duration
	Smooth, Consolidated	Breaking Up	Rounded, Well-balanced	Inwardized	Vigorous, Expansive	Neurotic, Inwardized, Troubled	Smooth, Consolidated	
1st	4 weeks	6-12 weeks	16 weeks	20 weeks	24-28 weeks	Birth	4 weeks	0.7 years
2nd	40 weeks	44-48 weeks	52-56 weeks	15 months	18 months	32 weeks	40 weeks	1.2 years
3rd	2 years	2½ years	3 years	3½ years	4 years	21 months	24 months	3 years
4th	5 years	5½-6 years	6½ years	7 years	8 years	4½ years	5 years	5 years
5th	10 years	11 years	12 years	13 years	14 years	9 years	10 years	6 years
						15 years	16 years	

standards. They are merely standards of reference to which a child can be compared. They must be used with the same judiciousness as norms of height and weight. Although these physical norms represent an average trend, we expect most children to exceed or to fall somewhat short of the specifications. Norms for height and weight must be applied intelligently, and often only the expert judgment of a physician can determine whether the child is actually undernourished. Intelligent parents have learned that such physical "standards" must be applied with discretion and caution.

Norms of behavior development, as measures of maturity, must be applied with even greater caution. The lay person should not attempt to make a diagnosis on the basis of such norms. This would constitute a misuse of norms. Refined and responsible application of maturity norms requires clinical skill based on long clinical experience.

Nevertheless, the lay person wishes to know how the child mind matures, how the patterns of behavior normally change with age. We cannot appreciate the changing psychology of personality without an understanding of the pathways and patterns of development.

Thus, for the orientation of the reader, we have drawn up a series of behavior profiles for advancing age levels. These are mere thumbnail sketches of maturity, but they are concrete enough to give bearings. And that is their purpose. They do not pretend to tell you exactly when things will happen, but they do give approximate times. *When the profiles are read as a consecutive series, they give a time-flow map of the way a child matures. It is not intended that a single profile should be used to determine whether a given child is bright or dull, good or bad. Individual deviations are almost as normal as they are numerous.* The norms enable us to detect the deviations.

The behavior profiles in Chapters 8 through 20, as a series, outline the sequences of development. By following this continuity the reader is in a better position to interpret the sequences and patterns of maturity in a growing child. *The path of growth is the most important thing to study and to understand, not the exact time at which any single behavior occurs.*

Babies and children go through similar stages of growth, but not on the same timetable. Variations are particularly common in postural behavior. For example, we observed five healthy babies, all of whom are now normal and effective adults. At forty weeks of age, one of these babies was backward in locomotion, one was advanced. The other three were near average. Baby One "swam" on his stomach without making headway. Baby Two crawled. Baby Three creep-crawled. Baby Four crept on hands and knees. Baby Five went on all fours. It would have been regrettable if the mother of Baby One had worried unduly over this bit of retardation, since the rest of the infant's behavior was quite up to par. Likewise the mother of Baby Five had no reason to be unduly elated, since the total behavior picture was near average expectation.

From this example it is clear that *age norms and normative character sketches must not be taken too literally, and that parents should not worry if their child is not in every way up to the normative behavior we describe.* Norms are useful if they are used flexibly. They are also useful in determining whether a child's behavior is well balanced in the four major fields of activity (motor, adaptive, language, and personal-social).

The behavior guidance and general management of a child should be based primarily on the maturity level of his personal-social behavior. If the parents, for example, find that their three- or four-year-old child is consistently functioning like a two-and-a-half-year-old, it will work advantageously for the child if his parents are aware of his level of maturity. Naturally he should be treated like a two-and-a-half-year-old child and not held up to three-year-old "standards." At this early age such a degree of retardation will have less serious consequences if his psychological care, as well as his later school placement, is determined by his psychological maturity and not by his chronological age.

The guidance of development must reckon judiciously with norms in one form or another. In the final analysis, the child himself is the norm of last resort. We are interested in his growth. From time to time—that is, from age to age—we compare him with his former self; and this gives us an insight into *his* method of growth. This is supremely significant because each child grows in his own way. A normative description of the way that behavior in general develops and changes from age to age does not mean that every child grows in exactly the same manner.

There is a principle of relativity which should afford us some comfort. It is whimsically stated in two stanzas by John Kendrick Bangs:

> I met a little Elfman once,
> Down where the lilies blow.
> I asked him why he was so small
> And why he did not grow.
>
> He slightly frowned, and with his eyes
> He looked me through and through.
> "I'm quite as big for me," he said
> "As you are big for you."

CHAPTER 3

EVERY CHILD AN INDIVIDUAL

How can we account for the striking individual differences in children's personalities? Why is one child in a family calm and sturdy, and another from the same family intense and easily upset? Why are some children basically happy, others gloomy? Why are some sociable, others aloof?

Theories abound as to where personality comes from. Some believe that the environment in which a child grows up, especially the emotional environment of his home, determines personality. Some believe that any child can be made into almost anything by the world around him.

Others believe, as we do, that behavior is to a great extent a function of structure—the way we behave is largely determined by the body we inherit. As Dr. Gesell has expressed it, "environmental factors modulate and inflect but do not determine" behavior.

Gesell at all times emphasized that "infants are individuals" and that every child is different from every other, even his identical twin, from the time of conception. This, however, does not preclude the fact that in real life it is difficult to think of heredity without at the same time considering environment. The two factors do not exist separately, but rather in interaction. The more we know about *inher-*

ited aspects of a child's individuality, the better job we can do in suiting the *environment* to his needs.

The Mother/Child Couple

That each infant is an individual, different in many ways from every other individual, has thus long been recognized. That an infant's or child's behavior can be strongly influenced by the way his mother treats him is also well recognized. But that each mother is strongly influenced by the way her baby behaves is a somewhat new notion, developed most effectively by Dr. T. Berry Brazleton in his excellent book *Infants and Mothers.*

Most of us realize that if a baby is exceptionally and prolongedly fussy, it can make his mother nervous and upset. If he is calm and happy, she tends to be more relaxed. Dr. Brazleton emphasizes that this interaction between a mother and her baby is more than a momentary, occasional thing.

He states clearly that each mother "must find her own way as a mother with her own special baby. Each mother and baby is an individual. As such, each pair is stuck with its own ways of interacting. Thus as a mother you may have done an excellent job with your first baby and thus have considered yourself an expert. A second, more difficult, baby may be much more trying and may elicit from you a quite different kind of mothering."

If you do have a difficult baby, keep in mind Dr. Brazleton's notion that each mother/baby pair is a couple, and that *you* may be responding to your baby quite as much as *he* is responding to you. Some babies are more difficult to mother than others.

Physical Appearance of the Three Body Types

But underneath all behavior there is always the child's own body. To a very large and somewhat predictable extent, people behave as they do because of the way their bodies are built.

The idea that the kind of behavior or personality a person exhibits is rooted deep in his physical structure is not new. It goes back to antiquity. The ancient Greek physician Hippocrates classified people into four types of personality based on the "body humor" dominating each. He called these four types of people sanguine, choleric, bilious, and phlegmatic.

Constitutional psychology (a psychology that explains the kinds of behavior to be expected from people of different body types) has come a long way since Hippocrates. The man who has done the most in this field is Dr. William H. Sheldon. Sheldon describes three main body types. Actually everyone has some of each but in most people one or the other of the three basic qualities predominates and so it seems fair, even though not entirely accurate, to speak of three different types.

The three are: the *endomorph*—the fat, round person; the *mesomorph*—the broad-shouldered, squarely built, muscular, athletic individual; and the *ectomorph*—who is thin, fragile, angular, flat-chested, and stoop-shouldered, with pipestem arms and legs.

In a little more detail, people of the three physical types contrast as follows: The body of the endomorph is round and soft; of the mesomorph, hard and square; of the ectomorph, linear, fragile, and delicate. In the endomorph, arms and legs are relatively short as compared with the trunk, with the upper arm longer than the lower arm. Hands and feet are small and plump. Fingers are short and tapering. In the mesomorph, extremities are large and massive, with the upper arm and leg equal in length to the lower arm and leg. Hands and wrists are large, fingers squarish. In the ectomorph, arms and legs are long as compared to the body, with lower arm longer than upper arm. Hands and feet are slender; fingers are fragile with pointed fingertips. (See Figure 3, page 34.)

Behavior of the Various Physical Types

The theory behind constitutional psychology is that the way a person behaves stems largely from the kind of body he has. According to

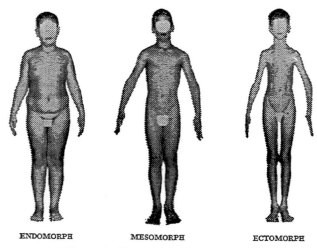

ENDOMORPH   MESOMORPH   ECTOMORPH

Figure 3   The three general body types.

Sheldon, the endomorph attends and exercises *in order to eat*. Eating ·is a primary pleasure.

The mesomorph attends and eats *in order to exercise*. What he likes best is athletic activity and competitive action.

The ectomorph, on the other hand, exercises and eats *in order to attend*. Watching, listening, thinking about things, and being aware are his most important activities.

Sheldon gives another good clue to differences among the three types. He states that when in trouble, the endomorph seeks people, the mesomorph seeks activity, and the ectomorph withdraws and prefers to be by himself.

Whatever kind of behavior you think about, each of these three kinds of people responds differently. The eating, sleeping, and social behavior that can be expected of each follows:

Eating. The *endomorph* loves to eat. It is one of his greatest pleasures. And when not eating, he or she loves to be cooking, planning meals, or talking about food and recipes. Such a person is what the Freudians call "oral erotic," that is, he likes to be kissing, chewing, smoking—

doing something with his mouth. The endomorph, in addition to loving food and cooking, loves homemaking.

The *mesomorph* neither dreams of food nor lives to eat, but he does have a demanding appetite and likes big meals. He eats a lot and likes to wolf large quantities of food at one sitting.

The *ectomorph* gets into trouble with his family about food because he cares very little about it and eats very little, usually less than people think he ought to eat. He might actually get along better with four or five small meals a day than with three big ones.

Sleeping. The *endomorph* loves to sleep, and sleeps limp and sprawled in any position. Sleeping, like eating, is not a problem for him. He enjoys both and does both well.

The *mesomorph* sleeps well but actively. He thrashes and kicks a lot as he sleeps. His bed is usually quite mussed in the morning. The child of this physique usually falls asleep quickly and easily. And, even more characteristic, he wakes quickly and easily, and jumps quickly out of bed, ready for action. He does not need as much sleep as do children of the other physiques.

The *ectomorph* has trouble with sleeping as with eating. He finds it hard to go to sleep but once asleep, finds it hard in the morning to wake up and get going. He needs a great deal of sleep, but it is hard for him to fall asleep unless he is close to physical exhaustion. He sleeps lightly and dreams a great deal. That is, his relaxation even in deepest sleep is incomplete.

Social Behavior. Strong differences appear with regard to the child's reaction to and feelings about other people.

The *endomorph* loves company. He has a tremendous appetite for people. He feels real emotional delight when he is surrounded by and supported by people. As Sheldon describes it, the endomorph experiences a "deep, persistent craving to have people about, a rich satisfaction in being one among many, and a strong sense of loneliness and weakness when cut off from other people." This kind of individual warms up and expands in company and feels frustrated and uncomfortable if alone.

The *mesomorph* likes people but is nowhere nearly as dependent on their company as is the endomorph. However, he does well with people, has plenty of friends, and is a natural-born leader of other people. He likes people well enough but as a rule other people have to adapt to *him*. He gets on well with others but often as their leader or as the one the others look up to. He likes others primarily because of the things they do, because of the activities he and they can enjoy together.

The *ectomorph*, in contrast to the other two kinds of individual, has a strong need of privacy. He likes to be alone and dislikes being socially involved. If he has a choice—which the young child does not always have—the ectomorph not only dislikes but avoids social gatherings. He tends to be distressed, uncomfortable, and unhappy in social relationships, especially those of a temporary and superficial nature. The concept of good-fellowship is strange to him. He likes to have one or two close friends, but shrinks from social contacts, especially new ones.

Problems. What things about each kind of child cause parents anxiety? Here are some of the most usual:

The *endomorph*, typically jolly, friendly, and well adjusted, does not as a rule pose any great problem to his parents. As a baby such a child is usually described as "wonderful." He eats well, sleeps well, and seems to love life. As he grows older, he gets on well with everybody, loves people, and they love him. This is a nice kind of child to have around.

If parents, too, are of this temperament, there is not much to worry about. But if parents are more driving, more competitive, and more ambitious, then they tend to worry that their endomorphic child doesn't try hard enough and doesn't compete. They consider him lazy, and his lack of drive may cause them (not him) anxiety. It is hard for some parents to accept the fact that great drive and extreme good nature seldom go hand in hand. This kind of child gets on best if his parents can accept him for what he is.

The *mesomorph*, on the other hand, especially in the preschool years, before he learns to channel his great energy into acceptable lines, can be a great source of anxiety to his parents. He tends to be constantly active, into everything, and highly destructive. His hands must touch everything he sees, and he seems to break nearly everything he touches. His mother is worn out just trying to keep up with him, and he easily earns the reputation of being the "worst child in the neighborhood." Though he usually gets on well with contemporaries (he bosses them around and is looked up to as a leader), he is often not too scholarly. He tends to lack sensitivity and thus may be hard to reach. One thing that makes him a lot of trouble to adults is that he is so loud and noisy. Parents must accept this characteristic and must try to provide acceptable outlets for his vigorous and aggressive motor drive.

The *ectomorph* causes anxiety for quite other reasons. As a baby he is likely to suffer from colic and other feeding disturbances. He often has sleeping problems. He may have more than his share of allergies. What worries parents most, however, is his oversensitivity, his social shyness, his immaturity, and the fact that he may not seem to need people—all of which combine to make it hard for him to find friends. The ectomorph has an especially hard time in high school, since he matures late and is still often quite childish at a time when others have started dating and enjoying themselves socially. Mothers often complain that the ectomorph "always has his nose in a book." They should not worry. Reading is a normal and natural activity for the ectomorphic boy or girl. Parents need to give such a child time to mature and they should not expect too early or too great social success.

Tempo

Another of the main components of individuality that should be mentioned here is the matter of timing or tempo. If you've ever tried to walk with somebody who walks much faster or slower than you do, you know what a nuisance it is. If you have a friend who consistently thinks more slowly, talks more slowly, moves more slowly than you do, so that you are always waiting for him to catch up, you know what a menace to friendship a strongly different tempo can be. Any parent or teacher of a very slow-moving child knows how exasperating it is to wait and wait for this child to finish his task.

Much time and effort are spent by adults in trying to get the slow child to speed up, or the very fast child to slow down and be a little more careful. Much of this time could be saved if people were aware that tempo is to a very large extent an inborn, inherited characteristic and that most people are fast, or slow, throughout their life span. No matter what other people try to do to them, most people do not speed up or slow down very much just because somebody tries to change their tempo.

One of our early studies checked the timing of a group of children from infancy through the first ten years of life. Much of their behavior was photographed and when the films were analyzed, it was possible to arrange these children in rank order from the quickest to the slowest-moving individual. Interestingly enough, the baby who crept most quickly and reached for things most quickly was also the one who crept earliest and reached for objects soonest of all the group.

In this instance, the speedy children not only moved speedily, but they grew and developed from one stage to another more quickly than did the slow-moving children. A most amusing climax to this study took place when four of these children were invited for a five-year-old's birthday party. (Not all were five on the same day, but a date was chosen *near* everybody's birthday.) Instead of one big birthday cake, individual cakes were furnished on a plate. When it came time to reach for these cakes, the child who as a baby had been the fastest creeper reached first. The second fastest creeper reached next; then the next to the slowest creeper reached for her cake; and finally the slowest creeper, an endomorphic boy, reached for the very last cake.

Slow children or parents of slow children have in the past consoled themselves with the notion that slow people are careful and accurate, quick people are careless and sloppy. Research does not particularly bear this out.

Keep in mind that speed or tempo of movement is to a large extent an inborn characteristic. You can help a slow child to be less awkward and more effective in his movements, but the likelihood is that you cannot substantially speed up the slow or slow down the speedy.

Sex Differences

One last area of individual differences is the always fascinating matter of sex differences. This is something that has never given the nonscientific person too much trouble. Such a person knows that boys behave differently from girls. Men behave differently from women. And why? Largely because they are built differently.

Scientists have sometimes gone to a great deal of trouble to becloud the issue. Some social scientists believe that boys behave differently from girls because we *expect* them to behave differently. True, we do have different expectations for the two sexes, but many of us believe that the expectations were drawn from the behavior, rather than that the behavior resulted from the expectations.

Many of the more important differences between the sexes are obvious and evident from the time of conception, or at least from the time that sex is determined, in the fetus. Thus it is generally accepted as a fact that boys are physically less strong than girls in the months before birth, and in the childhood years that follow.

As babies and preschoolers, boys tend to be much harder to raise than girls. They develop more slowly, tending to walk later, talk later, and be toilet trained later.

Studies in nursery school settings reveal that even as early as two years of age, boys tend to be more interested in wheels and cars, girls in dolls. Girls know people's names; boys as a rule do not. Girls can generally play longer in one situation than boys can without the play deteriorating. Boys tend to fatigue more rapidly.

By three and a half years of age, boys tend to engage in extremely masculine building play. As the school year proceeds, they become more and more affiliated with masculine roles and with grown-up male pursuits, such as being firemen, sailors, and such. Girls play mostly with other girls and prefer such feminine activities as playing house.

At four, boys are wilder than girls, and they play especially with blocks, cars, and trucks while girls continue with more feminine play.

On the average, boys tend to be about six months slower in their development than girls. Ideally, then, when it comes time for school, they should start kindergarten and first grade a good six months later than girls do. If they did, they not only would be more successful in school, but they might also avoid that awkward time in the early teens when girls are so much more mature than boys in the same school grade, both physically and socially.

The Ages Themselves Have Individuality

Infants are individuals, it is true, but there is more to it than that. Not only every infant and child but also each individual *age* has its own individuality. The three-year-old is not simply a slightly older and more capable edition of the two-year-old. The four-year-old is not just a more capable Three.

Every age is not merely a sum of the things the child of that age can do. Instead, each age has its own individuality, its own growth task, its own climate, its own way of being. And since growth does not proceed in a simple straight-line direction, the immature aspect of any behavior repeatedly recurring in alternation with the more mature, we must anticipate that ages of disequilibrium will alternate with ages of equilibrium.

Not only will ages of equilibrium and disequilibrium alternate but also ages of inwardized and outwardized behavior. There are ages in which the majority of children seem characterized by a general equilibrium and an easy outgoing adaptation to environmental factors and the demands of daily living. Other ages are just the opposite and seem characterized by a general disequilibrium or withdrawal. At such ages all areas of living may be affected and the child may have trouble with eating, sleeping, response to other people, and even to life in general.

When these stages occur, when their "good" child becomes suddenly "bad," it is difficult for most parents to remain objective. It is natural for them to seek an environmental explanation of behavior and to feel that somebody or something is to blame. But since this is the way of growth, since any one stage of equilibrium seems to need to break up before a new and more mature stage of equilibrium can be attained, we need not necessarily blame the environment or the child when things go less than smoothly.

Here in brief summary are personality sketches of the ages that will be described in more detail in Part Two of this book:

Four Weeks. This tends to be a quiet age. The infant shows, for one so young, rather conspicuous maturity changes when compared to himself just one month earlier. Muscles have better tone, behavior seems more organized. He is less given to startling. Breathing is deeper and more regular, swallowing is firmer, he does not choke or regurgitate so much. Though he still sleeps much of the time, the awake infant stares at faces and may quiet if picked up and held. He is surely on his way, though he still may spend more time supine and sleepy than otherwise.

Sixteen Weeks. Most have worked through the temporary disequilibrium that may occur around six to twelve weeks of age, and now are expansive and expressive. Sixteen weeks in many is an age of effective and expanding equilibrium. There is a delightful symmetry of posture, an interest in both objects and people. The baby smiles spontaneously. He is beginning to explore, both by grasping objects as he lies supine and by looking at them as he sits propped up.

Twenty-eight Weeks. At twenty to twenty-four weeks the baby quiets and pulls in a bit, but by twenty-eight weeks most are again responsively expansive, thrusting out into the world in all sorts of ways— new sights, new sounds, new activities enthrall. Baby now loves to sit and this posture frees his hands so that they can grab and manipulate. Prone, he is on the verge of pivoting. Socially he can discriminate a stranger, talk to his toys, smile at his mirror image, and be delightfully responsive to mother and father.

Forty Weeks. Following a brief withdrawn and often fussy period from thirty-two to thirty-six weeks of age, forty weeks again sees the infant in excellent equilibrium, on the verge of new worlds to conquer. He sits by himself with good control, creeps, pulls to standing—locomotor abilities now permit him to cover ground. He manipulates objects with interest and ease, and his eager socialization now includes such real words as "mama" and "dada." He has not yet, however, become a social person in his own right.

Fifty-two Weeks. And now he stands upright and may even walk with one hand held. Manipulation of objects is not only eager and skillful but permits him to enjoy such reciprocal nursery games as pat-a-cake and bye-bye. A new dimension, besides the upright, is the world of words. Many have two besides "mama" and "dada." They can imitate sounds, respond to their own name, reply to "No, no" and "Give it to me." A temporary period of disequilibrium from forty-four to forty-eight weeks has been replaced by excellent balance, both physical and social.

Fifteen Months. This in some is not an easy age. The ability to toddle takes the child into new terrain but his walking is not yet secure. If confined to his pen, he demands release. He casts his toys and then wants them back again. Activity is ceaseless. He is a motor-driven vehicle. An increased vocabulary is not yet enough to express effectively his many strong demands. Thus he and those about him may temporarily be in trouble. The fifteen-monther makes his presence known. He demands more and accepts less from the environment than when he was merely an infant.

Eighteen Months. The eighteen-month-old child walks down a one-way street, and this street more often than not leads in a direction exactly opposite to that which the adult has in mind. It is difficult for the child to mind when spoken to, to respond to commands, to keep within reasonable bounds. And he is extremely strong-willed. His immaturities in motor, adaptive, language, and emotional fields may lead to tantrums.

Two Years. Things are much smoother in nearly every field of behavior. Added maturity and a calm willingness to do what he can do and not try too hard to do things he cannot manage result in rather good equilibrium. The child is now surer of himself both motorwise and languagewise. Emotionally, too, he finds life easier (as his demands are not so strong as earlier), and he has developed an ability to wait and to suffer slight or temporary frustration if need be.

Two and a Half Years. This is an age of marked disequilibrium. The child of this age tends to be rigid and inflexible—he wants exactly what he wants when he wants it. Everything has to be in what he considers its proper place, everything done exactly so. He sets up rigid routines which he expects everyone to follow. Furthermore, he is domineering and demanding. *He* must make the decisions and his needs are very strong. His emotions are violent. And most of all, this is an age of opposite extremes. The child has no ability to choose between alternatives, so he shuttles back and forth endlessly between any two extremes: "I want—I don't want"; "I will—I won't."

Three Years. Things quiet down briefly at three for most children. Whereas the two-and-a-half-year-old loved to resist, three loves to conform. The child now likes to give as well as take. He likes to cooperate. He wants to please. He seems to be in good equilibrium not only with those about him but within himself. People are important to him and he likes to make friends. His increased language ability allows him to enjoy language and to respond well to language cues.

Three and a Half Years. In many, there is even more marked disequilibrium now than at two and a half. The child at this age exhibits an extremely strong will, and any sort of compliance is hard to obtain. He may resist any and every routine. He insists on having his own way and seems to resist for the sheer pleasure of resisting. Though quite unwilling to please, he is emotionally very vulnerable and is quick to question: "Do you love me?" He cannot stand to be ignored; but too much attention also disquiets him. "Don't laugh!" he commands.

Four Years. This is an expansive, out-of-bounds age. Motorwise the child may hit, kick, throw stones, break things, and run away. Emotionally, he exhibits loud silly laughter or fits of rage. Verbally he is extremely out of bounds: he lies, swears, boasts, resists. He loves to defy parental commands and seems to thrive on punishment. A terrible toughness comes over many: they swagger, boast, and defy. And yet within himself the child of this age does not seem to be in any great trouble, and he can be quite delightful and enjoyable in spite of his out-of-bounds qualities.

Four and a Half Years. Halfway between out-of-bounds four and calm five, the child of this age often doesn't seem to know where he is functioning and, as a result, his behavior can be extremely variable and unpredictable. It is this extreme variability and unpredictability that makes life difficult for the child himself and for those around him. This is a highly probing and questioning intellectual age. A favorite question is "Is it real?" Separating fact from fantasy is a real concern for him.

Five Years. A period of extreme and delightful equilibrium. The child of this age tends to be calm, stable, reliable, and well adjusted. He is friendly and undemanding with others. He loves to please. His mother seems to be the center of his world and he likes to be with her, to do what she asks, to please her. "Today I'm going to do all the good things and none of the bad things," a five-year-old will say. Five likes to be instructed, to get permission, and then to obey. He likes to help. For a brief period he is a delightful social being.

Five and a Half to Six Years. Equable five is followed by tumultuous six, the breakup behavior starting around five and a half. Behavior resembles that seen at two and a half in that the child is violently emotional and tends to function at opposite extremes: "I love—I hate." He himself is now the center of his own world and he wants to be loved most, to be first, to have everything. When anything is wrong he blames his mother, and takes things out on her. He cannot stand to lose, to wait his turn, to share. He has to be right, needs to win, demands praise. If things go well he is warm, enthusiastic, eager, ready for anything. If they go badly, he resorts to tears and tantrums.

Summary

The full story of individuality has not yet been told by anyone, though many books have been written, and such responsible and gifted investigators as William Sheldon and Henry Murray of Harvard have spent their lifetimes on the subject. This chapter offers only an introduction to one of the most interesting aspects of human living.

Though to a large extent the basis of any person's individuality is inborn and lies in his inherited physical structures (as Freud remarked, "Anatomy is destiny"), the possible variations even with this limitation are endless. To begin with, there is the interesting possible combination of innate individuality and whatever age the person has reached. When a calm, well-balanced individual hits a calm, well-balanced age, things can be smooth indeed. When a person who is not too well balanced hits an age also characterized by disequilibrium, things can be rough indeed. Thus if a child is by nature excessively well equilibrated, even an age like two and a half or three and a half may go by with relative ease.

And then of course there is the always unpredictable factor of environment. With a highly supportive environment, your boy or girl may find it possible to live up to the very utmost of his inborn potentials. With an unsupportive or destructive environment, only a few of his basic potentials may be able to find expression.

As we say, the possibilities seem limitless. But never forget that although you have the important responsibility of trying to see to it that your child has a chance to express his fullest potential, how he turns out is not *all* up to you. Genetic potential does make itself felt. Thomas Hardy writes truly in his poem "Heredity" when he says:

> I am the family face.
> Flesh perishes, I live on.
> Projecting trait and trace
> Through time to times anon.
> And leaping from place to place
> Over oblivion.

If any one of you has seen a child the exact "image" of a grandparent or great-grandparent, you may well know what this poem is saying.

CHAPTER 4

THE CHANGING CULTURE

Much that we wrote in 1943 about the infant in his culture holds true today, thirty years later. The world has changed a very great deal. Attitudes toward children are also changing. Yet the human organism, especially in the early years of life, is not tremendously different from what it has been all along. Thus, although we are able to amplify many of the things we told you earlier about infant and child, the basic story remains very much the same.

The human organism still develops through a series of patterned and to some extent predictable stages. Those persons making up the child's immediate environment, especially his mother and father, will now as then be able to handle him most effectively, will stand a better chance of helping him develop his fullest potential, if they know as much as possible about the ways in which his behavior grows.

The child as we see him seems not conspicuously different, in the way in which he grows and develops, from what he has been all along. But there have been marked changes in the culture in the past thirty years, changes that definitely do influence our babies and our children.

One of these changes, which perhaps is most important for parents, is that *early child behavior has suddenly become a number one topic of interest*, not only for parents and professionals but even for politicians. When the first edition of *Infant and Child* was published in 1943, there was considerable feeling expressed by colleagues that the home behavior of babies and small children was hardly a suitable subject for professional concern.

This attitude has now changed completely. Our contention has always been that if any psychologist or educator wished to really understand human behavior, he had no choice but to familiarize himself with what behavior is like in the earliest months and years. We are no longer alone in this contention. Most colleges and universities now provide departments of early childhood education and, in addition, major research concern is being devoted to the details of *infant* behavior.

Besides research in the earliest infant behavior, books, articles, films, and television programs are available for the information of parents who want to know more about their child's behavior. The first edition of *Infant and Child,* followed shortly after by Dr. Spock's famous *The Common Sense Book of Baby and Child Care,* were so far as we know the first books that talked to parents about the ordinary, everyday problems of child-raising and the ordinary, everyday changes in child behavior that they might expect.

Mothers and fathers today are almost swamped with advice from experts. The problem is more one of choosing among specialists, of choosing among the many (often conflicting) books of advice written especially for parents, than of finding any help at all.

Politicians, too, have been vitally concerned with the problems and rights of the very young. The 1971 Day Care Center Bill, which proposed that day care centers should be made available to all preschoolers —at no cost to those whose annual income was less than some four thousand dollars, at a small cost to those with larger incomes—though vetoed by President Nixon, is a clear example of the extent to which demands are being made in the name of childhood and accepted by many politicians.

A single paragraph from the vetoed bill will give a notion of the comprehensive nature of support for children to have been offered:

The government would involve itself in comprehensive physical and mental health, social and cognitive development services; food and nutritional services (including family consultation); special programs for minority groups, Indians and bilingual children; specially designed programs for emotionally disturbed children; prenatal services to reduce malnutrition, infant and maternal mortality and the incidence of mental retardation; special activities for the physically, mentally and emotionally handicapped children and children with special learning disabilities; training in the fundamentals of child development for family members and prospective parents; use of child advocates to assist children and parents in securing full access to their services; and other activities.

This proposed bill represents another very big cultural change that has taken place since *Infant and Child* was first published. Today *society has become sincerely concerned with the health (emotional as well as physical) of all children,* not just the middle- and upper-middle-class children whose parents might be expected to provide for them a comfortable and enriching cultural setting.

A major effort in the direction of seeing to it that the needs of the underprivileged, as well as the privileged, preschooler should be met had already been made through the much publicized *Headstart* program, initiated during the Johnson administration. Initial steps in this program were much too hasty, somewhat poorly conceived, and certainly overoptimistic. Headstart did not in a few summer months, as was originally promised, "improve the child's health; improve his emotional and social development; improve and expand his mental processes; increase his ability to get along with others in his family, thus strengthening family ties; develop in the child and his family a responsible attitude toward society."

However, as the years went by and goals and practices became increasingly realistic, much good and effective work was accomplished by local Headstart organizations. Also, Headstart effects were found to have a better chance of lasting if there was continuity between the Headstart effort and the home, that is, if parents were actively involved in seeing to it that the home provided an enriching experience for the child.

Excuses given by some for failure to accomplish the ambitious original goals were that this effort came too late and that the homes and parents were *not* involved enough. Following this line of reasoning, the government is now projecting a much earlier intervention, labeled Homestart.

Homestart programs, proposed and initiated in 1970–72 by the newly formed Office of Child Development in Washington, under the competent directorship of Dr. Edward Zigler, are just beginning. They offer much hope for the future of children in this country, especially children of underprivileged families. Through home visitors, parents will be helped in their homes to do a good job of parenting and also to take pride in their role as parents. Hopefully such programs will benefit young parents as well as their children.

The 1960s were, unfortunately, to a very large extent dominated by what Dr. Zigler calls the "environmental mystique." This maintained that one could, by providing the proper stimulus and encouragement, both speed up the sequential stages of development and make the infant or child more intelligent than he might otherwise have been. Such books as *How to Raise Your Child's I.Q., How to Raise a Superior Child, Give Your Child a Superior Mind,* and many others, as critics have put it, made the authors rich and many parents anxious. They did not, so far as one knows, speed up development or actually increase any child's intelligence. Little was gained, though many eager parents, convinced that it was their responsibility to introduce academic activities early, were led to push their preschoolers.

Homestart, as we see it, is not concerned primarily with so-called cognitive functions or with raising intelligence. Rather, it is directed toward helping those parents who need such help to be better parents and to provide for their infants and children a warm, responsive home environment in which parent and child live and interact in ways that will be rewarding and enriching.

There are many lower-class young people who do not believe that anything they might do would matter to their children because they themselves feel so worthless. Homestart will try to change their self-concept at the same time that it helps them to be good parents.

The Office of Child Development is also urging, as we ourselves do, that all school systems offer courses in child behavior or in "parenting" to all students, boys and girls alike, at some time during their high school experience if not earlier. Such courses would provide not only information about how children behave and how behavior grows but also practical experience with very young children in nursery school settings. Society is gradually coming to accept the truism that the mere act of producing a child does not automatically guarantee that a man or woman will be a good or effective parent. Parenting is a skill which requires both training and practice.

However, it is not only politicians or society in the abstract that is now making new and substantial efforts on behalf of children. In the years since the first edition of this book was published, parents themselves have increasingly banded together in groups oriented toward the many problems of children who are deviant or defective in some special way. Today we have societies for parents of retarded children, autistic children, emotionally disturbed children, perceptually handicapped children, and many others.

These parents meet to discuss their children's problems. They encourage and support research. They arrange that pertinent information be published and disseminated. They provide facilities, or encourage legislation which requires that special facilities be provided for their children.

More than this, in some communities parents of children *not* in trouble meet on a somewhat formal, or at least organized, basis to discuss *their* children's problems. An example of this kind of organization is San Diego's COPE (Committee on Parenthood Education), whose members meet in small groups on a regular basis to discuss "the problems, joys, and frustrations of raising children—supporting each other—serving as a sounding board—a resource for new ways of dealing with an old situation—group therapy." Meetings are held sometimes with, sometimes without, the children. At some of the meetings, outside speakers provide information on special topics.

Any list of cultural changes of the past thirty years that have vitally affected the lives of modern American girls and boys must include

the discovery and development of television. Though much of a negative nature has been written about the television programs available,
and much that is wrong with children has been blamed directly on
this medium, no one could question that it has had a very strong influence on the lives of many.

At the opposite extreme to those who feel that television is responsible for practically everything that has gone wrong with the American
child today are those who feel that educational programs such as the
much publicized "Sesame Street" are going to solve existing problems
and speed up our children's learning.

Our own stand is probably somewhere between these two extremes.
We do not expect miracles but we do feel that television has in general
been one of the influences most responsible for the fact that the child
of today lives in a world much widened from that in which his parents
grew up. We do not necessarily think that children are any smarter
than they used to be, nor do we think that they necessarily mature at
. a more rapid rate than in days just earlier. But there is no question
that they are better informed. Parents who complain about television
often ignore the fact that if their child watches too widely and too
much, they as parents do have it in their power to select and supervise.
Parents must help if the child, especially the very young child, is to
get out of television all that is available.

An important new influence in the field of child behavior, which
we would like to mention briefly, is the current notion of *behavior
modification.* Those who work with children from this frame of reference are no longer content merely to describe behavior. They propose
to do something about it. Those who practice and teach behavior
modification maintain that we can strongly influence child behavior,
and in fact can get children to do whatever we wish, by always giving
immediate and concrete reward to desired behavior and by totally
ignoring undesirable behavior.

Though we shall not discuss behavior modification techniques in
this book, we may note that there is no inherent quarrel or basic difference of opinion between our own developmental point of view and
that held by behavior modifiers. Our suggestion would be merely that

the more you know about the normal development of behavior, the more effectively you can practice behavior modification. This is especially true with regard to timing. If you know that a certain behavior that you may not approve, such as thumb-sucking, will in all likelihood run its course within the first three to five years of life, you may well feel that it is not necessary to step in earlier than that, with behavior modification techniques, in efforts to terminate it.

This chapter does not pretend to include or mention all the many other changes in the world around us that have affected our children. But we must take account of one phenomenon that has had a direct and extremely positive effect on the lives of both parents and children. This is *the tremendous change that has taken place in the practice of pediatrics in the past few decades.*

As late as 1943, the date of our original publication, with very rare exception pediatricians treated disease and not development. Pediatric emphasis was chiefly on diseases of infancy and childhood, and *behavior* was to a large extent ignored. Hard as it may be to believe, many pediatricians at that time even ignored serious signs of defect or behavior deviation as long as their young patients were physically healthy.

The change to an interest in the whole child, in his development as well as his physical health, came about in the late 1940s and in the 1950s. One of the strong stimuli was a major campaign waged by Dr. Gesell and forward-looking colleagues. Dr. Gesell firmly insisted that "development as well as disease lies in the province of clinical pediatrics." He urged that medical schools in their training of pediatricians include in their course work information about the normal behavior changes that come with age and about ordinary behavior problems met with by parents in the course of raising their children.

This effort has paid off splendidly. It may be hard for the parent of today, almost bombarded with help and information at every turn, to realize how little support was available just a few decades ago. This lack of help from pediatrician and professional child specialist was of course in earlier days made up for by the fact that many young parents were bringing up their children within easy reach of help and support from their own parents and relatives.

That many young families today are reduced to what is termed the "nuclear family"—mother, father, and one or two children—living alone or at a considerable distance from parents and close friends, means that they need more help from outside. Happily, now that supportive grandparents are often less available than formerly, supportive pediatricians have taken their place.

One of the very first pediatric books to give parents substantial help with their children's behavior problems, as well as with their physical health, was Dr. Spock's *The Common Sense Book of Baby and Child Care,* first published in 1946. Its tremendous success clearly speaks of the very great need parents felt for this kind of information and help.

Dr. Spock's book, as many of you know from your own reading, includes along with good pediatric advice much sensible information about behavior in general. What it does not contain is the kind of information that, increasingly in very recent years, is now to be found in effective books by pediatricians—information about growth and development, and most of all about personality differences. Nevertheless, it was a tremendous first step in an important direction.

Today there are several excellent books by pediatricians, all including the kind of pediatric advice that needs to be given—a combination of practical information about illness and even more practical advice about daily living with children. We would like to mention, and recommend, three of the best. The first, by Dr. Marvin J. Gersh, sets its tone by its jaunty title—*How to Raise Children at Home in Your Spare Time.* It is extremely amusing but also extremely practical. Above all it conveys the message that bringing up small children need not be deadly serious—in fact it can be fun. "Let us all relax," says Dr. Gersh.

A second, more serious, but equally helpful pediatric book for parents is Dr. Lendon H. Smith's *The Children's Doctor.* As Dr. Smith correctly asserts, "The role of the pediatrician has gradually changed from what it was a generation ago. . . . The new child-care specialist may spend less time on health and nutritional maintenance, and more time on the behavioral and emotional aspects of his patients."

Dr. Smith has not only an excellent understanding of the importance of age changes in behavior but a clear and respectful appreciation for the fact that when a child is in difficulty, "the root of the evil may be biological rather than psychological." As he says, "Just possibly your impossible, ornery, stubborn, irritable child has inherited all the wrong genes (from the other side of the family, of course)."

It is high time that this warning should come. For all too many years, Freudian-oriented psychologists have badgered parents with the notion that if a child is in trouble, it is probably *their* fault. Dr. Smith comes down hard on the side of biology and gives some of the very best advice available on how to deal with the allergic child, the stubborn, unruly child, the hypermotor child. He discusses calmly and sanely the possibility that some kind of medication and not simply improved methods of child-handling may be what is needed.

A third excellent book, *Infants and Mothers*, by pediatrician T. Berry Brazleton, though it gives much good pediatric advice, focuses primarily on the important subject of individuality: individuality of infant, of mother, and of what he calls the mother/child couple. (We have discussed his notions in Chapter Three, on individuality.)

The world that the child of the 1970s faces is in many ways a very different world from that of the 1940s, yet his own life with his parents in his home is in many ways only very slightly changed. The tremendous increase in abilities that takes place in the first year of life is about the same as it has always been—the infant looks, he reaches, he grasps, he sits, he creeps, he walks, he talks; sequence and substance are pretty much what they have always been.

And the parents' reaction tends to be rather what it has always been. The first smile, the first step, the first word still are greeted in most instances as though they were the most remarkable accomplishments of all time.

So it may be a different world on the outside, but the world of home and family stays surprisingly the same. Though we have added to and amended our earlier text, our original descriptions of behavior typical and characteristic of each of the growing ages still describe your infant and child today.

We have discussed the changing culture in some detail because, contrary to some of our critics' contentions, we do have great respect for the effect of the culture, or environment, on the behavior of any child at any time. Although there are those who believe that Gesell and his colleagues considered that the environment does not count, this is far from an accurate observation.

One of Gesell's earliest evaluations was that "environmental factors support, inflect, and modify, but they do not generate the progressions of development." Obviously environment does count. The culture does make a difference.

PART TWO

THE GROWING CHILD

CHAPTER 5

BEFORE THE BABY IS BORN

The First Baby

Husband and wife choose each other, but except when they adopt, they cannot choose their children. The parents cannot determine in advance the kind of children who will be born of marriage. That is the great adventure of life. The newborn infant is an individual in his own right and must be accepted as such.

Indeed, the individuality of the infant is to a significant degree determined before birth; well before the fourth month of gestation the prenatal child has taken on certain fundamental features of the individuality that will become apparent in infancy. Through no process of maternal impression or of wishful thinking is it possible to determine in advance whether this child will be blond or brunette, athletic or retiring; whether he will love the sea better than the mountains.

After the child is born, a parent with an overweening faith in the influences of environment may continue to harbor a preconceived image with excessive determination. In extreme instances there is a positive fixation upon a specific type of child. This fixation later impels the mother or father or both to attempt too strongly to make over the child in terms of this image. Matters grow still worse if the father has one ideal and the mother another. Such fixations are detrimental to the developmental welfare of the infant. From the very outset, parents must temper their wishes and school their affections. They must accept the infant for what he is. They should become consistently inquisitive about one permanent question, namely: *What kind of child is he—what is his true nature?*

This question is shrouded in darkness before birth, but will be ultimately answered in visible patterns of behavior. Even during the prenatal period the behavior characteristics of the future infant are undergoing a preliminary development. So-called quickening is more than a mere index of life. It is the product of a patterned behavior response made possible by the maturing nervous system. The twenty-week-old fetus is already so far advanced in his bodily organization and in the sculpturing of his physiognomy that he is distinctly human in his lineaments, and assumes in the fluid medium of the uterus postures and attitudes not unlike those that he will display when he lies safely ensconced in his bassinet.

Although the mother's imagery cannot be too precise, the realization that the individuality of the child is in the making puts her in a better position to identify herself during the period of pregnancy with the developmental welfare of the child.

The impending crisis of the first birth is sometimes so magnified that the anxieties and fears of the mother prevent her from building up a natural, constructive outlook. The supervision of the obstetrician may relate itself too much to the birth episode alone. Expectant parents would greatly benefit from a prepediatric type of guidance, directed toward the postnatal career of the child. For example, it is probable that breast-feeding would be more widely adopted in the interests of the child if both obstetricians and pediatricians encouraged the mother to nurse the child during his early months.

Such anticipations are especially important in the case of the first-born child, when the mother has so many new orientations to accomplish. These orientations are physical or biological on the one hand, and cultural on the other. The attitude and expectancies of the mother during the period of gestation, therefore, have far-reaching implications for the early career of the forthcoming child.

The care and management of the child will depend not only upon the practical details of technique, but also upon the philosophy of the parents. The welfare of the child is best safeguarded by a developmental philosophy which respects at every turn the individuality of the child and the relativities of immaturity. The foundations of this philosophy are best laid before the baby is born.

A Second Baby

The first baby makes the greatest demands upon the mother, both physically and psychologically. The second benefits thereby. The parents are now in a better position to see the meaning of birth and of child development in truer perspective. But the very fact that there is another baby already in the picture adds new problems which justify a little frank discussion.

Needless to say, the second baby is just as important as the first and just as much an individual. To a certain extent he, too, must be reared as an only child, entitled to his own distinctive rights. Parents sometimes envisage the second child as a reforming influence, who will be used to mitigate the selfishness and the aggressiveness perhaps mistakenly ascribed to the first child. If such motives determine the second pregnancy, the home may really not be ready for the newcomer.

Current theories may have exaggerated the dangers of a jealousy reaction toward the arrival of a new baby. The result is that parents, in their anxiety to forestall such a reaction, go to extreme lengths to build up fortitude and hospitality in the already entrenched first-born. Some of this build-up is nothing short of amusing (in the dispassionate light of what we know about child development). Perhaps a sense of humor can prevent us from going to unnecessary or unwise extremes in getting Junior ready for the new baby who several months hence will make him a senior!

To begin with, Junior has a very limited presentiment of events that have not taken place. If he is two years old he has no sense of the future. If he is somewhat older, he may be disappointed and bored by unending references to an event so distant that day after day it is heralded and yet never comes! His age, his temperament, and his maturity should determine how much is told and how it is told. It must be remembered that young children are not adept in thinking in words. They can scarcely be told anything for which they have not had equivalent experience. Or rather, they may be told, but they will not understand. Or they will interpret so literally that their imagery becomes a travesty of the truth you attempt to impart.

A little lesson on seeds and flowers will hardly elucidate the complexities of childbearing. Even with a bright child such a botanical approach has its hazards, as was illustrated by an incident in an Episcopalian cathedral, when a certain bright preschool child broke the solemn silence of a marriage ceremony by bursting out aloud with the question: "But, Mother, when is he going to put on the pollen?"

Concrete-minded children do not think in analogies. They think in terms of seeds in the stomach. An experimental child may swallow a tomato seed or even a prune pit in order to induce pregnancy. Then there was the girl (or was it a boy?) who swallowed two seeds because the objective was twins!

Such amusing misconceptions should remind us of the limitations of the child's intellect and imagination. His comprehension is dependent upon experience and upon growth, which proceeds by slow degrees. It is idle to give him information in advance of his capacity to assimilate. Too much information will actually confuse him. His questions are not as profound as they sound. They should be met with casualness rather than ecstasy. One need not resort to concealment and old wives' tales; but in general it is wise to respect the child's primitive notions and to give him a minimum response that will satisfy him for the present and provide him with a nucleus for another advance in his thinking. He cannot be told anything complex at one fell swoop. His adjustment to the new baby does not so much depend upon advance information as on a kindly planned protection of his sense of status and prestige.

The planning includes the spacing of children. Many factors bear on this question. One of these is the age of the first-born. Usually the three-year-old child is becoming psychologically ready to make a good adjustment to a new baby. He has just come through a stage of reliving his own babyhood emotionally and is well on his way to adjusting to the larger world beyond the home. The three-year-old may be ready to go to Grandmother's when his mother goes to the hospital. He thinks about the trip almost more than he thinks of the new baby. He may even stay on for an extra two weeks after his mother and the new baby have returned to their home. Frequent postcards hold his contact with his parents. If he stays at home, the mother's voice over the telephone continues a bond, although for some children this makes her absence more difficult.

For the younger child, twelve to eighteen months old, special preparations may not register at all. He may not react unfavorably to the mother's hospitalization or the homecoming of the baby, but unwittingly he may be deprived of many accustomed privileges and even some necessities if the household has not been careful to plan for him in his own right.

The two-year-old child can take part in a simple way in the physical preparations perhaps a month or two before the baby comes. The bassinet, the blankets, the baby powder and doll play help to initiate him into the impending event. At this age, he will probably cleave to his mother as the time for her departure draws near. It is hoped that he will have had a chance to become accustomed to his caretaker before his mother departs for her three to four days in the hospital. In general, it may be best to have him remain in his own home during this period, for to place him in unfamiliar surroundings might add to the strain of the separation from his mother. The daily homecoming of the father gives support to his sense of security. The two-year-old responds well to some physical token of his mother, such as a scarf or a pocketbook, and wants his repeated query, "Where's Mommy?" answered with the selfsame words, such as "Mommy's on Ivy Street in the big house." He may even come to answer his own questions himself if they are tossed back to him.

It is rather surprising to see how slow is the three-year-old, and even the four-year-old, to notice the enlarging of the mother's abdomen. At three and a half to four years he is often very conscious of marked deviations in the symmetry of the body, such as an amputated arm or a limping leg. But a slowly changing form before his own eyes does not register. If it is perceived he often gives his own immediate interpretations that his mother has eaten too much breakfast so that her stomach has grown large. He may even try to duplicate her prowess! The wise mother does not impose more knowledge of the coming events than the child has shown himself perceptive of and capable of handling. As with the two-year-old, the orientation of the three-year-old is accomplished through participation in the physical preparations a month or two before the baby arrives.

The four-year-old, and sometimes the three-year-old, is ready for further information and elementary interpretations. In Chapter 22, we shall attempt to outline the steps and developmental stages by which the young child grows into a deepening knowledge of the meaning of birth and babies.

A great fuss is naturally made when the new baby arrives home. This is the critical period, which calls for finesse. It is easier for all concerned if the older child, especially the three- or four-year-old, is away from home. Then the mother has a simpler home adjustment to make and can give all of her attention to the newborn infant. At whatever age the older child may be, the first sight of the new baby is the most difficult for him. He should participate in the fuss of welcoming and be given simple tasks, such as fetching diapers and administering the bath powder, to afford him a sense of participation. Perhaps much of the fuss should be strategically and ostensibly shifted from the new baby to himself. His prestige should be preserved at all hazards. Indeed, in the happiest households, the prestige of all members is equally safeguarded. When there are two or more children in a family, the most skillful mother plans separately for each individuality.

Whenever a second baby comes into a household, there is danger that we try to do too much and consequently overlook the simplest things, which are the most important. Explanations have their limitations. The shortest path to the young child is not through the intellect. He is not ready for a preschool course in embryology and obstetrics. There is even some danger in magnifying the role of the physician before the new baby is born. We know of a boy who betrayed unmistakable disappointment as he looked upon the florid face of his newborn brother. In his wisdom, the elder brother exclaimed, "I knew this would happen if you had a *country* doctor!"

We also know of a girl who had been beautifully "prepared" for the new baby but, alas, was visibly dejected when she saw the new arrival. Why? Because nightly she had prayed for an *older* sister!

Subsequent Offspring

Nowadays, even the mention of a third or fourth child is almost taboo. Since the population explosion is dictating a family of two or even fewer, many young parents are beginning to shift their sights. Many have chosen to restrict their offspring to two and are thus especially happy when they are granted a boy and a girl. Large families of six, eight, or ten are a thing of the past. "Cheaper by the Dozen" has no place in the modern scene.

The hard core of statistics and logical thinking, along with the automated edicts coming forth from the computer, all give the same directive of "No more than two children to each family group." But for those who do produce a larger family, it is interesting to conjecture about what we can expect of subsequent children. Unfortunately, very little research has been done on these later offspring. Geneticists steer clear of such research, wisely protecting themselves from the complications of "too many variables."

But there are those of us who in dealing with family groups over the years, though we may not be using research controls, have come to feel that there are innate differences between first, second, third, and subsequent children, highlighted by what some have called those "glorious thirds." By "glorious third" we are referring to the third pregnancy, not the third live birth. The possible glory of the third seems to stem from his sometimes seeming to be endowed with the best characteristics from each parent. So often he is highly adaptive, brings comic relief, and is easy to care for. (This does not mean that there are not occasionally "terrible thirds.")

In our clinical service we always ask about the whole family group. We ask about any miscarriages, abortions, or deaths. We ask the parents to appraise each child as they see him or her. We wish to help parents to individuate each child and to recognize what is innate and what the environment has done or needs to do, to and for each child. We try to help them realize that even a child's order of birth can become important.

We have come to feel that certain characteristics have been linked, at least in our own minds, with order of birth. The first child, we have often found, is well endowed, acquires speech early, and shows early gross motor abilities. His speech is clear, he repeats accurately what he hears, and is less apt to indulge in or simulate "baby talk." He may be interested in books very early and often teaches himself to read long before he enters first grade.

It is in the emotional realm where he may lag. He may show lack of emotional expression, or show emotional dependence on his mother. Intellectually he strides forth with portents of genius. This observation is borne out in the predominance of first-borns in the listings of *Who's Who*.

There is, admittedly, a wide spectrum to the possibilities of what the first-born is equipped to become. Retardation is at the other end of the spectrum from superior endowment. In fact, first-born children seem to show more variables and more extremes than any other sibling order.

As for the second child, it sometimes seems that one can predict to some extent by the quality of the first child. Nature has a way of rebalancing. A difficult first child is often followed by an easy second child, or vice versa. A less endowed or possibly retarded first child may be followed by a brilliant second child. In general, however, we find that second children often have a fuller emotional expression but sometimes more emotional difficulties than first children. They may become embroiled in emotions which mask a very good basic intelligence that lies dormant. If this intellect can mesh with emotions, then a very productive creative process can be set in motion. These are the children who often begin to thrive when an older sibling goes away to school, or even goes away for the weekend.

The "glorious third" has already been mentioned. High adaptability, in social, in mechanical, and in other aspects, seems often to be a part of their instinctive nature. They know how to respond without being taught. They may be slow in speech but high in comprehension; slow in reading but high in problem-solving. They need to be given time and thus allowed to move in their own way. Often they possess inherent wisdom.

We are not sure of our opinions or even of our guesses after the third child. However, we have seen a number of very unusual fourth and fifth children, especially in families where the first two were less endowed and more difficult to handle. It is almost as though the reproductive mechanism through practice steadily improves the outcome. But then we have seen just the opposite happen, when the first two are brilliant and well endowed and a retarded child crops up as number four or five.

Some parents report that their children seem to alternate as good, bad, good, bad. This, when it happens, may be nature's way of rebalancing.

With the population explosion and our efforts to combat it, how are we going to allow for the birth of these later offspring, hopefully of special and unusual quality? What if some parents choose to have only one child or none at all? Could not other parents then be allowed to have slightly larger families, at least a few extras?

Dr. John B. Graham of Chapel Hill has even suggested that each couple receive two tickets as their child allotment. If they choose not to use them, they could give these tickets to couples who desired more children!

CHAPTER 6

A GOOD START

Labor and Birth

When does the baby's mental welfare begin? Before birth. And not, of course, because of the effect of maternal impressions on the unborn child; but rather because the mother, even during her pregnancy, is developing attitudes, expectancies, and decisions that will inevitably influence the course of the baby's mental growth, particularly in the four fundamental months that follow birth. It is well to make a good start.

The mental hygiene of the child, therefore, begins with maternity hygiene. For this reason, the obstetrician has a more important role to play than he frequently suspects. Naturally his concern is focused upon the critical event of birth and the preservation of the mother's health in the face of this crisis. But granting this, the expectant mother still turns to him with many questions that have potential importance for her personal psychology and for the psychological welfare of the expected child. There are still other questions that she does not formulate at all, but that the obstetrician should formulate for her through his guidance.

The obstetrician has a big responsibility, which is not always carried out as effectively as perhaps it should be. The term "cultural warping of childbirth" is harsh, but may there not be some truth in it? Are obstetrical practices often more rooted in hospital and medical tradition than in human physiology? There was a time when parents-to-be put themselves in the hands of a trusted obstetrician and accepted whatever directives he gave.

But times are changing. Expectant parents are more knowledgeable than they used to be. Many wish to be more involved than in the past. They seek out and even shop around for the type of physician and hospital they feel they need in order to have the type of childbearing experience they want. They not only want a doctor who will support them in their efforts to have a prepared, natural birth with a minimum of or no medication; they also want a hospital that offers education for childbearing and a supportive family-centered atmosphere.

The demand for "rooming-in," a word coined by Dr. Gesell thirty years ago, has alerted many hospitals that a new type of mother is arising and that times are changing. Obstetricians also need to respond when the prospective parents ask for natural childbirth and no medication during delivery.

It is hard to account for the number of unphysiological practices that have become so much a part of American obstetric care that they have been accepted as normal accompaniments of birth. It is when we compare our infant mortality rate and our Apgar scores* after birth with those of other countries (the Netherlands, Sweden, and Japan to name only three) that we realize there is something more to be desired.

Our efficiency, the elaboration of hospital equipment, and the use of drugs are often working against the normal processes of birth and the safe delivery of an undamaged child. It is strongly recommended that the trend in many countries to have professionally trained nurse-midwives be followed here to relieve the obstetrician of a too heavy load and to support the expectant mother throughout labor, during birth, and after birth. The presence of the expectant father, especially if he has been trained with his wife in natural childbirth methods, can give emotional and physical support.

Too often parents are not sufficiently informed. They should be told

---

* A method of scoring a newborn's physiological competence (heart rate, respiratory effort, muscle tone, reflex irritability, response to catheter in nostril, and color) at sixty seconds and again at five minutes after birth.

that obstetrical medication may be to the disadvantage of their new-born infant. In our clinical service we have become increasingly aware that obstetrical medication is the possible source of minimal brain injury in the child who is showing difficulty in the learning process. It is important for mothers to be able to report on what medication they receive during labor. If they had realized the dangers, they might well have refused certain kinds of medication.

Simply stated, mothers who are "prepared" for the possibility of participating effectively in the birth process may experience significantly shorter labor, may require less medication and less obstetrical intervention, and may remember the experience of birth more favorably, than those who are not. An educative process is needed, such as is fostered by the International Childbirth Association.

Breast-Feeding

First and foremost comes the question of breast-feeding. Too often the decision on this crucial question is allowed to drift until a short time before the baby's birth. This dilatoriness has an adverse effect upon the mother's emotional orientation. It also tends to have an adverse effect upon her capacity for lactation. For one thing, the breast and nipples may require regular and systematic attention three months prior to birth, the anointing and massage of the nipples preventing the cracking that so often interferes with successful breast-feeding. This regular attention to the nipples also prepares the mother mentally for the duty of breast-feeding when the time arrives. Perhaps the word "duty" has been misplaced. Our culture in America in years not too long past showed a growing tendency to give the mother a choice between nursing and artificial feeding, and often weighted the choice in favor of the bottle.

However, within the last thirty years there has been an ever-increasing surge toward breast-feeding. Before that, mothers did not receive the supportive help they needed. Many had not fully realized the benefits of breast-feeding for both infant and mother. It is easier to make a choice when the mother realizes the advantages. Would any mother wish to deprive her infant of colostrum, the viscous substance that precedes the milk during the first two days after delivery, if she knew that this substance contains many protective antibodies? Early access to the breast, even in the delivery room, starts the process of interaccommodation between mother and child. We can destroy this by giving the infant fluid by bottle and separating him from his mother. The transitional milk can come in as early as twenty-four hours after delivery if the infant is allowed access to the breast when he cries.

The advantages to the child of a ready supply of nourishment from the mother, of a protein he can digest, of the close physical contact with the mother, of protection from illness (especially diarrhea) for the first six months before he has built up his own immunological protections, plus many other benefits, should alert mothers and physicians that breast-feeding may well constitute a fundamental requirement, not merely a method of choice. To be sure, the newborn can survive without breast-feeding, but only with certain very definite deprivations.

Fortunately the forces of influence are no longer restricted to those in authority—the obstetrician, the pediatrician. Grass-roots forces have been organizing in favor of breast-feeding since 1956 in the mother-stimulated La Leche Leagues, including two in Canada, one in Africa, and one in Mexico. The members give their personal service to those who have trouble continuing breast-feeding. There is a spirit in these organizations and a capacity to disseminate knowledge that defy all the forces which oppose breast-feeding.

A Rooming-In Arrangement for the Baby

Now let us assume that we take our point of departure from the internal physiological clock of the infant himself and give regard to his individual cries. We might then suggest a rooming-in arrangement, which would bring both bassinet and baby into the mother's room.

It is a movable bassinet which may be put in a secluded corner or more intimately at the foot or side of the bed, in accordance with the mother's wishes. Is it not desirable to place the mother on a reasonable self-demand basis? When her strength permits and when her wishes so dictate, it may prove very wise to keep the baby within her vicinity during the course of the day. After the evening or 10 P.M. feeding he might be best in an adjoining room with other infants, to ensure a better sleep for the mother. He can be brought to her as he awakes and cries.

A rooming-in arrangement will actually reduce the amount of manipulation to which the baby is subjected. It simply means that when he cries to be fed, he will be fed. It also means that the baby will benefit from the added oversight of the mother during the intervals between feeding. There is no evidence that under proper safeguards such a rooming-in procedure increases the hazard of infection. If anything, the hazard will be reduced because of attendant advantages.

The presence of the baby gives the mother a profound sense of security. Vague worries and misgivings as to the identity of her baby lose their insistence. She is in a favorable position to build up a sense of relationship with the infant, a sense of familiarity that will fortify her confidence when in the very near future she herself takes over the ministrations and infant care. She is spared the uncertainty that comes from being unable to visualize exactly where her baby is and how he is faring at any given moment. This proximity of mother and child is so natural and can be made so simple that it will dissipate tensions and much of the hospital haste and hurry.

The presence of the baby will serve in a salutary way to protect the mother against an influx of visitors. He sleeps most of the day. The mother keeps a weather eye on him. The incidental oversight makes her perceptive to his self-demands. All this increases the advantages of the self-regulatory program of care on which she and the physician have embarked. There is no excessive strain upon the mother. She is within easy reach of a push-button and controls the situation by summoning the nurse whenever she needs help. The rooming-in self-regulatory arrangement is not rigid; it is flexible and can be altered to meet the needs of both mother and child from day to day.

From the standpoint of the infant there are obvious advantages; that is, if we grant that the infant is subject to psychological influences in this early neonatal period. He enjoys more natural and diverse stimulations under rooming-in conditions. His rhythms will not escape notice and he will be spared unnecessary crying. He is in a position to be his natural self. He will communicate his individuality to his mother even in this short hospital stay of three or four days. The more intimate reciprocal relationship between them serves to give the mother more insight into the baby's needs as expressed in his patterns of behavior. The rooming-in arrangement, however, should be kept flexible. It may be adopted in varying degrees subject to the physician's judgment. In some instances, for special reasons it may be unsuitable either for the mother or for the baby.

We would like to recommend the keeping of a behavior-day chart, as illustrated in Figure 4, page 230. We originally tried to simplify the recording process to perhaps only once a day, around noon, but it is difficult to remember all of the changing happenings of the day if they are not recorded immediately. Each entry had thus best be made on the spot. There was a time when we anticipated that each mother would chart her child's daily behavior day so that she would know what was happening and possibly predict what was to come. But this proved too much of a chore for most. However, a sample chart is included for those who may be interested.

From Hospital to Home

There was a time, and this was true thirty years ago when this book was first written, when the mother spent a fortnight in the hospital after the birth of her baby. We were unnecessarily protective then. Gradually we have reduced the length of this stay, though in part because there is not room in the hospital for mother and infant to stay on.

Nowadays a three-to-four-day stay in the hospital sets the mother-and-child couple well on their way together, especially if they have been growing together in a rooming-in situation. The mother has thus seen so much of her baby that he is no stranger to her. He looks much less precarious because she has seen and participated in his adaptations from day to day. She has seen him dressed and undressed and has tried her own hand at carrying out his needs. She has watched him being sponged off and is relieved that a bath is often not in order before he is several weeks old, when he can enjoy it. This introductory familiarity with the details of infant care can stand her in good stead when she is thrown on her own after her homecoming. She may not even need the demonstrating services of a visiting nurse, but might indeed welcome the ministrations of a visiting homemaker.

The importance of planning for acceptable help, especially during the first six to eight weeks of an infant's life, cannot be emphasized enough. Europeans, especially the Scandinavians, have solved this problem through the existence of state-supported home helpers' agencies. New Jersey has developed such facilities, and it is hoped that other states will soon follow suit.

The need for spending the first three days at home in bed, in an extension of the hospital regime, could thus be more easily met. The protection from interruption during three one-hour naps each day could also be assured. This regime could also protect the mother from too many well-meaning visitors, especially relatives. A special time of day convenient to both mother and child could be adhered to for visitors. The demands of too much visiting can so exhaust a mother that her ability to breast-feed her baby may actually be in jeopardy.

Each family needs to work out a plan that is best for the whole family as it relates to the demands of the household, the presence of other children, the preparation of meals, etc. Fathers are now becoming more a part of this early adjustment period. Sometimes a father may even arrange his vacation so that he can be there in both an active and a supportive way. If the baby sleeps in a separate room during the night, though nearby, it may be the father who brings him to the mother for the night feeding. The domestic policy should be to divide the labors. The home waits on the mother and the mother waits on the child.

If proper care is provided to ensure enough sleep for the mother, enough fluid intake, and household help, especially during these first critical six to eight weeks, there is no reason why she should not be capable of continuing breast-feeding. (Her interest in breast-feeding may well be strengthened by the realization that it has a favorable effect upon the postpartum involution of the uterus.)

The Evolution of the Behavior Day

These first months are inclined to be somewhat stormy, but the weather will seem much less erratic and will take on much more meaning if the child's behavior is regarded not as erratic but as an expression of his organic needs and interests. A behavior-day chart, if the mother wishes to keep one, facilitates such interpretation. The baby's most articulate mouthpiece is his crying. Crying is essentially language, even though at times it appears to be indulged in for purposes of sheer self-activity. From the standpoint of a self-demand regime, the major task of the mother is to be alert to all forms of crying and fussing, to read their meaning, and to give as prompt attention as possible. Punctual response to crying in the early weeks reduces the total amount of crying, for if there is a delay in the response there is likely to be a resumption and prolongation of the crying after attention has been given.

(In the interests of closeness, some mothers have returned to the old practice of slinging their infants against their bodies—ventrally, or in front, until they weigh seventeen pounds or so, and then dorsally, or on their backs, to better accommodate their increased weight. This can quiet the baby with amazing speed.)

It is a comfort to realize in advance that ordinarily there is a steady reduction in the frequency and amount of crying. During the first eight weeks hunger crying is virtually universal. After this time the hunger cry tends to diminish in intensity and frequency. The child begins to substitute fussing for crying and he has longer intervals of quiescence because he is becoming interested in various forms of non-feeding behavior. His crying is consequently more intermittent, less sustained. By the age of sixteen weeks his hunger cry may be almost entirely limited to the morning feeding. During the first six weeks he also cries when his diapers are wet or soiled. He may even cry out for this reason during a sleep period. After about the age of six weeks he accepts this condition with a nonchalance that may continue to the age of twelve or fifteen months, or even later.

At about the age of four weeks a new type of cry emerges: the baby shows a tendency to cry prior to sleep. This is not a hunger cry. The cry is a mixture of cause and effect, a symptom of his growing capacity to stay awake. It is a developmental symptom of a thrust toward a higher level of activity. This wakefulness crying tends to occur in the afternoon and evening. It loses its prominence after about the age of ten or twelve weeks, forsooth because the baby has scaled the higher level. At about this time there is an increasing metamorphosis of crying into fussing and into "talking" vocalization.

With advancing age the crying that occurs toward the end of the day is frequently related to a higher order of psychological hungers. The child wishes to exercise his growing sense-perception abilities, to experience color, light, sound, musical notes, singing. He likes to watch movements, and to feel them through his kinesthetic sense perception. He may like to be talked to or even to receive play objects toward the end of the first four months. These new appetites or interests come in small snatches, often punctuated by brief intervals of crying and fussing. The mother is well advised not to overstimulate the child in response to this type of crying, but inasmuch as it is symptomatic of psychological growth needs, it deserves discriminating consideration. For similar reasons a little gentle rocking prior to sleep may assuage a fretful cry. While the mother carried her unborn child he was frequently subjected to translations in space. He does not suffer from mild transportations and an occasional jostle after he is born.

With increasing age the child cries less readily on provocation.

Whereas in the early weeks a startle was typically followed by a cry, he may, by the age of twelve weeks and later, startle without crying. He is building up margins of reserve and margins of exploitive activity. Viewed in perspective, his behavior is manifestly becoming more configured, more defined. He terminates meals more decisively by symptoms of positive refusal. His appetite is more clear-cut. His demand to be moved from the crib for a brief sojourn on the couch may become so clearly defined to a perceptive mother that he could not express it better if he had a vocabulary of spoken words.

His behavior becomes relatively so effectively defined that there may be a temptation to feed him solids even as early as twelve or sixteen weeks. Such a premature attempt to introduce solids during the first four months sometimes invites regrettable results. The baby's neuromuscular system is not mature enough to handle solids competently. His tongue projection and lip constriction patterns are so dominant that they interfere with normal swallowing mechanisms. Moreover, if supplementary food is added too early the mother's milk balance is upset. A premature administration of solids may result either in marked reduction or overproduction of the mother's milk supply, for the baby consumes less at the breast. Not until about the age of twenty to twenty-four weeks is he likely to be mature and interested enough to handle solids acceptably. Fortunately, at this period the mother is capable of maintaining an adequate milk supply over a full twelve-hour interval without the stimulus of the infant's nursing. This circumstance permits the introduction of solids without prejudicing continued breast-feeding and also gives more freedom to the mother. Breast-feeding continues to be advantageous to both mother and child. It is especially advantageous if the child persists in demanding an early-morning feeding.

The expanding behavior chart builds up a perspective that reaches into the future as well as the past. This sense of perspective is increased when the mother is informed in advance that her child at sixteen weeks is very likely to show well-defined behavior patterns. But she should understand that the trend toward focused and defined behavior is not altogether smooth and even—the baby has "bad" days as well as "good" days. And paradoxically enough, from the standpoint of development the "bad" days may be his best days because they are days of high tension in which he is making a thrust into a more advanced sphere of behavior. These are the high-tension days when his crying is expressive not so much of frustration as of "thrustration"! The pendulum is swinging to a new extreme. He is wriggling upward. He may briefly display a behavior pattern that will not become part of his established equipment until several weeks later. After a high-tension episode or a high-tension day he may revert to a lower level of apparently vegetative functioning which on the surface seems like a "good" day.

Actually both types of days have their justification in the economy of development. Development proceeds consistently toward a distant goal but it fluctuates from day to day while advancing toward that goal. It is therefore not surprising to find that after the baby has consolidated many of his abilities at the end of four months, he will begin in another month or two again to show perturbances and irregularities reminiscent of the first four months. Nevertheless, the trend of normal development is always toward increasing organization and consolidation. Realization of this trend has practical value because it gives the mother a sense of proportion. Things are not as bad as they seem. Patience does not cease to be a virtue; for the higher order of abilities cannot be hastened. Everything in season.

In the following chapters we shall try to outline in an orderly manner the behavior traits and the behavior trends which time brings to the growing infant. We have already emphasized that time travels in diverse paces with diverse persons. No two infants develop in precisely the same manner at precisely the same pace in every detail. But the ladder of maturity is made of rungs. The series of behavior profiles in subsequent chapters is simply intended to show *in a general and approximate way* how a somewhat typical child, as a representative of his species and his culture, mounts the tall ladder with rungs placed at advancing ages.

CHAPTER 7

SELF-REGULATION AND CULTURAL GUIDANCE

If we have demonstrated that the infant is indeed an individual, then a very practical question at once arises: How much shall we defer to his individuality? The very helplessness of the newborn baby and the obscurity that conceals his individuality make these questions somewhat poignant.

Individuals and Schedules

One solution for such perplexities is to lay down a fixed feeding schedule and to raise the baby by it. The schedule presumably reflects the wisdom of the human race. It is based upon much experience derived from the care of previous generations of babies. It also embodies the cumulative knowledge of the science of nutrition. The physician, as the carrier of this knowledge, lays down or sets up a schedule with a degree of acknowledged authority. The schedule thus becomes at once a symbol and a vehicle of cultural control.

The schedule, therefore, would seem to be the very essence of hygienic science and good will. In actual application, however, the culture often proves to be so inept and the infant so refractory that conflicts ensue between schedule and individual. Difficulties multiply when a hard-and-fast schedule is rigidly imposed without discriminating between babies with different tempos and different temperaments. Veritable contests may occur.

The culture, embodied in the parent, insists on feeding at a pre-established hour; the baby insists on sleeping instead. The baby cries when he should be asleep; he may even vomit when he ought to keep his meal down; he may be hungry when he ought to be satisfied; he may refuse to take solids when he should, etc. This child-versus-culture conflict is exaggerated when an overwrought parent and an overdetermined physician insist too strongly on schedules and procedures that are not adapted to the infant. It is at this near breaking point of emotional tension that the problem of self-regulation and cultural guidance comes to a genuine issue. Who is to win out—the schedule or the individual? And who is the wiser—the household or the baby?

The Wisdom of the Body is the arresting title of Walter Cannon's well-known volume that discusses the marvelous mechanisms of self-regulation whereby the human body maintains an optimal equilibrium in its chemical constituents and physiological processes. These mechanisms operate with considerable precision even in the newborn baby; but they do not operate with completed perfection. In many behaviors the baby is physiologically awkward. He does not know how to sleep, how to wake up, how to keep himself at a steady temperature. In many of these functions he is "learning," he is growing, his body is acquiring more wisdom. But all the time he is preeminently wise as to what he *cannot* do and what he *should not* do because of the limitations of his maturity.

He is in closer league with Mother Nature than he is with the contemporary culture. There are limits, physiological limits, to his tolerances. He is growing at an extremely rapid rate, which may add to his difficulties in adjusting to the demands of culture. He is in a somewhat unsettled state of progressive organization and reorganization. He has his ups and downs, his physiological needs seem to vary from day to day; no two days are quite alike, and each month differs from the next. He is under the constant necessity of keeping all his internal organs and body fluids working cooperatively to produce an internal environment favorable for full life and growth. It is not a simple task. He advances as he matures, but not by a straight and narrow path, nor by a simple timetable. *He fluctuates as he advances.*

Self-demands and cultural demands must somehow be brought into mutual accord. This can be done only by appreciating the essential wisdom of the baby's body and behavior manifestations. We must respect his *fluctuations* and interpret their meaning. The fluctuations express his developmental needs. The progress of the fluctuations from one week to another affords a clue to his methods of growth and learning. If we chart his naps and sleep periods over several months, we find that the total sleeping time per day varies in almost a rhythmic manner. The variations go up and down, but the downs in the long run exceed the ups, so that the average amount of diurnal sleep may fall from nineteen hours in the fourth week to thirteen hours in the fortieth week. This is what we mean by self-regulating fluctuation.

Development does not proceed in a straight line. It deviates now up and now down, now left and now right. Sometimes it even seems to go backward. But the total trend is forward. If the deviations and the slips are not too many and too extreme, the organism catches its balance at each step and then makes another step onward. The fluctuations are really not lapses: they are groping efforts to reach a further organization.

The enlightened culture attempts to recognize these efforts, and to go along with them. The child is in league with nature: but he is also growing into his culture. By reading the cues of the child's organism, culture also comes into closer league with nature. By registering his self-demands and by having them met to a judicious degree, the individual is able to accomplish a maximum of self-regulation.

Self-Demand Schedules

How does an infant register his self-demands? By his behavior. The well-being and the ill-being of his organism are summed up in his patterns of behavior and in the alternations of rest and activity that make up his behavior day. The infant's diary is represented in his behavior day.

The infant does not have words at his command, but he has two sets of signs and signals: the negative and the positive—those that express *avoidance* and *rejection* and those that express *seeking* and *acceptance*. The negative signals include crying, fretting, uneasiness, refusal, anxiety. The positive signals include quiescence, relaxation, satiety, cooing, smiling, and pleasurable self-activity. By such behavior language the infant reports his status and his self-demands. He tells us if and when he is hungry, sleepy, tired, contented, uncomfortable. By paying attention to these cues, the culture (through the parents) can devise a flexible schedule of care adapted to the infant's needs as they arise. This would be a *self-demand schedule* as distinguished from an imposed schedule. An inflexible schedule based on a more or less arbitrary norm would ignore the infant's signs and signals. It would insist on regularity of intervals despite the infant's irregular fluctuations. It would regularly insist on waking even when the infant insists on sleeping.

There are two kinds of time—organic time and clock time. The former is based on the wisdom of the body, the latter on cultural conventions. A self-demand schedule takes its departure from organic time. The infant is fed when he is hungry; is allowed to sleep when he is sleepy; he is not roused to be fed; he is changed if he fusses on being wet; he is granted some social play when he craves it. He is not made to live by the clock on the wall, but rather by the internal clock of his fluctuating organic needs.

Some parents have interpreted the Gesell philosophy as being ultra-permissive because of a misinterpretation of our self-demand and self-regulation method of dealing with the infant. Admittedly, at the very beginning of this regime the infant *is* fed when he is hungry. And in the earliest days or weeks, this demand for feeding comes rather often.

But the mother is not a passive participant in all of this. The behavior-day chart (Figure 4) shows how quickly, through self-adjustment and cultural guidance, the child works out his individual schedule, which gradually includes the expectations of the household as well as his own hunger pangs. He soon reduces his feedings from some seven a day to only three a day. The mother takes her first clues from the child's own demands, but the child quickly comes to regulate and adapt his own demands to the expectations of the culture.

(The same thing applies to the older child, and to situations other than sleeping and feeding. A developmental point of view, or, as it has sometimes been called, a philosophy of *informed permissiveness*, recommends that the adult be sufficiently informed about expectations for children at various ages and of differing personality characteristics that he can know what it is reasonable to expect and *not* expect of any given child. He then refrains from making demands that will be unreasonable for that child at that age, but definitely does make reasonable demands. We are permissive to the extent that we permit normal inadequacies and ineptitudes. We are not permissive in that we do make reasonable demands.)

Self-Regulation

This principle of self-regulatory fluctations is so fundamental in child development that it has vast cultural implications. We emphasize that the principle applies not only to such simple functions as sleeping, eating, and infant play, but also to the higher forms of learning and of mental organization. The organism during the entire period of active growth is in a state of formative instability combined with a progressive movement toward stability. The so-called growth gains represent consolidations of stability. The opposition between two apparently contrary tendencies results in seesaw fluctuations. Stability and variability coexist not as contradictory opposites, but as mutual complements. Therefore we must look upon many fluctuations as positive thrusts or efforts toward higher maturity. They may be construed as self-demands, which if adequately unsatisfied by the culture result in optimal growth of personality organization.

The cultural pattern must at first be adapted to the growth pattern because in the final analysis all individual development depends upon intrinsic self-regulation. There is no adjustment to culture other than self-adjustment.

But self-demand is only the beginning of the story of fostering the infant's healthy development. It is important to get a feeling early for the way that the mother at times needs to give in to the baby's demands and his immaturity—and at other times must require that he himself adapt to the culture's demands. It is important for the parent to learn the mechanisms of innate and cultural regulation within the first year of the child's life, when the patterns are relatively simple.

Thus a mother understands the urgency of the four-week-old child's hunger cries and knows that they can be controlled only with food. She realizes, when her child is sixteen to twenty-eight weeks old and this cry is less frequent, that he can wait for his feeding. His hunger pains are now less intense, his gastrointestinal tract is subordinating itself at times to other demands. For now the infant's overflow energy is diverted into active discovery of his own body, his hands, his feet, and also of those who people his environment. His own inner growth is a controlling and organizing factor.

But this inner ability to wait is specific rather than general. It fails to show itself at the age of eighteen months when it is time for food. There is a developmental reason for this behavior. The child is acquiring a new control, that of demanding food when he sees the table at which it is usually served. His mother, realizing the significance of this passing stage of maturity, manages accordingly. She knows that at eighteen months the child has an overwhelming sense of immediacy. She also knows that she can help him to wait when he is two and a half years old by saying, "Pretty soon." By three years he understands "When it's time"; and by four he may wish to help in the preparation of a meal.

The old and pithy word "curb" harks back to a control that was used in earlier days. The word lives with us in our curbstones. These ancient stones help us in the control of behavior quite as much as do modern traffic lights. The young child grows only slowly in his understanding of what a curbstone means as a limit of safety. His culture, having put him in a world of swiftly moving cars, must protect him from dashing out into the street at eighteen months. He needs to be harnessed. At two he not only sees curbstones but has the motor capacity and balance to walk on them endlessly as long as he has a helping and protecting hand available. It is not until two and a half years that he visually sees and is aware of the danger of a car backing up toward him. At three he continues to accept his mother's hand as he is crossing a street. At four he is more watchful, more conscious of objects coming from both directions, and longs for the independence of crossing a street absolutely alone. The culture knows that he often overstates his abilities at this age, but responds to his eagerness by allowing him to cross narrow, safe streets (though not thoroughfares) without holding of hands. By five he is less eager and more self-regulated, and accepts the new and helpful control of traffic lights with his ever-watchful eyes. He is now capable of greater independence.

If he cannot adjust in this orderly fashion, there may be two possible causes. He may be holding on to earlier modes of adjustment. The culture must then wait and watch, believing that the time will come when his behavior equipment will be ready. Often, however, the child cannot make the final step alone, but needs a lift from the environment at the moment when he is ready to accept the help.

Through all such mutual accommodations between culture and child, human relationships are improved at all age levels. The culture teaches the child, but the child also teaches the culture—makes it more intelligently aware of the laws, the frailties, and the potentialities of human nature.

The Cultural Significance of Self-Regulation

Does this philosophy of self-regulation elicit overindulgence or excessive individualism? By no means; for we always conceive of our individual as growing in a culture which makes demands on individual responsibility. In the infant the self-demand type of management builds up body stamina and a corresponding organic sense of secureness. The most vital cravings of the infant have to do with food and sleep. These cravings have an individual organic pattern. Only by individualizing schedules can we meet these cravings promptly and generously. By meeting them with certainty, we multiply those experiences of satisfied expectation which create a sense of security, a confidence in the lawfulness of the universe.

It is too easy to forget that the infant has a psychology, and that our methods of care affect his mental as well as physical welfare. The individualization of food-sleep-activity schedules is a basic approach to the mental hygiene of infancy. The education of the baby begins with his behavior day.

The first year of life offers a mother a golden opportunity to become acquainted with the individual psychology of her child. What she learns during that first year will be of permanent value, for throughout childhood and adolescence this child is likely to display the same dynamic characteristics that are obvious in early life.

The adoption of a self-demand-schedule policy creates a favorable atmosphere for the kind of observation that will enable the mother to learn the basic characteristics of her infant. She escapes the vexation that comes from forcing unwanted food and from waiting for long spells of hunger crying to come to an end. Instead of looking at the clock on the wall, she shifts her interest to the total behavior day of the baby as it records itself on the daily chart (if she keeps one). She also notes in what manner and in what direction these days transform as the infant himself transforms. This is a challenge to intelligent perception. Thus she satisfies her instinctive interest in the child's growth and gains increasing insight into the growth process and the growth pattern. It simply comes to this: the mother has made the baby (with all his inborn wisdom) a working partner. He helps her to work out an optimal and flexible schedule suited to his changing needs.

Although this seems very simple, it has profound consequences in the mother's attitudes. Instead of striving for executive efficiency, she aims first of all to be perceptive of and sensitive to the child's behavior. Thus she becomes a true complement to him, alertly responsive to his needs. The child is more than a detached individual who must be taken care of at stated clock intervals. And he is more than a treasured possession. He is a living, growing organism, an individual in his own right to whom the culture must attune itself if his potentialities are to be fully realized.

The first year of life is by no means all-determining, but it is the most favorable of all periods for acquiring the right orientation toward the child's individuality. During this first year one does not use sharp emotional methods of discipline. One comes to understand in what way the child's immaturity must be met. We expect the child to creep before he walks. We do not punish him for creeping. We do not prod him unduly into walking. Growth has its seasons and sequences.

The child must do his own growing. For this reason we should create the most favorable conditions for self-regulation and self-adjustment. But this means neither self-indulgence nor laissez faire. The culture intervenes, assists, directs, postpones, encourages, and discourages at many turns; but always in relation to the child's behavior equipment and maturity status. When the baby is young we meet his hunger needs promptly. As he grows older he is able to wait a little longer before his hunger is gratified. He thus acquires increasing hardihood by slow degrees as he is able to bear it. But this method of gradual induction is not possible unless we take fundamental notice of his self-demand cues and shape our guidance on a self-regulatory developmental basis.

This philosophy of child development and of child guidance assumes a democratic type of culture. A totalitarian type of culture would place the first and last premium upon the extrinsic cultural pattern; it would mold the child to this pattern; it would have little patience with self-demand. Cultural guidance, as outlined in the present volume, is essentially individualized. It begins in earliest infancy. It remains individualized not only in the home but in the nursery school and in the larger social world.

CHAPTER 8

FOUR WEEKS OLD

Behavior Profile

What is the mind of the four-week-old baby like? He cannot tell us; and you and I cannot recall what it was like. The inmost psychic processes of infant and child are always veiled from view. Nevertheless, we can gain a just and useful picture of the "psychology" of a baby, even at the tender age of four weeks, if we examine the different kinds of behavior of which he is capable. His behavior patterns, his behavior traits, tell us what he really is.

In four weeks the baby has made considerable progress. He is not quite as limp and "molluscous" as he was at birth. His body muscles have more tone; they tighten in tension when he is picked up. Therefore he seems less fragile, more organized.

Indeed, he *is* more organized. Growth is a process of progressive organization. It is not simply a matter of getting bigger and stronger. The four-week-old baby is much more mature than a newborn baby because his whole action system is more elaborately built up, more closely knit together. Multimillions of nerve fibers from millions of nerve cells have made new connections with each other and have improved their old connections with his internal organs and with his muscular system.

His breathing is deeper and more regular. His swallowing is firmer; he does not choke or regurgitate as freely as he used to. He is less susceptible to startling, jaw trembling, and sneezing. His temperature regulation is steadier. All his vegetative functions are under better control, because the chemistry of his body fluids as well as the "vegetative" part of his nervous system has made adjustments to his postnatal environment.

But he is by no means a vegetable. He evidences an unmistakable psychological interest in his bodily functions and bodily experiences. He gives manifest attention to the well-being that suffuses him after a meal; he enjoys the massive warmth and tingle of the bath; he responds to the snugness of being wrapped up or of being securely held. He reacts positively to comforts and satisfactions; he reacts negatively to discomforts and denials. By crying and other sign language he expresses demands and desires. He may quiet as he is slung in close contact with his mother's body. He is far from empty-minded. He is far from being a mere automaton. There may even be a trace of volition in some of his behavior. At any rate, we cannot think of him as being a mere bundle of reflexes. From the standpoint of four-week-oldness his behavior is patterned, meaningful, significant.

He stills sleeps most of the day and night—as much as twenty hours out of the twenty-four—but his waking up is more decisive and more businesslike than it was even a fortnight ago. His eyes roll less aimlessly; the twelve diminutive but all-important muscles that operate the movements of the eyeballs are assuming directive control. He is now able to hold both eyes in a fixed position, staring vaguely at a window or wall. This does not mean that he actually perceives the outlines of the window; the nerve cells of the brain cortex are not sufficiently grown for that. Yet he is especially regardful of the human face when it comes noddingly into his field of vision. His general body activity diminishes when this "interesting" optical and social stimulus meets the eye. In yet another month he will converge both eyes upon a near object. Then we may say he has truly begun to use his binoculars.

At four weeks his range of eye movements is limited by incomplete head control. He tends to keep his head to one side. You can entice him to look at a dangling toy held directly before his eyes, and he will follow it a short distance when it is moved toward the midline; but it will take another month or two before he will follow way across from one horizon to the opposite horizon.

At sixteen weeks his head will prefer the midline, facing the zenith. If during the first few months the head prefers the horizon or side position, it is for good developmental reasons. This position enables the baby to catch glimpses of his hand, for he often holds his arm extended toward the same side to which his head is directed, the other arm being flexed at the shoulder.

This sideward attitude of head and arm (sometimes called the tonic neck reflex) is a normal stage of growth which should not be tampered with simply because it appears asymmetrical. It is a natural form of asymmetry which serves to bring eyes and hands into coordination, and such natural postures are entitled to respect. At four weeks the baby's hands are usually fisted (another natural posture. How silly it would be to keep prying open the hands; they will remain open in due course when the baby is ready to reach).

Just now, at the age of four weeks, the baby is beginning to reach, but he does so with his eyes rather than his hands. The eyes take the lead in the organization of his growing brain. He cannot hold a rattle prolongedly until about the age of eight weeks; at first he merely holds without looking. In another month he both holds and looks; still later he seizes on sight. The coordination of hands and eyes is a long and complicated process. It takes time. It needs understanding.

The four-week-old baby is not ready for social stimulation. His vegetative needs, his sensorimotor experiences are most important. He is often busiest when he is apparently quiescent. His behavior patterns are undergoing organization and reorganization, through immobilization as well as through activity. He cannot tell us what is happening because his laryngeal vocabulary is limited to a few throaty sounds. But he makes his developmental needs articulate in many other ways. This will become clear when we describe the daily cycle of his home behavior.

Behavior Day

The behavior profile that you have just read summarizes the behavior capacities and characteristics of the four-week-old baby. How will he display these characteristics; how will he use his capacities in the course of a day? He answers this question for us in the form of his behavior day. If he could keep a logbook, he could record for us all of his activities and interests, and from such a record we could gain a picture of the manner in which he stores and distributes his energies.

On the basis of our own observations of the day-by-day living of the four-week-old infant, we can draw up a suggestive profile sketch of a more or less typical behavior day. We cannot set down any hard-and-fast hours because we must allow for many individual variations and because we shall assume for purposes of illustration a breast-fed baby on a self-demand schedule. The Egyptians reckoned their day from midnight, the Babylonians from sunrise, the Athenians from sunset; we shall reckon the baby's day from midnight and shall consider the full series of twenty-four hours that span the interval between two successive midnights.

Assume that the baby is sound asleep, at least on the first midnight. He may awake at almost any hour between 2 A.M. and 6 A.M. He awakes with a decisive, piercing crying. He awakes because his economy requires that once again he should have a ration of food. He wakes to eat. His cry is a more or less articulate statement of this extremely fundamental fact. Incidentally, it serves to announce his presence. Vaguely it may even express a sense of isolation, for he quiets momentarily when he is taken up, whether by his father or his mother. But crying renews if he is not soon put to the breast. He needs a little help to secure the nipple. Crying ceases when he establishes contact.

He nurses for a period of from twenty to forty minutes. He may be seemingly satisfied with one breast but often when offered the second breast he takes it with revived vigor. His eyes are closed during the nursing. As he approaches satiety the sucking becomes more intermittent and he gradually tapers off into sleep.

A similar satiety response occurs if his tiny stomach is distended by air. The wise mother, therefore, "bubbles" the infant when shifting him from one breast to the other and at the termination of the meal. The baby is now under the benevolent anesthesia of natural sleep. The mother exploits this opportunity to change the wet diapers. By postponing the change in this way, the baby's impatience is circumvented. If, however, the diapers were soiled before the feeding, the change is made earlier.

The baby is put back into the bassinet. He sleeps for a period of from two to five hours and wakes up as before for the prime purpose of feeding again. We call this a sleep period rather than a nap. A nap is a restricted and well-demarcated interval of sleep immediately preceded or followed by an equally well-defined period of wakefulness. But at four weeks the feeding-sleeping-waking-feeding sequence is so closely merged that the baby's day resolves itself into five or six zones of sleep, each terminating typically with a hunger cry. The baby has not yet learned to wake up for more advanced reasons. He does not nap. His capacity for wakefulness is very immature.

In the late afternoon (typically between four and six o'clock), however, he has a wider margin for perceptual and presocial behavior. This, therefore, is an optimal time, although not the conventional one, for his daily bath. Where he might show resistance in the morning, he now enjoys the experience of immersion in the tepid water. His eyes open wider; his general body activity may abate. He often gives tokens of pleasurable response to the sound of the voice and to the handling, which gives him a feeling of tactility, and to being tucked in when he is dressed and restored to the bassinet for another sleep period.

Whether the infant cries because he is awake or whether he is awake because he cries poses a philosophical problem. The four-week-old infant is maturing his capacity to wake up and to extend his areas of sense perception. Hunger is the chief cause of his crying but his cries are beginning to differentiate and there are distinctive features in the cries associated with various kinds of discomfort.

He frets or cries when his alimentary tract and his eliminative organs are not functioning smoothly. He basks with contentment when his physiological well-being is at least temporarily achieved. In these brief periods he has a margin for more advanced perceptual adjustments. He may give absorbed attention to his sense of well-being. He likes to gaze in the direction of his accustomed tonic-neck-reflex attitude and sometimes his fretfulness subsides if he is given an opportunity to fixate his restless eyes on some large and not too bright pattern.

Needless to say, these evidences of perceptual and presocial interest are slight and fugitive. Some children do not show them at all until the age of six or eight weeks. At times this early crying seems to be quite without reason, almost as though it were crying for its own sake. But the very fact that the baby quiets recurrently to slight environmental changes suggests that he is entitled to some of these changes. The handling should be restricted to his actual needs. He is not ready for social stimulation. At this age no two behavior days are likely to be identical. Some are stormier than others. Excess storminess may mean that the appropriate adjustments between the organism and the environment have not been attained. All of which suggests that it is well to be alert to such signals as the baby is able to give during the course of his behavior day.

The foregoing behavior day is not set up as a model, but as a suggestive example. This also holds true for the behavior days at later age levels presented in Chapters 9 to 20. They are merely illustrative behavior days. Individual differences are to be expected.

Further child care details for each age are given in the double-column text. [*Specific guidance suggestions are enclosed in brackets.*]

SLEEP

Onset—The baby gradually drops off to sleep toward the end of the nursing process, when sucking becomes intermittent. He will not accept the nipple when sleep is associated with satiety. If wakefulness follows one of the feedings, he may cry prior to the next sleep period.
Waking—The baby cries as he awakens. He may stop momentarily as his diaper is changed, especially when it is only wet. Crying usually continues until he is fed.
Periods—Four to five periods in twenty-four hours. The reduction from seven to eight at birth is accomplished by the merging of two sleep periods. Further reduction may be accomplished by the dropping out of a sleep period between two successive feedings.

[The infant should be cared for as soon as he awakens crying. If crying precedes going to sleep, release from crying into sleep may be assisted by mild and brief rocking of bassinet or carriage, perhaps accompanied by singing.]

FEEDING

Number—The infant spontaneously cuts down his feedings from seven to eight at birth to five or six at four weeks. This is accomplished by merging two adjacent feedings. This reduction may not hold for long and may return later.

Amount—The total amount may fluctuate between eighteen and twenty-five ounces from two to four weeks of age, after which there is a more rapid rise to thirty-two or thirty-six ounces by six to eight weeks of age. There may be no more than a one-ounce fluctuation in the amount of each feeding at four weeks of age, but this rapidly increases to a three-to-four-ounce fluctuation by six to eight weeks.
Duration—Sucking time varies greatly from child to child but is usually thirty to forty minutes and may even be longer during the evening feedings.
Breast- and Bottle-Feeding—Crying demands may be quieted by placing the baby on the mother's lap, but more frequently he is quieted after he secures the breast. He needs help to secure the nipple. The tongue has become more efficient in grasping the nipple and in exerting back-and-forth suction. With satiety the infant falls asleep, will not accept the reintroduction of the nipple, and may show transient facial brightening.

[The majority of infants know when they are hungry and are able to express their hunger by crying. They become more proficient in this innate ability if they are allowed to exercise it. Their proficiency is also promoted if their demands are answered with promptness and if satiety both for food and for sucking is ensured. This is most easily accomplished with breast-feeding.

Both breasts should be presented at each feeding. The first breast is alternated from feeding to feeding even though the child may refuse the second breast at times.]

ELIMINATION

Bowel—One to three or even four movements, on awakening from sleep.
Bladder—The baby may cry when his diaper is wet and quiets when changed. This pattern is only occasional and does not last beyond six weeks of age.
[If crying is associated with wet or soiled diapers, changing will quiet the infant. This cause of crying is to be differentiated from hunger crying.]

BATH AND DRESSING

The baby now enjoys the bath. He does not like to be dressed and undressed.
[Clothing should be as simple as possible. Preferably it should not be put on over the baby's head.]

SELF-ACTIVITY

The infant stares at lights and windows. He favors turning his head to one side or the other, according to his tonic neck reflex. He may become angry if turned on the side away from the light. He quiets as he is shifted toward the light. This desire for light and brightness, apart from sunlight, to which he makes a violent negative response, may be shown later at eight to ten weeks in an interest in red and orange colors. Intense crying may be controlled by having a bright-colored cretonne pillow to gaze upon.

Visual experience with light and bright colors is as important to the child as is the food in his stomach.

SOCIALITY

The baby stares at faces that are close by. If he cries in the evening —which is his way of asking for social stimulation—he quiets if he is picked up and held or if he is allowed to lie naked on a table where he can hear voices and look at lights for an hour or two. This demand is most frequent from six to eight weeks, and its total duration is so related to a growth process that the end results appear to be similar whether he is allowed to cry it out or his demands are satisfied. By eight weeks he likes to follow movement and enjoys seeing people move about the room.

When none of these usual methods work to control crying, slinging the baby against his mother's body often quiets him, especially when she moves about in her ordinary activities.

CHAPTER 9

SIXTEEN WEEKS OLD

Behavior Profile

The four-week-old infant was quite content to lie on his back. He could not support his head on his own shoulders. But the sixteen-week-old infant glories in the exercise of his growing capacity to hold his head upright. He likes to be transferred from the supine to a propped sitting position. His eyes widen, his pulse strengthens, his breathing quickens as he is shifted from horizontal to perpendicular. He holds his head quite steady while bolstering pillows or his mother's hands supply the necessary support for his wobbly trunk. For some ten minutes at a time he relishes his new commanding outlook upon the surrounding world.

He no longer stares blankly. He rotates his head freely from side to side as he lies in his crib—indeed, so freely that the rubbing produces an erosive bald spot. He moves his eyes in active inspection. He fixes them on this and that. He looks at his own hand; he looks at the kitchen sink; he looks at a toy that his mother dangles before him; he may even look from the toy to his mother's hand, and then back again at the toy, a sign of his increasing discrimination. He is becoming perceptive. He is also becoming more expressive. He smiles on the mere sight of a face. He coos, bubbles, chuckles, gurgles, and even laughs aloud.

The provocations for these vocalizations are both internal and external, but he is much less "subjective" than he was at the age of four weeks, much less wrapped up in himself. He is more bound up with his environment: he is sensitive to cultural cues, he "notices" sounds, especially those of the human voice; he "recognizes" his mother; he is so accustomed to certain routines that he expects certain things to happen at mealtime and bath time. He betrays these expectancies in his countenance and in his postures. So the household is also becoming sensitive to his cues. The two-way reciprocity of cues is the basis of acculturation.

Having gained elementary management of the muscles that direct his eyes and the muscles that erect and rotate his head, the next developmental task calls for a better management of his hands. (It is interesting to note that he can "pick up" a small object with his eyes long before he can pick it up with his fingers.)

At sixteen weeks the hand is no longer predominantly fisted. It has loosened up. The fingers are more nimble, more busy. The baby still looks at his hands on occasion, but he has a new trick; he brings them together over his chest, and engages them in mutual fingering play. His fingers finger his fingers! Thus he himself touches and is touched simultaneously. This double touch is a lesson in self-discovery. He comes to appreciate what his fingers are; and that objects are something different. Putting fingers into the mouth and putting objects into the mouth also help to clear up these fundamental distinctions. The baby has to learn his physics and his anatomy as well as his sociology.

And so in the next three months he lays hold of the physical world with his hands as well as his eyes. As once he showed visual hunger, now he shows touch hunger. He is ravenous in his desire to approach, to contact, to grasp, to feel, and to manipulate. Whether lying in a crib or seated in a lap, he shows a psychomotor eagerness when an object comes within reach. At sixteen weeks his shoulders strain and his arms activate as a toy is brought near. In another month his hands close in on the object, corral it, grasp it on contact. In yet another month or two he makes direct one-handed approach on sight. These advancing coordinations are organized through the steady process of growth. At sixteen weeks he clutches rather than prehends. He clasps his coverlet, pulling it over his face quite uncritically. This behavior pattern is immature but it foretokens more advanced forms of grasp and manipulation.

A baby is never complete. He is always in the making. But even his incomplete abilities are charged with potentialities. Accordingly there is much promise in the cooing, the expectant inspection, the excited breathing, the mutual fingering, and the coverlet-clutching of the socially smiling just sixteen-week-old baby.

Behavior Day

When does the sixteen-week-old baby awake? Any time between five and eight o'clock in the morning. One can scarcely list the clock hours of a typical behavior day at this age, because the organism is in a highly transitional stage of readjustment. Besides, the baby's waking hour may depend upon whether he was roused for a feeding at ten o'clock of the previous night. If he wakes at five or six o'clock he is likely to show in the next few weeks a steady trend toward a later hour. This trend is rather consistent. He does not exhibit the wide fluctuations in waking time characteristic of four weeks of age.

He may wake with a prompt cry to announce that he is hungry. But to say that he wakes simply to eat would do him an injustice, for often instead of crying he "talks" to himself for fifteen minutes or more. All his behavior, including his self-waking, is more demarcated. His hunger cry is businesslike. He quiets promptly when his mother comes; but he also breaks into a renewed spell of crying if his patience span is imposed upon.

His morning appetite is acute. He approaches the breast with mouth open and lips poised. He no longer needs help in establishing contact, and sucks strenuously.

His mother "talks" to him a little after feeding because he has a surplus margin of interest in sights and sounds. He is not perturbed by wet or soiled diapers, which, however, are changed before the next sleep period. The length of this period varies. If he is on a five-meal schedule he takes a short morning nap. After perhaps an hour he spontaneously wakes and once more begins to play. His wakefulness is more defined, more purposive in character than it was at four weeks. His sleep is less closely merged with feeding; it may be both preceded and followed by an active playful wakefulness. Such a sleep interlude is truly a nap, quite different from the vaguer vegetative somnolence of the newborn.

He awakes to play and he plays to be awake. In this play he exercises his growing sensorimotor powers: he deploys his eyes and rotates his head to inspect his surroundings, brings his fingering hands together, clutches his clothes, coos, laughs.

Another nap now follows. He likes to take this long morning nap in his carriage on an outdoor porch, or in an airy room, away from the din and activity of the household. He may resist briefly when a bonnet is placed around his actively shifting head, but if not further molested, he falls into a deepened slumber, to wake again both for play and for food. Play has become an occupation as essential for his psychological growth as sleep. He is working toward a three-phase cycle of play activity–feeding–sleeping–play activity–feeding–sleeping. But the phases do not always occur distinctly in this sequence. After the early-afternoon sleep, he may wake up with a rather prompt hunger cry. Then he will be ready to play only after he has been fed.

The most elaborate and well-defined period of wakefulness is likely to occur in the late afternoon or evening. Having been replenished, he plays by himself contentedly for perhaps a half hour. Then he may fuss, not for food but for attention and judicious stimulation. His wakefulness is deeper and wider. He likes to be shifted from the confines of his crib to the vaster expanse of couch or bed, perhaps with partial removal of constricting clothes. He enjoys the novelty of such change of scene; he may relish for a short period a well-propped partial sitting position, from which he sees and hears the world at new angles. Dangling toys intrigue him; he may hold a rattle for a few minutes. He is content with mild and brief variations of experience.

The curve of sociality mounts so high that late afternoon is a favorable time for the traditional "morning" bath. The bath has no greater sanitary importance at this transposed hour; but its behavior value may be enhanced thereby for both mother and child.

After his evening meal, which may include mashed banana, the baby "talks to himself." He may suck his fingers for several minutes, for the hand-to-mouth reaction is so strong at this age that it usually occurs after each feeding.

At night he is capable of a twelve-hour span of sleep. He is stretching the length of nocturnal sleep and the length of daylight wakefulness. In obedience to his private alarm clock, he sleeps till the following day. He wakes partly from necessity (to eat), partly from predilection (to be up and doing).

SLEEP

NIGHT

Onset—The baby falls asleep fairly soon after 6 P.M. feeding.
Waking—Time of waking varies, with different infants, from 5 to 8 A.M. Those who wake early do not usually cry, but talk and play with their hands or with the bedcovers until they are hungry. Desire to be fed is indicated by fussing. Not all sleep through the night.

NAP

Onset and Waking—The infant does not usually fall asleep at the end of a feeding, but talks to himself or plays with his hands for a while. Crying may precede sleep, though not at every nap period. If crying does occur, the child may need the quieting effect of back-and-forth movement of either carriage or crib, especially after the 10 A.M. and 2 P.M. feedings. He appears happy when waking from naps and does not cry.

Periods—Three naps in twenty-four hours are characteristic of this age, though there may be two or four instead of three.

Naps occur in the early morning, late morning, afternoon and evening. The early-morning nap may merge with night sleep, particularly if waking is late (around 8 A.M.). The late-morning nap may alternate with the afternoon nap. An evening nap is unusual and comes in only with a recurrence of the evening wakefulness characteristic of a younger age.

Place—The napping place has shifted from bassinet to crib. The baby carriage is usually the best place for the morning out-of-door nap.

FEEDING

Self-Regulation—A clear-cut crying demand on waking becomes less frequent from twelve weeks on, usually being associated only with the first morning waking. At other feedings the infant is more able to wait and can to some extent adapt to the demands of his environment. He may indicate a desire to be fed by fussing. At this age there may be occasional refusals (even to the extent of screaming) of the noon or 6 P.M. feeding. The poorer feeder may have a tendency to split one of these feedings into two parts, taking the second part after a one-hour interval.

There is often a decreased appetite for milk at this age and vomiting may occur with the poorer feeders.

Number—There are from three to five feedings at this age, the two earliest morning feedings often merging. The infant no longer spontaneously wakens for a 10 to 11 P.M. feeding.

Amount—The total daily intake may vary between twenty-five and thirty-two ounces. The poorer feeders do not fluctuate as much as the good feeders and are apt to hold close to twenty-five ounces. Individual feedings for the good feeders may vary in amount by five or six ounces; for the poorer feeders there is little fluctuation. Both breasts are preferred, except at the 10 A.M. feeding, when usually only one is taken. If the baby is still waked for a 10 P.M. feeding, then only one breast may be taken at the early-morning feeding.

Duration—Both breasts—fifteen to twenty minutes. One breast—ten to fifteen minutes. The 5 to 6 P.M. feeding may take as long as twenty-five to thirty minutes.

Breast- and Bottle-Feeding—The infant may fuss before feeding but often waits until approximately feeding time. Some cry vigorously in anticipation as the mother exposes her breast. When the nipple is presented, finger- or tongue-sucking gives way to poised lips and grasping with hands. Hands may come to the breast or may grasp at clothes as the infant secures the nipple with very little assistance from the adult. During nursing he may shift his regard from the breast, to his mother's face, to the surroundings—and especially to other people who may be present. Lips are pursed at the corners and sucking is strong. It may be so much stronger than the swallowing ability that choking results. In bottle-feeding, the infant is frequently called upon to adjust to the deflation of the rubber nipple. The harder he sucks, the flatter the nipple becomes until finally he is able to release the nipple and wait until air distends it.

After initial satiety the infant may release and resecure the breast repeatedly in a playful manner, with smiling. With final satiety he arches his back and may growl if forced back to the breast. He usually burps spontaneously after finishing the first breast. Though he may seem satiated as he is shifted to the second breast, his impatient eagerness usually leads him to make a good response to it. With final satiety he is apt to suck his tongue or thumb, and is often very talkative.

[Sucking demand is so strong at this age that it is best to satisfy it before solid foods are given.]

Spoon-Feeding—Tongue projection is still so marked that little food is swallowed unless it is placed on the back of the tongue. Many babies, especially if they are breast-fed, refuse solids or take them very poorly until they are as much as five or six months old.

Cup-Feeding—Approximation of the lips to the rim of the cup is still very inadequate and much spilling results. In spite of this, the infant often enjoys the process of drinking water or fruit juices.

ELIMINATION

Bowel—There are one or two movements a day, though a day is frequently skipped. The time of occurrence varies from child to child though it is usually consistent for any one child. The most common time is after a feeding. If the movement does not follow a feeding, it is apt to occur during the wakeful period from 6 to 10 A.M. If it occurs during a feeding, the baby may regurgitate.

BATH AND DRESSING

At this age the baby expresses his love of his bath by kicking and laughing. He does not like to have the bath too deep and may like to lie on his stomach as he is bathed. Around twenty weeks he may hold onto the side of the tub, and may express disappointment when taken out.

SELF-ACTIVITY

Waking periods are now longer and are often spent in physical activity, such as kicking, rotating the head from side to side, or rolling to one side. The infant is now able to grasp objects, and particularly enjoys a dangling toy. He also likes to clasp his hands together, and may suck his thumb or fingers before and after feedings. He is now very talkative, often vocalizing with delight, especially in the early morning and afternoon. Talking and crying may follow each other closely. He blows bubbles less than formerly. He enjoys a shift to a couch or large bed in the afternoon and may be good alone for as much as an hour, from 3 to 4 P.M., though he is also interested in people. He likes to have a light after 6 P.M. but no longer demands it. If it is left on it may keep him awake.

SOCIALITY

There is at this age an increased demand for sociality. This may come in relation to feedings, often before each feeding, though with some infants it occurs during or after the feeding. Demand for social attention is especially strong toward the end of the day, around 5 P.M. The infant likes to be shifted from his bed for this social period. He particularly likes to be in his carriage. There is, at twelve to sixteen weeks, a marked interest in the father and also in young children. Social play with the father may go more smoothly than with the mother since the baby does not associate food with the father. He likes to have people pay attention to him, talk to him, sing to him. He is apt to cry in supine and seems to prefer sitting. By twenty weeks he so much enjoys being talked to that he may cry when people leave.

[He is apt to be more demanding of social attention if he sleeps in the same room with his mother, especially if she stirs in the early morning.]

CHAPTER 10

TWENTY-EIGHT WEEKS OLD

Behavior Profile

The twenty-eight-week-old infant likes to sit in a high chair. When he wakes from a nap he is quite likely to lift his head, as though straining to reach a perpendicular position. He wishes to sit up and take notice; and above all he wishes to get hold of some object (a clothespin will do), which he can handle, mouth, and bang. Expensive or elaborate toys are not necessary.

This is a heyday for manipulation. The baby has "learned" to balance his head; he can almost balance his trunk; he knows how to grasp on sight; he is eager to try out his rapidly growing abilities.

His eagerness and intentness show that his play is serious business. He is discovering the size, shape, weight, and texture of things. He is no longer content merely to finger his hands, as he did at sixteen weeks. He wants to finger the clothespin, to get the feel of it. He puts it to his mouth, pulls it out, looks at it, rotates it with a twist of the wrist, puts it back into his mouth, pulls it out, gives it another twist, brings up his free hand, transfers the clothespin from hand to hand, bangs it on the high-chair tray, drops it, recovers it, retransfers it from hand to hand, drops it out of reach, leans over to retrieve it, fails, fusses a moment, and then bangs the tray with his empty hand, etc., throughout his busy day. He is never idle because he is under such a compelling urge to use his hands for manipulation and exploitation.

His hands are not quite as pawlike as they were. He is beginning to use his thumb more adeptly, and to tilt his hand just prior to grasp. But his fine finger coordination is crude compared with what it will be at forty weeks. He still is more expert with his eyes than with his hands; he looks keenly at a small object that he cannot yet pick up deftly.

His urge to manipulate is so strong that he can play by himself happily for short periods. At these times he should be left to his own devices. It is characteristic of him to be self-contained as well as sociable. He will show a similar self-containedness at a higher level when he is in the eighteen-months-old runabout stage.

Now he is sedentary. So he sits in his chair; he watches with interest the activities of the household. He vocalizes his eagerness, not to say impatience, when he spies a bottle or a dish and sees his mother preparing a meal for him. He may reach for a dish quite out of reach, because he still has something to learn about distance—and time, too. But his mouth and throat muscles are much more highly organized than they were at sixteen weeks. He can now "handle" solids, which before tended to make him cough or choke. Nor does he extrude his tongue with the infantile ineptitude of earlier days. His lips sweep competently over the spoon in his mouth; his tongue smacks and on satiety he keeps his mouth tightly closed. All this denotes a great advance in his neuromuscular organization.

But of course he cannot grasp a spoon adaptively by the handle or use it as a utensil. At one year he will be able to insert a spoon into a cup. Not until about two years can he put the burden of a laden spoon into his mouth unaided without excessive spilling. The spoon is a complicated cultural tool. The twenty-eight-week-old infant in his manipulation is laying the foundations for the motor mastery of this tool.

All told, the twenty-eight-week-old baby presents a mixture of versatility and transitional incompleteness. He is vastly superior to the sixteen-week-old baby in the combined command of eyes and hands; but he is only at the brink of abilities that will come to maturity during the rest of the first year. He is at the brink of sitting alone; at the close of the year he will stand alone. He can hold two objects, one in each hand; in time he will combine them. He is vocalizing vowels and consonants in great variety. Soon they will take on the status of words. Through his ceaseless manipulations, transfers, and mouthings he is building up a wealth of perceptions that will make him feel more at home in his physical surroundings. Similarly he is amassing a wealth of social perceptions; he is reading the facial expressions, the gestures, the postural attitudes, and the goings and comings of the domestic routine. These social perceptions are not yet very sophisticated, but they are sensitive; they are patterned; and they are essential to the continuing growth of his personality.

At this age the child's abilities are in relative balance. The behavior patterns of the twenty-eight-week-old baby are in good focus. His interests are balanced; he is both self-contained and sociable; he alternates with ease from spontaneous self-activity to social-reference activity. He likes to sit up (with support) but he is also quite content to lie supine. He likes to manipulate toys, but almost any object will do; or no object at all will do, for then he moves his hand across the field of vision for the pleasure (and educational value) of seeing it move. All in all, his behavior traits are well counterpoised. But the tensions of growth will soon again throw them out of their comparative equilibrium as he forges ahead to a still higher level of maturity.

Behavior Day

Our twenty-eight-week-old baby wakes up at almost any time between 6 and 8 A.M. He is reputed to wake up "soaking wet." His urinary output apparently has increased since the age of sixteen weeks. But he is quite indifferent and typically amuses himself with play of his own devices. Now and then an infant of lusty appetite may demand a prompt feeding on waking, but twenty-eight weeks is a relatively amiable and equable age, and mothers report that children of this age usually wake up "good," playing contentedly for twenty to thirty minutes. A corner of the blanket, a loose end of tape, or even his own free-moving hand will serve his playful purposes. He may vocalize but not as much as at sixteen weeks, for twenty-eight weeks is the heyday of manipulation and visual-manual play.

Breast-feeding is very satisfactory for the first morning feeding. The mother finds this early breast-feeding very convenient because there is considerable variation in the morning waking hour during the interval between sixteen and twenty-eight weeks, and often an immediate demand for food. Whether at breast or bottle, he displays increased efficiency in sucking.

Typically the period from 6 to 8 A.M. is one of pleasant wakefulness. During this period the baby is most comfortable in a room by himself. He will play alone contentedly for twenty minutes, then likes to be given a toy, and at the end of another twenty minutes or so is propped up in his crib to survey his surroundings.

At nine o'clock he is ready for a trip to the kitchen, where he is placed in a safe chair that gives him a commanding view of the preliminaries of his next meal. He is not without anticipation and he becomes excited when the food approaches. He is fed in his chair, or if his postural and temperamental characteristics so require, he is fed on a lap. He poises his lips cooperatively for the spoon and a smile of satisfaction and satiation terminates the meal.

His daily bowel movement may occur at this time or before the morning feeding. In the period from sixteen to twenty weeks he displayed some adaptive response to placement on the toilet, but thereafter he began to show a strenuous refusal. The mother has by this time accepted his refusal and is delaying systematic "training." He gives no evidence of being perturbed by soiled diapers.

At ten o'clock he is put into his carriage, which is wheeled out of doors or onto a porch, and after a draught at the breast or bottle he goes to sleep with relative promptness. He wakes at about noon or one o'clock. He wakes happily and again plays contentedly by himself in the carriage. If he fusses slightly he is readily appeased by a toy and later by being propped up in a supported sitting position.

By two o'clock he is ready for his vegetable meal followed by a breast- or bottle-feeding. Weather permitting, it is time for a trip in his carriage. He does not altogether acquiesce in the application of a bonnet but he definitely enjoys the sightseeing opportunities offered by the perambulator. This is the first age when the baby is very "good" on these trips.

The afternoon nap comes at about three-thirty and lasts about an hour. He wakes somewhat more slowly from this nap and shows somewhat less self-dependence. As at earlier ages, he likes a little afternoon sociability as well as orange juice. Five o'clock, therefore, proves to be a favorable hour for the bath, unless an early waking from the morning nap makes a noon bath more acceptable for the household. In any event, he enjoys the bath hugely. Divestment of clothes is both a pleasure in itself and an anticipation of things to come.

The last feeding comes at about five-thirty. It may be at breast but more usually at bottle. And so to bed at six o'clock, when he falls promptly to sleep for a twelve-hour stretch.

SLEEP

NIGHT

Onset—The baby tends to fall asleep directly after his 6 P.M.* feeding.

Waking—Very few babies of this age are awakened for a 10 P.M. feeding, and even fewer wake themselves at this hour. If they are awakened, they take very little milk or refuse the feeding entirely; but if they wake voluntarily they can be quieted only by a feeding. The majority sleep right through the night, for eleven to thirteen hours, waking around 6 A.M. or later. Babies of this age are usually "good" for half an hour or longer after waking before they demand a feeding.

NAP

Onset and Waking—There is now no difficulty in going to sleep or in waking. Sleep is usually closely associated with the 10 A.M. and the 6 P.M. feedings.

Periods—There is at this age a fairly wide variety of nap patterns. There are usually two to three naps a day. The midmorning and afternoon naps are the most stable. Some children have a consistent pattern of a long morning and a short afternoon nap (or vice versa), whereas others alternate the length, depending on the length of the morning nap. An evening nap does not usually occur unless it is defined by a 10 P.M. waking.

Place—Babies nap best in their carriages out of doors, for the morning

---

* We refer to a 10 A.M., 2 A.M., 6 P.M. feeding simply for convenience.

nap. Some have their afternoon nap while being wheeled in their carriages. If not, they usually have this nap in their cribs in the house, during the latter part of the afternoon.

FEEDING

Self-Regulation—Self-demand occurs mainly for the first morning feeding. The time of this demand fluctuates according to the hour of waking. Some infants demand this feeding immediately on waking, but most will wait for half an hour or so. Other feedings are accepted at the times determined by the mother in accordance with the baby's growing needs and the ease or difficulty of his adjustment to the demands of the household schedule.

Solids are now taken well; perhaps best at the 8 to 10 A.M. and 2 P.M. feedings.

[With the decrease in sucking demands, solid foods may now be given at the beginning of each meal.

From thirty-two to thirty-six weeks, the infant is very impatient as he watches his meal being prepared. This can be remedied by having the meal ready before he sees it.]

Number—Three to four a day. Four persists if the child demands a 6 A.M. feeding or if the 10 P.M. feeding is continued.

Amount—The total amount is now difficult to judge because of the addition of solid foods. However, the poor feeders still keep to a consistent level of intake without fluctuating more than an ounce or two at a feeding, whereas the good feeders may show as much as a ten-ounce fluctuation at a feeding. The early-morning and the 6 P.M. are the best meals (ten to eleven ounces), and the 2 P.M. is the poorest (four to five ounces). If the breast is given at the 2 P.M. feeding it may be taken poorly or refused.

Duration—Eight to ten minutes for breast- or bottle-feeding.

Breast- and Bottle-Feeding—The infant vocalizes his eagerness when he sees the breast or bottle. He places his hands on breast or bottle, securing the nipple with ease. He exerts good continuous sucking, with the lower lip rolled out and forward and with good pursing at the corners. During the feeding, hands repeatedly grasp and release the breast or bottle. This grasp and release is similar to the sixteen-week-old tongue pattern of grasp and release. The infant regards the nipple as he withdraws from the breast or pulls the bottle away from his mouth.

With satiety he tries to sit up, and when helped to sit smiles at his mother or at others present, and may shake his head from side to side as though saying, "No, no."

[Since the infant is apt to bite the nipple, especially after the 2

P.M. feeding, after taking only a few ounces, it may be best to omit this feeding.]

Spoon-Feeding—The baby at this age anticipates spoon-feeding with eagerness, poising his mouth as he reaches toward the spoon with his head. Hands may be fisted at shoulder level or may rest on the tray of the high chair—if he is capable of being fed in a high chair. He sucks the food from the spoon. With succeeding spoonfuls he shows increasing eagerness and may grasp the spoon or the adult's finger. With satiety he bites on the spoon, and he smiles after the feeding.

Cup-Feeding—The infant shows a new awareness of the cup and spontaneously makes demands to be cup-fed. He apparently associates the running of water with the filling of the cup, and on sight of the cup he reaches forward with head rather than with hands, and with poised mouth. There is better approximation of his lips to the rim of the cup, but he has difficulty when the cup is removed in retaining the fluid in his mouth. He is incapable of taking more than one or two swallows at a time. He definitely prefers water or juices to milk, and may refuse milk from a cup.

ELIMINATION

Bowel—One movement a day (in the diaper) usually from 9 to 10

A.M., though it may occasionally occur in the late afternoon. The earlier response to the pot is no longer present. In fact strong resistance to the pot may be shown. There is no demand to be changed except on the part of a few fastidious girls who cry vigorously until they are changed. Babies of this type are more apt to be trained easily and early to the pot, and this behavior, once established, is usually sustained.

Bladder—Urination is still frequent and so excessive in amount that the child is often very wet when changed. Sex differences are noted at this age in that some girls are establishing a longer interval—as long as one to two hours—after which they may respond to the pot.

Bath—The baby enjoys being undressed for his bath at this age, and he also enjoys his bath. His hands are so active that objects are no longer safe on the bath table. In the tub, the baby splashes vigorously, usually with his hands though sometimes with his feet. He may close his eyes at the sight of the washcloth. It may suit the demands of both child and household to shift the bath hour ahead to the noon hour.

[When the infant is unhappily conscious of the approach of the washcloth, it is wise to approach him from the rear, washing his ears and cheeks from the back toward the front.]

Dressing—The baby likes to remove his bootees and also likes to play with the strings of his bootees or of his sweater.

SELF-ACTIVITY

The infant again enjoys supine. He hummocks, kicks, extends his legs upward, grasps his feet, brings them to his mouth, pulls off his bootees and stockings. He likes to watch his moving hand. He brings his hands less often to his mouth, and this occurs mostly after feeding or before sleep. He enjoys play with paper, soft rubber squeaky toys, and rattles. These he brings to his mouth and bites on. He vocalizes happily to himself, gurgling, growling, and making high squealing sounds. He is happier alone in both morning and late afternoon during his wakeful periods, until he indicates, by fussing, a desire for companionship.

[Around thirty-two weeks, the infant may frequently cry and need help in getting out of some awkward position.]

SOCIALITY

Babies of this age enjoy people not only for themselves but for what the people can do for them. Once the adult has given a toy or propped the baby sitting, the baby can let the adult go and can enjoy himself alone until he makes his next demand. He enjoys being wheeled along the street in his carriage, and although he enjoys sitting up for short periods, he is also content to lie down. He is beginning to respond to more than one person at a time, and likes to be handed back and forth from one person to another. He also likes rhythm, and enjoys being bounced on someone's knee. He differentiates between people, and demands more of the one who feeds him. He is lively with those whom he knows but may be shy with strangers, especially in new places.

[Around thirty-two weeks, though the baby enjoys the company of others, he may easily become overexcited. Instability of emotional makeup at this time is expressed in the close interplay of crying and laughter.]

CHAPTER 11

FORTY WEEKS OLD

Behavior Profile

The forty-week-old infant no longer takes kindly to the supine position. For the sleeping infant it may do; but when Forty Weeks awakes, he rolls over and sits up. He may even raise himself to a standing position, pulling himself by the palings of his crib. Man was meant to be a biped. There is an unmistakable hind-legs urge toward the perpendicular, which puts the baby on his feet. But the horizontal alignment is still under better control. For a few months the baby remains a quadruped, using his hands for locomotion as well as for manipulation.

In the evolution of the race, the upright posture was assumed for the purpose of emancipating the hands, freeing them for nobler and more refined uses. The forty-week-old baby is developmentally in this transition phase of emancipation, and the higher uses of the hand are already well in evidence. He brings index finger and thumb into delicate pincerlike opposition; he extends the index finger to poke and probe, to palpate and pluck. He can pluck a string and give it a tug. He is beginning to grasp things more adaptively by their handle. His inquisitive index finger will take him further and further into the third dimension. He will probe into holes and grooves and into the depths of a cup. Through these more refined manipulations he acquires a sense of hollow and solid; container and contained; up and down; side by side; in and out; apart and united.

The forty-week-old baby, therefore, is not nearly so naïvely single-minded as he was at twenty-eight weeks. He is beginning to see and to handle things in the depth of perspective. The universe is less flat, less simplex. He is conscious of *two* as well as *one*. Indeed, he puts two things together. He needs two clothespins instead of one to satisfy his impulse to combine and to bring together what is apart. This dim awareness of twoness is reflected in his experimental exploitation of play objects. He is more discriminating and sometimes actually dainty in his manipulations.

Socially, likewise, he is more discriminating, more perceptive of small variations in sight and sound. This greater perceptiveness makes him seem more sensitive, as indeed he is. He is sensitive to more events in his social environment; he is becoming responsive to demonstrations and to teaching. He has a new capacity for imitation. Accordingly he "learns" new nursery tricks like pat-a-cake and bye-bye. He could not "learn" them when he was twenty-eight weeks old, because he did not have the same perceptiveness for the actions of others, nor was the appropriate movement pattern as yet in his repertoire. His repertoire of movements depends upon the maturity of his nervous system. He cannot imitate any action until he is already capable of that action as the result of natural growth. If at the age of forty weeks you try to engage him in a game of back-and-forth ball play, he may disappoint you by holding onto the ball and merely waving it. But of course one *should* not be disappointed. In due time he will mature the motor capacity of release, and then he will roll the ball to you. Everything in season.

Behavior Day

The forty-week-old baby wakes any time between five and seven o'clock. He is likely to be wet but his fussing is often primarily for social attention. He is also likely to be keenly hungry and he imbibes his bottle with dispatch. He holds and pats his partially propped bottle. Should the nipple become deflated during the sucking, he is now an expert in waiting until it reinflates. With the increase in breast-feeding, the present trend is to continue breast-feeding until the infant gives it up spontaneously, as early as forty weeks or as late as eighteen months. Most children give it up somewhere between nine and fifteen months. After his feeding he is wheeled into another room for partial isolation, unless he is already in a room of his own. If he does not have this isolation he is likely to be too demanding. He plays contentedly for an hour or more, if he has two or three shifts of toys.

At eight o'clock he is ready for breakfast. He may take this in his high chair. He vocalizes "mama" and "nam-nam" in his eager anticipation; but he has learned to inhibit some of his excitement and waits for the presentation of the dish of cereal. The demanding eagerness, however, returns if the mother is too slow in following one spoonful with the next. He associates an empty dish with the termination of the meal and he makes a ready transition to a period of play.

Between eight and ten o'clock he likes to be part of the household group. He is content to play in his high chair, playpen, or crib and may enjoy a shift from one station to another by way of variety.

He may have a bowel movement during this morning play period, or in some instances there is a toilet placement immediately following breakfast.

Ten o'clock often proves to be a convenient time for the bath. He greatly enjoys a bath and expresses eager anticipation when he hears the water running and sees the preparation. The bath is completed almost too soon for his preferences. He is likely to enjoy by way of playful contest the washing of his face with the washcloth, and will play with a water toy.

By about a quarter past ten he is ready for sleep. He sleeps well indoors. This is his long nap. He wakes at about 1 o'clock, usually wet. (Girls are more apt to be dry.) He may play contentedly for a brief period and then fusses for social attention.

He lunches at about one-thirty on spoon-fed vegetables. He opens his mouth decisively as the spoon is presented and swallows rapidly.

He eats with new efficiency, moving steadily toward the completion of the meal. He becomes playful toward the end of the meal, manipulating empty dish or spoon. He finger-feeds on spilled particles, thus exercising his new powers of precise pincer prehension.

At two o'clock, weather permitting, comes a carriage ride. He does not even yet accept his bonnet with full grace, but he enjoys sightseeing. Nevertheless, he is not totally preoccupied with the scenery. He is in the early stages of independent sitting and of digital manipulation. He therefore likes to occupy himself with a toy even on his outdoor trips. His propensity to stand may be so strong that he needs a safety strap.

If he returns home dry at about three o'clock, he may respond to placement on the toilet. By this time he may be showing signs of sleepiness. He falls asleep promptly and naps from half an hour to an hour. He may wake up dry at about four o'clock. His nap is usually followed by orange juice, which he relishes. This is typically the most social period of the day. He enjoys being a member of the household group. He enjoys social types of play, including the usual nursery games. His sociality may lead to overstimulation. He is beginning to show a temper by way of resistance or as a mode of communication, not to say environmental utilization. He is not yet using words but his vocalizations are more articulate, more insistent.

A supper of cereal and fruit follows at about six o'clock. He is usually ready for the night's sleep in a quarter of an hour. He may "talk" to himself for from fifteen minutes to an hour, or he may promptly fall asleep. He may cry out momentarily during the course of the night, without waking and without requiring attention.

SLEEP

NIGHT

Onset—The baby still tends to fall asleep directly after his 6 P.M. feeding. A few infants who have had more difficulty in going to sleep and who have previously cried before some sleep periods may now talk for fifteen minutes to one hour before falling asleep. Others respond to a close contact with their mother, by being slung close to her. They will often fall asleep in this position.

[If there is resistance to being

put to bed at the usual 6 P.M. hour, delay bedtime a half hour or more.]

Waking—Most infants sleep right through till 5 to 7 A.M., the trend being toward the later hour. Night waking seems to depend both on household conditions and on the child himself. The infant who sleeps in the same room with his parents may awaken when his parents go to bed, but usually falls right back to sleep after his diaper is changed. Some cry out in their sleep momentarily without waking, and require no attention. A few are beginning to have occasional wakeful periods of an hour or more between 2 and 4 A.M. During this period the baby may talk happily to himself or may crawl out from under the covers and play. Toward the end of this period he may fuss and may be unable to go back to sleep unless his diaper is changed or he is given the breast or a bottle.

Early wakers (5 to 6 A.M.) may want to be changed at once and then enjoy either vocal play lying down, or play with a toy sitting up. They are most contented in a room by themselves at this time and will remain so for one to one and a half hours provided they have two or three shifts of toys, before they fuss for their food. Late wakers (7 A.M. or later) tend to demand food shortly after waking.

NAP

Onset and Waking—The baby indicates his need for sleep by fussing, turning his head to one side, sucking his thumb or a piece of material, wriggling his pelvis, or pushing with his feet, and if he is put into his crib at such times he falls asleep fairly quickly. If no such need has been indicated, he may accept being put down at the usual time but may remain awake.

The morning nap most often follows the 10 A.M. bath period (if the bath is given then) and the afternoon nap may follow a ride in the carriage—around 3 P.M.

Periods—There is not quite such a wide variety of nap patterns as at twenty-eight weeks. There may be four short nap periods—one at each of the four periods of the day—or there may be only one long mid-morning nap. The most usual pattern is a long mid-morning and an unstable afternoon nap which comes and goes.

Place—This is a transitional period of sleeping indoors in preference to out of doors. Some infants give a clue to their demand for less light by placing their hands over their eyes, and usually sleep better indoors with the shades pulled.

FEEDING

Self-Regulation—The baby may indicate an early-morning demand, but this demand is as much for company as for food. Breakfast is not usually served before 7 or 8 A.M. This meal is often preceded by a solitary play period of one to one and a half hours.

The infant takes his bottle alone for the first morning feeding if it is given then. It usually needs to be propped, though the baby will hold it alone toward the end of the feeding. At other feedings he demands that his bottle be held, and often enjoys the bottle after he has had his solid food, sitting in his high chair. Most solid foods are taken well, and some preference is indicated by a razzing refusal of disliked foods. One ounce of milk may be accepted in a cup, but the tendency is to blow bubbles in the cup, with a very rapid satiety of drinking. Orange juice and water are, however, taken well from a cup.

Although he is still eager for his feedings, he is not usually as impatient when he sees his meal being prepared as he was from thirty-two to thirty-six weeks. He tends to vocalize in anticipation rather than fussing and crying.

[The infant still needs to have some sucking at breast or bottle. If he does not, feedings are more difficult and prolonged because he will suck his fingers between spoonfuls.]

Number—Three meals a day, with fruit juice in the midafternoon. A bottle may be given as an extra first morning feeding as soon as he awakes. Night bottles are very rare. Some infants receive only two bottles, at 7 A.M. and 6 P.M., and others continue on three a day.

Amount—The total intake depends to a certain extent upon how much is offered. The infant now has a sense of finishing his bottle and therefore asks for no more than his bottle of eight ounces. He also "cleans up" his dish and takes it for granted that that is the end. Some infants have eaten a larger quantity before this age, others are just increasing their quantity at this time. The point of satiety indicates whether too much is being given, and the absence of any satiety patterns may indicate that more could be given.

Duration—Three to four minutes for a bottle. Five to ten minutes for solid food.

Bottle- or Breast-Feeding—Bottle-feeding patterns are similar to twenty-eight-week patterns except that sucking is now more forceful and more rapid and the hands are taking more part in holding the bottle. The baby needs assistance initially when his bottle is full, but as it empties he tilts it with ease and is able to resecure it as needed. On the whole he prefers to have his bottle held. Breast-feeding produces none of these complications.

Spoon-Feeding—Most infants are fed in a high chair at this age. They express their eager anticipation with such vocalizing as "dada" or "nam-nam." They open their mouths as the spoon is presented, swallow rapidly as they draw in their lower lip. Lateral movements of chewing are just beginning. The infant may reach toward the dish or show eagerness if the mother is slow in presenting the food. Satiety is clearly expressed coincidentally with the emptying of the dish. If satiety precedes this, it is indicated by biting of the spoon or the infant's own tongue, by shaking the head "no," and by razzing good-naturedly but determinedly. The baby enjoys a short period of play with the empty dish and spoon.

[A few infants may still need to be fed on the mother's lap or half-propped in an infant seat.

It is best to provide an unbreakable dish that can be used for play at the end of the meal.]

Cup-Feeding—The baby drinks one ounce, one to two swallows at a time, with good lip approximation. There is still a tendency to spill out of the mouth as the cup is removed. The baby enjoys blowing bubbles and also enjoys playing at drinking from an empty cup.

Self-Help—The baby finger-feeds with spilled bits from his tray.

ELIMINATION

Bowel—One to two movements a day, at 8 to 10 A.M. and/or 6 to 7 P.M. The baby may respond to the pot, especially if the bowel movement occurs after a meal. Some, especially girls, fuss to be changed.

Bladder—The baby may be dry after an hour's nap or a carriage ride and may respond to the pot if put on at once. However, he may not urinate till just after he is taken off. He may fuss to be changed in the middle of the night.

BATH AND DRESSING

The bath hour may continue to be at noon or in the late afternoon, but a morning bath is often most convenient for the household. The baby vigorously expresses anticipation when he hears the bath water running. He often prefers to lie prone in the bathtub, creeps better in water than on the floor, or rocks back and forth. He may cry as his face is being washed, but many enjoy the combat of face-washing, which can be accomplished easily if the baby is occupied with water toys or is standing in the tub.

SELF-ACTIVITY

Vocalization is varied at this age. The baby has given up growling sounds. He now says "ama," "nana," "gaga," "dada." He enjoys making lip noises, vocalizing at a high pitch, and trying out a variety of pitches with some such syllable as "dada." He often stops short and laughs at his own sounds, especially the high ones.

He concentrates on inspection and exploitation of toys. He enjoys playing with a cup and pretends to drink. He brings objects to his mouth and chews them. He clasps his hands or waves them.

He recognizes the absence of objects to which he has become accustomed, such as his mother's wrist watch or a water toy. He enjoys gross motor activity: sitting and playing after he has been sat up, leaning far forward and reerecting himself. He resecures a toy; kicks; goes from sitting to creeping; pulls himself up, and may lower himself. He is beginning to cruise. He likes to roll to the side or to prone and may get caught between the bars of his playpen.

[Because of increased motor abilities, it is now dangerous to leave the baby unguarded even for a moment on a bed or bath table lest he fall off.]

SOCIALITY

Though the infant will play by himself for relatively long periods, he is quick to articulate his desire for a shift of toys or company. He particularly likes to be with the family group from 8 to 10 A.M. and in the late afternoon (4 to 6 P.M.) and happily stays in his crib, playpen, or chair at these times. He also likes a carriage ride in the late morning or early afternoon—depending on his naptime.

Social activities which he enjoys are peekaboo and lip play (which consists of patting his lips to induce singing), walking with both hands held, and being put prone on the floor or being placed in a rocking toy.

Girls show their first signs of coyness by putting their heads to one side as they smile. This occurs most frequently in the bath.

The baby is still shy with strangers and seems particularly afraid of a strange voice.

[The baby continues to demand more of his mother than of other members of the family. He is often better when alone with one person.]

CHAPTER 12

ONE YEAR OLD

Behavior Profile

The first birthday, of course, is a great occasion. The folk ways call for a cake and one lighted candle to punctuate the event; and properly so, from a chronological standpoint. But biologically speaking, this birthday does not mark an epoch; for the year-old baby is in the midstream of developmental changes which do not come to their fulfillment until about the age of fifteen months. It will help us to better understand his behavior characteristics if we think of him as a fifteen-month-old child in the making.

At fifteen months the modern child has usually achieved the upright posture; he can attain the standing position unaided; he can walk alone; he prefers to walk; he has discarded creeping and begun to jargon in a manner that promises the most human achievement of all—speech. The year-old child is still on the way toward these abilities. He can attain the sitting position unaided, but often prefers to creep; he can pivot in the sitting position; he can cruise and climb if he gets ample purchase with his hands. But these are quadrupedal rather than bipedal patterns. Many children near the close of the first year walk on hands and soles rather than hands and knees. This is the last of a score of stages that finally lead to the assumption of the upright posture. When feet become the fulcrum, the hands will soon be emancipated.

Nevertheless, the year-old baby is already capable of finer coordination in his eating and in his play activities. He picks small morsels of food from his tray with deft forceps prehension, and masticates and swallows with much less spilling from the mouth. Finger-feeding comes before self-spoon-feeding. But the year-old infant may seize a spoon by the handle and brush it over his tray. He can also dip it into a cup and release it; all of which shows that he is advancing in his mastery of tools and of the solid and hollow geometry of space. Watch his play closely, and you can tell by his self-activity what patterns of behavior are growing. One can almost see them sprout, he exercises his newly forming powers with so much spirit.

He likes to play with several small objects rather than a solitary one. He picks them up one by one, drops them, picks them up again, one by one. This behavior appears a little disorderly on the surface; but it is really very orderly from the standpoint of natural growth, for this one-by-one action pattern is a rudimentary kind of counting. It is not as complex as a counting-out game, but it is a developmental prerequisite.

The baby has another reason for this picking up and dropping manipulation. He is exercising his immature but maturing powers of release. Having learned how to grasp, he must now learn how to let go. If he seems to overdo it, it is because the extensor muscles are not yet under smooth control. Hence his expulsiveness; hence also his momentary inability to let go at the right time.

But start a simple game of back-and-forth rolling ball play with him and you will see what a significant advance he has made since the age of forty weeks. At forty weeks he perhaps regarded your overtures soberly, looking at your movements without actually reciprocating them. Instead, he held the ball, mouthed it, or surrendered it in an ill-defined manner. By one year his release is responsive; it has an element of voluntary imitation and initiation. In another month he releases with a slight but defined cast—all of which reminds us how complicated these simple patterns are and how much they depend upon maturation.

Socialized opportunities undoubtedly facilitate the shaping of the patterns and favor a healthy organization of accompanying emotions. The year-old child likes an audience. This is one reason why he is so often the very center of the household group. As such he shows a thespian tendency to repeat performances laughed at. He enjoys applause. This must help him to sense his own self-identity, just as he learned better to sense a clothespin when he brought it bangingly down against his tray. He is defining a difficult psychological distinction—the difference between himself and others.

He is capable of primitive kinds of affection, jealousy, sympathy, anxiety. He may be responsive to rhythm. He may even evidence a sense of humor, for he laughs at abrupt surprise sounds, and at startling incongruities. He may be a prodigious imitator. Demonstrate the ringing of a bell and he will wave it furiously by way of social reciprocity. But suddenly in the very midst of the waving he stops to poke the clapper with his inquisitive index! This poking was not part of the demonstration, but it is part of the child. We may be grateful that nature has protected him with this degree of independence. After all, we do not wish to swamp him with acculturation!

Behavior Day

The year-old baby wakes between six and eight o'clock in the morning. He usually wakes with a communicative call rather than an infantile cry. The call is a guttural "eh" or some equivalent vocalization. He may play by himself for as much as twenty minutes before he calls out. He jargons with some excitement when his mother or caretaker arrives. He wakes up wet and is changed and toileted, and put back into his crib, where he amuses himself with manipulative toys and satisfies his moderate appetite with a cracker.

Breakfast follows in half an hour or an hour, say eight-thirty. The breakfast usually consists of cereal, a strong preference being expressed for whichever kind he likes best. He eats with moderate appetite, but has a margin of self-activity through the meal. He likes to play with a toy in either hand, one toy a container and the other toy an object that he can thrust into the container. His manipulatory drive is so strong and uncritical that the dish is not safe unless it is out of reach. At the conclusion of the meal he pulls himself to a standing position. It may be that he takes his cup of milk in this position or while he is still sitting.

He may be toileted after the meal. A morning bowel movement at this time is common. He is content to be restored to his crib, where he romps and plays by himself with manipulative toys. Perhaps at ten o'clock he is put in his playpen in the yard, if the weather permits, or on the porch, where he is self-sufficient and happy for say another half hour, when he begins to fuss, partly by way of anticipation of his morning bath, which he greatly enjoys. If he kept a diary he probably would record this as the high peak of the day's routine. He prefers to sit in his bath and is no longer engrossed with mere aquatic play.

He is ready for a nap by 11 A.M. He may prefer to take his nap indoors in a semidarkened room. This midday nap is often two hours long. He usually wakes wet. In any event he may be toileted and changed. He is given a cracker and he looks on as his mother prepares the midday lunch. He usually takes his lunch, as he did his breakfast, in a high chair.

At two o'clock he is ready for a carriage ride, which he enjoys, but in a manner which reflects more than forty weeks maturity. At forty weeks his playthings still absorbed much of his attention. Now he enjoys following the movements of pedestrians and automobiles and inspecting the landscape. He may be dry when he returns from his journey.

Late afternoon again proves to be a social period. Although he has been relatively self-contained during the day, he now likes give-and-take play with adults and with children. If he is learning to walk he likes to take a walk up and down the room, hands held. Similarly he enjoys cruising from chair to chair. He is ready on the slightest cue to reciprocate in nursery games such as "Where is the baby?" or repeatedly giving and then taking back some object. By way of conclusion of this social play he likes to climb into an adult's lap, rubbing his face against the adult's hand or giving other tokens of affection.

A supper of cereal and fruit follows at about five-thirty. And so to bed at six. As a nightcap he has a bottle, which he may discard by the age of fifteen months. He falls asleep between 6 and 8 P.M., which neatly completes a twelve-hour cycle.

SLEEP

NIGHT

Onset—The year-old baby usually falls asleep sometime between 6 and 8 P.M. A few infants still have an eating-sleeping association. A number, however, refuse to go to bed before they are ready, then go happily and fall asleep quickly. Others go to bed at the usual time directly after supper, and play on top of their covers or walk about in their cribs before they fall asleep on top of the covers. A warm sleeping garment can take the place of covers.

Waking—Most babies sleep through till 6 to 8 A.M. They may be "good" for twenty minutes after waking but more usually they call for their mother by crying or by vocalizing "eh." After calling, they seem definitely to wait for a response, and when the mother comes they greet her with excited jargon and may even look behind her as though expecting the other members of the family.

After being placed on the pot, if he accepts it, or changed, the baby is given a cracker (which he now prefers to a bottle). He plays happily in his crib, eating the cracker and enjoying his manipula-tive toys for half an hour to an hour. Breakfast follows this play period without the baby's having made any demand for it.

NAP

Onset and Waking—If the nap follows a morning bath or an early lunch, the infant accepts it readily and goes off to sleep shortly, but if it occurs in the middle of a morning play period he shows his desire for sleep by fussing or pulling at his ears, and goes to sleep fairly rapidly after he is put to bed. As with the early-morning waking, he demands attention at once, is glad to see his mother, is put on the pot or changed, and may tolerate a half hour alone in the playpen with cracker and toys before his lunch.

[If the infant interrupts his nap by crying before he urinates, it may be best not to pick him up and toilet him, for he may not go back to sleep. If he is allowed merely to urinate in his diaper, he usually falls right back to sleep.]

Periods—Usually there is only one nap a day, from eleven or eleven-thirty to twelve-thirty or two. Occasionally an early-morning or a late-afternoon nap persists irregularly.

Place—The carriage is no longer a

safe place for the nap and babies sleep better and longer in their cribs in a darkened room.

FEEDING

Self-Regulation—Gross motor drives may still be so strong that it may be easier to conduct the feeding with the baby standing but strapped in his high chair. He may stay seated if given some toy, preferably two toys that can readily be combined, to occupy the margin of his attention. He does not usually demand to have the dish on the tray, where it is not safe from his grasp and would probably be turned over, so long as he has something else to occupy his hands.

Many refuse milk from a bottle at this age (or even younger), especially if some change, such as a shift in style of nipple, has been made. This does not necessarily mean that the baby takes the milk better in a cup, for some refuse milk from a cup off and on up to eighteen months or even later. The preferred bottle is the 6 P.M., which may still be clung to.

Preference for certain foods are becoming fairly well defined. Cereal may be refused in the morning but may be taken well for supper. A wheat cereal may be refused but oatmeal taken with eagerness. Or hot cereal may be refused and a cold cereal chosen. Certain vegetables may be preferred.

Number—Three meals a day with midafternoon fruit juice. A cracker may be given both on morning waking and after the nap. If a bottle is still given, it is usually only one a day, directly after supper or after the baby is in bed.

Appetite—Appetite is usually good for all meals, though it may be somewhat less for breakfast.

Spoon-Feeding—Similar to forty weeks. The baby shows less eagerness for food, and a margin of his attention is given to other things than food. He enjoys some finger-feeding of food and may remove food from his mouth, look at it, and then reinsert it. He may rub spilled food on the tray. Toward the end of the meal he often pivots in sitting, flexes his legs on the chair seat, and may pull himself to standing.

Cup-Feeding—Patterns are similar to those observed at forty weeks, but now the baby enjoys holding his cup alone. His hands are pressed flat against the sides or bottom of the cup. His head tilts backward to enable him to drain the last drop. [If only an ounce or two is given in a cup, the baby can have the satisfaction of finishing it.]

Self-Help—The baby usually finger-feeds for part of one meal, either lunch or supper. A few boys, of a dominating but emotionally dependent type, demand to feed themselves at this age. They absolutely refuse any help even though they need it and results may be very messy. These same boys often ask for help at two to three years of age.

ELIMINATION

Bowel—one to two movements a day, at 8 to 9 A.M. and during the afternoon. The infant may respond to a pot if the bowel movement occurs directly after breakfast. "Successes" on the pot are less frequent than they have been and more resistance is expressed. An earlier indication that the bowel movement is about to take place (grunting) may no longer be present, but the baby may fuss to be changed after the movement occurs.

Bladder—Dryness after nap, and occasionally when the baby awakens during the night and in the early morning, if he is put on the pot immediately after waking, is more frequent now, though some have relapses. Girls often laugh as they urinate, from forty to fifty-two weeks, are interested in the process of urinating and look in the pot afterward to see what they have done. They may want to put their fingers in the urine or to put toilet paper in the pot, and may desire to flush the toilet. Fussing to be changed is beginning to be the rule, though some show delay in this response.

BATH AND DRESSING

Bath—Bath is still a favorite part of the day's routine. It may be given at any time of the day that fits best into the household schedule, often in the late afternoon. Most babies prefer to sit in their bath at this age, and are no longer absorbed by play with the water or by their own gross motor activity. They are now interested in the washcloth, the soap, and water toys. They grasp and release these objects in the tub or extend them outside the tub; for instance dabbling water onto the floor from the washcloth.

[Bath toys can be controlled more easily than the washcloth. If the baby refuses to give up the washcloth, he can often be induced to place it in a container, which can then be put out of sight.]

Dressing—Hat, shoes, and pants are the chief interests in dressing, and there is more interest in taking off than in putting on. When asked if he wants to go bye-bye (out for a walk), the baby may pat his head to indicate his desire for a hat. Shoes are played with for themselves and their laces, as well as for the pleasure of taking them off. The infant of this age is beginning to pull his pants off by himself, especially if his diapers are soiled or wet, and he is alone in his crib. This does not occur often. He now cooperates in dressing, putting his arm into an armhole or extending his leg to have his pants put on.

[A baby with an excessive drive to walk with his hands held may be inhibited, after he has had sufficient opportunity to express this drive, by taking off his shoes. His attention immediately turns to playing with the shoe, and walking is forgotten.]

SELF-ACTIVITY

The baby enjoys gross motor activity in his playpen and crib, pulling himself to standing, cruising, standing alone, creeping. He enjoys creeping on the floor, rather than in the playpen. He will usually be good in his playpen in the backyard or in the house for an hour in the morning, occupied with gross motor activity and with playthings. He enjoys placing things on his head, such as a hat, basket, or cup. He often throws things out of the playpen and then has difficulty in resecuring them.

Activities most enjoyed are gross motor activities; putting objects in and out of other objects (for instance, putting clothespins in and out of a basket); and play with buttons, which consists of looking at the buttons and fingering them.

[A walking device may prove useful for those babies whose sitting and creeping are poor but who like to stand.]

SOCIALITY

Fifty-two weeks is the heyday of sociality. The baby enjoys social give and take, and social occasions are apt to come about spontaneously, without planning. He is usually out alone in his playpen during the morning, though there may be some play with the family group. Most of his sociality, other than in relation to regular routine, occurs in the afternoon. He enjoys his carriage ride—enjoys standing up in his harness, and is especially interested in moving objects such as automobiles or bicycles. His playthings no longer absorb his attention.

He enjoys walking with his hands held, and loves the game of being chased while creeping. He enjoys hiding behind chairs to play the game of "Where's the baby?" or waving "bye-bye." He is interested in opening doors. He says "eh" or "ta-ta" as he gives something to an adult, but he expects to have the object given right back. He throws things to the floor with the expectation that they will be restored to him. He whimpers or cries when things are taken from him.

He enjoys rhythms. He may be inhibited by "no, no" or may enjoy a game of smiling and laughing and continuing his activity in spite of such admonitions. He may be just coming into a period of being shy with strangers, or if he has gone through this period he may be friendly again.

CHAPTER 13

FIFTEEN MONTHS OLD

Behavior Profile

At about fifteen months of age the American baby becomes something more than a "mere" infant. He is discarding creeping for toddling. He is discarding his nursing bottle in conformance with cultural custom. By virtue of other cultural pressures, he says "ta-ta" on more or less suitable occasions; by gesture language he calls attention to wetted pants; he makes an imitative stroke with a crayon; he helps to turn the pages of a picture book, albeit several leaves at one swift swoop. Numerous patterns which were in the making at one year now come to relative fulfillment. He is ready for a new chapter of acculturation.

But having graduated from "mere" infancy, he does not by any means settle down. On the contrary, he seems to feel and to exercise his newly formed powers almost to excess. He becomes demanding; he strains at the leash. While being dressed he may have to be held bodily. In his chair he stretches forward importuningly for things out of reach. He wants to hold and carry something in each hand. He is beginning to insist on doing things for himself. He likes to take off his shoes. He likes to empty or at least to overturn wastebaskets, not once but many times. If he is not equally ready to refill the wastebasket, it is because his nervous system is not quite ripe for this higher pattern of behavior.

For the time being, his gross motor drive is very strong; he is cease-lessly active, with brief bursts of locomotion, starting, stopping, start-ing again, climbing, and clambering. He likes to go out for a ride by automobile or by baby carriage, but even then he is prone to stand up and to be on his own self-activated move. If confined to a playpen, he is very likely to throw out his toys.

Casting is a very characteristic trait. And what is casting but em-phatic release? The voluntary power to release hold of an object is a complicated action pattern which requires an elaborate development of the controlling nerve cells of the brain. It takes time to bring about these developments; the child must learn to modulate his release, to time it accurately, to make it obedient to his intentions. Like any other growing function, it needs exercise—practice, as we say, although the practice is primarily a symptom rather than a cause of the growth.

The year-old child could poise one block over another; the fifteen-month-old child can let go of the block, neatly enough to build a tower of two. Likewise he can release a tiny pellet into a bottle. The matur-ing power of release also enables him to play a better to-and-from game with a ball. Indeed, he can throw it after a crude, casting fash-ion. At eighteen months he can hurl it. Even primitive man was once awkward in hurling stones. It takes years of neuromotor organization before a child can throw in a mature manner. Casting is a rudimentary first step in the development of this complicated ability. It must be a very important action pattern, or it would not figure so strongly in the behavior traits at fifteen months of age.

We have said that the fifteen-month-old child is "demanding." Per-haps it would be more accurate to say "assertive"; because he is not so much demanding things of us, his caretakers, as he is demanding things of himself: he is asserting his embryonic self-dependence. He wants to help feed himself. He grasps the cup executively with both hands (and of course tilts it to excess). He boldly thrusts his spoon into his cereal and, upside down, into his mouth (of course with spill-ing). It will take almost another year before he inhibits the turning of the spoon in this maneuver. (It took primitive man a long time to master the principles of the lever.) The significant demands are those he makes upon himself.

Now, as always, it is necessary to achieve a working balance between the individual and society. The danger is that the culture itself will place too heavy repressions upon this growing organism which is graduating from mere infancy. He does not enjoy the same kind of protectiveness that he had at the age of one year. The fifteen-month-old baby is at the threshold of behavior capacities which already foretell nursery school and kindergarten. He is dimly aware of pictures in a book; he can fit a round block into a round hole; he jargons and gestures; he is actually beginning to build a little with blocks; he can imitate a stroke of crayon upon paper; he is no longer a "mere" scribbler. These are foretokens of his educability, but he is still very immature.

The temptation may be for the adult carriers of culture to press him too fast and too heavily in the direction of civilization. It is well to remember that nature requires time to organize his burgeoning neuromuscular system—postural, manual, laryngeal, and sphincter. Everything in season!

Behavior Day

The pattern of the behavior day is changing. It shows the accumulative effect of cultural impress. Even at fifteen months, although the child still needs constant care, he is not as much a baby as he was at twelve months. Our illustrative fifteen-month-old child wakes between six and eight o'clock in the morning. He does not demand to be changed even though he wakes wet. Nor does he need toys. He is content with simple self-improvised manipulative and postural play in his crib. But when he hears someone stirring, the pattern suddenly changes to alert anticipation, which becomes overflowing joy as soon as his mother or caretaker greets him. He is now very sensitive to visual and auditory cues that have a social meaning.

The task of dressing him may fall to the father. The baby enjoys the tug and pull of dressing.

He is now capable of bipedal locomotion and so he walks to his breakfast. (This is a new behavior-day event.) He nibbles his cracker while he observes the family breakfast, and at about 8 A.M. is ready for his own, usually stationed in his high chair. His morning appetite is strong. He accepts being fed with a spoon, and demands that the dish be left on the tray. His motor drive is under better control so that the dish is now safe on the tray though it may need to be guarded. He likes to hold the spoon and likes to dip it occasionally into his cereal. He is more competent with the cup.

At about nine o'clock he is changed and toileted. He is not likely to resist toileting at this age. He is then returned to his crib, where he amuses himself with manipulative toys—a ball, a doll, a tin pan, clothespins, or containers of various sorts. Vigorous hurling, banging, or casting of toys may be a signal for a change of scene. He is transferred to a playpen. At twelve months he was quite content when the pen was in the rear yard. Now he prefers it in the front yard or on the front porch. He likes to watch the traffic. He is about to graduate from the playpen and the scope of his interest is widening. He likes to look into the neighbor's yard or onto the neighbor's porch, particularly if on this porch there is another playpen with another preschool child. This tendency to penetrate beyond the pen can be anticipated by placing some of his toys outside of the pen. He manages to pull these toys into the pen, and having secured them in this manner, he is probably a little less likely to cast them out. Casting, however, is a developmental, and not a regrettable, behavior pattern.

He plays contentedly until about noon, when he is ready for his midday lunch. He definitely wants this lunch. He is not too much interested in preliminaries, but he is a little more eager to contribute his own self-help during this meal, even though the spoon is likely to enter his mouth bottom side up. He is quite ready to accept help in feeding toward the end of the meal, although he may insist on holding the cup to drink his milk or water.

At about twelve-thirty he is toileted and may have his first or second bowel movement, after which he is returned to his crib. The effects of acculturation now become evident. Typically he makes no protest against the impending nap. He snuggles down under his covers. He likes to watch the shades go down. He is happy to be in bed and with an inflection of satisfied conclusiveness he says, "Bye-bye," and falls off to a sleep of an hour or two.

He is quite likely to wake wet. He is changed and toileted. He usually wakes in high mettle, eager to get out of his crib to continue with his behavior day. Already he is making definite associations between times and events. He is building up a sense of his own behavior day, which was scarcely present in earlier infancy. He realizes that he will soon be enjoying a trip in the carriage and he waits with a certain degree of patience before the journey—the patience being supported by a cracker which he munches while he waits.

Having arrived in the park or in a neighbor's play yard, he likes to be set free on the wide expanse of a lawn or a sidewalk. He indulges in a diversity of play, postural and manipulatory. Somewhat acrobatically he bends over and looks between his legs; he picks up sticks and strokes the dirt; hands them to an adult with an inflected "ta-ta" and does not expect a return as he did at twelve months. He jargons; he has a more sophisticated interest in his own sounds. Where formerly he was somewhat startled by them, he now listens to them suggestively. In his jargon he thus communicates with himself as well as with others.

He returns home at about four-thirty and continues his characteristic play activities, utilizing the apparatus of the living room, with a special interest in all containers, particularly wastebaskets. But he also likes to listen to music, to dance in rhythm to it, or even with the help of an adult to look in brief snatches at a picture book.

The daily bath may come at five o'clock. It is preeminently a play period. He likes to continue in his bath for a quarter of an hour. A favorite activity is the pouring of water from a receptacle.

Supper follows. He helps a little in the feeding but amiably accepts administered feeding. Supper over, he likes to come back to home base in his mother's lap or his father's lap, giving tokens of affection. He holds out his hand to have it kissed or caressed. And at about six o'clock he is again happy to be back in his crib for a sleep of some twelve hours. He is making increasingly definite person-to-person contacts, and after he has been tucked in bed he extends his hand through the palings for a good-night greeting.

The fact that we have so many greeting and intercommunication patterns emerging during the course of a single day at fifteen months is a convincing reminder that acculturation is well under way and that much still lies ahead.

SLEEP

NIGHT

Onset—Bedtime now comes between 6 and 8 P.M. and follows the happenings of the day in a regular, orderly fashion. The order, for instance, may be supper, bath, bed. The baby seems to have acquired a sense of "time to go to bed," an expectation that going to bed will follow certain events on the day's program. (At a later age this order and timing may change.) There may be initial crying by some, but most seem to have a feeling of being glad to be back in bed again. There may be talking for half an hour to two hours. The more active children may crawl out from under the covers and may be very busy in their crib until they finally fall asleep, perhaps at the foot of the crib.

[If falling asleep has been delayed, it is better not to go in to the child until he has fallen asleep or is nearly asleep. Otherwise the presence of the mother may stimulate him and further delay his falling asleep.]

Waking—Night waking is largely an individual matter and more common with the active child. Many children awake crying (more frequently before midnight) and are usually not quieted merely by being held. They can often be quieted by looking out of the window at lights, or by having someone play "This little pig went to market" with their fingers and toes. It is unwise to put them back to bed before they are ready, and the transition may often best be accomplished with a cracker, or by letting them hold something such as a toothbrush which they may have fastened upon in the bathroom.

Morning waking occurs between 6 and 8 A.M. The child is usually good at this time, lying under his covers and talking to himself. He may later crawl out from under the covers and play around in his crib, without the need of toys.

NAP

The nap usually follows a noon lunch. A common indication of the child's readiness for sleep is his trying to get off his shoes. He usually settles down at once and goes right to sleep. A few children delay sleep, and play for a few minutes with toys before settling down on top of the covers. They awake after a two-to-three-hour period and are ready to get up at once.

FEEDING

Self-Regulation—The gross motor drive is now under much better control than formerly. The child is able to sit through his meals, and commonly demands to help feed himself. Boys still lead in these demands. They do an especially creditable job with finger-feeding, and this is definitely their preferred method. They still are apt to turn the spoon en route to their mouths, and are thus apt to spill the contents of the spoon unless the contents stick to the spoon. With fatigue they are more apt to allow the mother to feed them.

An even more usual demand is to hold a spoon and dip it into the food in the dish, which is now safe on the tray. The child accepts being fed as long as he is happily occupied. Spilled bits on the tray are usually finger-fed. Many children differentiate as to the preferred method of being fed at different meals. Breakfast may be accepted without any demands for self-feeding. Lunch may be accepted partially, with some demands for

self-feeding. Supper may be taken completely alone, with the one possible exception when the child may allow his father to feed him. Many also enjoy feeding the father or mother and may do better at this than at feeding themselves.

Those who have clung to their evening bottle—either on their own demand or because their parents have felt it is the best and easiest way to ensure an adequate milk intake—most frequently have this bottle on going to sleep and often call it "ba-ba." They may even ask for it in anticipation of going to bed.

Preferences and refusals have their ups and downs but are on the whole quite similar to the patterns described at one year of age.
Number and Appetite—Same as at one year of age.
Spoon-Feeding—This is an age at which a large majority of children make some demand to participate in meals and want to have a try at the spoon. They grasp it pronately near the bowl, and have difficulty in filling it since they dip it rather than scoop it into the food. What sticks to the spoon is then carried to the mouth, but the journey to the mouth is a hazardous one and the spoon may be turned upside down and the little contents there are may be spilled. If it does reach the mouth right side up, it is usually turned after it is inserted. The free hand is quite inactive and only comes in to help in an emergency. The child usually allows his mother

to feed him so long as he is allowed to do some of the feeding himself.

[The child will often best accept help from the mother if she fills his spoon from her spoon, and then supports the handle of his spoon as he lifts it to his mouth.]

Cup-Feeding—The child now enjoys manipulating the cup by himself, grasping it more with thumb and forefinger or with the tips of his fingers. He drinks more continuously (five to six swallows) and now tilts his cup by the action of his fingers rather than by the tilting of his head. However, he is apt to tilt the cup too quickly, so that some spilling results.

[Though the child demands to hold his cup alone, he may allow his mother to help by holding her finger under his chin to restrict the wide excursions of the chin.]

Self-Help—Demands are similar to those expressed at one year, with the addition that a demand to spoon-feed is coming in and the child may insist on feeding himself one whole meal, preferably lunch or supper.

ELIMINATION

Bowel—One or two movements a day, though occasionally a day may be skipped. With some children it still occurs in the morning, either on waking or around breakfast time. With a few it has shifted to a more consistent afternoon pattern, either after lunch or in relation to the nap. A resistance to the pot common from twelve to fifteen months is now giving way to an acceptance. If the child is put on at a favorable moment, such as after a meal—usually breakfast—he may have a bowel movement easily on the pot. However, at other times he will not "go" until he is removed from the pot even though he remains contentedly on it for as long as he is left there.

Another favorable time is when the mother observes that the child has suddenly become very quiet, or when he looks at his mother, or stoops as he grunts. He is beginning to be conscious of a bowel movement in his pants and may fuss, say "uh," or grasp at his pants to indicate his desire to be changed, especially when he is with an adult. He is less demanding of attention when he is in his crib or playpen and may even try to take off his pants by himself.

[Occasionally episodes of stool-smearing may occur at this age, when the child is alone either in his playpen or crib. It is important that his clothes fit securely and also that he be watched, preferably without his seeing the adult. Then he may be cared for immediately after he has had his movement.]

Bladder—The child may be dry after his nap if he is taken up immediately. At this age he appears to be more conscious of being wet than earlier. If he is in training pants and makes puddles on the floor, he may point to the puddles, use a special word such as "tee-tee" or "pee-pee," or may just say, "See." He may splash his hands in the puddle and may be interested in mopping it up with any nearby cloth. He responds fairly well to being put on the toilet, especially at favorable times such as after meals and before and after sleeping periods. He may not urinate or defecate until taken off the toilet. Resistance to the toilet is shown if he is put on when he does not need to be, or during the midmorning and the midafternoon. Some children may now be (temporarily) increasing their span to two or three hours.

[A "potty chair" may be the most successful toilet equipment at this age, particularly for those children who like to do things for themselves.

Since many children will not urinate or have a bowel movement until after they are removed from the toilet, it is best not to leave them on too long. Leaving them on for longer periods will not produce the desired results.

Punishment for wetting has little or no effect. If the child is punished, he is apt to stop telling after he is wet. Dressing him in diapers and rubber pants is preferable.

If the child resists being placed on the toilet, his resistance should be respected.]

BATH AND DRESSING

Bath—Now that the nap is usually in the afternoon and supper is at five o'clock, there is little time for the bath in the afternoon. It may be best to postpone it till just before bedtime. Then it is heartily enjoyed, especially if it is taken with an older sibling.

Washcloth and soap are still grasped. Water is often sucked from the washcloth, or the washcloth may be placed on the head like a hat. Favorite water toys are containers such as cups or watering cans. The child may try to drink the bath water. He may fuss when taken from the tub but usually quiets when given some distracting toy.

Dressing—Dressing can be very difficult at this age. The child's attention is usually on other things. This is the age when the parent needs to hold the child tightly and pour him into his clothes. In the morning he may be dressed best on his mother's lap with the mother seated beside the crib so that he may reach for and occupy himself with his toys. Or he may be dressed standing on a high restricted place with a shelf at chest height for his toys.

His chief clothing interests are still his hat, shoes, and pants, and these are usually in relation to specific times: the hat when going out, the pants when soiled or wet, and

the shoes when he is sleepy and
ready for his nap.

[After waking from his nap his
chief interest is often to go outdoors, clothes or no clothes. Therefore dressing him near a window or
open door, if weather permits, may
make the ordeal less difficult. Giving him a cracker often helps.]

SELF-ACTIVITY

The child occupies himself happily and contentedly at the following times: until he is picked up in
the early morning; for an hour in
his room or crib; and then for another hour out in his playpen in
the morning. He cannot stay too
long in one place at one time and
enjoys a shift. His demands increase
as the day goes on. He does not
demand toys on waking, but plays
happily, with gross motor activity.
He wants his toys when he is returned to his room and he likes a
little action, such as watching traffic or seeing people walk by, when
he is out in his playpen. His favorite playthings are balls, spoons,
cups, clothespins, boxes, and some
fitting toys. His best play with toys
often occurs in his room from 9 to
10 A.M. after his early gross motor
workout. Then he puts things into
things and takes them out again,
throws balls and goes after them,
and with fatigue throws his playthings out of the crib or playpen or
puts them behind him.

SOCIALITY

The shy period that occurs at one
year has usually passed, and the
fifteen-month-old child is eager to
go out into the world in or with his
carriage. Some still sit or stand in
their carriage and especially enjoy
the noises of the world. He hears
a dog bark, a horse trotting, the
whir of an airplane. A sudden sharp
noise may even cause him to whim-
per. He watches, too, but more than
that, he listens. Some, whose gross
motor drive is strong, fuss to get
out of their carriages after fifteen
to thirty minutes, and wish to push
the carriage themselves.

An hour's carriage ride is quite
enough at this age. The fifteen-
monther wants to be about his own
intimate business of walking, stooping to pick up sticks, bending over
to look between his legs, bringing
odds and ends to the adult, and
exercising what small vocabulary he
has. He delights in dogs and often
says "bow-wow." He enjoys imitating smoking, coughing, nose-blow-
ing or sneezing, and blowing out
matches.

In fact he is becoming so aware
that he has to be restricted in his
activities. He is apt to demand anything in sight if he is at the table.
He is "into everything" in the living
room and no longer plays the game
of "no, no," but boldly demands his
own way. If he plays in the living
room, things must be put out of
reach. His primary interest in the

living room, however, is the wastepaper basket. His eyes search around a living room and seem invariably to pick out wastepaper baskets. He enjoys pulling things out and, less often, putting them back in.

Toward the end of the afternoon he may enjoy looking at colored pictures and turning pages, and may also respond to rhythmic music with the swaying of his hips.

[When the child makes demands that cannot be met—such as a demand to walk in some forbidden place—he may respond favorably to being picked up. The shift in posture seems to cut off the demand at once.

Some children will not accept things directly from the adult hand but will accept them from a container.]

CHAPTER 14

EIGHTEEN MONTHS OLD

Behavior Profile

The eighteen-month-old is so charged with run-about compulsions that he prefers to push his baby carriage rather than ride in it. His locomotor drive is so strong that he is constantly running into nooks and corners and byways, or going up and down stairs by one device or another. For the same reason he likes to chase and be chased. He is constantly introducing variations into his movements, as though he were trying out the versatilities of his motor equipment. He walks backward, he pulls his carriage backward. He does this partly because he is "learning" to shift the gears of his physiological automobile— namely, his nervous system. This neuro-automobile is far from complete. He can start and stop pretty well (when he is so minded), but he cannot turn corners; and he will have to double his age before he can pedal his tricycle or stand on one leg.

He has not even fully attained the upright posture. He walks on a broad base, feet wide apart; he runs with a stiff, propulsive flat gait. He squats a good deal; his abdomen is rather prominent; his arms extend out bilaterally from the body, almost like flippers; he uses whole-arm movements in ball play and "painting"; his hands are not agile at the wrists; he has difficulty in coordinating hands and feet. He even has trouble getting his spoon to his mouth.

He lugs, tugs, dumps, pushes, pulls, pounds. When he seizes a teddy bear he clasps it grossly to his chest. He is also something of a furniture mover. Gross motor activity takes the lead over fine motor. There is a primitiveness about his postures and manipulations, as though a reminiscent touch of the stooped Neanderthal man were still upon him.

But there is no reason to despair. At two years he will be more nimble at the wrists, and will turn the pages of a book singly! Even now he can take off his shoes, hat, mittens, and unzip a zipper if it is not too fine. Much more will come soon enough. At three he will put on his shoes; at four he will lace them.

His attention, like his body activity, is mercurial. He attends to the *here* and the *now*. He has little perception for far-off objects. He runs into them headlong, with meager sense of direction. You may talk to him about the future, but he will not listen, because for the time he is color-blind to the future. He is immersed in the immediate; but even now the push of growth is lifting him out of the immediate by giving him a sense of "conclusions."

This spontaneous interest in conclusions is one of his most interesting psychological characteristics. He likes to complete a situation. He puts a ball in a box and then utters a delighted exclamatory "oh" or "oh, my," in a burst of conclusive satisfaction. He likes to close a door, to hand you a dish when he has finished, to mop up a puddle, to flush the toilet, to "tell" after he has soiled himself. When he sits down in a chair it is with a decisive manner, as though to say, "Now, that's done."

These are elementary judgments, even if they are not yet put in words and sentences. He is thinking with his body rather than with his larynx, and his mind is already operating on a distinctly higher level than it did at one year. His attention is sketchy, mobile, works in swift, brief strokes. In his play he likes to carry objects from one place to another. In this way he learns what a place is. He even likes to put things back in place—an embryonic orderliness soon outgrown. But this bit of behavior is a good reminder that a great deal of organization is going on in spite of the apparent aimlessness of his activity. How can you discover without exploring? And how can you explore without traveling? And how can you find out where you started from without going back? So there is a logic, after all, in this back-and-forth behavior—the logic of development.

This logic cannot be hastened by words. The child must begin with a practical logic. Things must be acted out first. He has only about a dozen words at his command. He relies on a more abundant vocabulary of expressive gestures and odd little clucking sounds (again reminiscent of a very primitive human). Favorite words are "all gone," "thank you," "bye-bye," "oh, my"—all of which register completions. He responds to a few simple verbal directions, but he must be managed chiefly through things rather than words. If he is to remain still, he usually must have an interesting object in his hands. The manipulation of this object serves to drain his locomotor drive. Music may do the same thing. He will stay on the spot, and sway accompaniment with whole-body rhythm. He may hum spontaneously. If he attempts singing, it is by repetition of a single word. He is not very sedentary, nor ready for the finer arts, though he likes to stroke in the dirt with a stick.

With such an action system, and with such very elementary insight into time and space, we do not expect elaborate or refined interpersonal relations. It is doubtful whether he even perceives other runabout children as persons like himself. He pulls, pinches, pushes, and strokes them as though they were objects for manipulation. He is quite content with solitary play, back to back with one of his contemporaries.

And yet he is laying the basis for a more intellectual grasp of what another person is. He does a great deal of watching. He learns by looking a hundred times a day. It is by brief strokes and spans of attention but they count up. Sometimes he even imitates the wonderful adults upon whom he gazes: he crosses his legs; he reads a newspaper! He likes to play more elaborate peekaboo games; to hide and be found. This reciprocal kind of play helps to build up an identification of himself as distinct from but like others. If he seizes a broom to sweep, he holds it by the end and shoves it shovelwise, a reminder of how much he still has to learn about spatial as well as human relations.

Behavior Day

The eighteen-month-old child is relatively self-contained even though he is often described as a runabout. He awakens between six and eight o'clock in the morning and plays contentedly until his mother arrives. He greets her, but not with the bubbling and excessive overflow of even three months ago. He is changed and restored to his crib with a cracker and toys. He is content to play for half an hour or more until breakfast, which comes at about eight-thirty, and may not begin until the father has left home. Breakfast is often served on a low chair-and-table unit. He likes the confinement of such a unit. He accepts feeding by his mother although he insists on holding his cup while he drinks.

After breakfast he is toileted. He may have a bowel movement, but irregularity is quite typical of this age. If it is summertime he spends a play period from about nine to eleven-thirty out of doors on the porch or in a protected corner of the yard. If his enclosure gives him a free run so that he can exercise his locomotor abilities and if it is provided with a sandbox and other toys, he is quite content to remain in it. He needs only marginal supervision. It may be necessary to go to him if he falls or cries, and he reacts favorably to shifts of toys when needed. He is so busy and preoccupied with his play activity that he does not need to be changed during the course of the morning. His rubber pants serve their purpose, and if he is interrupted he may resist toileting.

The noon luncheon may be served in the kitchen. He is more insistent on helping himself at this meal. After luncheon he is toileted and is soon ready for his afternoon nap of, say, two hours. He wakes happy and cheerful from his nap. He is anxious to be up and doing. He is even interested in dressing to the extent that he helps with socks and shoes. However, he is more skillful at undressing than at dressing.

After a snack of juice and crackers, he is taken out for a ride in his carriage. He does not like to stay too long in the carriage and is happier to get out and push. He may have to be restrained in a harness. He returns home willingly by carriage and plays perhaps for a quarter hour in the living room, dancing to the radio, looking at magazines, playing with the wastebasket. Being relatively self-contained, he is quite agreeable to being left in his room with the gate closed while his mother prepares supper.

Supper comes at about five o'clock. Having had his fling of self-feeding at the noon meal, he accepts a measure of help at the evening meal. He is toileted again and may have a second bowel movement.

His daily bath comes a little before six o'clock. He enjoys it as he did at fifteen months but he is somewhat less reckless in his play, more sedate and more wary. After his bath, he joins his father for a brief period of good-night play.

Shortly after six o'clock he is put to bed with his teddy bear or doll, to whom he jargons more or less sociably. In spite of his locomotor capacities, he stays under his covers and falls asleep sometime between half past six and eight, to awake in the morning for another active day.

SLEEP

NIGHT

Eighteen Months—Bedtime still comes between 6 and 8 P.M. The child of this age likes to take some of his toys, as his teddy bear or his own shoe, to bed with him. He may play for a while with this object before dropping off to sleep, usually under the covers. Evening or night waking occurs intermittently and is usually associated with an active or too exciting day. He is easily quieted by being talked to, given a drink, or toileted if that is necessary.

He wakes between 6 and 8 A.M. He usually stays under the covers, talks to his teddy bear or plays with his shoe, and when he feels that it is time to get up, he may fuss or call. He is happy to see his parent and is eager to be taken up.

*Twenty-one Months**—Sleeping up till now has gone quite smoothly, but this is often the beginning of a period of sleeping difficulties which may continue through thirty months. Difficulties

---

* The age level of twenty-one months is a transitional age. It has not been given separate chapter status, but is discussed separately in this section under the six behavior-day categories (Sleep, Feeding, Elimination, etc.).

occur not only on going to sleep and during sleep, but also on waking. Difficulty is especially evident on going to sleep, when the child, though he seemingly has settled down with a book, doll, or teddy bear, calls his mother back for the first of numerous demands for toileting, a drink, a handkerchief, a kiss, or anything that comes into his mind. Sleep is more disturbed at this age and there is more night waking, but the child usually quiets readily after being toileted, or given a drink or a cracker. A few children remain awake talking to themselves for an hour or more, early in the morning. Total sleeping time is further cut down by the fact that they wake earlier in the morning than they did when they were younger. They are apt to fuss, but if the mother goes to them and cares for them they may go back to sleep for an hour or more.

NAP

Eighteen Months—As at fifteen months, the nap follows the noon meal. The child may or may not take toys to bed with him, but is often so ready for bed that he goes right to sleep. A few children, as at fifteen months, may delay sleep. The nap lasts for one and a half to two hours. The child usually awakes happy and wants to get right up. Occasionally he awakes crying and then responds best to a motor workout of running about before being toileted.

Twenty-one Months—As with night sleeping, there is difficulty in release of consciousness, but most children play well by themselves and do not call their mothers. Sleep may be delayed an hour or more and is finally induced only by the mother's putting the child under the covers at an opportune time. He sleeps longer (two to two and a half hours) and although he usually awakes happily, he may awake fussing. If he fusses it is best to let him take his time and awaken slowly.

FEEDING

Appetite—Appetite may be decreasing and is usually less than the robust infant appetite. The noon meal is frequently the best meal. Appetite for milk from a cup is less than appetite for milk from a bottle.

[If giving milk from a cup instead of a bottle has markedly reduced the amount that the child will take, it may be better to continue at least one bottle a day.]

Refusals and Preferences: Eighteen Months—Refusals and preferences are fluctuating and not clearly defined.

Twenty-one Months—Preferences are becoming more positive. If canned baby foods have previously been given, the child may demand the continuance of a specific brand.

Spoon-Feeding—Grasp of the

spoon is pronate. The child holds the spoon horizontally, raises his elbow as he lifts the spoon to his mouth. The spoon is aligned to the mouth half-point, half-side, and may turn after it enters the mouth. The free hand is ready to help as needed, pushing food on the lips into the mouth or placing spilled food in the spoon. The child may even carry food from the dish with his fingers and place it in the spoon bowl before putting the spoon into his mouth. Discrete particles such as peas and pieces of meat are preferably finger-fed. Food that cannot be swallowed is removed from the mouth.

The child cleans off the spoon well by tilting the spoon handle upward as he removes the spoon from his mouth. He adjusts his head as with cup-feeding. There is a lateral chewing movement of jaw and tongue. The tongue selectively licks in bits of food from the chin or the side of the mouth.

Cup-Feeding—The child holds the cup with both hands, holding and tilting it securely. He now has good control of his fingers as he tilts the cup, and spills very little. As he comes up for air he exhales audibly. He soon returns to drinking and usually finishes his glassful. The hazard in cup-drinking lies in the fact that when through drinking, the child automatically extends the cup to his mother, and if she is not there or does not come at once when he calls, he is apt to drop the cup or to throw it across the room.

Self-Help: Eighteen Months—Most children enjoy feeding themselves and may be able to handle all three meals. The mother may need to help fill the spoon. Some children, who have previously expressed occasional desire to feed themselves, may now prefer to be fed. Each dish is handed to the mother as it is emptied. Cup-drinking is handled entirely by the child, except for the mother's accepting the cup.

Twenty-one Months—If the child feeds himself, he eats better alone, with his mother moving about the room but not paying attention to him until he calls. If more than one dish is on the tray, he loves to pour things from one dish to another. He is not really able to handle more than one dish at a time. He likes to have patterns repeated— the same bib, the same spoon.

[Since the child at this age is sensitive to peripheral stimuli, it is important not to have his meal interrupted by small or large distractions. The dessert within sight, too much interference on the part of the mother, or the father coming home—any of these may serve to interrupt and perhaps terminate his meal. It is therefore often easiest to control such stimuli by feeding the child alone in the kitchen.]

ELIMINATION

Bowel: Eighteen Months—There is a variety of times and contexts for the bowel movement at this age, but each child is fairly consistent to his own pattern. However, at this age fluctuation and incompleteness are the rule. Therefore, any one child may set up a meal relationship for a time, then shift to midmorning, then to midafternoon. This makes successful "training" difficult. The child is beginning to request the toilet either by a word or by fetching his pot, and often the mother may judge by his unusual quietness that he is about to function.

There appear to be two distinct types of children: one with a close meal association with the bowel movement, the other more irregular and functioning at some time between meals. Those who have a meal association are usually trained more easily. The two daily movements usually occur after breakfast and after supper. These children often have a high language ability and refer to the bowel movement by the name of the receptacle—e.g., "pot." The name is more commonly used after functioning than before.

Those who have an irregular time of functioning commonly have their movement when alone, most commonly in the midmorning, and preferably standing at their playpen or crib rail. They usually want to be changed, and therefore may tell afterward by making a meaningful sound ("uh-uh" or "k-k"). Or they may merely gesture by pulling at their pants. These children usually resist the toilet and often have occasional episodes of stool-smearing, initiated as they try to take care of themselves when alone in their playpen or crib. If they do respond to the toilet in the morning, they frequently do not finish, and then they may have one or two more movements in their diapers throughout the day, particularly when they are alone.

Twenty-one Months—Similar to eighteen months. More smearing episodes occur, especially after naps. Some children still refuse the toilet, while others are completely trained, especially those who have a regular time. Some who have been well trained earlier often have a relapse at this age, associated with a diarrheal episode. This may be related to teething, but may also be related to a new but too powerful release mechanism. Many are reported to have an explosive bowel movement, which indicates a forceful, casting release mechanism.

They are also quite conscious of the process and the product. Often, if they soil their diapers, they seem unable to move, and stand screaming in distress, and continue screaming while they are being changed. This response is not necessarily related to any previous punishment. Sometimes they are able to inhibit release when it has started too soon, which may also bring on a screaming response. When they are successful in responding to the toilet, they are often overjoyed at their success.

Some children, chiefly boys, are unable to have their bowel movement unless they are completely undressed. This may be associated with the twenty-one-month-old's tendency to undress and to run about naked.

Bladder: Eighteen Months—Most children do not object to the toilet at this age if they are not put on too often. They may even enjoy sitting on it. However, there are some who still resist strenuously. Some children now take the initiative themselves by occasionally asking in advance, in which case they use the same word that they use for bowel functioning. Or they may fetch the pot. They respond best to being asked whether they want to go, before they are taken. Their answer is usually quite accurate. The response to the toilet is fairly prompt.

If the child is in training pants and makes puddles on the floor, he continues to point to them, saying, "See" or "pee-pee," and enjoys mopping them up. This is the age when punishment and shame are often introduced by the adult, since something in the child's awareness makes the adult feel that the child could have done better. If punishment and shame are used, the child will point to the puddle and say, "Ooh-ooh," as though it were quite awful; and when asked, "Who did it?" he may blame it on the cat or on his grandfather, and when further asked if he did it himself, may reply, "No, nebber." Another shame response is to show undue and sudden affection toward the mother just after wetting.

The child is increasingly dry after his nap, but still more frequently wet than dry. Keeping dry may depend on how quickly he was put on the toilet after waking.

This is an age when picking the child up at 10 P.M. for toileting is often started. He is usually wet at this time, and may not awaken when changed or put on the toilet. He may, however, resist the toilet, in which case this practice should be discontinued. The child is usually wet in the morning even though picked up in the evening, but a few are consistently dry on waking with the help of this 10 P.M. toileting.

[Because bladder control is in a transition stage, it is still best to keep the child in diapers or in padded training pants and rubber pants, especially during the morning play period, when he does not like to be disturbed, and during the night, when they may prevent him from feeling wet and waking up. Training pants plus rubber pants are more comfortable, and if the child is away from home he may need them since he is apt to refuse to respond to a strange toilet.]

Twenty-one Months—Though the child may resist the toilet at specific times when he does not need it, there is very little general resistance to the toilet at this age. The child may use words or gestures, and many are beginning to go to the bathroom by themselves even though unable to care for themselves. Accidents are more common in the afternoon, when the span is shorter than the morning span of one and a half to two hours. Children are more apt to ask for the toilet at night after being put to bed than at naptime.

The majority are wet after their naps, even though they may have been previously dry. Dryness depends largely on how quickly the mother gets to the child after he has awakened.

Resistance to being picked up at 10 P.M. is strong with many, so that many are not picked up at this time. They are usually wet in the morning.

BATH AND DRESSING

Bath: Eighteen Months—As at fifteen months, the bath is usually given after supper. There may be occasional short periods of resisting the bath, the cause of which is hard to determine. Perhaps the child has fallen in the tub or has felt unsure on the slippery tub bottom, or has been disturbed by the noise of water gurgling down the drain.

[A rubber mat placed on the bottom of the tub may help to give a feeling of security.

Children who are stimulated rather than relaxed by a bath just before going to bed should have their bath at an earlier hour.]

Twenty-one Months—There is an interest in helping to wash out the tub, an expression of the child's urge to imitate domestic activities.

Dressing: Eighteen Months—The child at this age is becoming interested in the process of being dressed and is on the whole quite cooperative. He even tries to put on his shoes but he is better at undressing than at dressing. He takes off his mittens, hat, socks, can unzip zippers, and is beginning to have an interest in undressing for itself.

Twenty-one Months—The child undresses completely, down to and sometimes even including his shirt, if that is easily removed. He does this when alone, usually in his room or out in the backyard. It is a common sight to see a twenty-one-month-old child frisking about the backyard without any clothes on—only the chill and cold of winter inhibit this removal of clothes.

SELF-ACTIVITY

Eighteen Months—The child at this age is primarily egocentric. The majority of his reactions are to himself and his own activities. Humor is self-initiated and largely in relation to self. There are some social relationships, largely self-initiated, with adults. The child largely ignores other children. He defends and strengthens his sense of self by opposing others. "No" is his favorite word. His chief activities are motor.

The eighteen-monther is a busy-body. He is both secure on his feet and secure in his own interests. He is not yet enough aware of people to be overdemanding, and demands occur mainly when he gets into trouble with his own activities. He has usually graduated from the playpen, though if his motor drive and activity are low he may prefer his fifteen-month-old station of being in his playpen in the front yard. If he refuses the pen, his refusal is strenuous and should be respected. He will settle down to a happy playtime either alone in his room, on a closed-in porch, or in a closed-in yard space which is not too big but which gives him space to run around. He may prefer to be in any of these places for most of the morning, although he may enjoy being shifted from indoors to outdoors.

The success of his play depends upon the presence of interesting playthings and the absence of hazardous equipment. Because he is such a furniture-mover and is beginning to be such a climber, it is wise to remove chests of drawers and small tables and chairs that he can move, while he is playing in his room. If a chest of drawers remains, the drawers should be locked to keep him from getting into them, or the dresser turned to

face the wall. Windows and screens should be securely fastened.

Indoors, he endlessly shifts from pull toys to doll to teddy to pots and pans to balls to fitting toy to blocks or a hammer toy to magazines (especially those with colored advertisements). He hugs the doll one moment, drops it and runs over to finger the light plug the next, runs over to sit down and look at the magazine, tears out a page when he is finished, gets up and goes to his hammer toy. He may become angry when things do not work the way he thinks they should, but he does not usually call the adult for help. Out of doors on the porch or in the yard, he also enjoys his indoor toys, but most of all he enjoys play with sand and can sit for long periods filling and dumping sand, especially outside of the sandbox.

Besides the morning play periods alone, the eighteen-monther will accept being put alone in his room with the gate closed for fifteen to thirty minutes while his supper is being prepared, provided that he has had a happy social afternoon. If he is not to be put to bed at the usual six-o'clock hour, it is wise to build up an evening play period in his room if his parents have an early dinner hour. This is initiated best with a new toy and should not continue past the time when he starts to fuss.

[Toys that are too difficult to handle and that for this reason bring on crying should be removed from the child's room and reserved for social play periods. Books that the child can tear should be removed from his room, though he may be allowed discarded magazines for his tearing play.

Light plugs in the child's room should be either disconnected or covered over, because of the danger of an electric shock resulting from the child's inserting sharp metal objects such as bobby pins.

Twenty-one Months—The prolonged busyness of the eighteen-monther is now lessening because of the child's new awareness of people. His play periods alone are now more frequent but shorter. He likes to linger in the kitchen in the morning until nine-thirty or ten o'clock before he will go to his room or to his outdoor play space, and then he may stay only if he himself closes the door.

Indoors, a toy telephone, circles on a peg, or a small cardboard chest of drawers delights him. He enjoys acting out many of the household tasks he has seen performed, as dusting, opening drawers, or putting things on shelves. He still tears magazines, but his eyes may hit upon the wallpaper and he may have the kind of hands that become busy picking at it. There are apt to be more interruptions of the play period at this age. He is more likely to fall or to get stuck. He quiets with affection after a fall.

He may scream for assistance as well as from fright if he suddenly has a bowel movement in his pants. After his mother has come to him, the child may refuse to return to solitary play. However, he will later remain happily in his room as his lunch or supper is being prepared. He also may build up a longer evening play period, as long as one hour, during his parents' early dinner hour, though more often nowadays he remains with the family group.

SOCIALITY

Eighteen Months—This is the age when the child is "into everything" as soon as he is given the run of the house, and he never stays in one place for long. He is, however, becoming interested in the activities of the household, such as sweeping and dusting, and enjoys mimicking these. He is beginning to know where things are kept, likes to fetch things (father's slippers when he comes home), and especially enjoys putting things back. He can also go to places where things are kept and ask for them, if they are out of reach, by looking or pointing, making the sound of demand ("eh-eh"), or sometimes by naming.

His main time for social demand is not until after his nap. Then he wants to go out for a walk. He may even prefer to leave his carriage at home, though he may ride in it for a while and then want to push it. He likes to be on his feet and to go exploring. He darts into every byway that he sees or up any steps. He also rushes into the street. He refuses to be touched or to have his arm held, but generally tolerates a harness if it is used only when needed. The harness should be used with a loose rein except to break a fall, and the reins should be looped up whenever they are not needed. The eighteen-monther does not need to travel far from home since he so enjoys his weaving back and forth and his penetration into all by-ways.

When he plays indoors with an adult he can tolerate only a short time in the living room before he gets into things. He now enjoys dumping the wastepaper basket. He also enjoys turning the knob of the radio to get music to dance by. For a short period he may enjoy looking at picture books, turning pages, pointing to objects, and occasionally naming them.

But as soon as he fatigues, he is apt to grab objects and strenuously resists inhibitions. Then a sit-down temper tantrum may ensue, which can be terminated only by letting him have the desired object or by picking him up. Sometimes when he realizes he is taking something he shouldn't, he runs away and drops the object as he runs. After a very short time in the living room he plays happily with the adult in his own room, which is his favorite place.

After his evening play period of fifteen to twenty minutes, he enjoys coming to the dining room, and sits happily if confined, looking at a book or chewing on some food. He especially enjoys sociability with his father before bed, with a little roughhousing.

Twenty-one Months—At twenty-one months the child is not only more aware of people than formerly, but also knows what belongs to different people. He now understands "This is Mommy's," "This is Daddy's," and "This is Bobby's" (his own). A sense of property rights is dawning in his mind. He likes his own place on the bookshelf, his own drawer in his parents' desk, his own corner in his mother's room with some of his toys there. In fact each room acquires new meaning to him if he has something of his own in it. Then he always knows what to do in each room as he enters, and when he has exhausted the possibilities of his own things it is time to leave that room, for it is then that he begins to get into other people's things. He cannot be trusted alone in any room except his own.

He is now more aware of household activities and wants to participate in them. A favorite room is the kitchen. He likes to fetch things out of drawers, use them, and put them back. He delights in putting the groceries away and really knows where they go. After play in the kitchen he will happily go to his room for his morning play period, or else out of doors. He usually demands company by 11 A.M. and wants to go on a late-morning walk before lunch. But before he goes for his walk he will gladly help pick up his toys and put them away.

The walk is similar to that at eighteen months except that it involves more awareness on the part of the child. Whereas at eighteen months he went hither and yon impulsively, he now goes to the same places knowingly and with remembrance. His eyes are already picking out walls and it will not be long before he will want to walk on them. He responds less quickly to requests and is apt to do the opposite of what is asked of him, such as going in the opposite direction. This is especially true when it is time to go home. However, some incentive such as a constant repetition of "Go see Susie" (who may be the dog, cat, maid, or a doll) causes the homeward path to be taken in one direction.

The child is now both more responsive to and more demanding of the adult. He grasps the adult's hand and pulls him to show him things. He is more conscious of his acts as they are related to the adult and to the adult's approval or disapproval. He is conscious of disapproval of his tearing off the wallpaper, and very adroitly directs the adult's attention away from the marred place on the wall.

He also can control the adult by calling his name. Many, especially boys, do not call their mothers "mama" before twenty-one months. They now also have words for their desires, and combine the giver and the gift as when they call, "Mommy wa-wa" or "Mommy toidy."

This is the age when this new acquisition (language) may be used repetitively, and when going to bed is beginning to be fraught with frequent calling back of the mother. This is especially evident if the child has been put to bed at the usual 6 P.M. hour when he actually does not go to sleep before 7 or 8 P.M. The adult must then realize that the child has outgrown his infantile ways and needs a more mature type of handling.

CHAPTER 15

TWO YEARS OLD

Behavior Profile

At two years the child cuts his last milk teeth. He is no longer an infant though compared with a three-year-old child he is still very immature. There is danger of overestimating his capacities, simply because he is sturdy on his feet and is beginning to put words together. He is still an infant-child. He has so much behavior to coordinate, to organize in this third year that we must stress his limitations as well as his prodigious capacity for growth.

He does not yet walk erect. There remains a little of the angularity of the ancient man in his posture. Knees and elbows are slightly bent, shoulders are hunched. He holds his arms out and backward. His abdomen, however, does not protrude as much as at eighteen months. When he picks up something from the floor, he half bends at the waist as well as at the knees, whereas at eighteen months he squatted. Stooping is a more advanced behavior pattern than squatting. But the two-year-old still leans forward as he runs. Should he fall, he would bruise his forehead; at two and a half years he will hit his nose; at three and four years, his teeth. These are consequences of his physical makeup, just as his behavior traits are consequences of the makeup of his action system.

To get up from a sitting position on the floor, he leans forward, pushes up buttocks first and head second, instead of raising an erect trunk as he will later. He goes up and down stairs mark-time fashion, without alternating his feet. He can kick a ball, whereas eighteen months merely walked into a ball; but he cannot stand on one foot, as he will in another year. There is not much spring in his knees. The knee joints become flaccid or rubbery when one tries to slip on his leggings. He is rather hard to dress even though he is cooperative.

He is still geared to gross motor activity, and likes to run and romp, lug, push and pull, but with better coordination than at eighteen months. His fine motor control also has advanced. He manipulates more freely with one hand, and alternates from one hand to the other. He rotates his forearm, which enables him to turn a doorknob. He can crudely imitate a circular stroke. This increased manipulatory skill expresses itself in his marked interest in fitting one thing into another. "It fits" is a favorite and sometimes triumphant sentence. He also likes to take things apart and fit them together again.

The muscles of eyes and face are more adept. He moves his eyes more freely and is sensitive to marginal fields, whereas at eighteen months he ran headlong as though he had blinders on. He stops and engages in long periods of looking. The muscles of the jaw are coming under full voluntary control. Chewing is no longer as effortful as it was at eighteen months, and mastication is becoming more rotary.

The whole linguistic apparatus—mouth, lips, tongue, larynx, and thorax—is undergoing rapid organization. Jargon is dropping out, sentences are coming in. Soliloquy is taking the place of the babbling of the six-month-old child, as though on an advanced level the two-year-old is under a similar compulsion to exercise his vocal abilities, to repeat words, to name things, to suit words to action and action to words. Vocabularies vary enormously in size from a half dozen to a thousand words, but the third year is ordinarily the year when words burgeon.

The third year is also the year when the sphincter muscles of bladder and bowel are coming under voluntary control. Culture seems to conspire to increase the burden of development. For this reason home and nursery must be on their guard not to expect too much all at once in the correlation of postural control, fine coordination, speech, sphincter control, obedience, courtesy, and neatness.

The action system of the two-year-old is not yet sufficiently advanced to effect delicate and long-sustained interpersonal relations. He still prefers solitary play to parallel play and seldom plays cooperatively. He is in the precooperative stage, watching what others are doing rather than participating. He cannot share; he cannot as a rule let someone else play with what is his own. He must learn "It's mine" first. He does so by holding on and by hoarding. This is not a vice. How can he possibly acquire pride of ownership any other way? It is the method of development. Keeping and sharing are not separate virtues; they spring from the same developmental root. The hitting, patting, poking, biting, hair-pulling, and tug of war over materials so characteristic of two need to be handled with understanding and sensible techniques on the part of those who care for him. The infant-child is still too young to be reached by words alone; he must organize his experience through touching, handling, holding, clasping, and even a little hoarding and running away.

So to sum him up, what are his dominating interests? He loves to romp, flee, and pursue. He likes to fill and empty, to put in and to pull out, to tear apart and to fit together, to taste (even clay and wood), to touch and rub. He prefers action toys such as trains, cars, telephones. He is intrigued by water and washing. Although he is not yet a humanitarian, he likes to watch the human scene. He imitates the domesticities of feminine laundry work and engages in doll play. He has a genuine interest in the mother-baby relationship.

Behavior Day

The two-year-old child wakes somewhat slowly at, say, seven o'clock in the morning. He is happy to wake but not interested in getting out of his crib at once. He wakes wet but tolerates this condition and plays contentedly for about half an hour. He has a ready greeting for his mother, who toilets him and puts him in a bathrobe. He likes to go to the bathroom during this interim to watch his father shave. He is also content when he is returned to his room, where he munches a cracker and plays behind the closed gate. At breakfast he accepts considerable help from his mother but contributes in small dabs of self-help. (He will take over more completely at the noon meal.)

After breakfast he is toileted and is likely to have a bowel movement. He is dressed and again he offers some self-help. He plays in the kitchen for a while and then, at about nine-thirty he returns to his room and remains behind the closed gate without protest. If he should catch sight of his mother he may clamor for release. Otherwise he plays by himself for perhaps an hour. At ten-thirty he is toileted and, weather permitting, is taken out of doors. He makes no resistance to toileting because he takes it to mean a transition to new play experiences in his sandbox.

In his small enclosed play yard he engages in gross postural play activity, pulling toys and climbing on boxes, and near noon he has acquired a vigorous appetite for luncheon. This is the big meal of the day. He helps in its preparation. He also insists on feeding himself at this meal. He may even ask his mother to leave the room as he does so, calling her back for a next course.

After luncheon he is toileted and put to bed for a relaxation period that usually terminates in a nap, though sleep may be delayed until about two-thirty. The nap may last an hour. He wakes slowly. He usually wakes dry and responds to toileting. He takes some interest in dressing. He is beginning to show a well-defined liking for certain garments. He likes to listen to his mother's conversation and to make a few contributions of his own.

After juice and crackers, he is ready for outdoors. He prefers a stroller to a carriage. He likes to walk, does not object to being held by the hand. He likes to walk on walls. He is not averse to an auto ride, and particularly enjoys the traffic, assisting the stop-and-go lights with his own commentary announcements.

He likes to watch the preparations for supper. He may even help a bit. He feeds himself in part during the evening meal.

He is toileted again and may have a second bowel movement.

By six o'clock he is ready for a period of solitary play in his room. He likes to climb in and out of his crib when the arrangements so permit. He takes off his shoes as though by way of anticipation of going to bed. Frequently he has a brief session of play with his father. He is somewhat demanding about this bit of "life with father" for he insists that father should come directly to his playroom, without delaying to read the newspaper!

The daily bath comes after this play period. Here, too, the baby likes to offer some assistance and helps to wash himself with the washcloth.

He is off for bed at half past seven. He likes to have a book and some soft animal toy. After about a quarter hour of play he may call his mother, requesting the toilet or a drink. He resumes play and, after another interval, he is quite likely to call back again. By about eight o'clock he is ready to say "Good night," and this usually announces a release into sleep.

SLEEP

NIGHT

The time of falling asleep depends to some extent on when the child is put to bed, but his falling asleep is usually delayed till 8 or 9 P.M. The nap tends to displace night sleep, and if he has no nap he falls asleep earlier. His going-to-sleep patterns are similar to those at twenty-one months, there being many demands and requests. Children in whom these demands began at twenty-one months are often decreasing their demands by twenty-four months. Those who do not begin them till twenty-four or thirty months continue these pat-terns often until thirty-six or forty-two months. By twenty-four months, demands before going to sleep include a request for two or three stuffed animals, a book or two, and a pillow. The child still calls his parent back with various requests, though these may be decreasing. Going to sleep is not an easy thing for the two-year-old and tensional overflows may occur in various avenues—play, gross motor activity such as bouncing, calling for the mother, or demanding the toilet. The child may actually need the toilet three or four times and even if he does not urinate he very likely has sensations that make him ask. Having the door slightly ajar or a light on in the hall seems for some children to make the mother more accessible and relieves their anxiety.

If the child can handle going to sleep by himself he sings, plays with his toys, takes the case off the pillow, bounces, and may even finally crawl back under the covers by himself. When he is once asleep he often resists being picked up for toileting, and this waking may actually disturb his sleep pattern. Some, however, awake by themselves, especially girls, and demand the toilet as often as three to five times a night. They not only demand the toilet, but may also demand a drink of water or a cracker.

When the child awakes, between 6:30 and 7:30 A.M., he usually plays happily in his crib with his toys. If he calls, he is quickly satisfied with being changed and given a cracker and a few toys. He is then happily occupied until it is time to get up, when he especially likes to join his mother or father in the bathroom.

[This is the age when the child begins to hold on to the mother as he is being put to bed. This does not occur as much with the father and may occur even less with a baby-sitter. Thus bedtime may be smoother if someone other than the mother puts the child to bed.

Some children wake at the slightest disturbance during the night. In these cases it is best to make every possible preparation for the child's safety and comfort before he is left, and then not go into his room again.]

NAP

Going-to-sleep patterns are similar at nap time to those at night-time, with the exception that demands for the adult, at nap time, are put off till it is time to get up. Some give up sleeping at nap time for a few weeks or a few months, and others once or twice a week, but they will play happily in their cribs or rooms for an hour or more. If they do finally get to sleep, it is often induced by the adult's putting them under the covers, and they usually sleep well for two or three hours. Some do better if allowed to waken by themselves but too long a nap does displace night sleep and some children need to be wakened. When they awaken by themselves they often do so slowly and do not wish to be rushed through routines.

EATING

Appetite—Fair to moderately good. Breakfast is now relatively small. The noon meal is usually the best, but with some the one good meal is supper.

Refusals and Preferences—This is the age when the child is spoken of as "finicky" or "fussy." Now he is able to name many foods and has more definite ideas about what he likes. "Me want" or "Billy wants" is a common expression at this age. His affection is shown not only toward his mother but also toward the foods that he eats. His sense of form makes him prefer whole things—whole beans, whole pieces of potato—unless he demands the extreme opposite, i.e., the continuation of puréed foods. He does not like foods mixed up, such as gravy on his potato or milk on his cereal, unless, of course, he does the mixing himself. His preferences may be related to taste, form, consistency, or even color, red and yellow foods often catching his fancy. He is apt to repeat his demand for one food, but finally he drops that food completely and goes off on a different food jag.

[It is best to allow the two-year-old to have his food jags. Introduce new foods under new or pleasant situations. A great variety of foods is not needed by the two-year-old. If he holds food in his mouth, this may be considered a sign of satiety.]

Spoon-Feeding—The child now shows less experimental interest in the spoon and dish as play objects. The spoon is grasped more between thumb and index (more common with girls), and pronately. Filling of the spoon may be accomplished by pushing the point into the food without utilizing the free hand to push on the food. The point of the filled spoon is inserted into the middle of the mouth. There is still considerable spilling, and those who are disturbed by spilling may refuse to feed themselves, but accept food readily when they are fed.

Cup-Feeding—The child may now hold his cup or glass in one hand, with the free hand poised, ready to help if needed. He is able to lift, drink from, and set down the glass skillfully.

Self-Help—Some two-year-olds are able to feed themselves entirely and will accept no help. They seem to know that they do better alone, and dismiss the parent with, "Mommy way!" If the mother remains in the room she may have to be careful not even to look at the child.

There are some, however, who eat better when partially fed. They may eat their main dish better if they are given a spoonful of dessert now and then. With still others, who are the really poor eaters, the further distraction of stories, told or read, may be needed, especially when they are eating foods that they do not like.

The two extreme groups, the messy and the spotless eaters, are rather clearly defined at two years. The spotless are more apt to demand to be fed, to hold onto rituals, even to demand a special mat under their dessert dish if this has once been provided, and also to hold onto a repetition of certain foods.

ELIMINATION

Bowel—Accidents are rarer, though they come in periods, usually after meals. Those who have a nap relationship are slower in being trained. The child now differentiates bowel and bladder functions verbally. He may ask with whatever term he uses. Although he needs to be helped to go to the toilet, he wants to be left alone and often speaks imperiously to his parent with "Get out," "Go downstairs," or "Go away." But when he is finished he calls the parent back again to help him. Some children will not have a bowel movement if they are put on the toilet, but will only go if they put themselves on. [The two-year-old who will not have his bowel movement when placed on the toilet may do better if allowed to go by himself. This is often best accomplished by allowing him to run around in or near the bathroom without his pants on at the time when the bowel movement ordinarily occurs. Toilet facilities should, of course, be of a size and kind that he can use by himself.]

Bladder—There are fewer daytime accidents, though they may still occur in periods. The child's span is fairly long now (one and a half to two hours) and he often asks for the toilet. "I have to go potty [toidy]" or "Do wee-wee" are common expressions. He does not usually resist routine times before and after sleep, and midmorning and afternoon, except when he does not need to urinate. With most children there is an increased frequency period as short as twenty minutes between 5 and 8 P.M. Some are trying to go by themselves and may successfully remove their pants but cannot reach the bathroom in time.

They are now beginning to be proud of their toilet achievements and are apt to say, "Good boy" or "Good girl" when they have finished. They are also more concerned about their failures. They may suddenly cry as they urinate and find it difficult to move with wet pants on. Or they do something about it, taking off their wet pants and putting them in the hamper.

They are now more frequently dry than wet after their naps. Some may have a week's period when they wet daily and others may revert to wetting once or twice a week.

There is a good bit of variation in night wetting, with girls achieving dryness considerably ahead of boys. A few children are dry in the morning but the majority are wet even though they have been picked up at night.

BATH AND DRESSING

Bath—The child is now becoming more interested in helping to wash himself, and may prefer the washcloth to the bath toys. He is especially interested in washing and drying his hands, though he does neither very well.

[If the child refuses his bath, accept his refusal. He may, however, enjoy the change of having a sponge bath or of being washed on the hamper with his feet in a basin.]

Dressing—The two-year-old can take off his shoes as well as his stockings and pants. He may try to put on some of his clothes by himself but is not very successful. He almost invariably puts both feet into one pant leg and puts his hat on backward. When being dressed he is not only cooperative but definitely helpful. He finds large armholes and thrusts his arms into them, and lifts his feet to put on his pants. Some children still like to undress over and over again as a game and enjoy running about without their clothes on. However, at two years the recurrence of this undressing pattern comes only for short periods, as is true with so much of their other behavior.

SELF-ACTIVITY

If the snags of twenty-one months were not properly handled or ironed out, the child may be unable to adjust to a morning play period alone. Fortunately it is most frequently the child who is too stimulated by being with people who often does best alone, and the child who plays nicely beside the adult without getting in the adult's way who refuses to play alone.

The two-year-old may go happily to his room after a spell in the kitchen, if the doorway is guarded by a gate. But he may allow his door to be closed in anticipation of having something such as a letter or card slipped in under it.

He is now quieter at his play and has more continuity in doing things. He especially likes things that move and turn, such as little cars and wheels. In the kitchen the meat grinder and egg beater delight him. Screw toys and even a screwdriver, which he cannot handle alone, are also enjoyed. He now lines up his blocks and enjoys the blocks that stick together and fit into each other. The two-year-old often chooses little things like pebbles, pieces of string, marbles, beads, little bottles, and little books. Christmas cards are also cherished. Within the domestic line he now both feeds and toilets his doll and teddy and may even put them to bed or take them for a ride in a doll carriage.

It takes the thirty-month-old child to conduct a proper tea party, but the two-year-old enjoys the fitting together and matching of cup and saucer and the pouring of water. Out of doors, sand still holds his interest, with digging becoming more efficient. The addition of water is more than desired by the child, but is not the easiest thing for him to handle when he is alone, and always seems to lead to a demand for more water. Pushing a wagon or a baby carriage, along with other gross motor activities of running and climbing, are favorite out-of-door occupations.

SOCIALITY

The two-year-old child is now becoming quite an acceptable member of the household. With his further understanding of property rights, he gets into fewer things. However, he has now reached the stage of possessing as many things as he can, often with only the slightest reason for claim, and he insists upon his rights with "It's mine." The strength of his home demands is often in rather marked contrast to the meek compliance of his behavior away from home.

He enjoys helping in the house, running errands, helping make beds or clean the bathroom, and placing the table silver. He likes bringing ashtrays or passing things to people. He seems so mature in so much that he does that he is sometimes not watched closely enough. When left to his own devices, he can completely wreck a room, especially his parents' bedroom, in a very short time, by emptying bureau drawers, pulling scarfs off bureaus, and getting into powders or creams.

His walks are now more sedate. He likes to hold the adult's hand. He may stop to pick up sticks or pebbles, but he does not linger long. He delights in walking on walls or curbstones with his hand held. This is one way in which he can be given the sense of the boundary of the street. If he lingers behind his mother, he usually comes running when she starts off and says good-bye to him. He will now accept a ride in his stroller, and if he still uses a carriage he enjoys hiding back under the hood, especially as he passes strangers.

His afternoon play period in the house is happiest, with books and music. The nursery rhymes strike a responsive note in the two-year-old and any kind of tactile book demands repeated feelings. Dancing to music now includes running, turning in circles, and the beginnings of bouncing up and down.

The father is still a great favorite at this age, though the child may want his mother if he is any trouble or at night when he is tired, and especially during the night. He may show considerable dependence on his mother and is apt to demand all of her attention if there are others present. This is the age when affection is shown for parents or for those caring for the child, especially in the evening before bed.

The two-year-old with his increasing awareness of people goes through a shy period with strangers, especially adults. Indoors, he may put his fingers to his mouth, hide in the folds of the curtains or against his mother's skirt. Out of doors, he may act the same, or may walk a large circle around a passer-by, or hold the adult's hand and keep very close to her. But when he once becomes acquainted with a stranger, and especially if the stranger is of a preferred sex, he generously brings all of his toys and places them in the stranger's lap.

He is now enlarging his vocabulary from "baby" to "man," "lady," and even "boy" and "girl." He is delighted to be with other children and plays especially well with older children. He has passed through his earlier aggressive stage and is able to play parallel with another child. He almost always needs close supervision when playing with another child, especially after the first twenty minutes of play.

It is best for either the mother or the father to handle the child alone. This prevents conflicts.

CHAPTER 16

TWO AND A HALF YEARS OLD

Behavior Profile

If a group of parents should cast a secret ballot to determine the most exasperating age in the preschool period, it is quite likely that the honors would fall to the two-and-a-half-year-old, because he has a reputation for going to contrary extremes. The spanking curve therefore comes to a peak at about this time. Needless to say, we do not subscribe to this low estimation—or to the spanking.

The two-and-a-half-year-old is in a transitional period. He is fundamentally the same interesting child that he was at two; and he is growing into the thoroughly enjoyable child of three. Indeed, even now there is something delightful about his energy, his (apparently) misplaced exuberance, and his unmistakable tokens of embryonic sociability, helpfulness, and imaginativeness. If these tokens are sketchy and offset by their very opposites, it is because the two-and-a-half-year-old is at a crossroads stage in the growth of his action system. He has to do a great deal of intermediating between his own contrary impulses. Once more we must remind ourselves that he acts that way because he is built that way. And if he is managed rather than disciplined in terms of his peculiar limitations, he becomes tolerable and amiable.

Why does he go to such trying extremes? It is because his command of *yes* and *no, come* and *go, run* and *stop, give* and *take, grasp* and *release, push* and *pull, assault* and *retreat* is so evenly balanced. Life is charged with alternatives. Every pathway in the culture is a two-way street to him, because he is most inexperienced. (But remember, at eighteen months every path was a mere one-way street.) His action system likewise is a two-way system, with almost equally inviting alternatives, because he is so immature. His equilibrium is unstably balanced, because his inhibitory mechanisms are very incomplete. Moreover, life and environment are so complex, at this transitional stage, that he is almost obliged to go *both* ways, to experience both alternatives, so that he may find out which is really the right one. Do not despair if he tries out both, and tries you. When he is three years old he will be comparatively so much more mature that he will actually take pleasure in being asked to choose between two familiar alternatives.

At present his capacity for choice is weak; so he chooses both alternatives, not because of downright stubbornness, but because he lacks facility in balancing alternatives and of thinking of one to the exclusion of another. Instead of following one line, he follows two (and one of them seems obstinate to the observer). The nerve cell organization that presides over inhibition is poorly developed. This shows itself even in such "neurological" actions as grasping and releasing. He does not have his flexor and extensor muscles in check and countercheck. He tends to grasp too strongly and he releases with overextension. He has not learned to let go. He has difficulty in relaxing readily to go to sleep. And when he sleeps he may even show a tendency to sleep too much. Similarly he may not easily release the sphincters of bladder control and withholds elimination too long—another instance of going to extremes that can scarcely be set down to innate willfulness.

The peculiar limitations of his action system, therefore, account for his characteristic inability to *modulate* his behavior. He has such difficulty in making transitions that he tends to dawdle as though it were hard for him to go from the familiar to something different. He is so conservative that he combats innovations. He wants to have things done the accustomed way. He is a ritualist, particularly at home, and insists on having things *just so*. On these occasions he may be so insistent that he seems positively imperious. His "imperiousness" seems tyrannical, but it is simply an unmodulated intensity—the same kind of uninhibited propulsive release that he shows when handling objects. Even so, it is best to take this fictitious domineering with a grain of humor and let him be king within manageable bounds. By using a few of the techniques outlined below, you can *activate* him in the "right" direction. He cannot be forced; the activation must finally come from within himself. To handle him you must be something of a juggler. This means that he himself is something of an equilibrist entertaining opposite alternatives—trying to keep two balls in the air when he should be tossing only one. But he does this on account of his inexperience. Also he does it because it is the developmental method by which he learns opposites. Such behavior is the psychological equivalent of growing pains. It is helpful to think of him as a preschool edition of a slightly confused adolescent who has not yet found his way.

Nevertheless, in this very process the two-and-a-half-year-old is finding his way. His adhesiveness, his vacillation, his oscillations between extremes are temporary. By the age of three he will amaze us with his conformance, his desire to please, his interest in making not two choices but one. At present he is learning to make *one* by exercising *two*. And we can afford to be philosophical because he is giving us a glimpse of nature's favorite method of growth—the method of reciprocal interweaving by means of which she brings flexors and extensors, yes and no, come and go, grasp and release, push and pull into balanced equilibrium.

These characteristic traits are not, of course, equally marked in all children. They are particularly pronounced in those of a perseverative type. High tension and sudden fatigability sometimes evidence themselves in a kind of stuttering, which is later outgrown. Equable temperaments are least likely to show conspicuous symptoms; but it is relatively normal, from a developmental standpoint, for children at this age to show to some degree the extremes that have been suggested—the sudden shift from intense activity to passive quiescence accompanied by transient thumb-sucking; shifts from exuberance to shyness; from keen desire to possess an object to indifference when it is possessed; from clamor for food to rejection of it; from shriek and scream to whispering and monotone; from herdlike imitativeness to shrinking isolation; from laughing to whining; from precipitateness to dawdling.

These swings from one extreme to another are not so much mood swings as fluctuations caused by narrowness of base. The base will broaden as the child matures, as he makes an increasing number of distinctions between paired opposites and paired alternatives. Experience will organize the choices he will make with ease at three, four, and five years of age. He needs developmental time; he deserves discerning patience.

Moreover, is he not at least interesting, as he so transparently betrays his intellectual limitations? And is he not attractive with all his promising mixtures of exuberance and shyness, his overtures to adults, his friendly questions, his imaginativeness, his conquest of difficult words, his socialized imitativeness, his tribal chants, and his generosity? For he *is* generous when he eagerly shows his toys to a friend, and then cannot let him play with them. How can you possibly prize a toy without showing it to others? And how can you share it without keeping it? Life and culture are full of paradoxes for all of us. Two and a half years is the paradoxical age.

Behavior Day

The two-and-a-half-year-old child may wake up at almost any time between five and nine o'clock in the morning. He tends to waken toward the later hour, say between eight and eight-thirty. He calls for his mother fairly promptly after waking and is immediately toileted.

He enjoys the leisure of bathrobe and slippers while he takes a light breakfast. After breakfast he is dressed. Dressing is facilitated by the confinement of the bathroom. He ordinarily has to be helped during the whole process.

He is now ready for an hour's play in his room, which is set up and prearranged to meet the needs of his abundant self-activity. He talks to himself a great deal during a happy, active hour. The sound of heightened gross motor activity, during which he may turn over the chair in his playroom, calls attention to the termination of this hour of play. His mother comes and toilets him. He likes to linger in the bathroom, but he is also ready for a session of outdoor play.

The luncheon at noon is usually his largest meal. He likes to feed himself for at least half of the meal, during which he selects the foods that he most prefers. He may assert his self-dependence by asking his mother to leave the room, but he calls her back and accepts her help for the last meal of the day, reverting to self-feeding for dessert. He is toileted, and often has a bowel movement at this time.

The scheduled nap may begin at about twelve-thirty, but usually he consumes an hour or more in self-activity before going to sleep. He likes to have the side of the bed down and he may get in and out two or three times. He talks a great deal to himself during this prenap period. He may finally fall off to sleep after he has been tucked in by his mother. He sleeps for an hour or more, and wakens slowly, usually dry. He does not call for his mother until he has gone through a transitional period of progressive wakefulness.

By three o'clock he is ready for a walk or a visit abroad, though if he attended nursery school in the morning he may play from three to five o'clock in his own backyard. On his return from his walk he may have a snatch of play in the living room.

Supper comes at about five o'clock. He accepts more help during this meal than he did at luncheon. He may then enjoy a round of play with his father. It may be active play; it may be more receptive—listening to music or looking at a book.

The bath, which comes at about seven o'clock, is still a favorite experience. The two-and-a-half-year-old likes to handle situations in a somewhat commanding manner. He insists on certain routines, likes to have things done in an accustomed way, and likes to find things in accustomed places. By these demands he asserts his increasing insight into what he thinks is being demanded of him. He insists on comparable routines when he is put to bed. These are definitely "ritualistic" and may, therefore, be time-consuming. He continues his soliloquies and also talks to his teddy bear. He may call to his mother to render some specific help. He falls asleep at about eight-thirty. He may be picked up between ten and twelve o'clock and toileted without being awakened. He sleeps the clock around.

SLEEP

NIGHT

Bedtime depends very definitely on the length of the nap, which can vary from no sleep to a three-, four-, or even five-hour nap. It is not uncommon for the hour of going to sleep to vary from 6 P.M. to 10 P.M. Bedtime, therefore, has to be shifted according to the child's needs, but should preferably not be delayed beyond 8 P.M.

Going to bed is also complicated by a new intrusion, for the two-year-old's bedtime demands have often grown into an elaborated and rigid structure that may now take as long as one-half to one hour to enact. There is the going-upstairs ritual, the taking-a-bath ritual, the brushing-the-teeth ritual, getting into bed, pulling down the shades, kissing, and even a specially worded good-night ritual. If the plug is pulled out of the bathtub the wrong way, the entire going-to-bed routine may be disturbed and a temper tantrum may occur. Even the shades have to be pulled down to just the proper height.

The thirty-monther makes most of his demands before getting into bed. When he is once in bed and has said good night, he calls his parent back less often than at two years, and usually his demands express real needs. When he finally settles down he often sings and talks to himself. He enjoys snuggling under the covers. Those who fall asleep early are more apt to awaken during the night. They may or may not cry, and often ask for the toilet or a drink. The 10 to 12 P.M. picking up for toileting is more often successful at this age than formerly, but when it is unsuccessful, the disturbance it causes is very real.

Morning waking is as variable and has as wide a range as going to sleep. With some children, the later they go to sleep, the earlier they will awaken. Therefore, going to sleep at 10 P.M. may cause a 5 A.M. waking. However, the majority are "sleep-the-clock-around children" who do not awaken before 8:30 or 9:00 A.M. If they awaken early they will often play with their toys and look at magazines before they call the adult. Sometimes shifts of toys will help the early waker to stay in his crib, but after an hour or so he demands to get up. There is no problem with the late waker, for he is taken right up for his breakfast.

[The child will leave presleep activities more easily if he can have an active share in putting away play materials. The mother should not leave in the middle of presleep preparations to attend to some other household demand. Such preparations, once started, must be carried through to completion, or they will have to be started all over again. If the mother tries to complete them, after an interruption, without starting again, the child may have a temper tantrum.]

NAP

The nap is often a real problem at two and a half. Children of this age do not usually mind going to bed for their nap and enjoy taking a number of toys to bed, but they do not stay in their crib for long. They can now climb out with ease and keep coming out of their room, unless the door is tied. The thirty-monther does not usually mind his door being tied as long as he can freely get in and out of his crib and has his toys in the room to play with. *The windows must be very safe,* for he is apt to climb on the window ledge.

Many children refuse to nap in their crib at this age. They may nap better in another room on another bed, but the novelty of this may wear off soon and then they are much worse than they were in their own room. If some variation (under their own control) can be made in their own room, they will respond more quickly, more continuously, and with less interference with the rest of the household. They especially like to sleep on the floor, under their crib, or in a bureau drawer. If they cannot handle this themselves after preliminary arrangements and suggestions have been made by the parent when they are put into their room, they may respond to a little help from the adult around two or two-thirty, when they are more ready for sleep. Then the barricading of a blanket bed on the floor may be just the needed touch. Some will accept the bed if it is imaginatively turned into something else, such as a bus or a railroad train.

The parent must decide not only whether she should help put the child to sleep, but also if she should awaken him from his nap before he is ready to wake himself. A few children can have a long nap and still go to bed at the usual bedtime. With others, the displacement of the night sleep caused by a long nap makes evenings at home a bit troublesome for the parents. However, if the child cannot stand being waked at three to three-thirty and merely cries for the rest of the time when he would have been asleep, it is wise not to awaken him. Some will respond well to the ring of a telephone or to an alarm clock in an adjoining room when they will not accept being awakened by a person's voice. Trial and error is probably the only way these decisions can be made. And eventually the child will handle the whole problem for himself by not sleeping at all or by taking a shorter nap.

[If a child awakes crying from his nap, wait until the cry changes to a more agreeable note before going into his room. Engage in tasks such as pulling up the shade without approaching the child until he has made an approach, such as saying sweetly, "Hello, Mommy."]

EATING

Appetite—The appetite often fluctuates between very good and very poor. Usually one meal, either the noon or evening meal, is a good one.

Refusals and Preferences—These are quite similar to those of the two-year-old child, with the patterns of demand being held to more rigidly. In general, the child prefers meat, fruit, and butter, and dislikes green vegetables. He is now taking milk fairly well.

One may think of his preferences and refusals in a gradation of those foods he likes so well that he will eat them by himself, those that he likes well enough to be fed, and those that he absolutely refuses. As at two years of age, he still goes on food jags and a food that was once

in the first place of preference may be outrightly refused.

[It is best to allow swings in appetite. The parent may keep a chart if necessary to convince herself that good days balance poor days. Allowing the child to pour his milk from a pitcher may increase his appetite for milk.]

Self-Help—Patterns of self-help are also quite similar to those of two years. The parent can now readily set up a sequence of courses and can tell the child to "Call me when you are ready for your dessert" (for example). The child may feed himself half of his dinner and this will usually include foods that he likes. He will then be ready to be fed the remainder of his dinner if this does not include currently refused foods.

The ritualisms of the ritualist are at this age more clearly defined in eating as well as in going-to-sleep patterns. He demands the repetition of foods, of dishes, and of arrangement of dishes, and even of time when a certain food is given. If, for example, egg is given at suppertime it may be taken with relish then but refused at lunchtime.

This is the age when between-meal snacks are in greater demand; and often they interfere with appetite for regular meals. A few children eat very poorly at mealtimes but will eat well between meals.

[It is best to try to establish a set time for the between-meal snacks, such as 10:30 A.M. and 4:00 P.M., and to see if the child can be held off verbally until these times. Crackers and dried fruits along with fruit juices are probably preferable from the points of view both of ease of handling and of what is best for the child. Candy had best be out of sight and out of reach, even out of the house, or the demand may be very excessive at this age. Special infrequent occasions when candy is allowed establish it within the realm of treat and not within that of incessant demand.]

ELIMINATION

Bowel—The number of movements varies from one to two a day, with an increased tendency to skip one or even two days between bowel functioning. Accidents are rare. The general tendency is for the child to ask to go even though he needs no help. Some still tell after they have gone by themselves. They prefer a potty chair to the toilet seat. They still need help with taking off their pants. Those who have been slow to name the bowel movement often name it now with some such action word as "plop" or "bang poo-pee."

Very few now resist the toilet seat though some seem to persist in the postural need of functioning either standing up or lying down. If the child who still refuses the toilet seat or any type of receptacle shows a localizing tendency of going to a corner of a room or behind

doors, he is often ready to be shifted to the bathroom, where he may utilize a paper in the corner. Once he has begun to function in the bathroom, he more rapidly adjusts to a potty chair or the toilet seat, but should not be expected to adjust to the flushing of the toilet.

Even if the mother helps to put him on the toilet, he does not usually wish her to stay in the room and requests, as at two years of age, but now a little more personally, "You go away" or "Mommy go downstairs?" He now can leave on his shoes and socks and shirt, but wants his pants or overalls all the way off.

As was also true at two years of age, he will call out, "Mommy, all through," and wait to be wiped and put back into his clothes.

The time of occurrence has a wide variation, some still having a meal relationship and others being more irregular, with a definite trend to having the movement in the afternoon, especially in relation to the nap. The child usually asks to go at these times. Stool-smearing is relatively rare at this age.

[Though it is common for children to skip one or two days at this age between bowel functionings, the parents should check on this, and if the interval is longer than this, fruit laxatives may be given. It may help the child to have the adult remain in the room, or to look at a book.]

Bladder—There are very few daytime accidents. Most children go by themselves, according to the ease of removing their clothing and facilities available for climbing up on the toilet. Some, however, always tell beforehand, even though they need no help. They do need verbal help, however, such as being given permission to go. This is an age for long spans, especially with girls, who often have a morning span of as much as five hours (from rising till after lunch).

When they hold off too long they may start to dampen their pants before reaching the bathroom. They are very conscious of wet pants even though the wetness is only a drop, and want to be changed at once. (With boys this type of long span and holding off is more common from three to three and a half years of age.) Many find it difficult to urinate on a strange toilet.

[If the child has difficulty in urinating after a long span, he may respond to such helpful stimuli as the sound of running water, or taking a drink. It may help to tell him to close his eyes and listen for the sound that the stream of urine will make.]

Those who do not tell can be readily routinized. This function is now coming so much under the child's own control that he is beginning to be conscious of the control of others. He is interested in watching other people go to the bathroom and also is very much interested in watching animals out of doors. However, he usually reserves his comments until three years of age. Boys often urinate out of doors if they are allowed to.

It is difficult to generalize about nap dryness because individual differences are so marked. Some who have previously been dry, especially boys, are now wet again. Girls are more consistently dry. The length of the nap may have something to do with the relapse since the nap is now sometimes two or even three or four hours long. Therefore they may be dry if awakened from the nap, wet if allowed to sleep it out. The consciousness of being wet is probably most dependent on cultural handling, and with adult stimulation of shame, a contrary response of pride in a "methy bed" may be elicited.

Dryness at night is dependent upon a number of factors. The few children who remain dry may sleep through the night without waking or may call two or three times during the night to be taken to the bathroom. The majority, however, need to be picked up and even then may still be wet in the morning. If they are wet by 8 or 9 P.M., the chances are that they will wet two or three times more during the night. If they are dry at ten, the chances are fifty-fifty that they will be wet in the morning. If they are still dry at twelve, they will usually be dry in the morning. Picking up is, however, not a simple matter, for many children resist it. With any sign of resistance the practice should be discontinued until later acceptance. Picking up is more palliative at this age than instructive. Rubber pants and diapers are still in order to make the child more comfortable physically and emotionally, to restrict the laundry, and to eliminate the urinous smell that can be so distasteful in a child's room.

BATH AND DRESSING

Bath—The bath, which is now given around 7 P.M., is quite a favorite at this age. As with most of his activities at thirty months, the child "takes over" even though he is not capable. He wants to handle the faucets and the plug and to build up a ritual around them. He also likes to shine the fixtures and has often lost all sense of the bath as being a time when he is washed. He loves to slide back and forth in the water and would go on endlessly if not stopped.

Getting the child out of the tub is quite dependent upon the ingenuity of the parent. The removal of the plug with the subsequent running down of the water makes some children fearful that they will be sucked down, too. Therefore they hop out at once. But there are many who are not in the least fearful and who continue to slide back and forth even when the water is all out. Then tricks of getting out,

as counting or any other helpful transitional devices, need to be used.

Dressing—The thirty-monther is still better at undressing than at dressing. He can usually take off all his clothes but his dressing abilities are limited to putting on his socks and sometimes his shirt, pants, or coat. His dressing is not, however, very effective and usually needs correction. The heel of his sock may be on his instep, both feet in one pant leg, his shirt on backward, and his coat twisted. If he insists upon dressing by himself, he will usually accept helpful preliminary orientation of the garment— e.g., the shirt on the floor with the back uppermost. He will also accept some verbal help but will not allow his mother to touch him.

This demand for independence alternates with a demand for complete dependence, when he will not do the things he can do for himself, and even withdraws from the most rudimentary help with dressing, such as thrusting his arm into an armhole. At this time he may go limp and say he is a doll or a baby. If the parent is not fully aware of the swings of the thirty-month pendulum, or will not accept them, she will undoubtedly get into trouble.

This is the age when temper tantrums over dressing are common. Besides his demands to dress himself or be dressed, the child often runs away as soon as his mother starts to dress him. He particularly enjoys being chased and as soon as he is caught he runs off into another room or corner. He becomes violent if he is really caught and picked up, but usually comes running if he is left by himself with the suggestion, "Come to the bathroom when you are ready." If the mother closes doors behind her, this will almost immediately martial the child's forces to right-about-face and he runs in the direction the mother desires. He comes calling, "I'm ready, I'm ready." When he is once in the bathroom it is wise to close the door and even to lock it. A high hamper is a good place on which to dress a child of this age. He fools less because he does not want to fall off, and he wants to have dressing over with so as to get down as soon as possible.

[The game of discovering parts of the body, such as the head, hand, or foot, as they emerge from clothing is a delightful game at this age.]

SELF-ACTIVITY

The thirty-monther's morning play period at home takes on a new character of relaxation and of rediscovery. He is happy to go to his room after breakfast, but with his proficient ability to right-about-face, he will just as rapidly reverse his direction if his room is not sufficiently attractive and enticing. Therefore it is very essential to set up his room as though it were a stage, with the planned beginnings of spheres of interest—a doll corner here, fitting toys over there, a magazine on the bed, perhaps a tray of Play-Doh on the table.

The child is usually happy to linger in the bathroom washing his hands and making soap bubbles while the mother is accomplishing this bit of stagecraft. As a last touch she might hide something under a box for him to discover. His interest is quickly secured; he leaves his washing, and is whisked into his room. While the door is being shut, and tied if necessary, he is discovering his "surprise," and then happily sets about his morning activities.

His play is accompanied by constant talking. All of his past experiences are flooding in in bits of this and that. There is something enchanting about a verbatim record of the speech of a thirty-month-old child talking to himself in his room as he plays. Speech is now coming in with a rush and it is so uppermost in his mind that he uses it constantly. Words and activities that he has been hearing and observing at home and away from home are now put into practice in the simple security of his own room. Seeing his doll reminds him to put it on his lap the way grandmother does, or to tuck it in bed the way he saw some other child do it.

His play and equipment are similar to those of the two-year-old child. There may be the addition of a doll bed, an iron and ironing board in the doll corner, a few extra cars on the shelves, a simple puzzle, and sometimes Play-Doh. Scissors and crayons are not yet sufficiently under his control for him to handle alone in his room, though they are definitely in his realm of interest. Even Play-Doh may at times be too difficult for him to control, and he is then likely to spread it all over the room.

Some children want all their toys within sight or reach and have a strong sense of ownership and place for them. They are very orderly with their toys and stand guard as the room is being cleaned so that nothing will be disturbed. The majority of children, however, have only a momentary relationship with their toys. They actually do better with a shifting scene. Therefore the mother in her preliminary arrangement decides what is best for the child at the moment. He may even help her decide by asking for certain things. It is impractical to have either too many things in a child's room or too few. Some desire play with only one or two fitting toys whereas others demand variety.

When the thirty-monther has finished with a toy he drops it, often behind him. He may, however, return to it later. With fatigue, usually at the end of an hour, he shifts to more gross motor activity, jumps off a box, runs into a closet and closes the door, and finally may end by turning over all the chairs. He may occasionally return to wallpaper or plaster destruction. If he does he has improved his technique and is now using some object as a tool to increase his efficiency.

With the sounds of gross motor activity, the mother knows it is nearing time for shifting to out of doors. Nothing delights the thirty-monther more than to have his mother knock on his door at this moment and to invite her to "Come in." If she knows the ways of development she will not say, "My, what a mess your room is in"; but will rather say, "My, what a wonderful time you've had."

She will also know that this is no time for him to help in reordering the room. Toileting and out of doors, where space and bodily movements are freer, should follow immediately. His two-year-old outdoor play equipment is still of interest to him. He can also handle hollow boxes, which he loves to lift, carry, and jump from, and he enjoys paper cartons that he can climb into. A pail of water that he can dip into and pour on his sand delights the thirty-monther. He plays happily until it is time for lunch and then often does not want to leave his play. It is then up to the mother to lure him into the house without his realizing that he is being lured.

[Successful lures include the mother's mentioning some preferred food, giving the child something "important" such as a loaf of bread to carry into the house, or playing the game of "find Mommy" when he knows from previous experience what door she is hiding behind.]

SOCIALITY

The ritualism so characteristic of thirty months may weigh heavily on the entire household. The child of this age is likely to know where everything belongs and to insist that everything remain in its place. This is no time to rearrange the living-room furniture. Chairs must be placed at specific angles and certain pictures must remain on certain tables.

This is the age when father learns to hang up his coat, for his thirty-month-old child may not tolerate his throwing it down on a hall chair. The child is, however, much more efficient about handling other people's affairs than his own, which are often in a very chaotic state. He also may remember exactly how all household routines have been conducted and may insist always on an exact repetition. Father must put on his bedroom slippers whether he wants to or not. Milk cartons must be brought in only by the child. If he gets up late and finds the milk cartons in the refrigerator, the only thing to do may be to put them back out on the porch, close the door, and then go through the whole routine as though nothing had occurred.

His domineering ways are sometimes hard for others to accept. He may command one to sit here, another to do something else, and still another to go away. If the parent realizes that the child is only passing through a temporary regal, dictatorial stage, he may respond to the child's orders more graciously, more whimsically. The child actually needs to be treated with a little subservience to take him off his guard. A little humor added to the subservience may produce the desired effect.

Despite his imperiousness, the child may actually be a very useful member of society. He may be of considerable help in putting things away and in carrying out simple household tasks such as emptying the ashtrays.

He is usually more independent on his walks and is apt either to run ahead or to linger behind. He makes definite requests as to what he wants to do, and carries out going to a destination with real dispatch. However, on the homeward journey he is apt to lapse into dawdling or going up other people's steps. Therefore it is wise to have some means of conveyance, such as a wagon, a doll carriage in which the child can ride, or a stroller, to help him home again. Best either to stay close to home or to encompass distances in a car. The afternoon social play period in the house still includes music, dancing, and books. But the child also likes to color with crayons, to snip with scissors, and to do puzzles with help.

Most children at this age exhibit a definite preference for either father or mother, though the preference varies from child to child. Sometimes the child prefers one parent for one time of the day and for certain activities and the other parent at some other time of day. He is usually less dependent than he was at twenty-four months. His affection has not the overflowing warmth of the two-year-old's, but is often expressed in a rigid pattern of something to be gone through, such as a kissing ritual. As with the two-year-old, he is more apt to demand his mother when he is in trouble and during the middle of the night. However, he may quiet more quickly for his father, if he will accept the father.

The shyness and withdrawal of Two have now gone into reverse. However, the thirty-monther includes poles of shyness and withdrawal on the one hand and approach and aggression on the other hand. He responds according to the demands of the situation. He may demand his mother's hand when he meets a stranger on the street or he may suddenly "sock" a stranger with few or no premonitory signs.

He wants very much to be with people, both adults and children, but he cannot handle them. This is the snatch and grab age, especially when he is with younger children. However, the same child may swing from a period in which he is habitually too compliant to one in which he is too domineering. On the whole, he plays best with one child out of doors, and he does much better with a five- or six-year-old child whom he respects and also accepts. Play with children his own age is often best handled under supervision, away from home, and preferably with no more than two or three children in a group.

Some children play best at their own home with other children, others play better away from home. Those who play best at home are usually the ones who adjust poorly to new places. But they are also the ones who have difficulty in letting other children play with their toys. Therefore it is best to plan with them to put away their most prized possessions before another child comes to call. Then it is easier for them to share their less prized toys.

Those who play better away from home are more often the quick adjusters, the quick shifters. They want novelty and find it easy to adjust to the child who clings to the old. To lead these two types into a fuller realization of themselves, the environment helps the stay-at-home child finally to release his home and his things by going abroad, whereas it helps the going-abroad child to hold on a little tighter to the things at home by adjusting him to play with other children at home. This process of adjustment to others becomes more urgent at this thirty-month period.

CHAPTER 17

THREE YEARS OLD

Behavior Profile

Three is a coming of age. The strands of previous development converge and come to a focus. The conflicting extremes of a half year ago give way to a high degree of self-control. For one so young, the three-year-old has himself well in hand. Far from being contrary, he tries to please and to conform. He even asks, "Do it dis way?" as though he were sensitive to the demands of culture. He is susceptible to praise and he likes friendly humor. He is remarkably attentive to spoken words, and often displays a quaint seriousness. If a group of parents should again cast a secret ballot, to decide on the most delightful age of the preschool period, the honors would perhaps go to the three-year-old.

The greater self-control of Three has a motor basis. He is more sure and nimble on his feet; he walks erect, and he can turn sharp corners without going through the studied maneuvers of earlier months. His whole motor set is more evenly balanced, more fluid; he no longer walks with arms outstretched, but swings them somewhat like an adult. He likes to hurry up and down stairs, but he also enjoys sedentary pastimes that engage fine motor coordination. It is significant that he can delimit and orient his crayon strokes sufficiently to imitate the drawing of a cross. He has an eye for form, which suggests that the small muscles that operate his eyes are more facile than they were. He also has gained considerable inhibitory control of his sphincters; and he can almost toilet himself during the day. Not to overlook another domestic detail, he can unbutton buttons without popping them!

There is something "threeish" about the scope of his attention and insight. He can repeat three digits, he is beginning to count to three; he enumerates three objects in a picture; he is familiar with the three basic forms, circle, square, and triangle; he can combine three blocks to build a bridge. Many of his sentences and questions consist of three units. He likes to compare two objects, and this requires a three-step logic.

He listens to words with increased assurance and insight. He even likes to make acquaintance with new words, apparently intrigued by their phonetic novelty. He has learned to listen to adults and he listens to learn from them. He uses words with more confidence and with intelligent inflection, although he may not overcome infantile articulations until the age of four or five. For practice he soliloquizes and dramatizes, combining actions and words. He creates dramatic situations to test out and to apply his words. In this way he extends the range and depth of his command of language. These action-thought patterns, like his postural patterns, will come into evidence in his nursery school behavior.

The group life of the nursery school, for which he is now so ready, will also reveal the advances he is making in his management of personal-social relationships. These relationships are the most difficult and complicated that the growing child has to encounter. Nature has endowed the three-year-old with an interest in persons. He watches their facial expressions for the purpose of finding out what these expressions indicate. He is not reading from a book, but he is reading the expectations of his elders. He is making an important distinction between a physical obstacle and a personal one. Sometimes, however, he still strikes out at either, in spite of the fact that he generally desires to please. He is capable of sympathy. The infantile indifference has gone with other ineptitudes. Emotion as well as intelligence grows.

His sense of time is meager but well defined within his limitations. He distinguishes between night and day. He can say and understand "When it's time." Accordingly he can be put off a bit by the culture, and he can hold himself in anticipation. In other words, you can bargain with him, and he can wait his turn.

This constitutes a remarkable psychological advance and betokens well for the future—if the culture is able to organize his growing capacities for mutual aid behavior. These capacities and his limitations are revealed in the ordered freedom of a well-conducted nursery group. But it should be remembered that his cooperativeness is only in a nascent stage. He is still a preschool child. His collaborations in the nursery will be desultory, sketchy. He must also develop independence through solitary play. Too much must not be expected of him.

Behavior Day

The waking hour is still variable, although the margin of variation is not quite as large as formerly. The three-year-old child may wake at, say, seven o'clock. He may wake dry. Often he whines a little during this first waking and calls to his mother, who promptly toilets him. If he still seems tired, as often happens, he goes back to bed, perhaps to doze off for a supplementary nap. Such an awakening is a thawing-out process. By seven-thirty he may be ready to come into the parents' room, and now, being thawed out, he likes to romp rather actively on the floor or bed.

He dresses while his parents are dressing, needing only a little help along the way.

He breakfasts either by himself at his own low table or with the family, around eight o'clock, and manages the meal almost entirely alone. He may even toilet himself. He is growing more self-reliant and he likes to help others when he can. Accordingly he may lend a hand in clearing the breakfast table—he can carry the silverware.

Three shows a readiness for group activity in some form on two or three mornings a week. He eagerly gets ready for this expanding excursion. If he stays at home he is ready for a session of independent play at about nine o'clock. This play is somewhat less harum-scarum than it was a half year ago. When his mother comes for him he may help her put his toys away. He goes to the toilet on slight suggestion.

By eleven o'clock the day's program may permit him to accompany his mother to market, which he can now manage. It is a welcome experience. He also likes to go out of doors for a tricycle trip or for a round of play on a domestic backyard gym.

At the end of the play period, he goes to the toilet on a casual hint and washes his hands, after a fashion, by himself. Noon luncheon, as at two and a half years, may be his best meal. He manages most of it alone. He likes to have his mother near. She intercedes with occasional help but does not have to complete the meal for him to the same degree as formerly. Luncheon is still best served in courses.

At his next toileting he may have a bowel movement.

The routines of the day do not have to be rushed. The child makes comfortable transitions and adaptations. He feels his own increasing independence and may demand that his afternoon nap at one o'clock be merely a "play nap." This is a relaxation and rest period. He gets in and out of bed a few times and may or may not finally fall asleep. If he should not fall asleep, he presents himself to his mother as if to say, "Time is up." If it is not up, he returns to his play-napping, usually without protest.

He goes to the toilet again on suggestion around three o'clock. He needs very little help in this toileting. He likes to go on an excursion to a friend's house in the afternoon. He plays best out of doors.

On returning home, he is not likely to make any excessive demands. He likes to help in the preparation of the evening meal and even initiates suggestions as to the things he would like to have for his supper, which occurs at about five-thirty. He needs, perhaps, a little more completion help from his mother at this evening meal.

He plays contentedly until about six-thirty, often preferring dramatic or puzzle playing. He enjoys a half hour of play with his father. He is fond of quiet social play, listening to records and to stories.

The bath may still come at about seven o'clock. Again he is interested in helping with the arrangements but his "ritualisms" are much less rigid. They are developing into more adaptive cooperation. Time-consuming demands are abating and he is in bed by about seven-thirty, and may fall asleep within a half hour. He does not need much external assistance in achieving release into sleep, but his mother may tell him a simple bedtime story about what he did when he was a little baby.

He may not need to be picked up during the night for toileting. He sleeps the round of the clock.

SLEEP

NIGHT

There are many tag ends of thirty-month behavior that linger on into thirty-six months. The maturity of the three-year-old during the daylight hours seems slowly to leave him as night approaches and he again becomes, at least in part, what he was before. He is, however, giving up much of his ritualism and if he does continue it, it can be handled by such devices as the mother closing her eyes and saying she won't look until the child is under the covers. At two and a half the mother had to remove her whole person and shut the door. Now she has only to remove her seeing self by closing her eyes. As at two and a half, the child will often go to sleep faster for another person than for his mother.

The three-year-old does not usually mind being picked up for toileting at 10 to 12 P.M., though the majority of three-year-olds do not need to be picked up. Wakefulness is, however, common at three years and this is often the time when a night life begins. One type of child gets out of his crib easily by himself, goes to the bathroom, goes downstairs, gets some food from the refrigerator, "reads" a magazine after turning on the light in the living room, and may be found asleep on the couch next morning. Another type of child talks to himself for an hour or two in bed; and still a third type insists upon getting into his parents' bed. This is the age when dreams begin to be reported. Though they may wake the child, he is rarely able to tell them.

Morning waking is more difficult than going to sleep. As with two and a half, the time of waking varies between 6 and 8 A.M. The child is often tired on awakening, sucks his thumb, whines, and in general has a difficult time in starting the day. He is more apt to call to be taken up than to get up by himself. If he is allowed to come into his parents' bed (when it is time) to romp and play, he starts his day more gaily and more easily.

[Some children wake early in the evening while their parents are out, and cry until they vomit or until the parents return. Some may be able to accept being told ahead of time that their parents are going out. It may be sufficient for the child to be told just as his parents are leaving the house, or he may need to be warned even a day or two in advance. If such warnings are not adequate and the child continues to cry, the parent may have to stay at home evenings until the child can adjust at a later age.

If the child gets up and wanders around the house during the night without calling anyone, tying his door loosely may necessitate his calling. Many need to be toileted and be given food.

If the child insists upon getting into bed with his mother, it may be wise to accede to his demand, but to warn him ahead of time that after he has fallen asleep he will be put back in his crib. If he wakes and cries when returned to his crib, the mother may have to allow him to sleep with her. This type of demand is often self-limited to a week's duration. If, however, it continues, the child may respond better to having his father take the mother's role in the situation.]

NAP

This is the onset of the "play nap." Even the naming of this time when the child is resting in his room a "play nap" often seems to make it more acceptable. There may be a period of two to three months from thirty to thirty-six months of age when the child does not sleep. He often returns to a real nap at thirty-six months but this is not constant. If the child of this age does go to sleep, he usually falls asleep more quickly than at thirty months. The length of the nap is cut down to one or two hours and waking, though slow, does not involve the conflict that it often does at thirty months.

EATING

Appetite—The fluctuations of thirty months are now settling down to a fair appetite. Breakfast and supper are more frequently the best meals, though there are many variations. The milk intake is definitely on the rise.

Refusals and Preferences—These are less marked than they were at twenty-four to thirty months. Meat, fruit, and milk are now on the preferred list. Desserts and sweets are more desired, but cannot yet be used as a goal toward which to work (as they will at forty-eight months). Vegetables are now slowly being accepted. The child often wants foods that require more chewing, such as raw vegetables, potato skins, or meat on a bone.

Spoon-Feeding—The spoon is now grasped more between thumb and index. Some girls hold it adult fashion with the palm turned inward. Boys, however, are more likely to direct the palm downward. The filling of the spoon is easily accomplished both by pushing the point of the spoon into the food and by rotating it inwardly. The bowl of the spoon may be inserted sidewise or by its point. There is good rotation at the wrist and little if any spilling results. A fork is often demanded, especially to pierce pieces of meat.

Cup-Drinking—The cup is now held by the handle in adult fashion. The free hand is no longer needed to help. The head again tilts back to secure the last drop. This function will later be taken over by the hands alone.

Self-Help—Although the three-year-old child is eating well alone, he may not eat well at the family table. The situation may be too complex. He is apt to demand everyone's attention and wants to have everything in sight. Because of his dawdling he is either coaxed, fed, or left at the table to finish alone after the rest of the family has left, so perhaps it is better to feed him ahead of time.

He is now beginning to ask for special foods he likes during the preparation of his meals.

ELIMINATION

Bowel—The number of movements varies from one to two a day with only an occasional day skipped. If there is only one movement, it most frequently occurs after lunch; if there are two, the other more frequently occurs after breakfast. Very few have a bowel movement associated with their nap at this age. Many go to the toilet by themselves with or without telling, but still want help when they have finished.

Bladder—Most children go at routine times, with a fairly long span and no accidents during the day. If an occasional accident does occur, they insist upon having their pants changed at once. The most common asking is expressed in general terms such as, "I'm going to the bathroom."

The majority of children are consistently dry after their naps and also in the morning without being taken up during the night. A number of children are still dependent upon being picked up at ten o'clock and a few wet once or twice a week, or are alternately dry or wet for a few weeks at a time.

BATH AND DRESSING

Bath—Many of the thirty-month bath patterns linger on, though bath rituals are less complicated and more subject to change. Children are now more insistent upon helping to wash themselves at least in part. Getting out of the tub is still resisted, but surprising the mother by getting out while she closes her eyes usually works.

Dressing—Dressing at this age is likely to go more smoothly than at thirty months, as the child is more interested in doing what he can to help and is therefore less likely to run away. Undressing is still carried out with greater interest and ability than dressing. Most children of this age undress well and rather rapidly. Undressing is further facilitated by a new ability to unbutton front and side buttons.

Dressing includes putting on pants, socks, and shoes and sometimes sweaters or dresses. However, they cannot consistently distinguish the back from the front or button buttons, and though they may try to lace their shoes, it is usually done incorrectly. Self-help in dressing is also dependent upon their mood, for they do well one day and poorly the next.

SELF-ACTIVITY

The planning for the child's activity is now much more relaxed. Techniques can now be used with less rigidity and often the handling of a three-year-old is so simple and natural that no conscious techniques are needed. As with the younger ages, the mornings when the child is not at nursery school are best handled by play alone either in the child's room or in a closed-in yard. He happily accepts these places arranged for his own use as long as he does not have to stay in them too long. But he usually plays so happily and well that it is now the mother who may interrupt the play to suggest that he move on to the next activity. The child makes his own self-demand here and need only be helped more specifically with warnings in advance when it is time for the routines of toileting and eating.

A whole new imaginative world is opening up for the three-year-old. He now may have the addition of a fire engine, larger building blocks, a new puzzle, and if he is capable of handling crayons alone without scribbling on the wall, he may have a coloring book and crayons. This is the age when sex differences in choice of play materials are becoming more marked than earlier.

It is interesting to see a three-year-old's room after he has had an hour's play alone. It has none of the chaos of the two-and-a-half-year-old child's room. There are remnants of his play activity, and he may have stories to tell about what he has done. He likes to linger on and even helps to put his toys away though he has no initiative for this and only does it from a sense of comradery with the adult, and only on suggestion.

After toileting and maybe a midmorning snack, he is happy to be out of doors. His tricycle, which may be his latest acquisition, is often his chief interest. He usually knows how to ride it, but if he does not he likes just to push it around. Another addition to his play yard may be a gym with ladders, a swing, and trapeze rings. He can play endlessly on these and may find it hard to leave when it is time for lunch.

SOCIALITY

The three-year-old has fewer definite ideas about how the household should be run than does the thirty-month-old child. He is now more ready to accept suggestions, and may be of considerable help to his mother in wiping dishes, putting things away, and in running simple errands. He is an easier child about the house now that he no longer meddles excessively with things he should not touch.

He enjoys his afternoon excursions out of doors and often prefers to go on his tricycle. If a destination has been planned, he holds a definite idea of it in his mind, but he makes few spontaneous demands to visit his friends.

He is happy when the planned excursion is to another child's home. He actually prefers the afternoon companionship of other children, but cannot quite make his wants known unless it is usual for him to see a certain child quite often. Two

three-year-olds play best out of doors with gross motor equipment and may play alone well for twenty to thirty minutes. After this, they usually need supervision and guidance. If the three-year-old is not supervised, he is apt to withdraw from his companion or to attack him with biting, scratching, pushing, or kicking.

If he has difficulty in adjusting to children his own age even with supervision, it is best to handle him alone and to plan short excursions to see things and places, or to arrange his play with a five- or six-year-old who will demand a reasonable amount of fair play from the three-year-old but will give in to his immature wishes when he cannot be handled otherwise.

As discussed under thirty-month behavior, there is one type of child who plays best at home and shares poorly, and another type who plays best away from home and shares generously. The former is the child who does best with an older child.

The mother is more commonly the favored parent. The child enjoys speaking of himself and his mother together as "we." He has just come through a new emotional awareness of himself. From thirty to thirty-six months he has progressed past the feeling of "I" and its needs, and "you" with its demands from the other person. "I" and "you" are their own counterparts, for he sometimes demands to do what he cannot do and asks help from the parent with things he can do.

With growth and reorganization he partially loses this sense of "I" and "you" and somehow sinks back into babyhood. Emotionally he relives his whole life, with help from his mother. With fatigue he asks to be carried and wants to be a baby. He actually may say, "I'm a little baby. I can't talk, I have no teeth, and I have no hair." If he takes himself literally he may actually pull out hair. But if he holds more closely to his present reality, as is more usual, he may say, "I'm a little baby. I have to have a bottle. I sleep out in the carriage, but I *can* talk."

The wise mother helps the child to relive his babyhood. She answers all his questions and tells him about himself. He wants to know about what he wore and how he cried, how he talked and laughed, where he slept, how he was fed. He even likes to hear about the fears he has conquered. He especially likes these stories after he is put to bed and may enjoy hearing them over and over.

But finally, toward three, he is a little older and has relived step by step much of his past life until he has reached his present age. Then he is ready to go forth from the parent, to look forward rather than backward, to think of himself in his relation to the future, whether the future is tomorrow, the next school day, or the next holiday. Some cling to this reliving of their past lives and especially their babyhood even into the fifth year.

[The child may be ready at this age to choose between two alternatives and may enjoy making simple choices. For example, when he is slow to come in for lunch he may be asked, "Do you want to come in the front door or the back door?" Or, if he is slow in dressing, he may be asked, "Do you want to wear your blue overalls or your green ones?"

Those who cannot make choices need to have planning ahead of time. "We're going to buy the chocolate cookies at the store." If this type of child is allowed his own choice, he will be sure to shift his choice halfway home and have a temper tantrum because he does not have his way.

Do not divide authority about any specific situation between the mother and the father. The child should know that his mother decides about clothes, candy, etc.; his father, about the repair of toys, excursions to the railroad station, etc. Particularly do not allow the child to play one parent against the other.]

CHAPTER 18

THREE AND A HALF YEARS OLD

Behavior Profile

Something unexpected and confusing seems to happen to the smooth, conforming three-year-old as he turns three and a half. Where did all this turbulence and trouble come from? Why is there such opposition, so much refusal to obey or even to try?

An understanding of the mechanics of the three-and-a-half-year-old, who first thrusts out too far and then pulls in too near, may help a bit. And a readiness to weather the storm with a calm but brisk and matter-of-fact manner will stand the parent in good stead, because this is a very difficult period. Mother especially may keep on an evener keel if she can feel a keen interest in all the variable manifestations of this admittedly confusing and strenuous time. She will need to develop a capacity to marshal her ingenuity to circumvent or surmount the many difficulties the child expresses and experiences.

Whatever the task, whatever the situation, three and a half seems to find his greatest pleasure in *refusing* and in insisting that things be done a *different* way—*his* way.

Three is a conforming age. Three and a half is just the opposite. Refusing to obey is perhaps the key aspect of this turbulent, troubled period in the young child's life. It sometimes seems to his mother that his main concern is to strengthen his will, and he strengthens this will by going against whatever is demanded of him by that still most important person in his life, his mother.

Many a mother discovers that even the simplest event or occasion can elicit total rebellion. Dressing, eating, toileting, getting up, going to bed—whatever the routine, it can be the scene and setting for an all-out, no-holds-barred fight. Techniques and tricks formerly useful can no longer be guaranteed to work. The mother's equally resistant response may be tempered by knowing that soon, when he is four, her child will have developed a self-concept strong enough so that he can sometimes conform and sometimes enjoy going out of bounds and saying and doing things that he full well knows will not be permitted.

At times the three-and-a-half-year-old cannot seem to do even as simple a thing as taking a walk with his mother, which he has previously so much enjoyed. Now he characteristically will stop along the way, and insist that he is going not one step farther. He may actually not like to go for walks at this age, may prefer to stay indoors. Therefore the best technique may be to make a marked change in his day, to stay at home and build up new interests inside, especially in the kitchen. The activity related to the making of easy things like applesauce and gingerbread cookies, with their accompanying attractive smells, to which he is increasingly sensitive, may relax his tension.

Though three and a half is very resistant to what is being demanded of him, he is very demanding of others. He is free with advice and admonition: "Don't sit there," "Don't smile at Daddy," "Don't read your paper," "Play with me." He must be ruler of all he commands and seems to feel safe only when in control.

But he also gets caught in his own trap. He may control with his "Don't look" and his "Don't laugh," but later he wants you to look and laugh and feels left out when he doesn't secure your full attention. He makes his parent walk a tightrope. This is done to the extent that some mothers, even those quite skilled at parenting, find their greatest success by turning the child of this age over to a baby-sitter. It can be rather frustrating to an experienced and normally effective mother to see a young baby-sitter doing better with her child than she can. But the fact seems to be that three and a half is amazingly sensitive to the reactions of others. He *knows* that the baby-sitter really doesn't *care* if he eats or goes hungry, gets his rest or fatigues. With exquisite sensitiveness he deals out the grief to the person who does care, his mother. No mother of a child this age should hesitate to place the burden of daily routines on the shoulders of a sitter, who, for the time being, may be the best person for the task.

A parent can best relate to her child when she realizes the real difficulties he is going through. Though he climbed with ease at three, he is now afraid of heights and wants to be taken down. His previously sure coordination is being superseded by stumbling and falling. He is constantly asking the adult to "hold my hand," especially on going upstairs. The way this can be broken into might be to race him upstairs. In the end it will be the characteristic speed of the four-year-old that will resolve this temporary incoordination.

Fine motor coordination may now show a tremor. At three the child could build a fairly steady tower of ten small cubes. Now he has trouble in placing these cubes. Arm and hand tremble and his tower often falls by the fifth cube. His misjudgment of spatial relationships is also shown with these same blocks as he builds a three-cube bridge. He built it easily a few months earlier. But now the base cubes are too far apart and he has to slowly bring them in by trial and error until the top cube can span the space between the two base cubes.

His high, whiny, tremulous voice bespeaks his discomfort. When he feels in control and is enjoying himself, as he does in nursery school, his voice can become loud and piercing. But in a new and demanding situation his voice may become no more than a whisper. Parents sometimes fear that their three-and-a-half-year-old is deaf, but find surprisingly that he hears better when whispered to. The child of this age is actually very much aware of sounds and may have many auditory fears, such as the banging of a radiator, the sound of a siren, and especially the clanging of a fire engine bell or the sound of thunder.

Stuttering may become a very worrisome expression of incoordination. The very verbal child who stuttered at two and a half may have a return of stuttering. The child who is slower in speech may stutter for the first time at this age. Often this stuttering is a passing phase and should be treated without emphasis.

Vision may pose special difficulties. Not only does the child of this age fear heights, but he often complains that he cannot see when he is being read to in a group. He wants to be right on top of the book and often holds his picture book close if he is looking at it by himself. He does best being read to alone, preferably sitting on the reader's lap so that he can adjust the book and see it at his preferred visual distance.

With all these growing difficulties, it is no wonder that three and a half often says he feels confused. Sometimes his inner confusion mounts and mounts until he finally goes all to pieces. A mother may try to prevent such a happening, but if it does occur she can clear the air and gather up all the pieces as she gathers him in her arms. It is then that he may be able to express his true feeling of genuine love for her.

Fortunately all is not resistance, confusion, and darkness at this age. This same strong-minded and insecure little creature who can and often does make life so miserable for his mother can if so minded and for brief periods be a real joy and delight. He can be imaginative, inventive, with a real capacity for play. He can be aware of the other person's feelings and can become very endearing as he expresses his own affections. His language capacity is now full and rich and he has many things to talk about. His increased interest in books and storytelling provides much happy time together with a parent. The important thing is to avoid the pitfalls of this complicated age as much as possible. Then life together can be extremely rewarding.

Behavior Day

We have always been disturbed and intrigued by the changes occurring at this age, but it was not until we analyzed the age of seven years in our succeeding book, *The Child from Five to Ten*, that we realized fully the importance of behavior seen at three and a half, behavior which pretty much repeats itself at the higher level of seven years.

In order to bring the freshness of real living to a behavior day at three and a half, we would again have to saturate ourselves with the lives of many children at this age level. Alas, we shall have to content ourselves with the preceding general summary and the following detail as to different aspects of living.

SLEEP

NIGHT

Bedtime may be easier than it was at three. The child is less ritualistic than earlier but still likes quite a bit of time and attention from his mother. As with other routines, he may do better with someone other than his mother.

Many children now sleep right through the night. But if they do not, it saves wear and tear on parents if a night light is arranged so that the child can turn it on by himself, and if food (raisins or some other not too messy food) and something to play with are provided. Most will stay in their own rooms willingly but if not, tying the door loosely may prevent their wandering around the house and getting into trouble.

The majority do not need to be picked up for night toileting, but if this is needed, most accept it without difficulty. Bedtime is around seven with many, and an average of eleven hours sleep is usual. This means that waking is early. If parents plan effectively, many children will now get up and entertain themselves till it is time for adults to get up. A "surprise" (laid out by the parents when they go to bed) can keep many three-and-a-half-year-olds quiet till adults arise. Food makes a good surprise.

There appears to be some dreaming and some wakefulness and crying caused by dreaming, but only a few tell their dreams.

NAP

A few may still sleep at nap time but for the majority the nap is only a "play nap." Most are not too enthusiastic about this routine. It is best for those who do not sleep to have reasonable play materials available. Otherwise they are apt to do considerable damage to any damageable things in their room. Even for those who do not sleep, the brief time-out that the play nap provides is restful for the child and essential for the mother if she does not have baby-sitting help. A whole day without a break with a child of this age can be extremely demanding.

EATING

Appetite—Appetite tends to be reasonably good in most. It is not so much lack of appetite that makes trouble at mealtime as it is the child's strong-minded three-and-a-half-year-old need to dictate and dominate any situation, including mealtime.

Refusals and Preferences—The child at this age tends to refuse any food that is offered, and to prefer whatever is not available. As in other routines, the need to boss the parent and to have one's own way dominates any special like or dislike for certain kinds of food.

Thus a child may refuse either of two kinds of sandwich offered, may accept a third if the adult moves quickly, but then wants the sandwich cut in two. If the adult cuts the sandwich diagonally, the child may say he wants it cut "the other way." If the adult complies, the child may then complain, "Now it's in four pieces and I only wanted two pieces."

A fairly brisk, matter-of-fact approach on the part of the adult usually works best. Stay friendly and try not to become fussed or to get too deeply embroiled. If there are special foods that a child likes or dislikes (aside from his basic need to object to *whatever* is offered),

time and trouble will be saved by attending to these preferences. But even the most skilled and effective mother may find that mealtimes are difficult. As one mother of a three-and-a-half-year-old remarked, "I dread getting up in the morning, knowing that I have to force three meals into that child before bedtime." As with other routines, someone other than the mother may meet with less resistance when it comes to mealtime.

ELIMINATION

Bowel—Perhaps the majority of children have settled down to once a day, at some more or less regular time. Many still need to tell both before and after functioning. Most have little difficulty with this behavior. But at this age and even at four, a few children (usually boys) are still having trouble. A child may refuse to use the toilet and still "go" in his pants.

Best results usually come from taking off the pants and letting the child play in the bathroom at about the time he may be expected to function. (If this time has not yet settled down, this technique is obviously not workable.) Put a paper on the floor, perhaps in a corner of the room, and tell the child that when he gets ready to function he may use the paper. Often within a few weeks he is able to move on to using the toilet or a potty chair.

Bladder—By now many can take care of this themselves and have few accidents. A few, especially if there is a new baby in the household and/or if they are going through a stage of reliving their babyhood, may again wet and need help with toileting.

A substantial number can by now get through the night without wetting, either with or without being taken up at the parents' bedtime. However, since many perfectly normal children cannot stay dry all night till they are five or older, night wetting should not be a subject for concern. Merely pad the child up tightly, put on rubber pants, and use a rubber sheet to save washing bedding.

BATH AND DRESSING

Bath—For most children, the bath still comes just before bedtime and usually causes little difficulty. In fact this can now be a pleasant time for both mother and child unless the tangles of the day's many battles have put both in a bad mood. In that case, a child can be extremely difficult and demanding, to the extent that the mother may decide that "just this once" won't matter and skip the bath entirely.

Dressing—At this age, unlike three and again at four, dressing can be extremely difficult and can produce excessive problems. A child may so resist anything going on and off over his head that his mother may be induced to select only garments that button in the back. These she may be able to get on and off with a minimum of resistance. Speed is essential here; otherwise the child, in the contrary way characteristic of three and a half, may fuss and object to each article of clothing involved. As with other routines, someone other than the mother may be most effective in getting clothes on and off. The child is still not very skilled, especially with outer garments.

TENSIONAL OUTLETS

This is an age above all others when the child feels great tension, and expresses it through many and intense tensional outlets. Not only stuttering, but eye-blinking, nail-biting, thumb-sucking, nose-picking, rubbing of genitals, chewing at garment or sheet, excessive salivation, spitting, tics, and other simple compulsive patterns occur. The frequent whining at this age may also be considered a tensional outlet.

Some children also complain that they cannot see, even though a book may be held directly in front of them. This complaint may represent a real difficulty in handling the intermediate visual zone, as three-and-a-half-year-olds, when holding their own books, commonly hold them very close to the eyes.

SELF AND SELF-ACTIVITY

At three, planning for the child's activity was relatively relaxed. Not so at three and a half. Not only daily routines, but even the child's play, may give difficulty, since demands are so rigid and ability to adapt so slight. Nursery school is a real boon to a mother at this time and it is to be hoped that the child may have the privilege of attending. If not, baby-sitting help is essential.

Though the strong demands that the child of this age makes of others might give the impression that he is a strong-minded, firm, secure person, in all likelihood the opposite is true. It seems likely that the child makes strong demands of others and attempts to rule the roost because he actually feels insecure and is not certain of his ability to rule.

Possibly the main developmental task of the child at this age is to strengthen his will, and he does this by practicing domination. When he is a little more sure of himself, as he will be later, he will be able to give in and to adapt more easily to others.

Actually, difficult though playtime may sometimes be, it is in the long stretches of play that come between routines that the child is at his best. We now see much creative use of any or all play materials. Interest in books and in being read to

is strong. Children of this age seem to love games and toys that involve many different little parts, and mothers have to cope with picking up these pieces from all over the house. Puzzles need to be reassembled to preserve their totality.

Among the most delightful aspects of three-and-a-half-year-old play is the child's play with imaginary companions. The imaginative life of the child rises slowly until it reaches a peak at three and a half years. The amount of this play varies from child to child but in many it is very strong.*

This age frequently marks the beginning, particularly in boys who have been slow to develop and who have run a somewhat atypical course up till now, of a developmental spurt in which behavior for the first time is well rounded and well organized and up to age expectations. This is fortunate since at this age failure is very difficult for the child, boy or girl. He is quick to protect himself with "No" or "I can't" if he thinks a situation may be too difficult. He tends to protect himself by isolation from too many failures. But his feelings are easily hurt, by failure or if people ignore him or don't do what he wants them to.

This is also an age of emotional extremes. Just as the child may

---

* See pages 332 and 345 in Part Four, The Nursery School, for a full description of imaginary companions.

want your full attention at one moment and may insist that you do *not* notice him at the next, similarly he may first be extremely shy and then as a situation progresses may become exuberant and boisterous. His own variability may be an added source of difficulty for the often quite difficult child of this age.

SOCIALITY

Social relations are hard at this age. Gone is the friendly acquiescent "Me, too" response of the three-year-old. And yet to come is the boisterous exhilaration of four. Three and a half is very sensitive about social relations and has very high and definite standards as to the way things should go. But all the give has to come from the other person. The child himself has very set notions and shows little ability to adapt to the wishes or ways of other people.

Thus he is very strong, especially with his mother, in his insistence on "Don't laugh," "Don't look," "Sit here," "Do it this way." And if anything at all goes wrong in his life, as it often does, he takes things out on his mother. Her role is not an easy one at this time.

Nor is it only mother who has a hard time with him. He may also be extremely commanding and demanding with other adults. They have to do things *his* way. In disputes with other children, which are frequent, he calls for help from the adult. And he still wants the approval of adults, even though he is so difficult with them.

Added complication comes from the fact that at certain times the child does not want the adult, parent or other, to even look at him, but at other times he wants full attention, with a constant request of "Watch me." He may even be jealous if his father reads the newspaper, or his mother talks to his father. In general it is fair to say that the adult often finds it extremely difficult to keep up with the definite and differing demands of three and a half.

Friends are extremely important to the child of this age, but he is new and often not very skillful at dealing with them. At three a child often seems to like and to get along well with others, but somewhat indiscriminately. At three and a half there is the beginning of friendships for certain special people and dislike of or exclusion of others. (That is, excluding is not necessarily an immature response but may be an indication of increased observation of differences and of increased selectivity.) Friendships may consist of merely sitting beside the chosen friend. Or they may include verbalization and delicate, tentative, wishing-to-please overtures such as "May I play with you?" or "Would you like to do this?" A few who have known each other for some time may have already developed very solid two-somes.

CHAPTER 19

FOUR YEARS OLD

Behavior Profile

Three has a conforming mind. Four has a lively mind. Three is assentive; Four, assertive. Indeed, Four tends to go out of bounds both with muscles and with mind. And why should he not? If he remained a delightful, docile Three, he would not grow up. So he surges ahead with bursts of movement and of imagination. His activity curve again takes on the hither and thither pattern typical of eighteen months. But this is not a regression; for he functions at a higher level in all departments of his behavior: motor, adaptive, language, and personal-social. He covers more ground, not only in his running, hopping, jumping, skipping, climbing, but in the lively constructions and antics of his mental imagery.

If at times he seems somewhat voluble, dogmatic, boastful, and bossy, it is because he is a blithe amateur swinging into fresh fields of self-expression. For a while he can scarcely be too concerned about the feelings of others. He is not quite as sensitive to praise as he was at three and as he will be again at five. Instead, he praises himself through bragging. Besides, he is much less experienced than his brave verbal assertiveness might suggest. He has meager appreciation of disappointment and the personal emotions of others. He is inquisitively interested in death but has scant comprehension of its meaning. He is plausible because his words often outrun his knowledge.

His motor drive is high. He races up and down stairs; he dashes on his tricycle. He trapezes on the Junglegym, with flying commentary while he performs: "I bet you can't do this, I hope!" He can also combine talking and eating. At an earlier age he either talked or ate; now he does both more or less simultaneously. This is a new ability (Three had to stop undressing when he was speaking).

Four's motor equipment, including his voice, is under better control. He can throw overhand; he can cut on a line with scissors; saw with a handsaw; lace his shoes; stand on one foot. Although he enjoys gross bodily activity, he is able to sit for a long period at interesting manual tasks. Hands, arms, legs, and feet are becoming emancipated from total postural set. If his general postural development has been fortunate to date, his dancing and his hand movements now assume a natural, untutored gracefulness.

Four is a great talker. He is his own self-appointed commentator and often his own audience. He likes to use words, to try them out, to play with them. He likes new, different words (indeed, "different" is itself a favorite word for him). He also likes to perpetrate silly words, such as "marty-warty," "batty-watty," and "ooshy-wooshy" (to describe soft clay). Questioning comes to a peak. The endless "why" and "how" questions are not for pure pursuit of knowledge but are devices for practicing both speech and listening. Therefore, a bright, articulate four-year-old tends to run his topics to the ground, exhausting every verbal possibility. Just as he tries to climb high on the gym, so he climbs high with his vocabulary and grammar. Naturally his syntax often topples.

The key to Four's psychology is his high drive combined with a fluid mental organization. His imagery is almost mercurial. It moves from one form to another with careless ease. He starts to draw a turtle; before he is through it is an elephant or a truck. This same fluidity makes him a fabricator and a fertile producer of alibis. It also makes it possible for him to dramatize any experience that comes within his ken. A hospital bed scene is readily reenacted with very simple materials serving as properties. A block becomes a bottle of medicine, and in another instant a stethoscope. Such dramatic play with ever-running comments and dialogue is a stable form of nursery behavior.

Four is voluble, because his imagery is mercurial; and also because he wishes to express his experiences in more flexible and more mature phraseology. He cannot be content with the simple seriated sentences of the three-year-old; he wants command of conjunctions, adverbs, and expletives. So he uses them with creditable (and incidentally amusing) bravery: "you see," "you know what," "I guess," "maybe," "really," "not even," "enormous," "only," "suppose that," "still," "now see," "and everything." He is adept at picking up phrases from his linguistic culture, such as "You'll never guess in a hundred years." His use of numbers is experimental rather than critical: "There were seventy-seven people there." He "exaggerates" because he is practicing words. But sometimes (parents beware) he reports quite faithfully what happened at home, not sparing family disagreements: "Mother is careless with money."

Really (!), the four-year-old is very versatile. What can he not do? He can be quiet, noisy, calm, assertive, cozy, imperious, suggestible, independent, social, athletic, artistic, literal, fanciful, cooperative, indifferent, inquisitive, forthright, prolix, humorous, dogmatic, silly, competitive.

He is in a "growthsome" stage, particularly with respect to interpersonal relations and social communication. This is a period of acquisition, of rapid acculturation. At three years the child had consolidated earlier gains and was in relatively stable focus; at four he is moving on to another consolidation; for he comes into focus again at five years. It is not strange, therefore, that the four-year-old tends to go out of bounds, notably in the field of speech; but fundamentally he is striving (through his growth impulsions) to identify himself with his culture, and to comprehend its intricacies. He is more firmly based than appears on the surface.

Sometimes almost consciously he is trying to grow up. He is interested in becoming five years old; he talks about it. He does not, of course, have a concrete comprehension of a year as a unit of time; he is only beginning to understand that Wednesday comes after

Tuesday. But he is unmistakably interested in the march of birthdays. Birthday parties are a favorite topic of conversation. To be invited by a four-year-old, even months in advance, is a sign of social approval; to be expressly excluded denotes at least temporary disapprobation. Fragments and hints of tribal sociology appear in the group life of the four-year-olds when they foregather in the nursery school. They organize themselves into groups of three or four, often with segregation of boys and girls. Commands are given, taboos set up. Lines are drawn sharply and intruders barred. From a developmental standpoint, this negative behavior has a decidedly positive significance. The in-group feeling is a step toward understanding the nature of a social group. Mommy is the court of last resort and her authority is frequently cited: "My mommy told me to do that."

Social patterns are offset and in part defined by antisocial conduct. The four-year-old takes to calling people names: "You're a rat." He becomes defiant: "I'm mad!" "I'll sock you!" Refusals previously expressed by "No!" are now stated with a vigorous "I won't!" His boastfulness reaches towering egocentric heights. But all this bravado is not as drastic as appears on the surface. Four is feeling his powers and is trying them out. His inconsistencies are similar to the contrarinesses that he displayed as a younger child. Contrary extremes meet in the paradoxical logic of development. The cultural restraints of home and nursery school help to keep the extremes within normal bounds.

Basically, the four-year-old is more interested in socialization than in the resistance that absorbed him at three and a half years. He shows this in his great fondness for dressing up and acting like a grownup. That is one more efficacious method of maturing. He not only dons an adult hat, but he indulges in long telephone conversations, which echo the exact inflections of the adult voice. The incessant "Why?" is directed toward social as well as natural phenomena. The four-year-old takes a significant pleasure in listening to explanations. He also likes to make faces. This is still another method of identification with adults and of perfecting his skill in reading their facial expressions. He is reading into, talking into, and acting into the complexities of his culture.

Behavior Day

The four-year-old usually wakes up in a happy mood at about seven o'clock or a little later. He likes to get up and go to his parents' bedroom for greeting and conversation. He has lost the romping abandon of a year ago.

He dresses himself while his parents are dressing. He is able to do this without much assistance if his clothes have been laid out for him in advance on the floor or chair. He can complete the dressing with the exception of tying bows and buttoning back buttons.

He can amuse himself if necessary looking at books, and magazines. He may help set the breakfast table, and is most likely to join the family group for breakfast.

If he is registered at a nursery school, he usually spends three or four mornings a week away from home. He likes to attend regularly but is not unduly worried if he arrives at school somewhat late.

At home, he plays by himself contentedly indoors for an hour or two at a time. He favors a dramatic combining type of play. He is fond of building blocks and imaginatively converts them into multifarious animate and inanimate objects to suit his dramatic fancies. If he is a boy he likes to play with string, tying the chairs and furniture in intricate but to him meaningful mazes.

After indoor play he enjoys going out into the near neighborhood for a visit or an errand. He responds best if he has occasional supervision at critical points at the beginning and at the termination of an experience. He asks permission to go; he comes back to report. Although he now has a degree of self-reliance, the household does well to keep tabs on him!

At noon he may lunch alone or with the family. His appetite is on the rise. He eats neatly and adeptly, but again he needs an occasional cultural prod and incentive.

He toilets himself after luncheon. His regular bowel movement may come at this time. He attends to himself.

At about one o'clock he is ready for a play nap of an hour or two. He relaxes more readily than hitherto, reclines on the bed, looks at books, plays quietly. He may or he may not go to sleep, but he has acquired a rather accurate sense of time. He seems to know when the official nap period is over, and reports to that effect with clocklike regularity.

Even if he has attended nursery school in the morning, he craves company during the afternoon hours from three to five o'clock. He wishes either to visit at a friend's house or to have a friend come to his house. He generally prefers children of his own maturity, with whom he engages in gross motor and dramatic play. Two make good company, three a crowd that releases a tendency to vocal quarrel-someness.

At about half past five he is ready for supper. He may eat before the family dinner hour. He is able to amuse himself until it is time for a session of play with his father. He likes to be read to; he likes to build block structures with his father. He watches his special television programs. They now have more continuing interest for him.

The evening bath comes at about seven o'clock. He may be able to take it alone with the usual incidental cues, though he still needs a minimum of direction.

Although he is relatively self-sufficient, he may want to take his teddy bear to bed with him for dramatized conversation. He likes to have the light on for a short period, but when his parents return for a good-night greeting, he goes off to sleep without protest.

SLEEP

NIGHT

Going to bed is now relatively easy and by four and a half years of age the child may even ask to go to bed. He enjoys hearing stories before he starts for bed. He knows that the hour of seven o'clock is time for bed, and he can read that particular time on the clock. He responds better to the fact that the clock says it is time to go to bed than that his mother or father says it is bedtime. He may even respond more promptly if an alarm clock is set to go off at bedtime.

A few children need not only a going-to-bed time, but also a putting-out-the-light time. Without this extra fifteen to thirty minutes to settle down in their beds with the light on, they may be very demanding. The child likes to look at books or to color at this time. His teddy bear, or a whole family of teddy bears (mother, father, and baby) or dolls, are often his favorite bedtime companions. He wants to undress and dress them and treat them like real persons. He often wants to put them under the covers and puts the covers very carefully under their chins. A good-night kiss for the parent and a long strong hug means that the child is ready for sleep. He now falls asleep rather quickly.

The four-year-old usually awakens by himself if he needs to be toileted during the night. A few children are able to go to the bathroom by themselves, but they usually tell the mother first. They may need only verbal help, and the most difficult part of this procedure is often getting back into bed. Sometimes verbal suggestion is not quite enough and the mother may need to get up and help the child back into bed. By five years he is ready to carry through the entire process without the parent's help.

There is much less wakefulness caused by dreaming at four than there was at three and a half years; but by four and a half, the child may again have a period of dreaming about animals, especially about wolves. He may be especially sensitive to any light stimuli coming into the room and therefore may need to have his bed in a dark corner. If the child is afraid of the dark, a light on in the hall is often sufficient to allay his fears.

The four-year-old wakes around 7:00 to 7:30 A.M. He is now able to put on his bathrobe and slippers if they have been laid out for him, to close the window, to go to the bathroom, and to play in his room until it is time to go to his parents' room. When he goes into his parents' room he often likes to be read to or to look at books until it is time to get dressed. He finds it especially easy to make these shifts if there are whistles that blow or church bells that punctuate these hours.

[Children who wake up at night and have difficulty getting back to sleep may respond to stories about other children who used to wake up at night but who no longer do so.

The four-year-old is now ready to sleep in a big bed. This change from his crib to a big bed can be helpfully utilized in planning for needed improvements in sleeping patterns.]

NAP

A very small proportion of children nap at this age. They will occasionally take a nap preparatory to staying up late in the evening. This is in marked contrast to the two-to-three-year-old child, who, if he is told what is going to happen after his nap, will become so excited that he will be unable to sleep.

The four-year-old enjoys a play nap from 1 to 3 P.M. He may spend the first half hour or hour on his bed looking at books, and then spend the second hour out of bed. He may no longer need his door tied, goes to the bathroom if necessary, and frankly enjoys this time alone in his room.

Often these hours are very creative ones as long as the child has the proper media to work with. He needs to be alone, to have the pressure of other influences removed, that he may utilize his past stores of knowledge and ability. His inner time clock now seems to be more in tune with the time of the clock on the wall, for he senses when it is three o'clock and asks if it is time to come out.

EATING

Appetite—The four-year-old appetite is still only fair, but by four and a half it is good to very good, with no special meal leading another. The child drinks his milk well and rapidly.

Refusals and Preferences—There is some tendency to demand repetition. The four-year-old goes on either food jags or food strikes, which usually drop out by four and a half years, when the appetite is keener.

Self-Help—The four-year-old is beginning to help plan his meal and also to help prepare it. He enjoys helping to set the family table. Most four-year-olds have difficulty in not letting their talking interfere with their eating; they do not sit well through a meal, and may need to interrupt the meal (especially an evening meal) by going to the bathroom.

When they eat alone they are apt to dawdle but do not usually need to be fed. Such incentives as eating to get big, racing with the baby, finishing within a certain time allotment, or working toward a dessert goal may help. Planning ahead to ring a bell that announces the completion of one course and a desire for the next may be all the incentive the child needs. By four and a half years of age, he is picking up speed, is handling more meals with the family, can listen as well as talk, and is beginning to be sensitive to outside influences, such as those coming over television.

ELIMINATION

Bowel—One movement a day, after either breakfast or lunch, is a common four-year-old bowel pattern. Some children have more than one movement, and an irregular time of occurrence. Though some children still tell before they go, the majority tell only after they have gone because they need help in being wiped. A fair proportion take care of themselves completely. Though many are quite matter-of-fact about having a movement, others consider it a private matter which demands a closed bathroom door, and even a locked door at four and a half years of age.

Bladder—Children of this age are as a rule able to take full responsibility themselves and have only occasional accidents toward the latter part of the morning or afternoon when they have put off going to the toilet too long. In these periods of relapse they again need helpful suggestions and planning from the adult. They show less feeling for privacy than they do when they have a bowel movement, but are very much interested in watching other people in the bathroom, and show a marked interest in strange bathrooms. They are more apt to tell their mothers before they have to go to the bathroom in a strange house. This demand for the bathroom occurs not only because of real curiosity to see new bathrooms but also because the social situation creates tensions which seek outlets.

Relatively few children wet at night at this age, or need to be picked up at 10 to 12 P.M. Some still awake to be toileted during the night and may still need help, especially in getting back to bed.

BATH AND DRESSING

Bath—The bath is now an easy routine. The child is often capable of washing himself fairly well as long as the mother suggests part by part what he is to wash. He is apt to get marooned on one part of his body and keep washing it over and over again. He also lets out the water and washes out the tub on suggestion. He can now dry himself after a fashion. He is better able to make the necessary wrist and hand adjustments to do a creditable job of brushing his teeth.

The bath may well be shifted to before supper at four and a half years. The child takes his bath more quickly when he is less fatigued and may be looking forward to having his supper in bed. This shift in time is especially helpful in the winter months.

Dressing—The child of this age usually dresses and undresses himself with very little assistance, though he may need his clothes laid down on the floor, each garment separately oriented so that he can slip into it. He now can distinguish the front from the back, can lace his shoes, and some children can even button buttons. The child may for a while continue to dress parallel with the adult. When the novelty of this wears off, he often dresses best in a room alone. A few children become angry if things go wrong, and refuse any adult help at this point. Planning ahead with them as to how to put on a garment successfully usually controls their temper outbursts. Almost all children, even though they dress themselves poorly, enjoy dressing up in adult clothes, especially in hats, gloves, shoes, belts, and pocketbooks.

SELF-ACTIVITY

The four-year-old is ready for nursery school three or four days a week. He prefers to play with children rather than play alone. Therefore his play alone may be restricted to his play nap and an evening play period. He now combines his toys into a dramatic setting. People are added to his block structures, cars are placed in front of houses. Girls and even boys may indulge in considerable household activity, including the dressing and undressing of their dolls or teddies. Because of the speed of the four-year-old, he is a rapid utilizer of material, especially of paper and crayons and paste. He more often prefers to draw free hand than to color picture books. He is quite happy as long as he is amply supplied, and each new bit of material seems to stimulate him to new abilities.

He is now beginning to admire his products and wants others to admire them, too. He likes to have his pictures put up on a bulletin board (the back of his door is often the place he chooses, with Scotch tape taking the place of thumbtacks). He wants his block structures left up, and enjoys explaining their intricacies of building and of meaning. But his enthusiasm is not prolonged. When he returns to his room he will not add to his block structure. He wants to do something "different." If his mother has warned him ahead of time, he does not mind if she reorders his room. He is more likely to resist if he is present during this reordering, though he at times accomplishes it by himself.

He now resists confinement in either his room or his yard unless it is self-imposed. He does not want his door to be tied. If he can understand the "rules," he may be ready to stay in his room the allotted time, and to go back and forth to the bathroom as needed. Some children may have practiced being four years old when they were still only three, by having their door untied now and then when they asked for it. Although the majority of children need this type of restraint (having their door tied), there are some who do not need to have any more restraint than a closed door, and others who become resistant over a closed door that they themselves have not closed, and even panicky if their door is tied.

The four-year-old will manage to open his gate or climb over the fence if the gate is not left open. He now needs more scope, more rope, but he also needs the control of rules, for he is apt to go out of bounds so quickly. When he leaves his backyard and goes to the front, he will willingly announce this shift to his mother by ringing the doorbell. He is now allowed to ride his tricycle alone on the sidewalk. Most willingly accept boundaries in both directions as long as they are enlarged at intervals.

The four-year-old enjoys this slow receiving of new privileges, the response to "rules." He becomes surfeited all too quickly if allowed complete freedom, or he becomes resentful if he is held too tightly. With the latter type of handling he is more apt to go too far out of bounds. It is the four-year-old who runs away from home.

SOCIALITY

The four-year-old is a truly social being. He not only wants to join a play group every morning, but he wants to be with playmates every afternoon. He now so definitely prefers children that he may even refuse to go to places where there are no children. He is in fact so busy with his play life that his former interests in helping around the house have been largely given up. He will, however, run short errands outside the home which do not require the crossing of streets.

He is actually developing a strong sense of family and home. His mother or father are often quoted as authorities. Things that he sees away from home are compared with things at home, usually to the home's advantage. In fact he is given to boasting. Methods of management previously used by the various members of his family are now enacted in his social dramatic play. Some families may well be startled by this reenactment.

Though the four-year-old tends to be bossy and domineering, he does well either alone with one other child or in a supervised group. His play is smoother than that observed at three years because of the actual nature of the social dramatic play of house, doctor, etc., and because of his ability to shift rapidly. Although he plays well with one other child without supervision, he may find it difficult to adjust to a third child. The four-year-old still needs very watchful supervision. It is often at this age that too much is put upon the child. He may now be able to fight his own battles, and acquires more self-control because he can handle a situation alone. But many of the battles need never have been fought if proper supervision had been given in the first place. This also applies to the years after four.

Excursions and times with father are highly prized by the four-year-old. Saturday and Sunday take on new meaning because father is home and special things are planned with him. The father realizes that these excursions are still best taken alone with the child, who can adjust to a larger group especially on a picnic, but who is most relaxed and happy when alone with one adult.

CHAPTER 20

FIVE YEARS OLD

Behavior Profile

Five, from a parent's view, is one of the nicest ages of all. It is a kind of golden age at which for a brief time the tides of development flow smoothly. The child is now content to organize the experiences that he gathered somewhat piecemeal in his wilder fourth year.

At four it seemed as if the child was trying himself out against authority. He was definitely out of bounds. His experimentations carried him too far in almost every direction. At five, in contrast, he likes to be close to home, close to the tried and true, and, most of all, close to his mother. Mother is the center of the five-year-old's world and he likes best of all to be with her, helping her, watching her, playing along beside her. Unlike Four, he wants to do what is right and so he loves to ask permission. Even more, he loves to be praised for doing things "right."

Five is so often very much a mother's boy or girl that mothers sometimes worry, especially in the case of boys, that the child is *too* dependent. They need not, in most instances, be anxious. Time will bring not always welcome changes in the direction of independence.

This is an age much appreciated by most parents of preschoolers, coming as it does after the wild boisterousness of four, and following the in-between and somewhat uncertain age of four and a half, at which time the child does indeed seem betwixt and between. The transition from out-of-bounds Four to calm, confident, confiding, dependent, and dependable Five is not made easily by most. It is as if for a while, around four and a half, the child didn't really know whether he was four, with its exuberance, or five, with its calm, and he shuttles back and forth uncomfortably. One minute he is sure; the next minute uncertain.

The four-and-a-half-year-old is trying to sort out what is real from what is make-believe. He does not get as lost in his pretending as at three and a half and four years, when he really *was* a cat or a carpenter or an airplane pilot. "Is it real?" is his constant question. Making a *real* drawing of an airplane, he includes a long electric cord so that people can plug it in. However, he can still become quite confused as he tries to straighten out what he pretends, what happens on TV, and what is real. This mixture of reality and imagination can be quite exasperating to parents.

Four-and-a-half-year-olds are a little more self-motivating than they were just earlier. They start a job and stay on the same track much better than at four years, and with less need of adult control. When they start to build a farm with blocks, it ends up as a farm, not, as at four years, becoming first a fort, then a truck, then a gas station.

Four-and-a-half-year-olds are great discussers. Reading a book about fires might lead to a long discussion of the pros and cons of fire. They often have a surprising wealth of material and experience to draw upon, and seem to be prompted by an intellectual, philosophizing sort of interest. They are interested in details and like to be shown. Their desire for realism is sometimes entirely too stark for adults—they seem sometimes almost too frank as they demand the details about death, for example.

Children of this age are improving their control and perfecting their skills in many ways. Their play is less wild than at four; they are better able to accept frustration.

Their fine motor control, as expressed in drawing, is markedly improved and they will often draw on and on. They show a beginning interest in letters and numbers.

Four and a half also shows a beginning interest in seeing several sides of the picture. He is aware of front and back, inside and outside.

Four and a half, with its increased control and its interest in improving and perfecting skills, is a catching-up time with children, especially boys, who have been slow in motor and language development; or it may be an age of rapid intellectual growth for those who have already caught up.

But five, once the child reaches that comfortable island, is quite different. Now he is focal, factual, successful (since he tries only things at which he can succeed). He is sincere, smiling, responsive, and responsible. These are only a few of the favorable adjectives one might use to describe the child of this age. If only it could last forever, some parents wish.

For the time being, secure and capable, five is content to stay on or near home base, doing what he thinks his mother wants him to do. He does not seem to feel the need to thrust out into the unknown or to attempt things that will be difficult for him. Since he tries only what he can accomplish, he accomplishes what he tries. This brings success and increased complacency and self-confidence.

It is fair to say that the five-year-old feels truly at home in his world. And what is his world? It is a here-and-now world: his father and mother, especially his mother; his seat at the dining room table; his clothes, particularly that cap of which he may be so proud; his tricycle; his backyard, the kitchen, his bed; the drugstore and the grocery store around the corner; the street; and perhaps the big kindergarten room with other children and with his teacher, of whom he is usually very fond. But if his universe has a single center, that center is his mother.

He likes little responsibilities, but one must not be fooled by his air of competence. For instance, he loves to hold his baby brother or sister. He may be allowed to do this under supervision, but it is not wise to give him too much responsibility. Competent as he may be, or seem, he still needs a lot of help from the adult.

Five tends to be a great talker, and as a rule has overcome any infantile articulation. He uses connectives more freely when he tells a story. He may exaggerate but he is not, as earlier, given to over-fanciful invention. His dramatic play is full of practical dialogue.

In general, the emotional life of the five-year-old suggests good adjustment within himself and confidence in others. He is not without anxieties and fears, but usually they are temporary and concrete. Thunder and sirens awaken dread. Darkness and solitude cause timidity. Many a five-year-old has fits of fearfulness lest his mother should leave him, or not be there when he comes home from kindergarten. Sleep may be disturbed by nightmares, and it is not unusual for a child of this age to awaken screaming.

Though the world of the five-year-old is often seen as friendly, as evidenced by an increase in kind or friendly themes in stories he tells spontaneously, themes of violence do prevail as at other ages.

"Girl," "Mummy," or some animal are the chief characters in stories told by girls; "boys," some adult other than parents, or animals are prevalent in boys' stories. Mother tends to play a somewhat negative role in the stories of girls, but all boys see their mothers as helpful and friendly. Children of both sexes see fathers as friendly and helpful.

Girls, as always, and boys for the second age in succession tell stories with socializing rather than egocentric themes. As just earlier, the majority of stories are laid in somewhat distant places. Fantasy prevails in stories by boys, though a substantial number of girls have moved closer to reality.

The use of humor increases, humor taking the form of ridiculous actions, disaster or misfortune, silly language, or incongruity. As at all ages, there is a strong tendency to protect the self. Girls do this by having harm occur to siblings or boys, or by talking about violence that does not actually occur. Boys protect themselves by having objects or animals harmed, or by having the villainy of others punished.

If an earlier imaginary companion is still part of a child's life, this now tends to be a rather personal and private matter. Most do not talk about him (or her) to others as they did at three and a half to four years of age. However, five is so down-to-earth in his approach to life that we may assume that a former imaginary companion may be of little continued interest.

All things considered, the five-year-old tends to be in an excellent state of equilibrium. His health tends to be good, and emotionally he is comfortable. There are few temper tantrums, any refusal being expressed by a mere stamping of the feet or a "No, I won't." He is not fidgety. In fact, often we see unconscious grace and skill in both gross and fine motor coordinations. There is a finished perfection and economy of movement, which again suggests that five is a focal stage toward which the strands of development converge to be organized for a new advance—the breakup of equilibrium which characteristically occurs around five and a half.

Some parents do indeed wish, when the customary five-and-a-half-to-six-year-old breakup of behavior comes, and when their "good" little five-year-old turns into an often less-than-good little six, that they could have their docile five-year-old back again. Looking back in this way is, of course, fruitless. And a growing child needs more than five-year-old equipment with which to meet the world. He needs to branch out, as he does at six, though unfortunately in branching out he often thrusts into areas that cause a good deal of difficulty for all concerned.

Maturity Traits

A discussion of the maturity traits of the five-year-old can be found in *The Child from Five to Ten*, by Gesell and Ilg. In that volume, we have described the five-year-old in full detail, in relation to the years that come after.

PART THREE

THE GUIDANCE OF GROWTH

CHAPTER 21

PARENT AND CHILD

Nothing is quite as exciting as watching and fostering the growth of a child. It should be an enriching, challenging, and enjoyable experience. But think how often this experience is, for the parent, fraught with unknowing anxiety and exhaustion.

There was a time, at least with those who could afford it, when the care of the young was given over to a full-time, well-trained nanny or nurse. But such help is hard to come by nowadays even if one could afford it. An alternative in the early days of this country was the help of the family, as families were large and many extra hands were available with time to spare. Help is what the new mother needed in those days and help is what she needs today. She and the father too need help in all sorts of ways—help with knowledge, help with facilities, help with hands, and especially the help of caring.

Within the past thirty years, since the original publication of this book and especially within the past five or ten years, there has been a veritable proliferation of published material that can and does help a couple through pregnancy, through childbirth, and through the early trying months.

We hope that many couples come to child-rearing with some of the seasoning of time. A year or two of marriage without children could give parents that extra readiness. And when one sees the involvement of these more mature potential parents one feels secure for the child.

These couples do not delay seeking obstetrical supervision as soon as they know that the wife is pregnant. They want to provide all the care they can in nutrition, exercise, and otherwise during pregnancy. An ever-increasing number of parents are concerned about the birth process itself, especially if they have heard of natural childbirth in its various forms. The real glory of this method is not only that the mother comes to know the stages of labor she will be going through and how to become actively involved, but also that the father, once relegated to the waiting room, can also be involved and highly supportive. Young people today question the use of anesthetics and drugs during childbirth. Drugs may be essential at times, but our culture has been too prone to give drugs because they are so easily available. The undrugged newborn who makes his piercing cry as he fills his lungs with his first breath tells us that all is well.

Perhaps the word "natural," which after all means working with nature, summarizes the most important changes that have been going on in the past thirty years. We may well cringe when we realize how unnatural it is to take a child away from his mother at birth, how unnatural to bottle-feed, how unnatural to force solid foods too early, how unnatural to train a child in elimination before he is ready.

Mothers today seem more confident in themselves and less likely to overcontrol, to have that unfortunate urge to beat the child's own biological clock. General knowledge of the unfolding of growth forces can help to give a mother greater confidence. She comes to know that there is a time for everything, a time when it is too soon, a time when it is just right, and a time when it may be too late. Not that she can't test readiness, but she soon learns that if she tries to impose some order or demand too soon, the resistance and frustrations produced can obscure or delay the readiness that would have come naturally.

The simplicity and naturalness of breast-feeding cannot be overly emphasized. The well-nursed infant seems quite capable of determining his own schedule, his intake, and even his eventual acceptance of solid food. When he is well satisfied with breast milk, he may refuse solid food even into the fifth or sixth month. Weaning also is more easily controlled by the child when he is allowed to continue breast-feeding till he is tired of it.

Regulation of elimination poses a somewhat different kind of problem, but here again, when the mother works with the natural forces expressed by the child, control becomes a natural step. In our original study, we documented all the relative evidences of readiness for elimination control on which the mother might capitalize. But this often fostered wasted energy on the part of the mother and resistance on the part of the child. Disposable diapers have now made it easier for the mother to delay. And the rapidity of success sometimes between the second and third birthdays, when the child knows what he is doing, gives him a new status in the family. His success can be shared and praised by all.

Sleeping problems, especially going to sleep at night, have been somewhat reduced over the years, especially with a lessening of tensions. In some families children are not put to bed as early as they once were. In fact, too permissive delay of bedtime occurs in many households. Parents still need to establish some order in bedtime, and they find that bedtime routines can be more easily carried out if the child has had a satisfying playtime before bedtime. The return of the children's hour, a real children's hour (preferably without television), can do much for a household. The look on a child's face when he is fully ready to release into sleep must make a parent know that these happy activities are the kind of nourishment needed.

We might here put in a warning that many sleeping problems stem from a too early shift from crib to bed, especially when a new baby is expected. Four years of age is the ideal time to make this shift, and the planning for it can be a large part of the fun. All sorts of new things might happen. The child himself might decide that once he is in his big bed he won't wet the bed anymore. Give the child a chance to capitalize on this momentous shift in his life.

Among the greatest helps for the mother of an infant or preschooler today are those within the realm of what we call household engineering. She can now take advantage of many safeguards and methods of containment. Playpens, gates, window bars, fences, car seats, and safety straps all have their places as they are needed. The living area of a house, the kitchen, a family room with eating area can be ideal for a preschooler. The kitchen area needs to be made safe from his exploring. Gates can be used to keep him out of trouble.

How the activities of the day are planned will be determined by the mother. Whether the child eats with the family group or is fed ahead of time might vary according to age and family situation. Many feeding problems arise unnecessarily when the family group is too stimulating for the preschooler. Families need to face the success or failure of his inclusion at the family table.

A wise mother makes careful plans for the activities of her child's day. She brings out certain toys to be played with at certain times of the day. She stores some toys rarely played with, which can be brought out later on, when they may be received as though they were new. This is all a part of household engineering.

We said little in our earlier edition and still cannot cover adequately the troublesome problem of the interaction of siblings. Since families are getting smaller nowadays, many common problems may no longer arise. Too many children too close together have always produced difficulties that are hard to solve. Reducing the size of the family, separation, and time alone with either parent are among the best measures we know of for controlling quarreling.

Play groups and nursery schools will be discussed in Part Four. Outdoors is very important to the child. That's why we need play areas and parks for him to enjoy. Small children need and benefit by the informal atmosphere provided by outdoor space and outdoor activities. When the four-year-old is asked what he likes to do best, he often replies, "Play outdoors." And how he loves to watch the activity of construction sites, especially when bulldozers and cranes are in action.

Raising children is not easy and the child's need of his parents, especially of his mother, is very evident in these early years. It is so important that a mother should ideally be willing to pledge herself to the earliest years of a child's life. Substitute parents are possible, but then very good planning on the part of the mother is needed. If the mother must work, a part-time job may be preferable, especially at first.

It is becoming evident that a child needs to be talked to and played with in the first few years of his life. He needs to be interpreted in that early period before speech comes in. Only a mother who has been with her child will know what he has experienced and what he wants to say. She needs also to help him through his temper episodes, which she can usually interpret and respond to either by giving in or by circumventing them.

Perhaps the biggest change that has occurred in the past thirty years is that parents now view their children with a better perspective. There was a time when many parents were upset, and met force with force, only to become exhausted and defeated. Today's parent may smile inwardly as she sees the inevitable appearance of temper tantrums, and may cleverly mobilize her forces to stem the tide. She avoids her own exhaustion and with practice learns how to switch off her angry child. Some simple statement such as "But you forgot to get your shoes" might turn the trick.

Informed parents can also provide the help and safeguards needed at the different ages as they understand the detail and complexity of growing behavior. At no time is the mother more needed than at three and a half years of age, when the child is trying to understand the structure and confusion of his world. As tangled as his relationship with his mother may be, he needs her there to smooth out his days and to answer his many questions: "Is tomorrow today?" "Is it breakfast? Is it supper?"

The welling up of hate and anger at four needs to be dealt with on the spot. And love is hate's counterpart, as is shown by the child who says, "I love you so much that I hate you." This love-hate combination may even be so strong that a child will uninvite his mother to his own birthday party.

Anger met with anger seldom works out. Mothers have come to know when their children need supportive handling. Another important thing that many mothers now realize and admit is that it is often best to bring things out into the open. And there are times when shock techniques are needed, such as clapping one's hands and saying, "Stop it!"

Many parents today, with their improving perspective, can accept what their children say without shock or embarrassment. As ever, children tend to say what is on their mind. The realm of sex brings this out especially. One four-year-old girl explained to her mother, "But you can't say 'penis' around people 'cause they're kinda shy and they'd say, 'Oh! Who said "Penis"?'" The quiet smile on this mother's face indicated how far some of today's parents have come. And the child's awareness of the feelings of other people suggested that she had had a good upbringing.

The place where some parents still lag is in their lack of knowledge about growth in the cognitive and intellectual fields. They may no longer be pushing the more basic areas of behavior, but many now push intellectual learning. And how often parents feel the need to correct grammatical errors in their child's speech, especially when he is four years old. Somehow they have forgotten or never knew that the race went through these same steps in growing up. The acquisition of irregular verbs occurs slowly in most children. We might enjoy their errors ("I build it"; "Didn't I told you?"; "I brang it to you"), write them down, and look back on them with amusement in another six months.

Correct grammar, like completed toilet training or good sleeping habits, takes its own time, and in a supportive environment will work itself out without undue self-conscious pushing on the part of the parent.

Hopefully the specific information about behavior to be expected at the successive *age levels,* presented in Part Two of this book, and the discussions of the important *areas of behavior* in the present section, will help parents not to push. Hopefully it may also help them toward more effective functioning as they appreciate more fully what they can and cannot expect of their growing boys and girls during the exciting and rapidly changing period of infancy and the preschool years.

CHAPTER 22

THE GROWTH COMPLEX

Sleep

Sleep is behavior. One is accustomed to think of sleep as a cessation of behavior; it is, however, a positive function. It is not a mere stoppage of machinery; it is a readjustment of the whole machinery of the organism, including the central nervous system, to protect the total and remote welfare of the organism.

Perfect sleep is a total response. In this sense sleep differs from other forms of behavior. All other behavior represents an adjustment or an adaptation to more or less specific situations. Sleep, on the contrary, is a response which is as inclusive and fundamental as nutrition. Indeed, it can be envisaged as an expression of nutritional economy.

When we undertake to study the characteristics of sleep in infant and child, we find that sleep behavior is genetically inseparable from nutrition. Sleep is not a simple function in spite of its apparent simplicity. It is so complex that physiology has not yet succeeded in establishing a satisfactory theory of sleep. The very abundance of

---

In deference to the senior author of the first edition of this book, Dr. Arnold Gesell, we have left much of this chapter in his own words, as in the original edition. Readers looking for more specific advice on what to *do* in relation to these routines are referred to any of the good pediatric books now available. We particularly recommend Marvin Gersh's *How to Raise Children at Home in Your Spare Time*, L. Emmett Holt, Jr.'s, *Good Housekeeping Book of Baby and Child Care*, Fitzhugh Dodson's *How to Parent*, or Lendon H. Smith's *The Children's Doctor*. Or our own Ilg's and Ames's *Child Behavior* and *Parents Ask*.

theories indicates that we really do not know very much about its actual mechanism.

Many of the misconceptions concerning sleep arise from the fact that it has been oversimplified. In the care of infants and children, it must be recognized that sleep is not a well-defined, uniform response, but that it varies enormously with the individuality of the child and still more with his maturity. The biological function of sleep is to preserve the integrity of the total organism and its entire life cycle. Sleep, therefore, undergoes significant changes with age. The sleep of the fetus, if indeed the fetus does sleep, is quite different from the sleep of the adult; the sleep of infancy is different from the sleep of youth. In later maturity sleep assumes new forms, some of which are reminiscent of childhood and infancy. These grosser changes in the rhythms, nature, and depth of sleep should at once remind us that in child care we must be prepared to find variations in sleep behavior from time to time; sometimes from day to day. Such variations betray the complexity of sleep as behavior.

The child has to learn to sleep in the same manner that he learns to grasp a spoon or to creep and stand and walk. Just as prehension and locomotion undergo clear developmental changes as they mature, so do patterns of sleep change with maturity. Perfect sleep must, then, be defined as a form of positive inhibition which embraces the entire organism and which serves best to protect its developmental needs.

Such perfection is ideal. Sleep may be more or less partial. It is quite conceivable that in defects and deviations of development, certain organ systems do not get an adequate quota of sleep. Sleep may be disintegrated, incomplete, just as the positive behavior of the waking child may be disintegrated and incomplete. Indeed, a normal balance must be achieved between waking behavior and sleep behavior. The organism must acquire adequate methods of going to sleep and emerging from sleep. From this broad point of view, sleep behavior is closely related to attention. Certain forms of attention, idling, dawdling, periods of abstraction, naps, "play naps," to say nothing of lethargy and mild forms of hibernation, are all in some manner related to the function of sleep, if we recall our definition that sleep is a biological device for inducing inactivity in order to protect the organism's capacity for later activity.

And what is meant by the fighting of sleep, an interesting form of behavior sometimes found to an intense degree in vital, perhaps generously endowed children? What is the philosophical rationalization of such a contest against an adjustment which nature apparently designed for our best interests?

Sleep has often been compared to death. Shelley speaks of "Death and his brother Sleep." Even Shakespeare called sleep the "death of each day's life," but in the very next breath he also called it "great nature's second course,/Chief nourisher in life's feast." This last characterization is scientifically acceptable, for sleep is more than a sweet restorer. It is a nourisher. It is allied to nutrition.

The early association between feeding and sleep is extremely close. The baby eats to sleep and he wakes to eat, which promptly puts him again to sleep, so that the two functions almost overlap. A young premature infant may not stop sleeping at all: he may not even be arousable. His whole muscle tone is limp. Indeed, his "sleep" is very shallow, as though it had no structure. He may fluctuate in a thin twilight zone, without definitively sleeping or waking, as though he did not know how to do either, which is true. As he grows older his muscle tone becomes firmer and lasts longer. He is less fragile in every way. His sleep becomes more defined, more clear-cut. He falls off to sleep more decisively, he wakes up more decisively. All of this means that sleep is a complex function which requires developmental organization from the moment of birth (and before). It will never cease to need such organization, for, as we have said, it is articulated with the total economy and makeup of the human action system.

The newborn infant, accordingly, has a few elementary differentiations to make between eating, sleeping, and waking. He knows how to nurse. Having "learned" how to sleep, he must learn how to wake and to keep awake. At first he wakes up from sheer necessity (need of food). This requires no special mechanism, other than a subcortical wakefulness center. He wakes with a demanding hunger cry. Is it pain or is it rage?

As he grows older, he is no longer so purely subcortical. His cry may be delayed a little after he opens his eyes: it takes on a more cultivated fussing quality. In time it becomes intermittent. It intersperses short periods of wakefulness. He is "learning" to stay awake and to enjoy it. His cortex (the higher nerve centers of the brain) is growing rapidly: millions of cortical nerve cells make connection with his eyes, ears, and the twelve oculomotor muscles that he uses in his staring and looking. This keeps his cortex wide awake. He is developing nerve centers for a "wakefulness of choice."

There are, accordingly, three distinguishable phases to the sleep cycle: (1) going to sleep; (2) staying asleep; and (3) awakening. It is not always easy to distinguish between the first and the third phases. The first depends upon a higher cortical control which enables the child *to release into sleep;* the third upon an active wakefulness nerve center. Is failure to go to sleep due to faulty release or to excessive activity of the wake-up center? Between release *into* and release *out* of sleep lies an intermediate stage: the consolidation of sleep. The task of development is to bring about a proportionate balance between these three phases. As the child grows up, the first, or release-into-sleep, phase seems to give him the most trouble; the third the least. We shall consider each phase in turn, beginning with the third phase, which appears to be the first to which the baby gives his developmental attention.

1. *The Awakening Phase.* As we have seen, the young baby does not wake up smoothly or expertly. He often wakes with a sharp cry. His waking seems to depend upon an internal prod, a nudge from the gastrointestinal tract or some other incitement from inside. Significantly enough, he does not respond readily to a prod from the outside. He does not arouse easily to a pat or a shake, which confirms the suggestion that waking depends upon an internal mechanism operated by his own private nervous system.

As the weeks go by, he occasionally wakes up more smoothly: he does not always cry, or his cry is briefer and softer. He also wakes up oftener. He becomes more facile. By sixteen weeks his waking mechanism is working with comparative efficiency. Thereafter, it does not, as such, make much trouble for the culture. At two and a half years, however, he not only has difficulty in going to sleep; but he has difficulty in getting out of sleep. The two difficulties seem to be related to each other at this highly unsettled stage of maturity. He temporarily loses the knack of waking up. He regains it; but at adolescence he may again show a similar developmental clinging to sleep. Further aspects of waking behavior are considered in connection with the other two phases of the sleep cycle.

2. *The Consolidation Phase.* It does not pay to be too clever at waking. That would, as we say, interfere with sleep. The child must "learn" to stay soundly asleep in sizable stretches. This is the consolidation phase, and it is subject to growth processes. Figure 4 is a behavior-day chart, which plots the progressive organization of sleeping and waking periods for three age levels. (The dark strands represent sleep; the white, waking.) Viewed in perspective, these strands are comparable to narrow streams which at first flow separately and finally become confluent in wider streams. The night sleep becomes less broken, the day naps coalesce. At first they are short and irregular; but by twelve weeks, two or three adjacent naps have consolidated into one. The long process of achieving a monophasic sleep-waking cycle is under way. At twelve weeks the infant may have four to five sleep periods in twenty-four hours; at twelve months, two to three; at four years, only one. As an adult, he can remain awake from choice eighteen hours or more. This process is not merely one of quantitative reduction of sleep; it involves complicated pattern transformations, adjustments to the schedule of the entire behavior day, and readjustments to the ever-changing interests and abilities of the growing child.

All sleep is, so to speak, vulnerable; how vulnerable depends upon two factors: the constitution of the child and the maturity of the child. He is especially likely to show disturbances of sleep behavior during transitional periods of disequilibrium, when growth changes are most

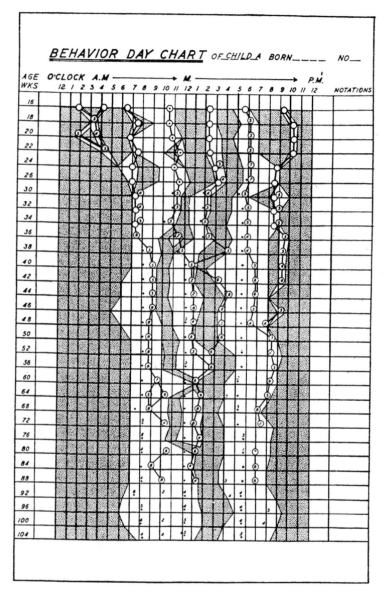

Figure 4 A typical behavior day chart of a child on a self-demand schedule, showing the early shift from six to two sleeping periods and from seven to three meals a day. Hours from midnight to midnight are plotted horizontally. Sleep is shown by shaded areas; waking and activity by unshaded areas. Bottle- and breast-feedings are shown by circles. Reading across the page, one sees the daily cycles; reading from top to bottom, the changes with age.

actively taking place. It is as though the organism had to assist in making readjustments even during sleep. Some of the apparent disturbances may actually have a positive usefulness in the economy of development. (The reader may be reminded that in this chapter we are attempting to interpret all behavior in its relation to an ever-changing growth complex.)

Up to the age of sixteen weeks, the variabilities of the gastrointestinal tract tend to discompose his slumbers. Later it may be wetness, or some bodily discomfort, or noises. Still later it may be emotional experiences—change of scene, undue excitement, new fears. At fifteen months, and at twenty-one months, the child often wakes during the night and, in an almost whimsical manner, remains awake for an hour or two. The three-year-old is apparently a little less settled during the night than during the day. He may get up out of his bed. He is disquieted if his mother goes out for an evening. Dreams become more frequent at three and a half and four and a half years, a reminder that sleep varies greatly in depth, in scope, and in integratedness; though we must be mindful of Freud's suggestion that dreams are the guardians of sleep. The organism does the best it can even through dreams. Indeed, it works while you sleep. In the recurrent periods of equilibrium, the organism is under the least stress and strain.

The sleep disturbances just outlined are the common lot of humanity. No man, no child escapes from himself merely by going to sleep. But some individuals have a much firmer grasp on sleep than do others.

"Poor sleepers" are comparable to the "poor eaters" who will be discussed in the following section. They do not hold fast to the sleep that they acquire, and they do not consolidate their gains readily. All the foregoing disturbances are intensified in degree and protracted in time. Poor sleepers do not shift readily from one maturity stage to another. They do not tolerate changes in accustomed routines and orientations. Even at the age of sixteen weeks a shift from bassinet to crib may not be accomplished with ease. The infant may accept the crib for a daytime nap, but rebels at night. It may take two weeks to wean him to this apparently simple change. At thirty-six weeks or later, the same child suffers derangement of sleep if his crib is moved from its accustomed position, or if a favorite blanket or pad is removed. Throughout the preschool years, he may be unusually dependent upon an adult, sometimes a particular adult, in his sleep adjustments. He persists longer than normally in a given stage of adjustment, and does not adjust by slow degrees but in a somewhat abrupt manner. His symptoms tend to exacerbate during periods of disequilibrium. Although his behavior is atypical, it follows normal sequences. It is best understood as a deviation from the normal rather than a perversity. It requires unusual patience and even compliances, for the simple reason that deviations of this type are grounded in the growth complex, and do not respond to rigorous, disciplinary measures. An appreciation of the developmental trend of the deviations makes for sympathetic and wise management.

3. *Release into Sleep.* The newborn infant, as previously noted, apparently has no difficulty in going to sleep. He is already there, and his sleep is so intimately bound up with his eating that transitions are easy. Moreover, his sleeping, like his waking, is at a subcortical level. He has neither inhibitory mechanisms nor inhibitory problems so far as sleeping is concerned. But as he acquires wakefulness of choice, these very problems—and mechanisms—begin to take shape. His cortex appears on the scene, and once it becomes active, he must learn to inhibit its activity. This is the task of release into sleep.

As the child grows older this task becomes more and more complex, for the cortex is both the agent and the storer of his ever-increasing experiences. And our high-geared culture keeps urging the cortex to cumulative rather than rhythmic activity. Not even the cosmic rhythm of night and day can compete with that relentless stress. Therefore, instead of being a simple, vegetative function, which ought to take care of itself, sleep creates, in our modern culture, a host of vexatious putting-to-bed problems. Under more primitive conditions of living, fatigue and ennui play a more prominent role in the regulation of sleep. Under modern conditions, the tyranny of the clock and the tensions of life complicate the reconciliation of sleep and waking. Some of the difficulties, however, it must be emphasized, are definitely based on maturity factors. The organism, in its nervous system, lacks the equipment for complete voluntary control. Recall how long it takes the child to acquire the simple ability to let go of an object at will. By trying, he can, at fifteen months, place one block on another, and relax his hold of it; but even then he tends to release awkwardly, with too much intensity, and with poor timing. This is physiological awkwardness. The same kind of awkwardness complicates his sleep mechanisms, particularly during periods of tension and disequilibrium. Going to sleep from choice is a release act, a voluntary inhibition of the wakefulness center. It is like prehensory release.

The ability to release into sleep tends to be at its best during the recurrent periods of equilibrium when the muscles of flexion and extension and other opposing functions are in check and balance. Accordingly, the sixteen-week-old child releases smoothly into sleep. Even during his waking hours, as he lies in supine symmetry, he gives a picture of composure. He has come through a period, at eight to twelve weeks, when the growth tendency toward wakefulness was pronounced. He did not release so well: he may have needed some judicious soothing—through rocking, singing, or a light to gaze upon. (Of course, the soothing will not work unless it is so nicely adjusted that he himself contributes just the right amount of self-hypnosis, which is but another name for the function of release into sleep.)

DIFFICULTIES AND DEVIATIONS

It is in this same period from eight to twelve weeks that *thumb-sucking* has its onset. This sucking, as we shall see, is related to the control of feeding behavior as well as of sleep. When the linkage to feeding is primary, the sucking may run a short course. If, however, for personality or other reasons, it establishes its main linkage with sleep, it is likely to continue longer and the tie-up with sleep will become more rather than less tenacious. Being well grounded in the growth complex, it runs a longer course. It may have its onset at variable times throughout the first year. It tends to recede somewhat during periods of equilibrium. At twenty-eight weeks, for example, mouthing of objects may take its place. Sometimes it may come to a sharp termination, as though a developmental hurdle had been passed. This again suggests that a combination of personality and growth factors is at work. When the sucking is still strong after the first birthday, it tends to run a long but resolving course, vanishing anytime between two and five years. This type of pattern is not only related to sleep and hunger, but becomes a generalized tension outlet, utilized for escape and relaxation in situations of fatigue, embarrassment, frustration, fear, and also excitement.

Thumb-sucking in many reaches its peak between eighteen and twenty-one months, when some children will spend hours, busy with thumb in mouth, either alone or watching other children but not partaking in their activites. Between the ages of two and three years, the pattern begins to break. It is less absorbing. However, it is most tenaciously associated with sleep: it not only induces but it accompanies sleep. There is an exacerbation of intensity at two and a half years, but by three years in many it definitely begins to fade out during the day, and returns to its older linkage with hunger and sleepiness. The three-year-old tolerates removal of the thumb after he has fallen asleep (not so the two-year-old), but he sucks again when he wakes. At four years the sucking may occur only prior to sleep, a mere minute or two with the thumb sufficing for some. By six or after, the child is able to verbalize the situation and often will cooperate with his parents in any plan of action. If in the preschool years the habit has been associated with some accessory article such as a blanket or teddy bear, weaning can sometimes be encouraged by a well-timed removal of this object.

Thumb-sucking functions as a real component of the growth complex. The fact that in complicated cases it pursues a characteristic developmental course and undergoes spontaneous extinction suggests that artificial curbs and restraints have doubtful value. There is no conclusive evidence that thumb-sucking, if discontinued by the age of five or six years, has a permanent deforming effect upon dentition and occlusion.

A similar sucking behavior, which may be associated with sleep or may occur at any time during the day, is the sucking of a pacifier. Styles of thought with regard to the pacifier change with time. For the past several decades, pacifiers have been much frowned upon as being germy, as looking "funny," and as encouraging a perhaps undesirable sucking habit. In the last few years, public opinion has changed and nowadays many quite responsible parents do permit their use.

This brief recital illustrates that behavior deviations, as well as normal behavior traits, are subject to developmental sequences. A behavior deviation should always be considered and approached in terms of the total growth complex. This gives rationale to any corrective measures that are used. It overcomes the temptation to unwise "discipline."

Whether the thumb is sucked or not, the release into sleep presents ever-changing problems as the child matures. It is not a specific, press-the-button mechanism, which simply needs training and regularity. It is a complex communication system, which must be hooked up with a network of ever-changing higher controls. The sleep-release mechanism is not a thing apart.

On the whole, sleep release during the first year is relatively simple. The child is almost able to ask for sleep as he goes along. The mother knows exactly what he means by a certain querulous cry and wriggling at the age of forty weeks. He readily accepts being placed on his back in his welcome crib. Indeed, until about the age of twenty-one months, he tends to accept the whole bedtime situation as a matter of course. He contrives various presleep devices he may need to put himself to sleep. He takes one or two toys with him; he talks and sings to himself; he brandishes his hands before his eyes; he may even indulge in a brief workout wrestle with his bedclothes.

Rocking on hands and knees, and bed-shaking, are common forms of deviation. Head-banging and head-rolling also have their origin in this period from forty weeks to twenty-one months. They may run a transient course; they may be superseded or elaborated in the next growth period. However annoying they may be, it is apparent that they are but variants and exaggerations of normal methods of sleep release.

When an infant or child does rock, placing the crib on a deep-pile carpet away from the wall can at least control the noise. A postponement of bedtime to increase fatigue can also be a helpful measure. If the rocking persists into the second and third years, a dramatic termination may occur when the child is shifted from the accustomed crib to a new bed.

As the child approaches his second birthday, a new and important factor comes into the picture. It may exaggerate already deviant behavior. It is bound to complicate normal and ordinary behavior. The child is becoming more dependent on the adult.

Hitherto he has managed the sleep situation largely through his own resources. Now he relates himself to someone else at bedtime. We should, perhaps, be grateful for this new manifestation because it represents a growth in maturity. He is yet too young to go to bed "like a little man" and forget everyone else, including his mother. So he does not fall asleep so readily. He calls her back. He requests toileting. Sometimes the culture regards this as a clever ruse, a perverse form of filibustering; or as "stalling," which it thinks must be severely and arbitrarily handled. (Strict discipline has a way of becoming very arbitrary with young children.) Actually his presleep behavior is probably accompanied by a transitional instability in the control of the sphincters of the urinary system. Sphincter control, like sleep control, involves inhibitory and release mechanisms.

At the age of two and a half years, going-to-bed and going-to-sleep *rituals* are strong and elaborate. The young baby simply falls off to sleep; the young child walks a winding path along the precipice of wakefulness before *he* falls off to sleep. It is as though he had to pick his way, before he finds just the right spot for the plunge. Rituals must have some such rationale. They cannot be senseless, even though they become grotesquely extended in the deviating child who inveterately finds difficulty in making transitions. He may be overconscious of his mother in his ritualistic demands. It is often better for him as well as for her to have someone else put him to bed. He then has to modify his ritual, and in the process he can contract it. That is the guidance precept for rituals. Respect them, but by wise maneuvers, well timed and nicely modulated, restrict the area of the ritual. In time, it contracts to a vanishing point; it loses its vitality in the growth complex. Unwise combative measures, on the contrary, may lead to a deeper ramification of the ritual into the growth complex.

In ordinary and normal course, rituals are shed by processes of growth. They have a lighter hold after the age of three years. The four-year-old is usually ready for a change from crib to bed. The change is regarded as a social promotion. It is made the subject of advance planning and conversation. It connotes so much cultural prestige that the change may bring about a sharp termination of persistent bed-wetting. The five-year-old has his sleep behavior, as he has everything, better in hand. New developmental changes may be expected prior to and during adolescence.

It is probable that many sleep difficulties are man-made rather than child-made, and arise from overrigid methods of management. Primitive peoples have experimented with various methods of binding and cradling their infants to restrict mobility and to induce the distinctive immobility that goes by the familiar name of sleep. Modern cultures are engaged in similar experimentation, employing such gadgets as sleep harnesses or slumber bags. Sometimes the gadget works deceptively like a charm. The child becomes completely conditioned to the device. Another untamable youngster will rend it with the ferocity of a feral child. Yet another child becomes so conditioned that he cannot endure a single omission: he must have this man-made envelope, night in, night out, without exception, summer as well as winter. Such minor complications in very reasonable children show how complex and personalized sleep behavior has become in our culture.

Knowing so little about the mechanisms of sleep, we ought to pay more respect to the physiological self-demands for sleep, not only in infancy, but in early childhood. Half, and over half, of every behavior day is expended in sleep during the early years. It is important that science should further our insight into the determinations and modifiability of this engrossing, powerful function, which is so pervasively identified with the growth complex, with the organization of personality, and with the conventions of culture. The mounting tensions of civilization make this a fertile field for cultural control, because sleep is by nature an inhibitory adjustment—a beneficent terminator of tensions. With increased insight, daytime as well as night sleep will be brought under greater personal control and this will be accomplished during infancy and the preschool years.

Feeding

In the beginning of the baby's life there is much sleep; but also there is hunger. When sleep is deepest, respiration is regular, tonus relaxed, the body motionless. But on the least diminution of oxygen intake, breathing hastens, tonus tightens, muscles stir; for air hunger is the most fundamental of all hungers—and there are many hungers.

Food hunger comes next. This is so imperative that the total body posture alters: mouth opens, eyes open. Crying and seeking movements ensue. The baby wakes to eat, and he eats to sleep. But as we have already shown, in due season he wakes for other reasons; he also eats for other reasons. At first, food satiety alone suffices. His alimentary tract, invested with a mucous membrane over two thousand square centimeters in extent, affords him some inward glow to which he pays blissful attention. Somewhat before the age of eight weeks, his smile becomes less introverted. His sensorium is less completely alimentary: it includes vision and sound. His smile accordingly migrates from his alimentary tract to his mother's face; he may even vocalize with a quasi-gastric chuckle on her social approach. Thus horizons widen and the feeding situation proves to be a growth matrix out of which other forms of adaptive, language, and social behavior emerge as though they were so many branchings from a main stem. In truth, feeding behavior with its manifold ramifications constitutes a major network in the organization of mind and personality, throughout infancy and childhood. It lies at the core of the growth complex.

This network, in the early periods of development, is closely related to that of sleep behavior. The developmental factors that organize feeding behavior are not unlike those of sleep. The feeding pattern may be considered in three aspects as follows: (1) appetite; (2) retention; and (3) self-help and acculturation. Appetite is the first phase: the child must seek food and want it. Secondly, he must hold fast to it. This is the phase of retention. Originally, he is entirely dependent upon others for the satisfaction of his hungers, but he desires increasingly to become self-dependent, and the culture encourages him in this desire.

1. *Appetite.* Appetite lies at the basis of self-regulation. In Chapter 6, we have shown concretely how simple principles can be put into application in the first four months to initiate a good start for mother and child. The same principles apply throughout the period of childhood.

At first, the physiological impulsion behind growth is so intense that virtually all children, whether reared on the breast or on the bottle, after an initial adjustment, can make their hunger known. With time, sheer craving gives way to variations in appetite. Appetite varies in intensity within a behavior day. It also varies from age to age. It differentiates in manifold changes of food preferences. There is an almost inextricable mixture of maturity factors and individual equations.

Appetite is especially strong in the period from eight to twelve weeks—so strong that problems of retention, as we shall see later, begin to manifest themselves. Ordinarily, the infant's feeding behavior is well organized by sixteen weeks. He eats with moderate vigor: he retains well what he eats. His sucking ability is competent. His sucking propensity is so strong that it tends to interfere with the acceptance of solids at this time.

In the period from twenty to twenty-eight weeks, his appetite curve again shows irregularity. He demands an extra feeding, often in the early hours of the morning, but there is a decrease in the sucking demands, and he is able to adjust to solids before he takes the bottle or breast. At thirty-six weeks there is a noticeable increase of eagerness for food. His appetite is reinforced by the mere sight of the food in process of preparation. At forty weeks his appetite again comes to a high peak. He eats what is given to him, and he cleans his bowl. Between one and two years there is a decrease in vividness of appetite and in the amount of food taken at each meal.

After eighteen months appetite becomes more sophisticated. The two-year-old child begins to name foods; preferences define themselves; he indulges in special runs on foods that he fastens on; he is intrigued by certain colors; he shows bits of fastidiousness as to service; he likes to have his dishes match! By all these tokens, we can see that the food complex within the total growth complex is expanding, differentiating, and taking on environmental specifications. Brute appetite is being civilized through the culture. One hardly knows where appetite stops and acculturation begins. But from time to time, the child initiates food behavior which is so self-assertive that it seems to spring from the organism rather than the cultural milieu. He indulges in whims; he goes on food jags (Dr. Clara Davis reports a child who, on a self-selection regime, sometimes ate several eggs at one sitting, and went on an egg spree twice a year, in spring and fall!). He tries one food and then another; he adopts favorites, and normally he steadily widens his range of choice. He goes from milk and cereal to fruit and meat, to vegetables, to combinations and salads. The five-year-old has acquired a catholic appetite.

Such, in brief, is the course of a normally developing appetite. There is a sizable and diversified group of children who do not conform to this developmental pattern. Many of them have appeared in child guidance literature as the horrible consequences of poor management. It is quite possible that parents, in some instances, have been overcriticized. There is evidence that some children are constitutionally *poor feeders* by usual cultural standards. They are also under-weight, but their muscular tone is good; motor activity, motor coordination, and intelligence may be superior. They are often good sleepers as well.

The poor eater may manifest himself as early as twelve weeks. His intake is low per meal, and he rarely goes above a low limit; he does not show the ordinary fluctuations, but holds close to his low optimum. He may be a vomiter; he may or may not be a thumb-sucker. But his margin of tolerance is narrow. He insists rather orthodoxically on being fed the same food, the same way, in the same place, by the same person. He is slow in making a shift from food A to food B, and having accepted B, he may for a while reject A: he does not combine foods progressively in the ordinary manner. He clings long to purée (he distinguishes like a connoisseur between brand G and brand H). He is a poor chewer. He may not be allergic by clinical tests at the age of two or three, but proves to be so on tests made at a later age. This vaguely suggests a generalized preallergic status.

In any event, his behavior from year to year indicates a sluggish gastrointestinal equipment, or an equipment that has not been fully incorporated into the total action system. It is somewhat as though the latter and the former were developing in slightly separated streams. The dissociation, however, is not complete; and by one device or another, including some very dramatic accessories, the child is fed and grows up. At five or six years of age he may have outgrown much of his indifference. He is able to throw himself more fully into the task of eating.

But in the earlier years he eats abstractedly, almost unconsciously, while his caretaker may be amusing him with toys, books, pictures, and reading. Up to the age of two years, he eats best with his mother; thereafter, he may do better with someone else. More often a group is too much for him. He does not like to see others eat; he gags on slight provocation; he cannot abide the sight of slimy foods, etc.

To what extent these peculiarities of behavior are due to faulty management is by no means clear. When the difficulties are chiefly the result of constitutional factors, parents are well advised to respect the child's weakness in this particular field. They should not be too disturbed by periods of stationary weight. It is a mistake to over-stimulate the child. It is better to go along with him in his conservatisms, and to wait for an opportune moment to introduce a variation and to widen his diet. He should be handled through things and externals rather than through emotional appeals and dramatic diversions. If complicating personality factors are present, they should be reached by indirection and flank approach, but not through the feeding situation. One should be interested in the total growth complex rather than the specific behavior deviation. Although this deviation may cause enough household annoyance, it should be treated without excessive anxiety. Somewhat like thumb-sucking, it runs a developmental course, which is based on maturational, constitutional factors.

It is significant that appetite should be subject to so many developmental changes. If we knew all the factors that determine these changes, we would have a deepened insight, because they are related not only to caloric and dietary needs, but also to psychological traits. For that matter, the subtleties of body chemistry and child behavior are one.

2. *Retention.* Food must not only be sought and taken. It must be retained. Even this is not a simple matter. The gastrointestinal tract is more than a passive receptacle. Its walls are muscular and active. They move in rhythms and waves which must be coordinated, seriated in the right direction, and brought under partial voluntary control. These are retention problems which can be solved only through progressive developmental changes within the central and vegetative nervous systems.

There is a steady rise in intake up to the age of from eight to twelve weeks, which may reach a maximum of nearly forty-five ounces in one day. It seems that the organism has to stoke up for the exacting growth changes that are in progress. There is a tendency to overload. The alimentary tract does not handle its increased task smoothly. There is more gastric distress and passage of gas in both directions. Premature solids and cod liver oil fed to the infant at this time may exacerbate his difficulties. He regurgitates; he may even vomit, the vomiting, if due to neuromotor instability, being in the nature of an excessive deviation of regurgitating.

Intake and retention have to be balanced. Peristalsis has to be kept going in the right direction throughout the entire alimentary tract. The organism must also acquire the protective ability to reject and to regurgitate. This poses a definite developmental problem, which brings into prominence a group of infants who have a more or less inherently defective peristalsis control. These infants must be differentiated from those who vomit from birth because of partial closure of the pyloric end of the stomach—cases of pyloric stenosis and pylorospasm, which need medical treatment.

Some of the thumb-sucking at about the age of eight to twelve weeks seems to be more closely related to feeding than to sleep behavior. It is induced by hunger; it continues after the feeding, as though the child, for reasons of his developmental economy, needed additional sucking activity. Or the supplementary sucking may be a physiological device which keeps peristalsis moving in the right direction. It serves as an antivomit stimulus. He may continue to suck when hungry up to the age of about three years. Thereafter, the sucking is mainly linked to sleep.

In most infants, the early instability is limited to regurgitation and proves to be relatively transient. They usually settle into equilibrium at sixteen weeks, and are then even able to expel gastric gas without help. This new ability is evidence of stability. It means that the excessive expulsion tendency is coming under control. A favorable growth change has taken place.

In less favored cases, the vomiting recurs and may not terminate until six months or even until two years of age. In these cases, the principle of self-demand again shows its importance. Taking cues from the child, it becomes evident that he does better with a reduction in the number of feedings. He benefits from longer rest periods, which he uses to build up his retention. If young, he needs careful bubbling. He retains better if he is put in a semipropped position for an hour after his feeding. For similar reasons at twenty-four weeks or later, he may prefer to take his bottle in two stages. There is a physiological sanction for the split bottle: he is building up retention.

The tendency to vomiting may be based on a specific neuromotor susceptibility or on more generalized personality factors. In the latter case, vomiting at the age of four or five years may be used as a threat or as an act to dominate the environment. This is an infantile type of hunger strike, a kind of neurotic utilization. There are many grades and forms. Some individuals have a very effective and discriminating equipment for rejecting adverse food intake. They use their ability when it is really needed. They may be very stable persons.

Gastric instability tends to show itself also at about the age of three and a half years, often in connection with school situations. The first signs are those of abdominal pain which, at four years, may develop into frank vomiting. The child is unequal to the stress of transition to school. He reacts by a rejection or distaste response: he vomits. The reaction is not limited to the gastrointestinal tract, for step by step it invades the domain of personality: he vomits not only in the schoolroom; he vomits on the way to school; later he may even vomit at home on the mere mention of school. This type of vomiting seems to be rooted (if vomiting is ever rooted!) in a sense of insecurity. It often disappears very readily with a little moral support. The mother or a friend accompanies the child to the schoolroom door, or a neighborhood playmate is allowed to join the strange school group. Then all is suddenly well. The vomiting vanishes. Abdominal pain or vomiting, however, should always be regarded as a significant symptom, which demands and repays careful investigation, particularly of associated personality factors.

3. *Self-Help and Acculturation.* Although the alimentary tract is racially the oldest part of man's anatomy, it has always preserved a connection with his highest and most recent brain organization. The whole process of feeding is inseparably linked with his manners and customs. Feeding customs and mealtime mores constitute an important chapter in cultural anthropology.

It will be interesting to trace in outline how the infant writes himself into that chapter. We have already noted how his earliest smiles emerge out of satiety and lead to a lengthening of the waking period in a sequence as follows: sleeping–eating–satiety–smiling–sociality–wakefulness–drowsiness–sleep. Thus, from the beginning, the egocentric act of eating has, nevertheless, a socializing aspect. The socialization of the child is in large measure built around meals. Which, incidentally, makes one wonder whether it is culturally wise to shake a baby out of deep slumber in order to have him eat. It seems to violate the more amiable pattern of nature. One of the tasks of development is to dissociate sleeping and eating with an intervening smile.

The development of feeding behavior in the human infant is a story of progressive self-dependence combined with cultural conformance. The course of this development is not a smooth one. Eating utensils are complex; dining room decorums are exacting; and modern parents are often extraordinarily insistent on tidiness in table manners. Every household works out its own compromise in this task of accommodating the culture to the neurological and psychological limitations of the child. Needless to say, our practices would improve if we recognized these limitations in advance. Even weaning problems are greatly simplified if our procedures are not imposed arbitrarily but are adapted to the child's immaturity. Under favorable conditions, he weans himself into ever-increasing self-dependence. He does so in primitive tribes; he can do it in more complex cultures.

If bottle-fed, he begins to pat the bottle while he is sucking as early as twenty weeks. Transitions to solids are readily made now because the maturity of the nervous system so permits. At thirty-six weeks he can usually maintain a sustained hold of the bottle. In another month he may sit up and hold and tilt it with the skill of a cornetist. He can feed himself a cracker. At forty weeks he also begins to finger-feed, plucking small morsels. At one year his strong drive to stand interferes with the further refinement of sedentary eating habits. Wise mothers learn to accept these postural drives when they make their unmistakable appearance in the growth complex.

Upright posture, for the moment, is more than meat; and there is no difficulty in feeding him while he is in the standing position.

At this time, an independent child may, of his own initiative, refuse a bottle. He weans himself with dramatic suddenness. He does not shuffle off a coil, he casts it off. By simple and graduated devices, weaning from bottle to cup can be achieved without traumatic damage. A few children who show unusual attachment to the bottle continue with it as long as eighteen months to two years; in some cases still longer. Breast-feeding takes on a similar timetable of release, varying with the child. In general, however, breast-feeding tends to continue into the twelve-to-fifteen-month period if the child is allowed to choose his time.

By fifteen months he has "learned" to inhibit his former instinctive grasping of dish and tray. One of the first steps in the fine art of table manners is to resist grabbing the bowl that holds your porridge. This new inhibition is based not so much on practice as on a maturational change in the neuromotor connections of hand and brain. There is a pretty cultural corollary of this pattern of independence: the child insists that his mother should *not* put *her* hand on the tray. He also handles his spoon manfully and begins to feed himself in part, though not without spilling; for the spoon is a complex tool and he has not acquired the postural orientations and preperceptions necessary for dexterity.

This surge of independence is a growth phenomenon. It is, of course, counterbalanced by other trends. Indeed, a child who is assertive at fifteen months and feeds himself well for a year or two may then ask for help from his mother and accept spoon-feeding. At two years he inhibits the turning of the spoon as it enters the mouth and feeds himself very acceptably. However, the new ability is complex and only delicately supported by his nervous system. Therefore, he feeds himself best when he handles only part of the meal and the food that he particularly likes. Given too much range, he messes and mixes.

It is well to recognize how really difficult these complex acts of motor skill are in their early stages. The child's command of time, space, form, and order are correspondingly immature. If we had a clearer view of the growth complex at the moment, we would pay more attention to details of placement and service, we would see the value of simple arrangements and single courses. It may be a mistake to further complicate the child's tasks of coordination and adjustment by trying to assimilate him too soon into the mealtime family circle.

There are, however, two more or less clearly defined types of children who do not acquire self-help by the ordinary progressions. They are the *poor feeders* already discussed and the *perfectionists*. The poor feeder does not have a lusty gastrointestinal tract that is closely integrated with his personality. He therefore lacks the drive toward self-help, which normally comes from this source. The source is somewhat separated from his motivations. He therefore fails to show an interest in self-help.

The perfectionist also remains dependent. His self-help is retarded and awkward. Apparently he suffers from a diffuse or generalized motor insufficiency which gives him an excessive amount of caution and disinclination. He will not blunder; he will not undertake an act before he is quite sure of himself. He has an extraordinary sense of form, and sensitivity to incompleteness of form. He cannot abide untidiness. A spilled drop must be wiped up before he proceeds. He does not even finger-feed. He does not like sticky fingers! But he likes ice cream, and at the age of four or five years he can be inveigled into feeding himself this delicacy. By slow stages the self-feeding spreads to other foods, and his onlookers heave a sigh of relief.

Because the deepest and the most vital cravings of the infant and child have to do with food and sleep, his daily schedules of feeding and sleeping assume great psychological significance. We are too accustomed to think of these schedules from the narrow standpoint of physical regimen and to underrate their effects on mental welfare. Only by individualizing the regimen on the basis of growth needs can we meet his organic needs promptly and fully. By meeting them with certainty, we multiply those experiences of satisfied expectations which create an increasing sense of security, the first essential of mental health.

Bowel Control

The excretory functions are controlled by a complex combination of voluntary and involuntary mechanisms—and by cultural proprieties. These proprieties are expressed in customs, in strict taboos, and in repugnances colored by more or less intense emotion. Anthropological literature is replete with details showing how different peoples react to these natural functions. For a time, parents in this country tended to place excessive emphasis on early toilet training, euphemistically called "habit training."

Such habit training was based on the naïve theory that practice makes perfect, and that by beginning in time, the desired cleanliness can be established early. In its zeal the household often went to extremes in this particular field of acculturation. Punishment, bribes, shaming, scolding, and relentless instruction were resorted to, and yet the child did not learn. Was there some fault in the child? Or some weakness in the theory of habit formation?

Bowel control is in fact an extremely complicated function. The involuntary act of evacuation consists in peristaltic contractions of the colon, governed by the vegetative nervous system; but the voluntary delay and initiation of the act under variable conditions requires a marked degree of inhibition by the higher centers of the brain. This inhibition cannot be acquired by steady straight-line progression, by mere habit training, because the control of the bowel involves not only the sphincter muscles but the entire child as a total organism. Voluntary defecation is not a simple localized reaction but a total response; and the entire child changes from age to age. Therefore the total response is different from age to age, in its neurology, in its psychology.

This is the reason that cultural control is so difficult, cultural intervention so often misguided. Far from being a simple physiological reflex, bowel control is a complicated behavior pattern profoundly influenced by maturity factors.

The growth of patterns of bowel behavior, therefore, is marked by irregularities, by ups and downs, by self-regulatory fluctuations, comparable to those that characterize the early patterning of sleep and feeding. As the child matures there are changes in the frequency of bowel movements, in the times of occurrence, in promptness of release; in postural attitudes, in self and social reference, in perceptual interest, in anticipatory adjustments, and in the accompanying verbalizations. These changes, to say nothing of personality differences, are developmental in nature. To a significant extent they are beyond cultural prescription; yet they determine the difficulties, the failures, and the successes of so-called toilet training.

The acquisition of bowel control, therefore, must be interpreted in terms of growth and maturity, rather than from the narrow standpoint of habit and learning. The parent's (and the physician's) guidance should be shaped with reference to the developmental factors. The shortcomings of the young child cannot be regarded as perversities; often they are paradoxical but positive steps toward ultimate control. It is the discrepancy between the cultural pattern and the maturing behavior pattern which is at the root of maladjustment. The maladjustments are greatly reduced if the lawful developmental factors are recognized in advance. It is the purpose of the following summary to present these factors concretely in their time sequence and in dynamic perspective.

In the first few weeks bowel movements are extraordinarily numerous. They occur somewhat sporadically; but by *four weeks* they are more closely associated with the act of waking, as though they were emerging out of sheer vegetativeness and entering into the conscious life of the infant. They tend to occur in the daytime and their number falls to three or four daily. By *eight weeks* there may be only two movements and they come not only on waking but also at the close of a feeding and occasionally during a feeding. The infant gives visible evidence of attention, which suggests still more clearly that at least the sensory aspect of this behavior is coming within the scope of adaptive attention. In other words, even now the act is not purely automatic.

By *sixteen weeks* there may be a definite interval of delay between the feeding and the evacuation, as though nature were intent on making a more clear-cut distinction between eating and elimination. A vigilant mother may note this delay and may seize upon it.

But alas, this is the very transitional time when the baby is undergoing an almost revolutionary change in his postural-perceptual makeup. He is beginning to sit up, with support. The neat little "habit" of regularity, which he has just acquired, was suitable to a supine infant and no longer fits neatly into his new behavior equipment. So he "has to learn all over again." And that is precisely what he is constantly doing throughout the whole period of his rapid growth. Changes in his postural, prehensory, adaptive, and emotional behavior are reflected in changes in his bowel behavior. If he had remained on a twelve-to-sixteen-week level of maturity he would remain "trained."

At *twenty-eight weeks* his movements show temporary irregularity. They are no longer closely associated with waking or eating. One may occur early during the morning in the play period, another late in the afternoon. A few infants, chiefly girls, fuss when soiled; but most infants are indifferent and usually are resistant to "training."

By *forty weeks* the capacity to sit has been well mastered, and for a period of several weeks the infant responds to training; that is, he reacts adaptively to toilet placement. He grunts and looks up at the mother's face during the act; all of which means that the behavior pattern is undergoing progressive elaboration, and becoming more completely incorporated into the child's action system.

But by *one year* postural developments again introduce complications. "Successes" are less frequent; resistance again appears; the relation of looking at the mother also is lost. Some of these irregularities and apparent losses may be ascribed to the assumption of the upright posture. The irregularities occur because the nervous system is undergoing a reorganization which simultaneously has to take care of the several sphincter controls, the mastery of standing up, and obedience to cultural directions. If the various developments proceeded on an even front there would be no fluctuations, no necessity for interweaving with its alternating rhythms and accents.

By *fifteen months* standing upright is already well achieved and the irregularities and resistances lessen. The child now likes to go to the toilet. Some children of this age instinctively assume a squat position, as though they had just come by inheritance into an ancient pattern. On the toilet they often show prolonged sphincter contraction; they release this contraction on removal, as though waiting for the stimulus of the diaper. This again is a temporary phase, which reveals that the developmental task is to achieve a working balance between contraction and relaxation. Each at first comes under voluntary control separately. Coordination of the two comes later. First A, then B; then A:B::B:A.

By *eighteen months* contraction is sometimes too strong, at other times release is explosive. Words, also, are coming into the total behavior situation, and they play no mean part in personal and cultural control. The articulate child who is able to say "Toidy" and to relate it to the bowel movement thereby increases his voluntary control. This is the type of child who thenceforth may have few accidents. He is trained, because he has matured all the requisite components for a pattern which is at once personal and cultural.

A second type of child with the same amount of "training" is slow in "learning." He does not use words as aptly. He is more interested in sounds and nonessentials. He does not fasten on the salient features of process and product. He has to progress by more intimate and direct experience. He may even dabble with the feces. Occasional episodes of "stool-smearing" have their inception in this circumstance. He does not relate the act to a social setting; he does not relate it to his mother. He relates it to his own taking care of himself. He is likely to have his movement in midmorning while he is alone, standing in his crib or playpen. Occasionally he may cry out in distress as though he did not know what it is all about. There may be a simple guilt sense, but we are inclined to ascribe such symptoms to a combination of physiological and personal awkwardness.

At *twenty-one* months there may be a transient period of physiological lability manifested in a form of diarrhea which is not traceable to mucoid irritation. During the same period there may be a marked increase in the frequency of urination. This suggests another transitional stage during which higher nervous controls are being incorporated.

The *two-year-old* is often quite trainable if he is permitted to take over himself. The parent removes the child's pants and then leaves him to his own devices. Some children manage best when divested of all clothes. This freedom apparently favors a more totalized response.

At the paradoxical age of *two and a half years,* the child naturally shows a tendency to extremes and exaggeration. At this period he may not have a bowel movement for a whole day or a succession of two days. The organism is acquiring an increased span of retention, but in so doing it temporarily exaggerates a constructive growth trend. Fruit laxatives are a legitimate cultural aid.

By the *age of three* there is an increased ability to withhold and to postpone. The daily bowel movement tends to occur in late afternoon or even after supper. The child accepts and even asks for cultural help.

By the *age of four* this function has become a private affair. The child manages almost completely for himself. He insists on a closed bathroom door, but is inquisitive to ascertain how this function occurs in others. He has curiosity about animal behavior and is somewhat perplexed by their indifference to the conventions of human culture. He has a childlike interest in volume, color, consistency, and conformation. This interest is wholesome and intelligent, not immodest. In all his aspects the four-year-old is a frank, forthright individual. In spite of his independent competence, he may occasionally have an accident, by way of tension outlet under excitement or strain.

Training for bowel control goes reasonably well in most children, and by three or four this area of behavior is usually taken for granted. The exception is that troublesome sort of child, usually a boy, who seems to be making no progress whatever toward having his bowel movements while on the toilet.

Once you have checked with your pediatrician and ruled out any physical reason for the delay, we recommend permitting such a child to play in the bathroom, with his pants off, at about the time you expect him to function. (If his functioning has not yet settled down to any particular time of day, you will just have to admit that you still have a long way to go.)

Put a newspaper on the floor in a corner of the room, and tell the child that when he is ready to function he may use the paper. Often he is able to get this far in just a few days—a few weeks at most. Once he has succeeded with this, it is often just a small step to get him to use a potty. From there to the adult-size toilet is usually fairly easy.

Slight incontinence occurs at six years of age under the stress of school life. By this time the child has become a member of a social group ready to cast aspersion on any member who shows lapses in the field of elimination behavior.

Culture has put opprobrium on any weakness of this kind, and yet in the phrase "intestinal fortitude" it makes half-humorous acknowledgment of a human frailty. The fact that under excessive strain even the adult may show such frailty should make us more sympathetic to the developmental difficulties of the young child.

The foregoing developmental survey is not intended either to overstate or to minimize these difficulties, but admittedly many of the disappointments and the emotional tensions that parents encounter in toilet training are self-afflicted. If the complexity of the growth mechanisms involved is recognized, the tensions subside and the child is spared unnecessary confusions.

Although the developmental sequences that have been outlined are typical, they will naturally be modified by individual differences in psychic constitution. Occasional and transient stool exploitation (stool-smearing) has already been mentioned as one deviation. It may occur at any age from one to two and a half years. It may occur once or twice, intermittently, or in some instances two or three times a day. It usually originates in a clumsy effort at self-care; it may have the novelty of self-discovery and the stool is naïvely exploited as though it were so much plasticine; it may even be neatly disposed on the door trimmings with some respect for design.

When the propensity is unduly prolonged and does not yield to common-sense measures, it may be regarded as a symptom of poor personality organization. The child is functioning in a fragmentary way and is not assimilating his toilet behavior into an integrating action system. He does not have a sufficiently vigorous sense of self when he is alone to subordinate this, to him, interesting and half-autonomous behavior. Significantly enough, when he is with another person he does not indulge in this behavior.

The more frequent and milder manifestations of this malbehavior are readily overcome by providing plasticine for exploitation, by dressing the child in impervious coveralls, and by encouraging self-management by slow degrees. Needless to say, marked emotions and severe disciplinary measures harm rather than help.

In the whole task of toilet acculturation parents are in danger of expending too much emotion and too little wise tolerance. When we take a long-range view of the underlying developmental mechanisms, we immediately see the child's growth problems in a more rational light. That is the basis of intelligent guidance.

Bladder Control

The mechanisms which govern the bladder are comparable to those which govern the bowel. In both instances we are dealing with an involuntary mechanism, into which voluntary control is incorporated through the slow and devious processes of development. The vegetative nervous system and the higher brain centers are coordinated to bring about this control. An extremely elaborate network of nerve cell connections must be built up during the first five years of life. And even then the controls are not perfected; growth continues through adolescence, and the bladder walls and sphincter always remain very sensitive to the psychical activities of the individual, whether in infancy, childhood or adult years. The bladder is a component of the genitourinary system and inseparable from the total organism. Voluntary urination is not a simple local reaction, but a total response of a total organism which is subject to the manifold changes of growth and maturity. These changes are reflected in times and modes of elimination, in postural attitudes, in motor and verbal adjustments, and in psychological orientations.

The acquisition of bladder control, therefore, is marked by the same variabilities, the same ups and downs and regulatory fluctuations that we have noted in tracing the development of bowel control. Indeed, our studies have demonstrated a significant correspondence in the growth of these two functions from age to age. There is almost a parallelism which is based upon common, coinciding maturity factors. Naturally the guidance and "training" procedures will also have much in common.

At about *four weeks* of age the infant may burst into a brief cry during sleep on the occurrence of micturition. It is as though the passage of the urine and the consequent wetness punctured the unconsciousness of sleep with a glimmer of wakefulness. The infant must learn to wake, and these early experiences in bladder and bowel response may represent faint acts of attention. Indeed, the whole development of voluntary bladder control consists in the formation of increasingly specific and elaborate patterns of attention.

By *sixteen weeks* the number of daily micturitions has decreased and the volume of certain micturitions has definitely increased. Nature is channelizing the output by the same developmental methods whereby she channelizes and consolidates the baby's naps.

At *twenty-eight weeks* this is evidenced by soaking-wet diapers. Intervals of dryness from one to two hours in length now occur.

At *forty weeks* it may be noted that the baby is dry for a whole hour after a given nap or after an hour's ride in his carriage. Capitalizing on the import of these dry periods, the mother may toilet-place him immediately after the nap or the ride. A few children can be "trained" in this way as early as twenty-eight weeks. But the control is limited to one or two episodes during the day, and is subject to lapses. The results are not permanent or deep-seated and they do more credit to the mother's vigilance than to the baby's self-control. They are not permanent because the new postural abilities create new complications, which require further reorganization of his total behavior equipment. It must always be remembered that a single function such as bladder control, feeding, or sleep is always part of an ever-changing growth complex; and that any individual function or "habit" is inevitably modified by ever-changing contexts. Habits do not grow. The child grows.

As he grows he acquires experiences that direct his further growth. At forty weeks and later, it will be recalled, his index finger becomes a prying instrument for exploring his environment and for penetrating into the third dimension. Accordingly he probes on occasion into urine that he has produced. Although he does this only a few times, it helps him toward an understanding of what is actually a complex situation.

At *one year* dryness after naps may persist. He may show intolerance of wetness at certain times of the day. Often he responds to toilet placement, and would appear to be a good candidate for training; but the development of standing and walking apparently introduces difficulties and resistances. Past learnings prove ephemeral.

At *fifteen months* postural difficulties have lessened. He likes to sit on the toilet, and responds at optimal times. But at other times he resists. This is because he is in a transitional stage in which contraction of the sphincters of the bladder eclipses relaxation. His retention span has lengthened to two or three hours. Placement on the toilet may stimulate him to withhold urine. He exercises this capacity while he sits. The moment he is removed, he promptly releases urine. This is a common household phenomenon. The mother, unaware of the growth factors at work, interprets the whole performance as willfulness. If exasperated she may resort to unwise discipline. It should be recalled that the same type of behavior shows itself in bowel situations. This also is the time when the child has not yet gained modulated control of manual release. Having seized an object, he may hold it in his hand and "let go" with exaggerated release. It takes time for the nervous system to attain smoothly working balances in its inner machinery.

But all the time he is widening the basis for ultimate control. He is just learning to talk and he promptly brings speech into the expanding behavior pattern. He points, not without pride, at a puddle and says, "uh, uh" or "See!" He uses the same word ("uh") indifferently for the product of bowel or bladder. Not until some months later will he make a distinction. By way of further verification, he sometimes pats the puddle. Patting is characteristic of this age of maturity; he pats his picture book in the same manner. There is nothing portentous in this passing exploitation. (It is obvious from the foregoing description that the use of training pants would possibly be premature. The present trend is to wait until the child shows more spontaneous readiness.)

Language assumes an increased role at *eighteen months*. If he is asked whether he needs to go to the toilet, the child can respond with a discriminating nod of his head or a "No." Using his recently acquired word "uh," he can even occasionally ask in advance. Words that are rooted in the child's own experience are instruments of control. He is becoming susceptible to "shaming." He understands when he is asked to get a cloth to wipe up a puddle. He goes on the errand with alacrity. At this age, in contrast to his fifteen-months response of overcontraction, he now may respond with explosive overrelease to toilet placement. He may also report any "accidents."

At *twenty-one months*, likewise, his natural tendency is to report, unless he has been unwisely spanked. Such reporting is part of the learning-growing process. He reports or announces not only after but occasionally before. He tells. He is greatly pleased with his successes.

The developmental pendulum is swinging from the contraction phase (withholding) to a relaxation phase. The number of urinations greatly increases. Lapses multiply; and the child calls his mother back frequently after he has been put to bed. To the head of the family it all looks like sheer backsliding. This is the time when father steps in and applies stern punishment. And of all times, this is the worst; for the child is in the midst of a constructive growth transition during which he is bringing the opposing functions of sphincter contraction and relaxation into more stable balance (A:B::B:A).

By the age of two years these functions are in better equilibrium. The *two-year-old* therefore shows a definite advance in control. He offers no resistance to routine toilet placements. He definitely tells in advance. He may go to the bathroom by himself and pull his pants down. He expresses pride in achievement, saying, "Good boy." He is beginning to differentiate between products of bowel and bladder by whatever onomatopoeic term or slang the household has adopted. But he is not overprecise—he may call a puddle "Bad boy!"

In spite of the definite gains in voluntary control, night fluctuations persist. If the developmental pattern is one of quick shifting, he may be dry for two nights, then wet, then dry again for two nights. Or if he is a "slow shifter," the fluctuating intervals may be two weeks long. These fluctuations themselves are part of a yet further consolidation of gains.

The retention span is lengthening. It may stretch to five or more hours by the age of *two and a half years*. This is the period when the contraction of both the bowel and the bladder sphincters is in the ascendancy. Girls, who in general are ahead of boys in sphincter control, may wake up dry even after relatively long naps. The child is now learning to stop and to resume in the midst of a micturition. This is a new elaboration. However, he still has difficulty in initiating release; he is dependent on the conditioning circumstances of his own bathroom and cannot command his emerging abilities in strange surroundings. He may need verbal props from his mother. But he is consistently advancing; he is more sophisticated, he watches with great interest the elimination behavior of others, including animals.

The *three-year-old*, as we have so often observed, is in focus. Accordingly he is well routinized in his bladder functions. He accepts assistance. Accidents are infrequent. He demands to be changed if they occur. Some three-year-olds sleep dry throughout the night; some even wake up by themselves and ask to be taken to the toilet. Others can be taken up for toileting without being roused out of sleep.

The *four-year-old* likewise remains routinized, but he more or less insists on taking over the routine himself. He makes it a private affair, behind closed doors, although he is frankly inquisitive about the same affair in others. He also displays an almost amusing degree of interest in strange bathrooms. This, after all, is a natural growth symptom. At two years he was resistant to or even fearful of strange bathrooms and unaccustomed plumbing.

Although the four-year-old is blithely self-reliant, he makes errors of judgment, due to his immature time sense and the low threshold of his voluntary control. The result is that he is often caught in predicaments which produce panicky dismay. The culture might well spare him some of these unpleasant experiences by more thoughtful planning.

The *five-year-old* again shows more aplomb. He does not feel the same childish interest in novel bathrooms; he takes them as a matter of course. He is not so subject to surprise and tension outlets. He sleeps dry; and if he rises at night he can take care of himself. His thresholds are higher; he is not as likely as the four-year-old to suffer lapses with the onset of a cold or the beginning of cold weather.

Ordinary individual differences and deviations in the acquisition of bladder control are correlated with constitutional differences in thresholds and in modes of growth. The developmental sequences, outlined above, are grounded in the architectonics of the nervous system and therefore should prove useful in interpreting individual deviations. Maturation of the nervous structures does not always advance at an even pace, or one component lags while another goes forward. Some children seem discouragingly slow in training, but on some fine day, perhaps under the stroke of a stimulating personal event, a missing connection is shunted in and control is achieved with dramatic suddenness. Something has been added; maturation had taken place after all. Having "clicked," these children usually stay controlled.

In other children, control is not so durable. The physiological threshold of their urinary system is low and the tensions of even slight vicissitudes find their outlet through this system. The wriggling and susceptibility that is normal enough in a four-year-old when he is excited persists into the later school years. These children develop various forms of wetting, which should be distinguished from the serious degrees of clinical enuresis. Simple physiological awkwardness should be considered, before ascribing the weakness to more profound personality disorders.

So far as night dryness goes, we find great variation from one child to another. Some children stay dry, almost as a matter of course, by three or four years of age. Many others are dry by five. However, some children, perfectly normal in all important respects, do continue to wet their beds till they are six, seven, and eight years of age or even later.

Since individual variation is so very marked, we prefer not to step in with admonition or interference in the first six or even seven years of life. It may be best all around to wait, since normally a full bladder will cause a child over the age of four, five, or six (depending on how rapidly he is developing) to wake and go to the bathroom before he starts wetting.

But in some children the simple message that the bladder is about to be emptied is not relayed to the brain. The child seems unaware of what is going to happen, stays asleep, and wets his bed. If you have waited till your child is six or seven, and he has not managed dryness at night, and if you have checked with your pediatrician to be sure that nothing is physically wrong, you may be well advised to get hold of one of the many good conditioning devices* now on the market.

These devices are simple in structure, and work on a well-known principle based on the findings of Pavlov, the Russian psychologist, who discovered that if he showed a dog a piece of meat and rang a bell at the same time, the dog would eventually salivate at the sound of the bell alone. Thus if it can be arranged, and it can be, that whenever the child's bladder is full a buzzer rings so that he does wake, he will gradually become conditioned so that he does not need the sound of the bell to wake him. A full bladder will suffice.

A basic device consists primarily of a sheet that has been treated

---

* If your local medical supply house cannot furnish one, you may write directly to the Dry-o-matic Company, 1055 Nadine, Huntington Woods, Michigan 48070; to Uritrol, J. G. Shuman Associates, Box 306, Scotch Plains, New Jersey 07076; or to Astric Dry-Beds, 3889 West 31st Avenue, Vancouver 8, B. C., Canada.

in such a way that even a few drops of urine will set up a short circuit and cause a warning bell or buzzer to ring.

Actually the whole problem of bladder control is so charged with developmental factors in normal as well as deviated children that those factors should have primary consideration both in interpretation and in treatment. All things considered, it seems that our modern culture still has much to learn from the child himself in this delicate sphere of personal-social behavior. The culture is inclined to be too meddlesome and too emotional. We would not advocate more neglect, although this would often be less harmful because it would give the wisdom of nature a fuller scope. What we need, rather than neglect, is timely help with a light rather than a heavy hand; and above all with a discerning hand. But how can the hand be deft or discerning without a knowledge of the ways of development?

Personal and Sex Interests

Under this heading we consider a group of problems that concern a very personal aspect of the development of the individual. The problems are complex but a simple factual statement of the sequences of development as observed in actual children should help to put them in their true light. They are not as portentous as they may seem.

The problems of personal and sex interests in infant and young child are, after all, not essentially different from those that have already been discussed. The principles of development and guidance that apply to sleep, feeding, and elimination apply in precisely the same manner to the patterning of personal and sex behavior. There are no special or unique laws for the organization of emotions. Indeed, so integrated and unified are the processes of psychological growth that an intelligent management of feeding, sleep, and elimination behavior in itself almost ensures a favorable organization of other fields of behavior. The problems of so-called sex hygiene may be approached with confidence, and without an undue sense of mystery.

The newborn infant has no personality problems. He is so deeply immersed in the cosmos and in the culture which has accepted him that in his nonage he neither needs nor craves a clear sense of self-identity. But as he grows up he must disengage himself from this universality and become a well-defined individual. By the time he is five or six years old he must see himself for what he is. There are many stepping stones along the way—articulate and inarticulate. Here are some of them:

Johnny—that's me. . . . I am I. . . . That is my mother. . . . That is my father. . . . He is a man. . . . I am a boy. . . . Susan is a girl. . . . She has a father and mother, too. . . . I was a baby. . . . I grew. . . . I came from my mother. . . . I am going to get bigger. . . . I am going to go to school. . . .

These thirteen propositions cumulatively create the outlook of a school beginner. They make a logical sequence, but they are by no means automatic axioms. They are complicated judgments which the young child has to achieve through the slow and steady processes of growth, aided by experience, which sometimes is bitter. Each successive proposition represents one more step in a progressive differentiation that disengages him more fully from the culture in which he is so deeply involved. Paradoxically this very disengagement also identifies him more fully with his culture; he transforms from a mere ward to a working member.

The process of disengagement entails a continuous reorganization of his emotions. He is "attached" to his mother, to his father, to the household. He feels this attachment vividly when fatigue or helplessness causes him to seek comfort and refuge. Affection has its root in such dependency and protectiveness. But he also feels detachment, particularly when he exercises some new power that gives him a sense of independence. He is driven, as it were, toward two opposite poles: to cling to safety and to emancipate himself from its restrictions. He must at least have enough defiance to grow. Normal emotional growth requires a proper balance of affection and of self-reliance.

But, as already suggested, his developmental task is not simply emotional; he must achieve judgments as to his place in the social scheme, he must identify himself as one kind of person, his mother as another kind, his father as still another kind. He must distinguish between parent and child, between male and female, between senior and junior, between conformance and defiance. *These judgments, although strongly tinged with personal emotions, are essentially intellectual. They require perception, discrimination, and intelligence.* It is this part of the story that needs emphasis, for here lies the key to understanding and successful guidance.

At *four weeks* of age the baby's face is generally impassive. By *eight weeks* it breaks into a spontaneous social smile at the sight of another person's face. Whether at that moment he is more conscious of his interior smile or of the external face might be debated. In any event, this double reference is at the basis of the child's socialization and personalization. At *sixteen weeks* the social smile is spontaneous or self-induced.

By *twenty-eight weeks* he already reacts differently to a stranger's face. This discrimination shows that the development of complex personal perceptions is already under way. He has already made an elementary distinction—a personal-social judgment.

By *forty weeks* or a year he has made significant advances in self-discovery. Whether he is sitting up or lying down, his arms and hands now have more freedom of movement, and he uses them to explore his own physical self. At sixteen weeks they were at his mouth; at twenty weeks they engaged above his chest. Following the head-to-foot trend which is characteristic of development, the hands at forty weeks (and later) come down to the thighs. Just as he used to indulge in mutual fingering, he now makes contact with his genitals when not clothed. Ordinarily his exploitive manipulation is a more or less transient event in the course of his physical self-discovery.

In the period from *one to two years* there is an increasing amount of social reference. Although the infant-child is capable of long stretches of self-absorbed activity, he is also given to numerous social advances, which are the charm of this age period. He extends a toy to a person; he holds out his arm for the sleeve; he says "ta-ta"; he hands an empty cereal dish to his mother; he tugs at her skirt to bring her to an object of interest; he asks for food, drink, and toilet; he echoes back the last two words of conversation. By all these tokens and devices, he builds up a vast body of specific perceptual experience which ultimately enables him to draw the momentous conclusion that there are other persons in the world more or less like himself. The urge to discover these persons is a growth phenomenon. It shows itself in various personal and sex interests which follow in natural sequence.

This discovery of other persons is of such great magnitude that it must come piecemeal, and gradually, otherwise he might be overwhelmed. Even so, he seeks increased refuge in giving and receiving affection. He is willing to be called "darling"; he will spurn it later. He is willing to be held by the hand; he will refuse it later. He likes to nestle on occasion in his mother's lap. (She may remember this period as the time when he used to be so much more affectionate than he is now!) The stern fact is that affection is related to the varying balances of security and insecurity. For example, at eighteen months he seeks and shows affection when he suffers from the physical (and mental?) discomfort of having wet himself. At about twenty-one months he grows more tender toward the end of the day. He expresses affection by kissing, particularly at bedtime. Children are affectionate by nature, but the amount, the times, and the depths of their affection vary with the necessities of development. Affection is not a diffuse, general trait, but it is a structured network of attitudes, shaped within a total growth complex. We must be prepared to see changes in its structure as the child matures.

Two years is a transitional period when the child both clings to moorings and cuts from them. Johnny is his name, and in his inarticulate psychology, the spoken word "Johnny" which he hears is nothing more or less than he himself! His name *is* Johnny as a person.

He will soon use the pronouns "you," "me," and "I"—a further indication of a fundamental change in the psychology of his self. But he still refers to himself by name (Johnny) rather than pronoun, and if one wishes to secure his *personal* attention it is advisable to address him by "Johnny" rather than "You." All of which proves our thesis that we are dealing with a complicated growth process—the growth of intricate perceptions.

The two-year-old thinks that all the world is peopled with "mommies" and "daddies" and that all the children are "babies." This flight of generalization does him no little credit but he has much more to learn. He has to differentiate between *the* mommy and *a* mommy. He also has to make a sharper distinction between his mother and his father. In the natural course of household events he has observed differences in their clothing and their methods of toileting. His early distinctions of sex are based on dress, hair style, and possibly voice.

At about the age of *two and a half years*, having acquired more comprehension of his own urinary functions, he is interested in the difference between boys and girls in their mode of micturition. This might be called a genitourinary interest, because that is the point of departure, and it leads to a new awareness of genitalia in self and others.

Now the keenness and suddenness of that awareness will depend upon several factors: the age and sex of the child; the child's temperament; the presence or absence of brothers and sisters; the bathroom and beach folkways of the household in which he is reared. These folkways vary tremendously in our American culture, from extreme modesty and deception to undiscriminating lack of reserve. The latter can scarcely be recommended from the standpoint of the guidance of growth. If the parents note undue interest and extreme awareness at this age, it is wise to graduate the experiences of the child to his capacity to assimilate them. It is not a question of concealment, but of common-sense adjustment, particularly to the needs of oversensitive or oversusceptible children.

The two-and-a-half-year-old child has a more vigorous sense of self.

He says, "*I* want"; "*I* need." He is negative as well as positive. He says, "I don't like." He can state his own sex by negation: "No, I'm not a girl."

This is an age at which the organism is in sensitive equilibrium. Nature must check and countercheck. If his sense of *I* and his will to power waxed too strong, he would go off on a developmental tangent. Besides, his sense of *I* needs content. A full sense of *I*-ness demands an appreciation of the biographic *I* in which the present two-and-a-half-year-old *I* had its origin. Accordingly he becomes spontaneously interested in his own infancy. Nature provides for his instruction in a charming way. She has this budding child relive his babyhood. Through question and answer, pictures and stories, he is enabled to relive in short scenes and acts the infantile parts which once he played. For even he has a past. The revival of that past consolidates his sense of self, gives it substance, and even flatters it with a feeling of superiority; for he is no longer a baby like that!

Such reliving seems to us not a backwash of regression, but a method of growth. It takes on ominous import only in the oversensitized child who lingers too long in the retrospect, and whose constitutional style of growth is so deviated that he shows similarly faulty mechanisms along the whole course of maturing. It is not abnormal for a child, say, thirty-three months old to wish to be carried as though he were a baby. It is a passing phase, part of the dramatic recapture of the infancy now being superseded.

Even by the age of *three years* the child has attained a well-balanced sense of self. He has no marked preference for either sex, although earlier he may have shown a fixation upon one sex in a manner suggestive of a possible temperamental trend. He knows his own sex with assurance. His interest in human anatomy remains strong; he talks freely and naturally about differences which he has observed. He has a rather catholic although fragmented interest in the structure of family life. He wants a baby in somewhat the same way in which he wants a tricycle.

By the age of *three and a half years* questions about marriage begin.

Both boys and girls show an intellectual interest in brides. (Bride-grooms and fathers scarcely figure at all in the marital interests of the next few years!) Weddings are vaguely explored in questions and dramatic play. Children, more or less regardless of sex, propose marriage to their fathers and mothers.

An articulate child of three or so may ask where he was before he was born. He may ask other questions that seem to bear very profoundly on the origin of babies. In reality the questions are usually not deep. Extremely simple answers satisfy his rather fragmentary curiosity. His mind has just thrown out a pseudopod; he is not absorbed in the eternal verities. He wants an answer that makes sense for *him* and not for you. To find out what makes sense for him, counter with a few naïve questions of your own. His naïve answers will indicate how you may shape your replies. You are guiding his growth. This is not the time to get out a picture book on Life and its Origin, which "explains" the whole story from Genesis to Exodus.

Even the blithe and boisterous *four-year-old* is none too ready for complete information. On occasion, with bravado, he would like to be a man of the world; but he really is still closely bound to his mother. He cites her as authority in cases of dispute. *My* mommy says so! He will, therefore, believe her if she tells him how babies are born; but for the time being he might almost prefer to compromise on the fiction that the baby was bought at the hospital, and that it cost money (which lessens the fiction!).

At any rate, the four-year-old may well not be ready for the whole story of reproduction. He has, nevertheless, some interest in growth, including the period of prenatal growth. He likes to weigh and measure himself and by dramatic gesticulation to boast how he is getting bigger and bigger.

Indeed, the mental organization of the four-year-old is somewhat fluid. He is quite likely to worry about how the baby "gets out." He may spontaneously decide it is through the navel. The navel is an enigma to him, and may become the focus of his modesty and secretiveness. If he is given to exposure, it is the navel, as well as the genitals, that he exposes. His urinary function, it will be recalled, tends to show some instability. Under the excitement of being in a strange house, he asks to go to the toilet. Under stress he tends to grasp his genitals. The urogenital system is a frequent tension outlet at this age.

Between *five and six years* the child again comes into developmental equilibrium and focus as he did at three years. He does so at a more sophisticated level. He has lost some of the sophomoric traits of four-year-oldness, and has more sense of status and propriety. He has a better appreciation of the folkways of culture. He shows the conservatism of youth in deferring to them, and citing them to his parents for their consideration. He does not want to be different from humanity. Boys and girls alike at this age talk freely about having babies of their own (without making any reference to marriage or the father's role). They also ask their parents directly for a brother or a sister.

And so the spiral once more comes to a full turn. By slow and not altogether painless stages the five-year-old has achieved the thirteen sequential judgments that register his cultural maturity. He has even foreshadowed a fourteenth judgment, which vaguely prophesies that when he grows up he will be a parent as once he was a baby.

There are a few children who show a strange lack of interest in life origins and in sex, even at the age of seven or eight years. Wise parents may plan simple circumstances that will bring the interest into focus; but the interest cannot be imparted. The impulse must come from within the child.

The greatest source of serious deviations in this field of personal-social behavior is the oversensitive child in combination with an overzealous parent. This leads to overawareness on both sides. The patience and moderation of a normal developmental tempo are sacrificed for the purpose of outwitting development. The policy of excessive, ill-timed frankness may create difficulties instead of solving them.

A tabular summary of the sequences of development that have just been presented is given on the following pages. The sequences are listed in two parallel columns to emphasize the close correspondences between the growth of the sense of self and the growth of an understanding of sex and reproduction. Both involve a process of self-discovery, in which the child relates what he perceives in others to what he knows concerning his own self. At first his identification may be limited to hands and face. Later it takes its departure from the organs and functions of elimination and reproduction. The information in the comparative growth table may help you to determine how much your child is ready to understand at any given stage of his development.

Parents often feel anxious and insecure when faced with the problem of telling their child about sex. It is important to keep in mind that you do not have to give this information all at once. The child's first questions are simple and easy to answer. You *do* know the answers. And his curiosity as a rule does not go very deep.

It is important in giving information not to give too much. Answer the child's questions as he asks them, but do not pursue the subject unless his questioning continues. And try not to feel embarrassed. Your child will not be.

Typical of the average child's matter-of-factness about sex is the answer one five-year-old girl gave to a friend who asked her, "Are you old enough to have a baby?" "Goodness, no," replied the little girl. "I can't even tell time yet."

So be calm, answer questions when they are asked, but do not try to tell it all at once. At the same time, realize that you are not giving information once and for all. The child may ask, seem to absorb your answer, and ask again later on.

COMPARATIVE GROWTH SEQUENCES

Self	*Sex*

8 Weeks

Social smile at sight of another person's face

Genital erection is common in boys even from birth.

12 Weeks

Regards own hand
Vocal social response
Knows mother and recognizes her
Enjoys evening play with father

16 Weeks

Fingers his own fingers
Spontaneous social smile

20 Weeks

Smiles at mirror image
Cries when someone leaves him

24 Weeks

Smiles and vocalizes at mirror image
Discriminates strangers

28 Weeks

Grasps his feet
Pats mirror image

32 Weeks

Withdraws from strangers

36 Weeks

Responds to his own name

40 Weeks

Waves bye-bye and pat-a-cakes

44 Weeks

Extends object to person without release

Again withdraws from strangers

52 Weeks

Gives object to another on request

18 Months

Hugs and shows affection toward doll or teddy bear

21 Months

Calls all other children "baby"

2 Years

Can call himself by his own name

Calls all men and women "mommies" and "daddies"

27 Months

Says "I want"

30 Months

Calls self "I" and has an increasing sense of "I," especially in relation to immediate abilities

Defines his sense of "I" by his very imperiousness

Calls other people "you"

A few, who have a slowly developing awareness of self, confuse "I" and "you"

Calls women "lady" and men "man" as distinguished from mommy and daddy

40–52 Weeks

When clothes are off, handles genitals. This may be the onset of masturbation.

When urinating, girls look at their mothers and smile

Fusses to be changed when wet or soiled

18 Months

Affectionate toward mother when tired, in trouble, or if pants are wet

No verbal distinction between boys and girls

2 Years

Kisses at bedtime

Unable to function in strange bathrooms

Distinguishes boys from girls by clothes and style of haircut

30 Months

Conscious of own sex organs and may handle them when clothes are off

Interested in watching others in bathroom or when they are undressed

Distinguishes boys from girls by different postures when urinating. Notices these differences but does not verbalize them

Beginning of interest in physiological differences between the sexes

30 Months (con't)

Calls other children "boys" and
  "girls"
Knows he is a boy, like father,
  and that he is different from girls
  and mothers (and vice versa)
Says "I need," "I don't like"

Inquires about mother's breasts
Nonverbalized generalization that
  boys and fathers have a distinctive genital and stand when they
  urinate; girls and mothers do not

33 Months

Relives his babyhood verbally.
  May even want to be a baby

3 Years

Sense of "I" increasing
Combines self with another in
  use of "we"
Can tell difference between boys
  and girls but makes no distinction in his play
Says "I like"

3 Years

Verbally expressed interest in
  physiological differences between the sexes and in different
  postures for urinating
Girls make one or two experimental attempts to urinate standing
  up
Desire to look at or touch adults,
  especially mother's breasts
Expresses a general interest in
  babies and wants the family to
  have one
Asks questions about babies: what
  can the baby do when it comes;
  where does it come from; where
  is it before it was born?
May not understand answers
  mother gives that babies grow inside the mother
Asks where he was himself before
  he was born

42 Months

Beginning of temporary attach-
  ments to some one playmate,
  often of the opposite sex. Girls
  are more often the initiators
  of these attachments
Interest in marriage and marrying.
  Proposes to parents and others
Says "I love"
Interchange of parent-child role
Imaginary playmates
Child plays the role of animals

4 Years

Expanding sense of self indicated
  by bragging, boasting, and out-
  of-bounds behavior

4 Years

Under social stress grasps genitals
  and may have to urinate
Extremely conscious of the navel

4 Years (con't)

Tendency in play groups for a division along sex lines, boys playing with boys and girls with girls

Beginning of strong feeling for family and home

Exhibits some self-criticism

May play the game of "show," either exposing genitals or urinating before another child out of doors

Verbal play about elimination and calling names, such as "You old bowel movement"

Interest in other people's bathrooms; demand for privacy himself but extreme interest in the bathroom activities of others

May believe mother's answers as to where babies come from but may cling to the notion that they are purchased

Questions about how babies get out of the mother's "stomach." May spontaneously think that the baby is born through the navel

5 Years

More secure in sense of self. No longer brags

5 Years

Marked interest in anatomical difference between sexes is often dropping out

Questions as to how babies got in as well as how they will get out of their mother's "stomachs"

Interest in parents' babyhood; in having a baby brother or sister; and in having a baby himself when he grows up (boys as well as girls)

6 Years

Beginning of value judgments about his own behavior; setting up standards for himself

6 Years

Boys may ask factual questions about their testicles

Factual questions about having a baby: does it hurt?

May be the beginning of slight interest in the part the father plays in reproduction

Self-Activity, Sociality, Self-Containment

The growth complex never stands still. It is comparable to an ever-moving stream—a very intricate stream full of currents and crosscurrents, eddies and pools, and yet a stream which manages to carve itself a channel and to reach a destination. Should the stream congeal, life itself would stop. The currents within the stream have their checks and counterchecks. At times the flow may slow down as though to gather force for an onrush, which in turn slows down.

Or the growth complex is comparable to a complicated melody, of varying tempo, with crescendos, diminuendos, legato, staccato, turns, and inverted turns. In spite of momentary disharmonies, the melody has structured form and moves forward with more or less rhythmic pauses.

In Chapter 2 we described the phenomenon of recurrent equilibrium which is characteristic of the psychological growth of infant and child. The organism makes a forward thrust at its growing margin, producing new patterns of behavior, often quite disharmonious. These innovations are then integrated into the total action system; there follows a period of relative equilibrium, followed in turn by another forward thrust: innovation–disequilibrium–integration–equilibrium–innovation–disequilibrium–integration–equilibrium–innovation.

Such seems to be the formula of growth, for separate areas of behavior and also for the entire organism over a period of time. The culture somewhat heedlessly (not to say ignorantly) tends to insist on a continuous state of equilibrium in the child. This leads to aggravations of all kinds, because it is contrary to an insuperable mechanism of development.

It is helpful, therefore, to think of the growth complex in terms of opposite trends which counteract each other, but which are progressively resolved in recurring phases of relative equilibrium. The developmental stream keeps flowing onward, seeks an optimal channel, and finds it. A discerning culture can ease tensions along the way.

To some extent *self-activity* and *sociality* are opposing tendencies. Nature through maturation and culture through guidance bring these tendencies into balance and proportion. Excessive self-activity would make the child an isolationist. Excessive sociality would lead to extreme conformance.

Now let us look back on the panoramic scene and locate, if we can, the areas of recurrent equilibrium. Conveniently, they tend to coincide with ages that have been delineated in the behavior profiles: four, sixteen, twenty-eight, forty weeks; one year, eighteen months, two, three, four, five years. These are key ages for the interpretation of the growing child. The intermediate ages give many evidences of developmental innovation and disequilibrium. The two-and-a-half-year-old and three-and-a-half-year-old levels are particularly instructive for this reason.

In the survey that follows, it must be understood that all normal children do not show with equal definition the recurrent phases of self-containment and of readjustment. Constitutional differences reflect themselves in this very respect.

Some children are, by nature, in rather good equilibrium at almost every age. Others express equilibrium for only very short periods. They seem to go from one stage of disequilibrium to the next with only brief intermission.

Also, the way a child is dealt with by his home surroundings has its own influence. Even a child who, in a stage of disequilibrium, has difficulty with himself at every turn may not give himself and others too much difficulty if he is dealt with skillfully by a parent who understands both his basic temperament and his state of disequilibrium. Unskilled handling can, conversely, create difficulties even at a stage of equilibrium.

These three things must be kept in mind at all times: the child's own basic temperament, the stage of equilibrium or disequilibrium that he may have reached, and the way his parents treat him. When all three are favorable, things go well indeed. But the possibilities of some sort of disequilibrium do exist, especially at certain ages and with children of certain temperaments.

The broad trends that we shall now trace are characteristic of human growth. The sequences are significant. *The age designations are, of course, approximate.* Having made ample qualifications, we shall stress, as in an earlier chapter, the alternation of disequilibrium and self-containment as a basic function of the patterning of behavior in infant and child.

Compared with the irregularities of the early neonatal period, the behavior status of the *four-week-old* infant is stable and coordinated. He shows less stress and struggle in his brief waking hours. But at six or eight weeks he displays a new kind of discontent in his evening crying, as though he were making a groping thrust for some new experience. He is less self-satisfied. He apparently wants some social contact. His responsive smile on sight of a face will prove to be a partial fulfillment of this vague striving. The culture does not always know just what to do for the baby in his obscure fretting innovations. But even so, he incorporates new experience into his action system, and some fine day at about *sixteen weeks* of age he basks for a while in self-containment.

Gone are the indistinct strivings and frettings. He smiles spontaneously. His postures are symmetric. Tremors and startles are rare. He brings his hands competently and comfortably to his mouth. Confusions are gone. His oculomotor muscles are under improved control. He can look and hold at the same time. He is content with the self-activity of mutual fingering. He enjoys his caretakers, beams alike on father or mother, laughs aloud for personal as well as social reasons. All things considered, this is a period of self-containment. For the time being the culture has less perplexity. In his self-activity and sociality he seems to know what he wants and he is getting it.

But naturally, this is a passing phase. In another month there are evidences of transitional disequilibrium. He begins to discriminate strangers. He is sensitive to brusque changes. He cries when someone at whom he has been looking suddenly disappears. The householders can no longer drift in and out of his room as they used to in the good old days of sixteen weeks! The baby now has tiny timidities associated with his new powers of perception. He would like to sit up and be sociable but he is not quite equal to combining his self-activity with sociality. Even on his stomach he may not be content. He would like to get into a low creep position, but he has (to us) amusing difficulties in coordinating his fore and hind quarters. Such faulty coordination is a symptom of developmental disequilibrium.

But in accordance with nature's blueprints, all these difficulties will be resolved in the fullness of time—indeed, at about the age of *twenty-eight weeks*. The twenty-eight-week-old infant presents a classic picture of self-containment, whether supine, prone, or seated. He can combine his perceptual and prehensory abilities with the posture at his disposal. He can look, manipulate, and smile all at one time. Anything satisfies him as a toy. He makes friends easily. He can be handed from one lap to another with impunity and without warning. (What equanimity!) He can play contentedly by himself. Or he can alternate between solitary and interpersonal play, between self-activity and sociality, with the ease of a virtuoso. He is so harmoniously and amiably constituted that culture has a breathing spell which coincides with his developmental equilibrium.

At about *thirty-two weeks* the smooth waters begin to ruffle again. He loses his postural aplomb. He strives to sit without the support he formerly accepted; he strives to go from the sitting position to prone. He gets caught in awkward positions and entangled with himself in his crib. (Culture has to intervene to disentangle him.) He has a fear of strangers. He gets too excited by social contacts and cannot readily shift from sociality to self-amusement. In the prone position he is more likely to go backward than forward. Life is not as simple and straightforward as it used to be.

But at *forty weeks* sailing is again smoother. In prone he can now creep forward and secure the object that formerly only baffled him. He can sit alone. He can pull himself to the thrilling heights of standing. He can play alone, combining objects ad libitum and exploiting them with fine motor coordination. For the first time in his eventful life he can correlate gross postures, fine motor control, and social behavior. He is contented in his playpen. He enjoys a rich though temporary measure of self-containment.

In another month or two he displays new fears, which so often accompany new powers. He becomes frightened at some of his own self-activities; he may be terrified of his own new loud sounds. He is frightened by strangers, particularly if they touch him. He has a fear of the doctor's office. Such timidities remind us of the difficulties, detailed earlier in this chapter, which the child encounters in making valid differentiations between himself and other selves.

When he is in equilibrium these difficulties do not trouble him. This is the case at *one year* of age, when he maintains a delightful rapport and easy give-and-take commerce with the household. His action system is in such nice balance that he is ready for almost any two-way nursery game. He likes to-and-fro play, in which there is a reciprocating social and self-reference. He likes it over and over again, for when a top is in fine balance, why should it not spin round and round and round again?

At *fifteen months* this circularity gives way to tangential and pro-pulsive behavior. He has become a biped. He likes to dart and dash. He has a great propensity to cast objects, heedless of their destination. (At one year he liked to have the objects stay in an orbit so that they would return to him.) This is a dynamo stage, a unidirectional stage. As yet this active baby is capable of starting but not of stopping. From a cultural standpoint he is not in equipoise. He needs constant shifts and assistances, unless he is confined by chair, crib, or playpen. Out-doors he takes free rein. He is at extremes rather than in even balance. Culture has to anticipate and plan for his dogmatic one-way tendencies.

At *eighteen months* he is still very active; but he has himself in better hand. He has become more of a person, who can be easily traf-ficked with on his level. To be sure, he can wear out his mother with the exactions of the daily routines, but otherwise he accepts almost any stranger as companion on his excursions. He is so self-sufficient that he will play by himself for two consecutive hours. He manipulates things with competence and assurance. Persons do not give him undue concern. Consequently he shows a high degree of self-containment, in spite of his mercurial bumbling demeanors.

At *twenty-one months*, with his increase of maturity, he comes into a new awareness of persons again, and with it comes a fear of strangers. He clings closer to the familiar adults of the home circle. He has a new sense of ownership of things which complicates life for him, because the culture is rather blind to the patterns by which he manifests his rudimentary possessiveness. He has poor command of words, but he has much to say so he "bawls" in what is said to be a most unreasonable manner. He may also speak with temper tantrums. In some ways his behavior is reminiscent of an older deaf child who likewise is so often misunderstood, and in a similar manner. He lacks, moreover, a flexible command of time and space relationships, which makes him cleave to routines. He is not equal to reorientations. No wonder he lacks equipoise.

Now the *two-year-old* is in better equilibrium, with a less precarious orientation in time and space. He adjusts more completely to familiar places. He is more at home with himself, content to play quietly in smaller spaces and with smaller objects. He is capable of parallel as well as independent play. Indeed, he enjoys it and is content not to disrupt the play of other children. He is not excessively dependent on his mother, but he likes to have her around and greets her from time to time with an approving smile. He is emotionally attached to her but not overdependent on her. He is self-contained.

But in another six months this composure all but vanishes; for he is then *two and a half years* old. And this age is distinguished for its dramatic manifestations of unsettled equilibrium. If twenty-eight weeks affords the classic example of self-containedness, thirty months is the classic example of its polar opposite. It is almost as though the pyramid of personality were trying to rest on its peak rather than on its base, and therefore wobbled on the slightest provocation or no provocation at all. In our behavior profile of this age we listed some of the numerous and diametric opposites that struggle for mastery within the child's complex action system. If, like the fabled donkey and the haystacks, he were precisely at the middle point between all these opposites, he would be the essence of neutrality; but he is just enough off center to be the epitome of double contrariness and disequi-

librium. What he wills to do he can't; what he can do he won't. Yes
and no; affection and resistance; running away and clinging; holding
on too hard and giving up too easily; whispering and shouting—these
and a host of other opposites alternate with such poor timing that the
child is at home neither with himself nor with his environment. And
the culture is often out of gear with him as well.

He is not sure of himself. His salvation lies in his routines. These
are his old and established self. These he has mastered. Accordingly
he insists on them with spirit and with repetitiveness. He converts
them into life-preserver rituals. Being in the midstream of a growth
transition, he has a very small margin of tolerance; *but he has a little.*
It is a wise culture that recognizes how little and concedes the rationale
of the ritualism. However, by utilization of the small margin of tolerance, the ritual is varied gradually. It loses its vitality (to the parents'
relief) when it has lost its necessity.

Lo and behold, this same child in another six months, at the age of
three years, may become a paragon of self-containment. He has re-
captured the power of choice through his winning battles with the
warring opposites. He is sure of himself. He is emotionally less turned
in on himself. With his widened margin of tolerance, he has a fund
of good will for mankind. The culture can bargain with him on even
terms. He is at home in the domestic circle, at nursery school, on the
playground, at a picnic down the river. He has flexible personal relations with his father, as well as with his mother, as well as with other
children. Self-activity and sociality are well apportioned. He takes his
routines sensibly. He uses his behavior equipment in culturally acceptable ways. Or more precisely, he has an effective behavior equipment because, for the time, he is in good working equilibrium. The
rest follows.

But it does not endure. For in yet another semester, at the age of
three and a half years, there are new growth signs of unsettledness.
Even his general motor control, which one might well think would
be by this time stabilized, betrays signs of weakening. His penciled
strokes waver; his voice quavers; he is prone to stutter. He overcomes
the tendency to vocal tremor by speaking in loud high pitch. He gives

vent to his motor tensions in endless scrubbing and rubbing activities. His inner life of fantasy betrays stresses and insecurities. He has many fears. He may dread deformities and darkness. Dreams multiply and intensify. He spends hours and days with imaginary playmates. In dramatic fancy he exchanges the roles of parent and child. He becomes the parent. He may trot about all day in the privately impersonated role of a horse or a dog. He takes this role seriously. He wishes the culture to take it seriously, too; he will extend his paw but not his hand. And when he shouts, "Don't laugh," some heed should be paid, for these are developmental devices whereby he, almost without the aid of culture, initiates himself into the complexities of culture with its manifold human relationships. Imaginary roles, like more infantile rituals, are scaffoldings for emerging patterns of social behavior.

The *four-year-old* is already a more patterned person with increased savoir faire. He has, as once before noted, a fluid organization, but he is in relatively stable equilibrium. This fluid organization spreads in all directions and includes with almost equal force all fields of his behavior. The expanding periphery pushes across frontiers and thus his horizons are widened. His fine and gross motor control has greatly improved. He is no longer fearful of the high rungs of the gym as he was a half year ago. He is well oriented to his family. He likes nursery school and wants to attend every day. He is capable of sustained cooperative play. He is sensitive to the hints, the commissions, and the commands that come from his culture.

But once more six months of added maturity bring about a difference. The *four-and-a-half-year-old* child tends to go out of bounds. He is, as it were, pushed out of bounds from the unregulated momentum of his expansion into widening horizons. He tells tall tales. He boasts. He shows off. He stands on his head. Inwardly, however, he is not so brave or composed. He has his fears, symptomatic of another transitional stage of disequilibrium, which inevitably produces insecurity. He dreams of wolves. He is afraid of jails. He is afraid of the red traffic light, which means danger to him. He is afraid of the policeman, who is perceived as a threat rather than as a patron of protection.

The *five-year-old*, on the other hand, has so matured that he sees the policeman in his truer light, as both a mentor and a guardian. This added mite of maturity brings with it a more catholic outlook, an ability to see two sides and to weigh them proportionately. The five-year-old has a much more balanced awareness of himself in relation to other persons. He is conscious of differences in hierarchy and prestige. He accepts the social scheme. He goes to and from kindergarten like an embryo citizen, as indeed he is. We need not celebrate his virtues again. He has completed the first long lap on the pathway to maturity.

It has indeed been a long journey marked, as we have now seen, by a succession of phases of recurrent equilibrium and intermediate stages of relative disequilibrium and readjustment. The whole purpose of this chapter has been to bring these almost rhythmic alternations of readjustment and self-containment into sequential perspective. The interludes and the transitions are all but meaningless if they are regarded as separate episodes or fortuitous variations. They have a profound logic when viewed in the continuity of the single, biographic growth career. They show that everything that the infant or child does has a functional or symptomatic significance in the economy of development. Nothing is sheer nonsense, sheer deviltry, or sheer obstinacy. Every patterned action must have a rationale in the physiology of development. Growth as a process is as lawful as metabolism, digestion, respiration, secretion, or any living process. It is in fact the sum of all the living processes of the organism. And when we are concerned with nothing less than the growth of a human personality, this all-inclusive process is the greatest challenge to culture. The culture did not create this process, but it determines its products—within the limitations of the law of recurrent equilibrium, and all other laws of development. That there is an element of recurrence in this equilibrium should give all parents and all philosophies a modicum of optimism.

One more glance at the panorama. Let us look not on the developmental stream but on the cultural landscape. We then see that during these first five years the child has steadily penetrated into the cultural milieu and thereby has widened his physical horizons as well as his psychological orientations. With each expansion he has formed a new niche. His first translation was from uterus to bassinet, and then in quick succession from bassinet to crib, to high chair, to playpen. The playpen itself has its gradients. At first it is in the living room with mother nearby. Stage by stage it migrates into the playroom, onto the porch, and into the vast space of the yard. As the child draws closer to the civic community the playpen is moved to the front yard. Further excursions are made by perambulator and stroller and velocipede. More formally the excursions may take him across the threshold of the nursery school, at first on one or two days during the week, later thrice, later daily. At five years he is able to attend the kindergarten, usually without escort. He has almost graduated into member status in the community. These gradations reveal the stage-by-stage progression of the complicated process of acculturation. Each stage is dependent upon an increment of maturity in the behavior equipment of infant and child.

PART FOUR

THE NURSERY SCHOOL

CHAPTER 23

NURSERY SCHOOL BEHAVIOR AND TECHNIQUES

Introduction

Initial readiness to expand beyond one's home is already evident in the child of seven to eight months when he wishes to sit up and view the world around him as he enjoys his carriage rides. By fifteen months his eagerness to get dressed for an outdoor excursion is very evident. By eighteen to twenty-one months he may even verbalize his desire with a long three-word sentence of "Hat—coat—out." There is no question as to what he wants.

We once even thought that the eighteen-monther might be ready for a short group experience of one hour a week in nursery school. We soon realized that he was too young. In fact, experience has shown that not even the two- or two-and-a-half-year-old boy or girl may be fully ready to get the most out of nursery school.

We ourselves have come to settle for a three-year-old group as our beginning group. Three is not only the tricycle age but also, to us, the ideal nursery school age. By three and four a regular nursery school experience is welcomed by most children. We recommend a schedule of two or three mornings a week at three, and of three or four mornings a week at four. There will, of course, still be some three- and even four-year-olds who will be unable to separate from their mothers.

If so, the child should not be forced, or put through a long and strenuous attempt at separation. He needs to be reassured that he will be ready at some later date. This emotional unreadiness almost always indicates a general unreadiness and need for extra time. If a child has repeated colds, this also could be an indication that he is not ready for a group experience. And parents should be warned that even though a child may have given up his nap at four years of age, he may need to return to it on the days he goes to school.

The availability of a nursery school experience at public expense for children of three or four whose parents desire it might be a blessing to both parents and children. But we would prefer this not to be in a day care form. We still wish to have the home be the center of the young child's experience. In fact, nursery school should be, and often is, an extension of the home. What happens at home becomes important to what the child does at school and affects his ability to adjust. That is why an ongoing communication between home and school is extremely important. That is why a home visit from the teacher often reveals the child in his own right as related to his home experience. Also, this visit can often foster a closer, more personal relationship for child and teacher.

We would wish that public nursery school groups could be conducted on the lines of the best of our private nursery schools, with highly individualized attendance. Federal subsidy of accredited nursery schools could help them to function more effectively. But it is hoped that these younger groups, if established, would not be a part of the regular school system. The child of four is still too young to be part of a big school with older children. And the danger of *teaching* the child too soon will undoubtedly be a temptation if he enters the regular educational stream. When the child is not under pressure to learn beyond his readiness, he no longer shows the tensions of crying, refusing to go to school, and other upsets that sometimes occur.

Nursery school, if it does not come too soon, offers opportunity par excellence for the child to enjoy a socialized experience outside his home. It also offers us an ideal opportunity for observing characteristics of the ascending age levels, and the lively and very definite changes that come with age. Away from home and mother and grouped with others of approximately his own age and level of interest, your typical two- or three- or four-year-old often reveals himself most clearly as the special little individual he really is.

Age characteristics stand out vividly when one sees a whole group of two-year-olds playing silently side by side with very little interpersonal reaction; a group of two-and-a-half-year-olds all vigorously defending each and every toy that they are playing with, have played with, or might in the future wish to play with; a group of friendly, sociable three-year-olds interacting with pleasure and enjoyment.

They stand out vividly when we observe a roomful of two-year-olds attempting each to get more than his fair share of a teacher's attention while ignoring contemporaries; see three-year-olds dividing attention and interest between teacher and playmates; see four-year-olds all but ignoring the teacher in their enthusiastic interaction with each other.

A nursery school teacher finds that only when she really understands the characteristics of each and every preschool age can she deal most effectively with her lively charges. Techniques that work beautifully with a two-year-old do not get very far with the more boisterous and obstreperous four.

Even if your own boy or girl may not be attending a nursery school, information about what nursery school behavior is like can be useful to you in better understanding the child at home, since both at home and at school, behavior grows and changes in a highly patterned, predictable way that has much in common from child to child and from place to place.

For each age level, in the pages that follow, we discuss general kinds of behavior, techniques that can be effective, cultural and creative activities that are enjoyed, and, when appropriate, sense of time and space as well as storytelling and imaginative abilities commonly expressed.

Eighteen Months

BEHAVIOR

Though it would be most unusual for a private nursery school to have an eighteen-month-old group (most start with two-and-a-half or three-year-olds), as day nurseries proliferate it is becoming somewhat more usual for groups of eighteen-monthers to gather. It may thus be helpful for teachers or supervisors of such groups to have some idea of what may be expected, socially, from eighteen-monthers when gathered together.

Actually, what may be expected is not very much—usually quite a bit less than "early intervention" specialists and optimistic and eager child psychologists hope for.

The usual eighteen-monther is not much interested in other children. He has nothing to say to them and very little to do with them. He is primarily interested in himself and his own concerns, and in the adult insofar as the adult can administer to those concerns. To a large extent, so long as opportunity is available for him to express his own drives and wishes, other people in social and play situations are quite unnecessary.

Much of the child's activity at this age is gross motor. He may seem never still, bumbling from one part of a room to another as now this and now that stimulus attracts him. But even when he has attained some attractive goal—a doll corner, a pile of blocks—his attention to it tends to be momentary. Figure 5 shows how much ground may be covered by a typical eighteen-monther in seven minutes of nursery school play.

Interest in the teacher is so slight at this age that a child may ignore her even visually. He may grab an object from her without so much as regarding her.

When the eighteen-monther does pay attention to the teacher, it is mostly to show her things and to name them: "car," "nose," "truck,"

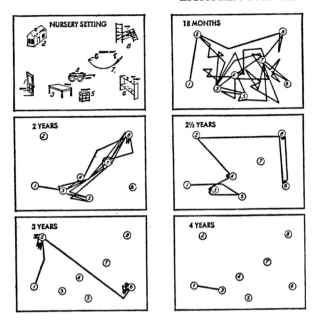

Figure 5 The ground covered by typical preschoolers in seven minutes of nursery school play.

"ball," "hat." Or he may ask for "coo" (cookie) or "water." If he wants to ask about something, his request may be simply phrased: "Eh?" Often he merely points or gestures to ask for objects or to ask for help. The one word he uses more than any other in response to comments, requests, or suggestions from others is "No!"

Since attention to other children is very slight, most eighteen-monthers would probably be quite as content if no other children were present. If they do attend to others it may be merely to shout "No!" at whatever the other child is doing or trying to do. Or they may demand an object another child is holding by pointing and saying, "Eh! Eh!"

There is virtually no response to approaches of other children for the simple reason that few approaches are ever made. For the most part, children simply ignore or attempt to grab objects from each other.

The child grabbed from may let his object go or may tighten his hold almost reflexively.

As a group, children mostly play in isolated, very mobile units, having little contact with anyone else. They may occasionally stare at each other; and if one goes over to the teacher, others may follow. Two may play near the same object but with almost no attention to each other.

One may wonder as to the value of assembling children in day nurseries *if* the object is socialization. Also, it is probably not true, as some hope, that the child will be "readier," later on, for social interchange because he has had this early experience. Social interaction seems to come more from added maturity than from added time spent in the company of other children.

We would prefer a child of this age to be at home with his mother, but hopefully to have access to a park where simple gross motor activities of swinging and sliding and playing in sand are available. An hour's excursion to such a park both in late morning, before lunch and nap, and in midafternoon, after the nap, gives the child's day a feeling of expansion and new conquest.

TECHNIQUES

PHYSICAL ENVIRONMENT

Simplify the physical environment to prevent overstimulation. Provide gross motor equipment, such as stairs with railing, and slides, to suit the child's gross motor drives. Manipulative materials are also necessary.

The simplicity and freedom of the outdoors are suited to the psychology of the eighteen-month-old child. Outdoor activity reduces tensions and resistance. He enjoys the outdoors and this puts him at his best.

A sandbox is a necessity at this age, providing, as it does, a focal center capable of holding interest without the restrictions of bounds, as well as an opportunity for filling and dumping play.

ADJUSTMENT

Adjustment should be effected at this age through things. It often consists of gradually luring the child away from the mother by rolling rings which he follows, by moving manipulative toys farther and farther away from the mother, or by centering his interest on some part of the room or on toys at a distance from and if possible out of the sight of the mother. This gives her a chance to slip out. This is not an age for formal good-byes. "Out of sight, out of mind" applies here.

ROUTINES

Do not attempt to set up elaborate routines (as toilet, washing hands, resting) too soon after entrance. These activities are not only associated with home and mother but are often not yet well established and the child may resist them in school for several weeks or longer. His adjustment to school may be jeopardized if these routines are pushed. Diapers and rubber pants to keep the child dry, or a short stay at school to avoid the necessity for toileting, are desirable.

The one routine that is accepted and heartily enjoyed is the mid-morning snack of juice and crackers.

The eighteen-monther also enjoys some participating in undressing, such as taking off his hat and mittens and putting his clothes in his cubby; but the rest of undressing and dressing has to be done by the teacher.

The child at this age has a strong desire to "put things back" and enjoys clearing up the room before midmorning snack.

TRANSITIONS

Avoid resistance to sudden changes by utilizing methods of gradual transition. (Verbal transitions are usually futile at this age.) Allow the child to take a favorite toy with him. Use the toy as a lure to get him from one room to another. Utilize his responsiveness to gross motor humor by picking him up like a bag of rags. He may accept this, while resisting simpler touching such as having his hand held. He likes chasing someone and being chased. Do not expect to control him through hypnotism or solemn discipline.

TEACHER

For his safety, each child needs the close and constant physical supervision of an adult teacher. Children of this age are quick and adventurous and frequently tumble. Therefore groups should be kept small.

Direct the child through objects and physical orientations and gestures. Use language sparingly.

When contacting the child, it is important for the teacher to be on his physical level by squatting, or sitting on a low chair or on the floor.

The teacher's role is more passive for this age than for the ages immediately following. Her chief role is protecting and supplementing.

Once the initial adjustment is made, this is one of the easiest ages to handle because the child goes on his own steam and is not likely to get into conflicts with his contemporaries.

VERBAL

Use language sparingly. Simple well-chosen words such as "all gone," "Thank you," "Bye-bye" are most effective. The child responds better to one word or a short phrase than to complicated explanations. For instance, "Hat?" or "Outdoors?"

Use the child's name in addressing him rather than the pronoun, as "Bobby wash hands."

Situations can be terminated by "Thank you" or "Bye-bye."

It is important for the teacher to employ a rising, expectant inflection when she speaks to the eighteen-month-old child. Gestures are often needed to reinforce language.

The eighteen-month-old has an immediate time concept and only understands "now" or association with routines, such as "after juice."

HUMOR

Children may respond to gross motor humor, as hiding and peek-aboo, and being lifted in bag-of-rags fashion. Such humor can be used in effecting transitions.

OTHER CHILDREN

The eighteen-month-old child tends to treat another child as an object rather than as a person. He resorts to experimental poking, pulling, pinching, pushing, and sometimes hitting. The teacher needs to be on guard to direct this experimentation into harmless channels. She should not attempt to force socialized cooperativeness at this age.

GROUP ACTIVITY

These children are not ready for group play. Most of their time is spent in solitary activities. For the most part, they play in isolated, individual, very mobile units with very little contact with anyone. A child may look at other children but generally merely stares in their direction without verbal or physical contact.

CULTURAL AND CREATIVE ACTIVITIES

BOOKS

1. Attends to pictures of familiar objects in books.
2. Listens to short rhymes with interesting sounds, especially when they are accompanied by action or pictures. Likes to have them sung.
3. Enjoys tactile books such as *Pat the Bunny* or *The Tactile Book*.
4. May look at books upside down.
5. Needs supervision while looking at books, as he frequently tears them at this age. Cloth and heavy cardboard books are recommended.

MUSIC

1. Spontaneous humming or singing of syllables.
2. Wide range in tone, pitch, and intensity of voice.
3. Very much aware of sounds such as bells, whistles, clocks.
4. Rhythmic response to music with whole-body activity.

PAINTING

1. Whole-arm movements.
2. Very few strokes on a page, often in the form of an arc.
3. Shifting of brush from one hand to the other.
4. Satisfied with only one color.

BLOCKS

1. Carries blocks around the room, pounds them together, or dumps in a mass.
2. Only building may be a tower of three or four.

POSSESSIONS

1. May have a special toy, blanket, or other object to which he is attached. Unable to sleep without it.
2. Definite relationship of possessions to their owners—takes hat or pocketbook to its correct owner.

EXCURSIONS

Enjoys short walks; runs ahead of adults; interested in all byways.

TIME AND SPACE

The *eighteen-month-old* child lives in the immediate present and has little if any sense of past and future. He cannot wait. No time words are used by him, but he responds to the word "now" and his time psychology is founded in the present. There is some slight sense of timing; he may roll a ball and wait for it to stop before he pursues it. The sight of juice and crackers may bring him to the table.

He spontaneously uses such words as "up," "down," and "off," dealing chiefly with his own basic movements in space. "Come," "go," and "gone" also refer to his own activities or the presence or absence of objects in which he is directly interested. The child can, if requested, obey two directions with a ball, putting it on a chair and giving it to his mother.

The *twenty-one-month-old* child still lives chiefly in the present. His chief time word is "now." Projection into the future begins. He will wait in response to "In a minute." There is an improving sense of timing: two children may rock in rhythm, or the child may sit at the table and wait for food.

There are still no space words in response to questioning, but "up," "down," "on," and "off" are used spontaneously; also the size word "big." Also most characteristic of this age are "All gone," expressing interest in absence or departure of an object, and "Here," suggesting the "here and nowness" of this age. A child frequently merely looks in a direction indicated, does not actually move.

Two Years

BEHAVIOR

The two-year-old child is barely ready to take advantage of, or enjoy, the nursery school situation. Most Twos, in a school setting, are primarily occupied with their own individual activities. Most can keep themselves more or less happily occupied in rather simple play with the toys provided. They often talk to themselves as they play: "Whang whang whang," "Zoom zoom zoom." They may give verbal directions to themselves to describe what they are doing: "Jump," "Rock," "Go up this way." Or they may chant or sing, smile or laugh in accompaniment of their own gross motor activity.

Though other children are to a large extent ignored—certainly they are not conversed with—most do pay quite a lot of attention to the teacher. They may ask for help nonverbally by pulling her to another part of the room. They tell her about things: "Mummy be back soon," "Ann climb up"; show her things: "Telephone," "Choo-choo train"; ask for things: "Wan get down," "Wash my hands," "Read books." They ask for as well as give information: "What is this?" "Where's baw?"

Some like to have the teacher watch their activity: "Watch me," "Look at this." They emphasize completion by telling the teacher, "Aw finished." They are most interested in things *they* say *to* the teacher, but may also answer when she speaks or may take part in very simple conversations. They may or may not obey the teacher's suggestions, but do like her company. They may just like to play near her or may involve her in simple imaginative play, such as handing her an imaginary cup to drink from.

Though they show most interest in their own activity, or in simple interchange with their teacher, children often will play voluntarily *near* some other child. But there is little social verbalization and often little attention to other children except for an occasional aggressive attack or a brief skirmish over property.

Relations with other children are tentative. Though they may play side by side, and sometimes watch each other, any talk is chiefly directed toward obtaining or protecting play objects. A child may grab something he wants but is more interested in the object obtained than in the person from whom it is obtained. Children this age cannot share. They are now consolidating their sense of self by obtaining and hoarding possessions, and this need will become even stronger at two and a half. "Mine" is a favorite word.

Play is for the most part more parallel than social, even when children are playing side by side with similar materials. Children may protect their own property but are most likely to go to the adult for help.

Several may flock together, following the teacher, but the response here is more to the teacher than to each other. Behavior is largely highly individual. Though there is some tendency to gravitate to the place where others are playing, and as many as half a dozen children may play within a very small space, there is often not even visual attention to each other.

TECHNIQUES

PHYSICAL ENVIRONMENT

Eighteen months' equipment can all be used at this age. In addition, there should be a doll corner and climbing apparatus.

ADJUSTMENT

This is perhaps the most difficult age for adjustment. The child is increasingly aware of and affectionate toward his mother and therefore finds it hard to leave her. He is also shy of new people and new places. If there is difficulty, it is often best to have some relative or neighbor bring him to school instead of his mother. Adjustment is effected through *people* at this age. Therefore one special teacher should greet the child, stay near him, and help him to initiate activity. One visit to his home by his special teacher may assure his ease of adjustment.

A teacher should be on hand to help in detaching the child from his mother if she is the one who brings him. Distraction helps some. Others need some simple formula each time, as "Shall we go and see the bunny?" Children like to have their names mentioned: "Good morning, Nicholas. I'm happy to see you."

The initial adjustment may be better outdoors, and it may be necessary for the teacher to carry the child out and attempt to interest him in sand, filling and dumping, rolling toys, etc. There may be crying at first, which usually stops quickly as soon as interest is caught and held.

ROUTINES

Toileting and Hand-Washing. The child accepts elaborate routines at this age, though he may still resist toileting, or may be unaware of the problem and may come to school in diaper and rubber pants. The teacher must look for readiness, and the child who has become aware of his toileting functions can sometimes profitably be taken to the bathroom on some pretext or other (to wash his doll in the basin) and thus he can see others who are using the toilets. Taking the child who is not trained to the bathroom along with one who is is sometimes helpful, but the teacher should not push the child who is not ready.

When the child shows interest in the toilet, it is best to have him come to school in training pants rather than diapers. Training pants are easily changed, and allow the child to notice the puddles he makes.

Boys sometimes need help in aiming. Some boys prefer to sit down for urinating. Some insist on privacy and some refuse to use the school toilet at all.

Most like to wash their hands but have a tendency to prolong the operation, and may need the teacher's help in stopping. The child may respond to "Good-bye, water," combined with having the plug removed from the basin.

Milk and Crackers. Midmorning snack is the high point of the morning. Most can wait for the group to collect, and enjoy having everyone there. The snack at this age should be rather early to keep up energy. A child should not be expected to conform to one cup of juice and one cracker, though often he will respond to "One [cracker] for each hand." He should be allowed a second helping and is usually satisfied when he sees that the supply is "all gone." Some may demand, and need, more than others. Children like to try pouring their own milk and should be allowed to do so, while the teachers keep a hand ready to steady and direct those who have difficulty. Conversation will be at a minimum; the teacher will have to initiate and for the most part carry on simple conversation.

Rest, Music, Books. The child is not yet ready for a midmorning rest, but music and books provide a period of relaxation. Most enjoy music time and do not mind singing the same songs at each successive session. "Chug-chug-chug, I'm a little tug" represents the usual level of accomplishment.

At story time, children may mill around the room a good deal, and many teachers' or mothers' laps are needed to suggest to them that they can enjoy a book without having immediate contact with it. Ten minutes is quite long enough for story time.

Of primary importance is simplicity—large, clear pictures with few details, a situation of minimum complexity, simple language with no abstract words or ideas. Two loves to have one idea repeated over and over. He likes books about everyday activities—getting up, getting dressed, eating breakfast, taking a walk, going to bed.

Twos are not good listeners and may wander about, look at books only briefly, talk aloud as the story is being read. They may prefer to look at a book of their own rather than listen to the teacher.

Dressing. Two is interested in dressing and undressing though he does not help himself beyond removing his hat and mittens, and zipping and unzipping zippers, which are a new interest at this age.

TRANSITIONS

Two is prone to dawdle, but can be shifted by such devices as:

1. Leading him away, if he is not resistant.
2. Talking of the next thing: "Go find the soap." "Time to get crackers now."
3. Telling him to "Say good-bye."
4. Leading by means of an enticing toy.
5. Picking him up bodily and carrying him to the next situation. Two often dislikes to be touched—led by the hand—but he can be picked up bodily, as at eighteen months.
6. Warning him in advance of a proposed transition: "Pretty soon we'll go to the bathroom and then have juice."
7. Since most are ready to leave for home when the time comes, there is usually little difficulty with this transition.

TEACHER

Very often a two-year-old adjusts to school primarily through his relationship with a single teacher: she must toilet him, sit near him when he has crackers and milk, comfort him when he is frustrated, provide a lap when he feels insecure. Most two-year-olds demand a more motherly relationship with a teacher than do older children.

The teacher of a two-year-old must know the simple repetitive games that show him how to play, doing the same thing over and over. Gradually the child will achieve more independence from his teacher, and as he moves on toward two and a half will show increasing interest in playing by himself or even with other children. On occasion, stimulating play and widening the scope builds up the play of the group.

The teacher is now more of a person to the child and he usually knows her name. He usually responds to one teacher in preference to any of the others.

Sometimes the teacher can work through other, perhaps older children when a child refuses to comply. "Betsy, will you bring Jane to wash?"

VERBAL

Verbal handling is now beginning to supersede physical handling. It is important to keep language simple, concrete, and repetitive. There is no need to fear boring the two-year-old with repetition. The world is all so new to him that repetition helps him to feel comfortable. But keep language at a minimum. The adult who talks too much to the two-year-old inevitably uses words he does not understand. Such verbosity from adults may set up in the child patterns of not paying attention.

The teacher's language should be modeled on the level of the children. Typical useful phrases are: "Have clay after juice." "When it's time." "Now John can have it." "Find your mittens." "This is where it fits." Emphasize important words with a calm, reassuring tone.

Be ready to shift verbal techniques to a level above or below the child's age as the situation requires. Often eighteen months' verbal techniques, as "Good-bye, water," to terminate washing, or "Good-bye, turtle," to terminate play with a turtle, are useful. Some children, however, will be ready for Two-and-a-half's verbal techniques.

Often it is necessary to follow or support verbalization with action. Thus, rather than simply saying, "Go wash your hands," a teacher may lead a child to the washbasin as she speaks.

Try to get the child himself to substitute verbal for gross physical approaches to other children, such as screaming or hitting in disputes. Say "Jane can *talk* to Jimmy. Jane, say, 'no, Jimmy.'"

Imitation of the other children's activities may be induced by use of a repetitive phrase, such as "Ann is drinking her juice. Judy is drinking her juice."

Interest in specific rather than general concepts is characteristic. The child may not respond to a general statement, such as "Let's put the toys away," but may respond to "Teddy goes in the bed"; "Cars go on the shelf." Also, the teacher can use the specific when two children are fighting over a toy, to direct one of them to a similar toy. "Ann could find the *blue* carriage."

Use such popular words as "again" and "another."

And there may be need for continued use of supplementary gestures to make clear the meaning of new words.

HUMOR

Humor is largely gross motor, as peekaboo and chasing. It may, at this age, be initiated by the children rather than just by the teacher, and may be carried on by them without adult support.

OTHER CHILDREN

Two shows an awakening interest in his contemporaries. Children at this age are both an absorbing interest and a thorn in the flesh to each other. Play is still predominantly solitary but affectionate approaches such as hugging, patting, and kissing often occur. Parallel play is beginning. They also spend much time just watching each other.

Children engage in a good deal of physical exploration of each other, especially aggressively. Hitting at this age does not necessarily mean dislike. It may be the one form of social contact that the child knows. A child may begin by stroking another child's hair because he likes the way it looks, then may pull it to see how it feels. A teacher must realize that she is going to have to teach two-year-olds the absolute fundamentals of getting along with other children. Often it seems that the two-year-old might enjoy school more if the others were not there, and the teacher's main task may be to get children to tolerate each other.

One of Two's chief difficulties is his dislike of giving things up and of sharing. He likes, however, to find substitutes for other children to use. He will usually respond to "If you have the car what can John use? He could use the train. I'll hold the car while you get the train for John." The two-and-a-half-year-old may be able to respond to just the first part of this sentence, but Two needs more specific suggestions. Do not expect disputes to be settled "fairly" from an adult point of view. "It's mine" may have to be respected in a demanding child at the expense of a more docile child, though this may violate the adult's command "*Johnny* needs it."

Social relations can be interpreted in a positive way: "How nice that he made you a cake"; "He likes to do the puzzle with you." Or, instead of hitting another child, the would-be molester may be encouraged just to touch or stroke him.

GROUP ACTIVITY

There should not be too much planning for group activity. Since solitary or parallel play naturally predominates, group activities should be spaced and brief. All children should not be expected or required to cooperate. Flexibility is needed in music, reading, and similar activities. They need to see the record going around; they need to touch the book that is being read. Groups that can be kept within touch are best. Some children will stray immediately. Juice time is the best time for collecting the whole group.

A two-year-old group tends to warm up as a morning progresses. This warm-up takes place day after day and does not as a rule carry over to a following day. Improvement during any given day is not necessarily a steady improvement. A two-year-old group is often at its best from ten to eleven, and after that the children may start to go to pieces. They fall down, droop, their noses may run, and they are likely to cry if their mother does not come right on time. Thus, ideally, a two-year-old's morning at school should not last more than two hours.

So far as seasonal changes go, two-year-old groups usually have their greatest difficulty at the beginning of the school year, and generally improve and find life easier toward spring.

CULTURAL AND CREATIVE ACTIVITIES

BOOKS

1. Enjoyment of simple pictures with few details and clear color.
2. Likes to talk about pictures, having adult turn back the child's "Whassat?" with "What is it?" or an explanation. Likes to have the adult ask, "Where is the kitty?" etc.
3. Enjoys having stories simplified by interpreting them to him, using his vocabulary, people and experiences he knows, and especially his own name.
4. Interested in sound and repetition, as in *Ask Mr. Bear.*
5. Likes listening to nursery rhymes and repeating them with the adult.

MUSIC

1. Sings phrases of songs, generally not on pitch.
2. Enjoyment of rhythmical equipment, such as rocking boat, swing, and rocking chair. These often stimulate spontaneous singing.

3. Such rhythmical responses as bending knees in bouncing motion, swaying, swinging arms, nodding head, and tapping feet are favorites.
4. Likes holding something, as block, bells, or another's hand, while walking to music.
5. Interested in watching phonograph operate while listening to records.

PAINTING

1. More wrist action than at eighteen months.
2. Less shift in handedness, though often paints with a brush in each hand.
3. "Scrubbing" paper with little regard for color. Paints several colors over each other vigorously, with muddy effect.
4. More variety of strokes when only one color is presented.
5. Process, not end result, important to the child.
6. Easily distracted and does not always watch hand movements.
7. Social enjoyment of painting on same paper with another child.

FINGER PAINTING AND CLAY

1. Initial objection to feeling of paint and getting hands dirty, but enjoys it after a few trials.
2. Manipulates clay, pounding, squeezing, and pulling off small pieces; often hands to adult.
3. Often experiments with the taste of clay.

SAND, STONES, WATER

1. Fills pails and dishes with sand and stones, dumping and throwing.
2. High interest in water play—extensive hand-washing, washing clothes, filling and emptying dishes.

BLOCKS

1. Used manipulatively, filling wagons, dumping, and rolling.
2. Some building of towers and lines, often combining various sizes of blocks in random order.
3. Preference for colored blocks.

POSSESSIONS

1. Pride in clothes, especially shoes, socks, and handkerchief.
2. Strong feeling of ownership in toys. "It's mine" is a constant refrain.
3. Difficulty in sharing toys; hoards them.
4. May bring small token such as marble, orange section, etc., to school and hold on to it all morning, objecting to anyone's taking it.
5. Enjoys naming possessions of others, and telling to whom they belong.
6. Much interest in money but almost no understanding of its use. Likes to use it manipulatively, carrying it around and handling it.

HOLIDAYS AND FESTIVALS

1. Birthday—Enjoys a party with just family or perhaps one other child. The best time for this is the child's regular mealtime. The food is the party for the two-year-old.
2. Christmas—The tree is important. He enjoys Christmas cards and plays with them long after Christmas.
3. Valentine's Day—Enjoys receiving valentine cards and may carry them around for days.
4. Easter—Interest in the Easter Bunny.
5. Halloween—Not much interest in this day.
6. Thanksgiving—Has little meaning except for the turkey. May not enjoy the day because shy with guests.
7. Religion—Some are ready for Sunday school if it is run on nursery school principles. Enjoy repeating the last phrases of prayers.

EXCURSIONS

1. Out for a walk, he is interested in touching things he sees along the way. Picks up sticks and stones, touches animals. Likes to walk on curbs or walls. Dawdles and concentrates interest within a small area.
2. No thought of destination.

STORYTELLING AND IMAGINATIVE PLAY

If we can come to conclusions about the child's sense of self and surroundings from the kind of stories he tells, we may assume that the two-year-old sees himself as living in a somewhat friendly world. Nearly half the children questioned by us, more than at any other preschool age, told stories with friendly themes. Conversely, though 64 percent did mention some violence, this was less than at any other age.

Closeness to mother is shown by the fact that she is the outstanding character and, happily, in three-quarters of the stories of girls and in all of those of boys, she is presented in a friendly light, more so than at any other age, though boys see her more positively than do girls. And father, more than at any other age, is seen as friendly, caring for, or providing. Girls, however, see him as more friendly than boys do.

As at many ages, girls tell stories centering around some socializing theme, whereas the stories of boys tend to deal with the boy himself. Stories of both boys and girls at this age are based strongly in reality—children, eat, go to bed, fall down, cry. There is very little humor in stories told by two-year-olds, which emphasizes the fact that the boy or girl of this age is a rather serious little person.

"Baby," "girl," "Mummy" or some animal are the chief characters in stories by girls; "baby," "boy," or some animal in stories by boys. Children of both sexes stick very close to home in their stories, going certainly no farther than their own yards. Life has a rather narrow setting for the child of this age and home and parents pretty well bound it. And stories deal with extremely *real* subjects—fantasy and imagination are seldom expressed.

In active play, the child of this age demonstrates only a beginning imaginativeness. He shows this when he talks to, feeds, toilets, or puts to bed his teddy bear or doll, or otherwise plays house in rudimentary fashion.

TIME AND SPACE

An important advance takes place at this age. Though the child still lives very much in the present, several words that denote *future* time (especially "gonna" and "in a minute") become part of his own spoken vocabulary. He will wait in response to such words as "wait," "soon," and "pretty soon." The child now has several different words to indicate present time: "now," "today," "aw day," "dis day." He uses no specific words implying past time, but is beginning to use the past tense of the verb, often inaccurately. The two-year-old cannot answer questions involving time concepts, but he comprehends simple sequences, as in the adult's promise, "Have clay after juice."

The child uses space words both spontaneously and in response to questions. Although two years is not a particularly expansive age, note the expansion from earlier "here and nowness" implied in the use of such words as: "there," "where," "other side," "outdoors," "upstairs," "up high." The more complex notion of container and contained comes in with "in" and "out." "In" is used more than any other word in answer to questions about space. "All gone" is still strong. There is great interest in having things in their proper places. Also, the child can answer such space questions as "Where is Mummy?" "Where is Daddy?" "Where do you sleep?" He can obey four directions with a ball: putting it on a chair, under a table, giving it to mother, giving it to an examiner.

Two and a Half Years

BEHAVIOR

Though children of this age occasionally play alone, talking to themselves as they play, solitary play is no longer a leading type of activity. The largest number of social approaches, verbal or otherwise, are now between teacher and child, and usually child-initiated.

The child of this age likes to talk to the teacher about what he is doing or is going to do: "I'm gonna paint." "I want to climb." He asks for help when it is needed—"I need to get down. Help me"—but likes to announce his own independent ability: "I can take my own coat off." He tells her, "I want the big bike. I'm a big boy now," or he tells about things at home: "I even have a mommy at home." He likes to call her attention to his prowess: "Hey, watch! Hey, lookit!" "I climbed all by myself. I'm way up here, see!" He is very quick to complain of and ask for help against other children: "She's got my toy." "He pushed me down."

By far the greatest amount of socialization and verbalization is with the teacher, but for many the sense of self is now consolidated to the point where it can be strengthened in interpersonal relations (or interpersonal rivalries) with other children.

Parallel play still prevails. There is little cooperative play, and self-initiated relations predominate since the child is still extremely egocentric. His chief interpersonal relation with other children is in getting objects from them and in protecting any object he himself may be using, has used, or might use. The child now wants everything to come to him. He says "me," "mine," "I need." But obtaining objects from others is no longer easy, since the child grabbed from may resist vigorously, both physically and verbally.

He may defend his possessions with "Get off, this is my place." "You can't have my dolly." "Don't touch. Go away!" "I want that; that's mine." Or "I'll hit you if you don't watch out." "Don't be like that. You go down 'fore I hit you so hard!"

This is an aggressive age, and play with objects as well as with others tends to be quite violent. A child may say of her doll, "I'll kill her dead" or "Let's tumble her out. I like her to hurt herself." In fact aggression, both verbal and physical, predominates. Some is for the purpose of protecting possessions; some seems quite unprovoked. There is much hitting, slapping, pushing, screaming. Or a child may walk up and push another child over and then knock his house down. Children may bump into each other intentionally. Materials may be torn or broken in the course of a dispute. Most children are more aggressive spontaneously than in response. Some do not fight back even when toys are snatched. They are seldom able to solve their own altercations.

There is now a bare beginning of cooperative play: "Who's ready for dinner?" "How about some ice cream?" (Imaginary dinner; imaginary ice cream.) Some call the attention of other children to their own activity: "See, I made a birthday cake." "Neil, look! Johnny has a new cart." Any two may group together briefly and tentatively in parallel play, though even here there will be more watching than talking. Cooperation may succeed at the simple level of chasing each other and laughing, but even if one starts a simple conversation, the other, as a rule, does not respond. The most frequent interchild exchange is quarreling over materials.

There is little group activity, though several children may group together near the teacher, or over materials at the teacher's suggestion. Five or six children or even the whole group may work individually, isolated in different parts of the room, all at about the same level of noncooperation. There is not much structure to the group, but rather rapid change of locale and very little more than temporary grouping except when groups are teacher-arranged around clay, phonograph, books. The fact that all children seem to be at rather a uniform stage of noncooperation and relative isolation gives the group an appearance of unity and one-levelness, as if all were on about the same plane.

TECHNIQUES

PHYSICAL ENVIRONMENT

Environmental handling is most important at this age. Doors should be shut, distracting materials removed.

Two small rooms are preferable to one large one. This makes possible shifting the group from one room to another, or the isolation of one child, or of small groups.

Climbing apparatus indoors as well as out is most desirable.

ADJUSTMENT

Some children adjust easily at this age, but others are apt to make trouble about leaving their mother and may hit out at mother or teacher. A variety of adjustment techniques may need to be called on here. For some it is necessary that the mother say a definite good-bye, but with others it works best if the mother slips out unobtrusively as the teacher distracts the child.

Some need a good deal of immediate attention from the teacher but the shy child may adjust better if she pays little or no obvious attention to him and makes her approaches indirectly.

ROUTINES

Children at this age tend to enjoy and to accept most routines.

Toileting. Only a few have accidents now. About half ask for toileting when they need it. Those who don't care if they are wet have such a long way to go that it is a mistake to work very hard on this problem.

The child's general pattern of negativism at this age may operate with regard to toileting even though he is supposedly "trained." If he resists, try picking him up and talking about something else as you carry him to the bathroom. But if real resistance persists, abandon your effort.

Milk and Crackers. Even nonconformists at this age seem to accept and enjoy their milk and crackers. They like to eat. Most enjoy the occasion boisterously. They bang their feet on the floor, squeal, dunk crackers. Rather than forbid these activities, a teacher can get attention by telling an interesting story, by whispering, by showing another way to eat crackers. She may say, "One cracker at a time. There are enough for everybody." When they leave the table, which some do sooner than others, a teacher should see that they have some special place to go. They should not be left to wander around.

Dressing. Teachers still have to do most of the dressing. Usually there is too little time to make much of a game of dressing, or to wait for self-help.

Resting, Music, Books. The ability to rest varies, but in any event rest time should be short and may be more relaxing if accompanied by music. Children of this age probably relax best merely by sitting in a comfortable position looking at books. Shifting to a room other than the playroom is conducive to relaxation.

Children like to sing simple, repetitive songs and take much pleasure in bodily actions to accompany music. They like running, jumping, crawling, or may enjoy simple group activities such as a lineup for a train, or dancing in circles for ring-around-a-rosy.

Children of this age listen to stories better than earlier, but their attention span is still brief and they may wander around the room, look at their own books, talk, or, if permitted, leave the room. Attention is best held if most can sit near the teacher and if she keeps the stories very simple and gives much attention to the children. She should of course hold the book so that they can see. Simple stories of everyday activities, and books with short stories and many pictures, help.

TRANSITIONS

This is a perseverative age. Transitions are difficult. Expect a slow adjustment to new materials, a strong holding on, and slow release even after interest has waned.

Do not try to hurry children too much, since two and a half is a strong dawdling age. If rituals have been set up by the child, make use of them instead of trying to break them down.

Verbal handling alone can be used to effect transitions much more successfully than at two, when verbal handling had to be supplemented by physical handling or by a lure.

Children at this age often make a fuss about leaving. They either don't want to go at all, or insist on "Just one more turn," or may try to hide. Mothers may be embarrassed and may then talk too much or try too hard. The teacher can help by offering a "surprise" to lure the child to the car. Or she may ask, "Will you show me your car?" or "Let's find your car."

TEACHER

Do not trust the child too much. He appears self-reliant and unneedful of restraints, but cannot really be relied upon. His repetition of a rule or prohibition does not mean that he can carry it out. This is no age for promises from the child. "Me do it myself" cannot always be carried out. "You do it" may express a real need for help.

Children may require adult direction in their play at this age. They are often not sufficiently mature to carry out their own ideas unaided, and deteriorate without adult assistance.

Give yourself and the child leeway so you both will not lose face in situations. By saying, "You have to wash your hands before juice," you may get resistance from the child, and the adult may have to back down. Save face by suggesting, "You need to wash your hands," and if the child resists, say, "Maybe tomorrow you will be ready to wash your hands."

Never make too much of an issue of discipline with Two-and-a-half. Comprehension is low at this age and disciplining emphasizes contrariness and fosters repetition.

Do not expect children to respond to direct questions or to direct commands. Do expect them to respond to a statement that has meaning to them, if it is made with assurance. For example, "Now it's time for juice. First we wash hands," or "First we wash our hands and then we have juice."

Questions such as "Where does your coat go?" can be good motivators. But it is important to avoid questions that can be answered by "No," such as, "Do you want to . . ." In general, it is best to avoid choices, for children tend to find, as soon as they have made a choice in one direction, that the other is highly desirable.

However, choices about things that do not matter may act as motivators, as "Do you want the blue one or the red one?"

Talk about some neutral topic can sometimes distract a child so that you can give him the help he needs but does not want (such as putting on his snowsuit for him).

Compliments are foolproof at any age. "You have such a pretty dress. I hope you won't get it dirty" can motivate toward cleanliness. Verbal expressions of affection, as well as praise, can be highly effective.

Use other children in the group, as in noisy situations. Say, "Dicky doesn't like so much noise. It hurts his ears." "Dotty uses a whispering voice." These suggestions often do not work immediately but are for future reference. The immediate action is to take the noisy child out of the group—preferably outdoors.

The child at two and a half deteriorates easily and the group follows in a negative mercurial flow. A complete shift is essential when this happens.

VERBAL

Verbal handling has now superseded physical handling. The child's rapidly increasing comprehension and use of language make it possible for both the teacher and himself to express themselves through language.

(The reader will note that most of the techniques discussed at this and following ages are verbal in character.)

Certain key words help to organize the child's vacillating tendencies and thus give him a thrust in the forward direction. Some of the most potent words are "needs," "have to have," "when he's finished," "it's time to," "you forgot."

Questions may be used advantageously to activate the child if they demand answers that he already knows, such as "Where does your coat go?" "What did you forget?" "What do you do with your cup?" Avoid questions that can be answered by "No," such as "Can you hang your coat up?" which is usually answered by "No."

HUMOR

If you treat the more annoying characteristics of the two-and-a-half-year-old, such as perseveration, vacillation, and negativism, by using them in humor, you not only give them a legitimate outlet but also loosen their grip. Use these characteristics as foils for activating techniques; for example:

Perseveration and vacillation—"No, no, no." Adult: "Yes, yes, yes," etc., with laughter.

Negativism—Ask silly questions that are answered by "no": "Does Nancy go home with Panda?" "No." "Does Nancy go home with Daddy?" "No." "Does Nancy go home with Mary?" "Yes." (When Nancy has had trouble, formerly, going home with Mary.)

OTHER CHILDREN

The teacher needs to have a wealth of techniques to draw upon, because more disputes occur at this age than at any other. Disputes are best handled with the teacher on hand to give the children sufficient suggestions, but also sufficient leeway to settle things according to each individual's needs. Often at this age the more mature child gives in to the less mature. The solution will often not conform to adult standards of justice.

A great deal of physical separation is needed. Teachers should try to anticipate and thus protect children from too many situations where they need to be negative, aggressive, possessive. If trouble is too complex, simply remove the child to another part of the room.

At two it was important to keep talk simple. Now a long flow of words directed to a child may calm him even when he doesn't understand all that is being said.

Substitution is still one of the best methods of handling disputes. "What else can you use?" or "What can we get for Bill?" Some cannot give up their own toy but can find a substitute. After a period of this sort of suggestion, some may start substituting on their own. They protect the toy they are playing with by offering something else to the aggressive child. This ability increases at three years of age.

GROUP ACTIVITY

The quality of two-and-a-half-year group activity is fluctuating because of the unpredictability of the individuals composing it. Some of the stormiest days, which appear tangled and give the guidance teacher a sense of failure, may in reality be the precursors of more coordinated group activity.

Rising tension at this age may be relieved by the adult's setting up parallel group play, with each child using identical material such as clay, beads, etc.

Though parallel play still predominates, there are glimpses of cooperative group play including two or three children. Children may sit momentarily in a block train, may bring medicine to a "sick" child, or may pull others in a cart.

Cultural and Creative Activities

BOOKS

1. Pretends to pick up objects from pictures, pats kitty, etc.
2. Spontaneous language (of the child) is often rhythmical and repetitive.
3. Enjoys rhythm and repetition in rhymes and stories.
4. Wants repetition of same story day after day.
5. Slow acceptance of new story.
6. Attends to short, simple stories of familiar subjects, as *The Little Family* and *The Little Auto*.
7. No demand for plot in stories but enjoys a simple one, as in *Cinder*.
8. Likes books giving simple information about animals and transportation, as *Ask Mr. Bear* and *Saturday Walk*.
9. Enjoys having an adult improvise a story about what the child

does throughout the day or what his contemporaries are doing.

10. From thirty-three to thirty-six months wants to hear elaborate details of his babyhood and later of each member of his family and friends. The story of *Little Baby Ann* is a favorite during this stage.

11. Reading in which he takes some part holds him longer, as naming kinds of animals or filling in words or phrases of a sentence he knows.

12. Enjoys looking at books alone.

MUSIC

1. May know all or parts of several songs which he reproduces at home or spontaneously at school, but is often inhibited in singing with others at school.

2. Spontaneous singing on minor third of such phrases as "coal man, coal truck."

3. Absorbs music and particularly enjoys repetition of old, familiar tunes.

4. High interest in listening to instruments or phonograph.

5. Enjoyment of marked rhythm, as in Ravel's *Bolero* or band music.

6. Musically talented children with sensitive ears may show *fear* of phonograph at this age.

7. Less individuality in rhythms because of imitation and awareness of others.

8. Majority of group will run, gallop, swing, etc., to music, watching others.

9. Enjoys simple group activity, as ring-around-a-rosy.

PAINTING

1. Experimenting with vertical and horizontal lines, dots, and circular movements.

2. Good form at beginning but generally quick to deteriorate.

3. May go out of bounds, painting on table, easel, floor, own hands, other children.

4. May paint many pages with little variety.

FINGER PAINTING

1. A better medium for this age than painting on easels because hands are in direct contact with the medium and do not have to adjust to a tool and container, such as brush and paint jar. Since this is a tangled age, the simpler medium is preferable, because it does not add complications.
2. To see the enjoyment of a child having his hands legitimately in paint makes one know the wise choice of this medium.
3. Needs more supervision than at any other age. Stimulus of groups in school controls it somewhat, but apt to go far out of bounds at home.
4. Pure enjoyment of manipulation and color with little feeling for form.

CLAY

1. Excellent medium for this age because each child can have identical materials for parallel play, thus reducing to a minimum the characteristic desire for the equipment of others.
2. Good medium for working off tangles and surplus energy by pounding, squeezing, and poking.
3. Affords relaxation as it inspires a long span of attention, which is seldom true of other materials.
4. Out-of-bounds behavior can be legitimatized and interest span lengthened by using other materials in combination with clay, such as tongue depressors, play cars, and toy animals.
5. Like to pass products around to each other, naming them pies, cakes, etc.

SAND, STONES, WATER

1. Makes pies and cakes with sand and mud, patting and smoothing them.
2. Continued high interest in water, which is also an excellent medium for this age. Likes blowing soap bubbles, "painting" with water, washing clothes and hanging on line, sailing boats, and scrubbing.

BLOCKS

1. Continued vertical and horizontal building with beginning of symmetry.
2. Some simple structures are named, as bridge, bed, tracks.
3. Sometimes blocks are used imaginatively as coal, ashes, lumber.
4. Uses larger blocks more than when younger.
5. Some color matching with blocks.

POSSESSIONS

1. Brings favorite toy to school to show to others, but generally not able to share it with others. May bring same toy each day. Is happier if toy is stored out of reach of others until time to go home.
2. Clings to favorite possession when insecure.
3. May cling to old clothes and dislike new ones.
4. Especially fond of hats and mittens.
5. May go through elaborate rituals with possessions at home.
6. Interest in acquiring possessions of others, but seldom plays with them.
7. Likes to have a few pennies in pocketbook and is very possessive about them.

EXCURSIONS

1. Enjoys going to the park to see other children or to use play equipment.
2. Likes short excursions to nearby farms to see animals or flowers.
3. Enjoys watching trains go by at a distance.
4. Beginning to have thought of a destination in mind, and may even insist on going along a special route.

IMAGINATIVE PLAY

The child of this age is still rather close to home, but imaginative play, begun in a small way earlier, continues and elaborates. Thus the child may pretend he is a baby, may play with imaginary objects, or may play house imaginatively with a doll or teddy bear, and in this play may animate the object, pretending it is alive.

TELEVISION*

At this age as just earlier, many children do watch quite a bit of television. It can be an interesting though not necessary and usually minor part of their lives at this time. As a rule, it presents no special problems since parents can still pretty well control any viewing, determining both time of watching and programs seen.

TIME AND SPACE

Though the child's vocabulary of time words may still be very limited (comprising probably not more than twenty or so different words), a definite advance takes place at this age in that he now freely uses words implying past, present, and future time, having numerous different words for each. Thus the finer divisions of time—"morning" and "afternoon"—have been added to "day" to indicate present time. The future may be indicated by "someday," "one day," "tomorrow," and several others. There are fewer different words for past than for future. Past time is usually designated as "last night." Though "tomorrow" is used, the word "yesterday" has not yet appeared. Altogether, time expressions sound quite versatile in spite of the smallness of the child's time vocabulary. He freely uses the names of the days in the week.

The use of space words is very much in keeping with the rigid, patterned, exact behavior of the age. Many space words are rigid, exact words and many appear at this age only. Thus we have: "right," "right here," "right there," "right up there," "right home," "right down," "right in." Also note at this age, for nearly the first time two space words combined give more exactness to location indicated: "way up," "up in," "in here," "in there," in addition to the use of "right" and

---

* At this and other ages, television viewing is included with other cultural and creative activities though it normally takes place at home.

some other words. "Near" represents a definite advance over the earlier "in" or "at." A beginning interest in more distant places is expressed by "far" and "far away."

Also, the most new space words are added in the period from two to two and a half years of any six-month period in the preschool years, both in spontaneous verbalization and in answer to space questions (this in contrast to the most new time words, which come in between two and a half and three years). Words used most are: "in," "on," "up in," and "at." There is great interest in and marked insistence upon having objects in their proper places.

Three Years

BEHAVIOR

Three is the first age when the child pays as much attention to other children as he does to his teacher. In fact, attention in general seems to be about evenly divided between the two. There is relatively little solitary play now, though some climb alone or play with blocks alone, but only on occasion do they talk to themselves (as they did earlier) when so playing.

There is a good deal of interaction and conversation with the teacher, though now in perhaps the majority of instances this conversation is initiated by the child and not by the teacher. Children tell the teacher what they are doing: "I'm going to make a worm," "This is a garage"; they ask for help: "Me want a turn, just a little turn," "I want you to do it"; announce their own independent ability: "I'm older. I can put that up," "I can go by myself"; or talk about their imaginary role: "I'm a kitty, too, but I found my mittens."

They ask her for information and sometimes give information, tell the teacher about things that happen at home: "My daddy dressed me yesterday"; call attention to their own prowess: "Hey, watch this!"; request or demand help; offer to help her; complain about other children: "When I make a bubble he breaks it."

The less mature the child, the more teacher-oriented, but nearly all at times ask for help, announce behavior, show off, or announce termination of an activity.

And of course there are still many nonverbalized relations with the teacher. They may look at her roguishly when acting wild, may retreat to her for help if in trouble. Or with the basic niceness and me-tooness of three, they may just like to gravitate to near where teacher is. She is a very important person in their lives even when they may seem temporarily caught up in their own concerns.

A good proportion of conversation, and attention, is now directed to comtemporaries. There is much social, self-initiated conversation. Some still protect their own property: "Dat's mine. Get out of there." Some argue over property ownership, and some call names: "You bad boy"; "You naughty girl"; "You're dumb." Children may now use earlier, teacher-instigated techniques on each other: "You get another train. I need this one."

Earlier threats may now be replaced with polite requests: "You have it and then it's my turn." "I need it. I'll give it back when I'm all through. All right?" "I'm getting *this* ball for Michael. You bounce that one." Some may even ask permission for an object or activity: "May I have these?"

Much conversation is social and friendly, having to do with the carrying out of real or imaginary play activity: "Make b'lieve this is a boat." "You're the doggy; say 'Bow-wow.'" "Have some cake." Or one child tells something, as "Mummy's coming for me," and then others tell that *their* mummy is coming for them. Even at this age there is a beginning of a friendly heterosexual approach: "Michael, I wonder—I wish you'd come to my house sometime."

There is a beginning of the excluding, unfriendly commands that will be so much more prevalent six months later: "You can't come in here. Nobody else can come in here." There is less aggression than earlier but more excluding.

Probably the majority of verbalization is still self-initiated, but many now do converse, meaningfully, with others. They may give or withhold permission, make a reciprocal offer when something is offered to them, take part in rather complex imaginary or housekeeping or other group play. Maturity is shown by the fact that some children can now separate activity and conversation. They may be playing with clay but talking about when they were babies, or about something that happened at home.

Cooperative play is still rather rudimentary. Two children frequently play together but often do not *do* very much. Thus both may simply stand inside of their "store" with heads out of the "store window" being "store men." Several may, though, work together on the same block or other structure. Social relations seem tentative and experimental. Most contacts do not seem to go very deep or to last for very long.

Any altercations are more easily solved than earlier, both because children are beginning to use techniques such as asking permission and suggesting turns, and because their own interests are more flexible and not as rigidly adhered to as in the past. However, if their own devices fail they quickly turn to the teacher for a solution and, if needed, for protection.

Group behavior is extremely different from what it was at two and a half years. There are more different activities going on simultaneously, which gives less of an impression of everyone being at about the same level. Thus activity in one playroom may range from solitary, to conversation with the teacher, to aggressive play between some two, to relatively cooperative play between two or more. There are many different kinds of subgroups and many different degrees of cooperation.

Most children seem to like to play physically near each other but many are still only on the verge of cooperative play. There is some giving and receiving of directions and suggestions, but only for brief periods. Groupings are fluid and they shift rapidly. There is little structure to groups since personnel and/or activities change quickly. Imitation is strong. If one child starts an activity, others are likely to follow.

Group play at this age is more than parallel, but less than cooperative, as any child may stop play at any time to insist that the house all have been working on is "Mine!" This demand may if necessary be reinforced by pulling, hitting, pushing, or kicking. However, children are much more ready to adjust and are much less defensive and aggressive than earlier.

Twosomes last longer and get on better than do larger groupings. In any size grouping the activity seems to be of more interest than the cooperation of other children.

TECHNIQUES

PHYSICAL ENVIRONMENT

Fewer environmental restrictions are now necessary. Since the gross motor drive is reduced, children can hold more to spheres of interest in various sections of the room. They can be helped to hold to these spheres of interest longer through verbal suggestions from the adult; e.g., "Is your supper ready?" when playing in the doll corner; or "Does anybody need any groceries?" when playing in the store.

More materials for dramatic play, such as a costume box, and more constructive materials, such as large blocks, are important at this age.

ADJUSTMENT

Difficulties in adjusting to school at the beginning of a session are rare at this age, and when they occur can be handled through "surprises" or through favorite toys. As the school day moves on, the happy adjustment of the three-year-old often depends on finding a friend. If he does not do this on his own, a teacher can help.

ROUTINES

Children at this age move easily through such routines as washing, toileting, midmorning snack, and rest. They can handle undressing almost entirely by themselves but need some help in dressing, mostly in starting their ski pants and jackets. (More help is usually needed at home than at school.) Dressing and undressing can both be speeded up through humor.

Toileting. There are still quite a few who object to toileting at school, but most are trained and are no problem. They will tell when they are going and will ask for help if they need it, chiefly in pulling up pants. Routine toileting is needed only for the younger Threes. Most ask when they need, or go by themselves.

Milk and Crackers. A child may like to sit by special friends. Most like this routine, but may be boisterous and silly. They may wiggle, spill milk, shout, bite graham crackers into the shape of guns and shoot with them. As a rule, the group can be controlled by distraction. Very simple conversation will do this, as "Do you know what?" "I have a secret." "Do you know what kind of book we're going to read next?"

Any sentences using the words "surprise" and "different" can calm them down, as can calling favorable attention to their clothing. But some boisterousness should be allowed.

Most can now obey simple rules such as not having their cup too full or not pouring milk back into the pitcher. Some milk will be spilled. This should not be a cause for concern.

Rest. Very few refuse to rest on cots at this age, but they will not rest for more than ten to fifteen minutes. Relaxation can best be accomplished when music or stories are used.

Cleaning up. Children do not put toys away spontaneously, but enjoy doing so in a group if the putting away is dramatized and they can pretend that they are lumbermen, movers, or other specific persons. The whole group often works together in the spirit of a game.

TRANSITIONS

Transitions are seldom difficult at this age. New ways of doing things, of going from one place to another, can be used. Since the gross motor drive is now more under the child's control, the suggestion to run, jump, or hop into the bathroom or elsewhere becomes a new game.

Often mere verbal suggestion will effect a necessary transition. If toys must be picked up in a change from one type of activity to another, children will frequently help with this. When it comes time to go home, most are happy to leave and there is little difficulty about this. Some need to perform just one more trick or have one more turn, but will now accept the "just one more," so that it can be permitted.

TEACHER

This is a social, imitative, "me, too" age. Therefore it is better to point out positive rather than negative factors (referred to more safely before three), as children are apt to do the thing mentioned. "We stand on the floor" gives them the positive suggestion rather than "We don't stand on the table."

VERBAL

The two-and-a-half-year-old child's demand for repetition of the same words and phrases is now giving way to an interest in many new words and new uses of words.

1. Key adjectives—"new," "different," "big," "strong." "Could you make a different kind?" stimulates the child within a situation without giving him a specific idea. "Can you carry two big ones?" may be the needed challenge to put the blocks away.
2. Key nouns—"surprise," "secret." "When you finish going to the bathroom I have a surprise for you" may organize a scraggly group.
3. Key verbs—"help," "might," "could," "guess what," "needs." "You could help John fill the cart" may produce not only the desired action but also the satisfaction as expressed in "I'm helping."
4. Key adverbs—"maybe," "how about," "too." "You could help, too" helps the child to join in the group activity, which he craves.

The three-year-old listens well when he is reasoned with. He will sometimes do things he does not like to do if he is given a good reason; e.g., "Let's pick up the blocks so we'll have more room to dance." A good reason for doing something should include a specific step-by-step suggestion. Children withdraw from general demands such as "Pick up your room" or "Tell me what you did at school today." They respond readily, however, to the more specific "First let's pick up the big blocks and then . . ." or "Did you paint at school today?" It is still wisest to avoid "Do you want to . . . ?"

The use of "maybe," "you might," "perhaps," "you could" gives the child a graceful way of refusing in situations where complying is not important; e.g., "Maybe you could help Bobby pull the wagon."

One of the best ways to simplify a group pressure situation is by whispering to the child. The same question, such as "Where does your cup go?" that may not be responded to when spoken out loud may receive an immediate response when spoken in a whisper. The whispering not only gives the enjoyment of a secret, but also restricts the child's influence to only one other person.

HUMOR

The gross motor humor of the two-year-old is steadily giving way to verbal humor by three. Simple repetitions, such as "golly, golly, golly," tossed back and forth between the child and the adult like a verbal ball, give a joyous air to activity.

Humorous wrong guesses from the adult delight the child. For example, as the child is taking off his outer things the adult may ask, "Are your socks purple today?" "No," says the child with a smile.

Adult: "Then they are red?" "No."

Adult: "Then they must be blue." "No, wrong again," and the child laughs as he hurries to take off his snowsuit to show the teacher that they are white.

OTHER CHILDREN

The teacher's role in helping children play is now less active than earlier. She can enrich and elaborate play by standing near and offering creative ideas. But she does not need to help and demonstrate as she did with the younger child. Such questions as "Who'll be the doctor?" or "Now I wonder who's going to cook the dinner?" can be enough to start elaborate sickroom or domestic play.

With language equipment and a better-developed sense of the other person as expressed in his use of "we," the three-year-old can solve his own problems more adequately and needs less adult guidance than does the two-and-a-half-year-old. It is sometimes advisable to let children settle their own disputes by fighting it out if they are fairly evenly matched and the aggressive child does not always win. The adult should sense the point beyond which her "ignoring" the conflict would be detrimental to the children involved.

The three-year-old is apt to respond more to the other children than to the adult. Therefore the adult may often use a child to help another. "John, you may go in to rest with Bobby." Group squabbles are often best settled by the leader, as when a boy and girl in a group of three were fighting over an armchair. The teacher's stock techniques of "Who had it first?" or "You could take turns" made no impression upon them. Then the teacher turned to the third child, who was the "hostess," and asked her what she was going to do about it. Whereupon she replied immediately, "Only daddies sit in chairs with arms. You sit over there, Nancy." And Nancy complied at once.

Teachers can now talk effectively about "friends," and a great deal can be done with this concept. If there is sufficient mention that a person is a friend, that person tends to become a friend, though twosomes still tend to predominate over threesomes. A child can be persuaded to imitate the positive thing a "friend" is doing. Some can learn to come to school without crying, be toilet trained, play happily, because the "friend" is doing these things.

Cooperation, sharing, and taking turns now seem to come more naturally and with less help from the teacher. She may still occasionally need to use such phrases as "When he's finished," "His turn," "He needs it," but the three-year-old can wait better, can understand that "Bill is using it now," and may often take his cue from the teacher. "Ask Bill when he is going to be through with it." Bill may answer, "In two minutes," which may mean "Almost at once."

Since three-year-olds are much more social than formerly, other children can be used successfully to take charge of a difficult child or to help make new adjustments. A seven- or eight-year-old child visiting for a day may raise the level of behavior considerably and may have a carry-over for some length of time.

In general, the teacher's role at this age in adjusting children to each other is more to encourage or start friendships, to give ideas for elaborating play, than actual disciplining or giving children techniques for getting on with each other.

GROUP ACTIVITY

Three is capable of continuing group play more smoothly and longer than Two-and-a-half, and there is more spontaneous group play. The teacher can often keep play from deteriorating by elaborating it with suggestions such as "Is supper ready?" or "Who's going to be the conductor on your train?"

Rising tension at this age may be relieved, as earlier, by the adult's setting up parallel group play with clay, etc., which satisfies the "me, too" characteristic of the three-year-old.

There should be a balance or alternation of quiet and active group play. A suggested schedule for a three-year-old group is as follows:

Outdoor play	1/2 hour
Indoor free play	1 hour
Music, singing, and rhythms	20–30 minutes
Milk and crackers	10 minutes
Stories	10–20 minutes
Outdoor play	Until they go home

The group may need to be subdivided to separate conflicting personalities. This will help to prolong and support group play.

Clear-cut daily changes in adequacy of adjustment are not usually seen in a three-year-old group, but during the course of an entire week there tends to be a change toward less individual and more integrated behavior. Though this might seem in some ways desirable, actually as a group children manage better before they become too high-spirited and too integrated. Children of this age are so extremely imitative that *all* may go too far in imitating the high spirits of some one child.

A three-year-old group, if children are more or less of one age, not only starts the fall season rather well but may steadily improve till about Christmas time. There may be a slight lag after that, during which the teacher may feel a strong need to introduce new activities and new materials.

By spring the group is likely to have become quite high-powered and high-strung: children cry, act aggressively, are hard to please. This, of course, may be related to the fact that many are around three and a half years of age by then. Fortunately the group is more often than not out of doors in the spring, and the added freedom that this provides tends to calm tensions, and provides extra outlet for vigorous behavior.

Cultural and Creative Activities

We have combined our information on these topics for three and three and a half years. Thus the reader is referred to page 341.

STORYTELLING AND IMAGINATIVE PLAY

In stories told spontaneously by children of this age, as at other ages, themes of violence predominate. Children obviously are much concerned about, if not preoccupied by, thoughts of violent action. People, objects, and animals in their stories come to much harm. But there is a strong sex difference here. Girls seem equally interested in friendly, gentle activities and actions but now only half as many boys tell friendly tales as tales of violence and disaster.

"Girl," "mummy" (or other adult), and animals are the things talked about most by three-year-old girls; "boy" or some animal are the favorite characters of boys. Two-thirds of the girls, as compared to all of the boys, see their mother primarily as a friendly, companioning, protecting person. All of both sexes, at this age only, see their father as a friendly, kind, caring for, protecting person.

As earlier, girls tell stories with primarily social themes; boys talk about themselves. Girls in their stories still think of themselves as being close to home, in their own houses or yards. Boys are already spreading out—to school, store, zoo, movies.

Sense of humor is increasing. Substantially more children than at two introduce some humor into their stories, though this may be no more than the use of silly language: "Choo choo, floo floo, boo boo," or "The girl shook when she took a look."

This is the last age in which realism dominates over fantasy. Two- and three-year-olds not only live (in their minds) close to home but in rather real worlds. However, imaginative play with doll or teddy bear continues as earlier, and the child may play with an imaginary object (an object that is not actually present) or may impersonate an animal. And in the more advanced and possibly somewhat superior child, one may see a good beginning of the play with imaginary companions so strong in many at three and a half years of age. The imaginary companion or playmate may be an animal or a person. The child may have one such playmate or several. Play with this companion may occur only now and then or may be a somewhat dominating theme in his daily life. This kind of imaginative play reaches its peak, in many, at three and a half years of age and will be described somewhat fully as we discuss that age.

TELEVISION

Perhaps three-quarters of the children studied by us now watch television. Those who do not, for the most part just don't have a television set in their homes.

Perhaps half still accept their parents' ideas as to what programs they should watch and how long they should view. Others either decide for themselves (in extremely permissive households) or make a fuss, argue, and tease to watch more often or for longer periods than parents think they should.

Most parents who do permit television-watching feel that it does add to the child's life. Programs watched most are "New Zoo Review," "Sesame Street," "Lassie," "Mr. Rogers," "Captain Kangaroo," and "The Flintstones."

TIME AND SPACE

More different time words come in between thirty and thirty-six months than in any other six-month interval. Most of the more common basic time words are now in the child's vocabulary. Past, present, and future are all referred to, though there are still more different words for expressing future than past. There is now nearly as much spontaneous verbalization about the past and future as about the present. Expressions of duration, such as "all the time," "all day," "for two weeks," come in.

There is now a pretense of telling time, and spontaneous use of clock time phrases, usually inaccurate. There is much use of the word "time," alone or in combinations: "What time?" or "It's time," as well as "lunchtime," "puzzle time," etc. Phrases beginning with "when" are very common. The child of three can answer a few questions involving time concepts. He can tell how old he is, when he goes to bed (in terms of some other activity), and what he will do tomorrow, at Christmas, in the winter. At this age especially the child may tenaciously answer all questions about time with some one in-appropriate clock time or some one number, as "fifty-nine."

As to space, most of the space words used at two and a half are continued in use except for a few of the more exact and rigid words, such as "right there," "right up there." A few of the new words that come in, though not as exact as the two-and-a-half-year words, express an increased refinement in space perception: "back," "corner," "over," "from," "by," "up on top," "on top of."

A new and marked interest in space and direction detail comes in at this age, particularly in response to questions. In telling how to get somewhere, the child may give an actual direction; e.g., "Turn left and then turn right." In telling where his daddy is he no longer says merely, "At his office," but spontaneously may describe where the office is. In telling where he sleeps he may tell where his crib or bed-room is located. "To," with a city name, shows increasing expansion of space interest. The three-year-old can tell what street he lives on, though usually not the number. He can put a ball "on" and "under" a chair. "In," "on," "at," and "to" are space words used most.

Three and a Half Years

BEHAVIOR

At this age there comes a big change in nursery school socialization. At three most children seemed to share their attention more or less equally between teacher and other children. Now, for the first time, other children receive the major part of attention. Nearly all boys and girls are extremely social and aware of each other at this age.

This does not mean that the teacher is ignored. Most are still strongly aware of her. They talk to her about current, completed, or intended activities. They ask for information or help; announce their own independent activities or abilities; call her attention to their activity or prowess, boasting about size or adequacy. Some conversation is merely social and friendly, or may involve an offer of help.

Thus the child may say, "My, I'm awfully tired." He may offer, "I fweep it all up for you." "I'm seven years old—not a baby." "Please show me where the paint is." "I couldn't put my shoes on last year and I can't this year. No child as old as I am can put on shoes." "Do you have any sisters?" "Look what I made. I made a whale."

Most conversation and attention, however, is directed to other children. This still consists frequently of statements of ownership: "My own ball. Get out." But now there is a little sharing talk: "Let me have yours and you have mine. That would be a good thing." There is also some asking of permission and some talk about taking turns.

There is a good deal of imaginative conversation accompanying play: "I'm a monkey." "Come on, children; we're running an elevator here." "I'm the store man. Steena, would you like some apples?"

Some make friendly invitations to others to take part in play, as "Will you come down to my house?" and much conversation is now engaged in as part of cooperative play: "We got everything we need, haven't we? We need more berries?" "O.K. I got blueberries and flowers. This is the way we make our cake." With boys, activity is strong, but for many girls much of their loved cooperative house play consists of little action and *much* talk.

Earlier it was objects that were the major bone of contention. Now it seems to be people. Children are much concerned about whom they play with and whom they do *not* play with. For the first time we find a great deal of *excluding* of some other child: "We don't like him, do we?" "He can't play with us." "Get out. We don't like you."

Children are beginning to be interested in friendships, and one of the ways they establish whom they will play with is by emphasizing whom they will not include. Just as they are very emphatic about their exclusions, so they are also emphatic about inclusions. A strong feeling of togetherness with a chosen child is expressed by use of such words as "we" or "we both." Though frequently these friendships are between two children of the same sex, heterosexual friendships, with girls often the aggressors, are characteristic of this age.

The query "Do you love me?" which is so often addressed to parents at home, may also be addressed to contemporaries, as in the case of the child who asked another, "Do you love me like Karen?" only to receive the reply: "Yes, I love you like carrots, I love you like spinach, I love you like cabbage."

In spite of marked interest in other children, many on occasion still seem to prefer solitary activity. This may be one way of protecting themselves when the going gets too rough. But in general there is now little isolated play and fewer twosomes than earlier. Most children now play much of the time in groups of three or more, in lively imaginative play. Groupings are important but very fluid. There is much imitation: if one child does something interesting, the whole group is likely to follow.

TECHNIQUES

ADJUSTMENT

Three-year-olds as a rule have very little difficulty in adjusting to school. At three and a half many revert to earlier difficulties, especially when it is the mother who delivers them to school. At this age, whatever mother wants is likely to be what the child does not want, so that actually someone other than the mother may be the best one to take a child to school. If she is the person to do it, it may work best if she drops the child off and leaves as quickly as possible. Once the teacher has taken over, there is usually little trouble, as children at this age tend to be more amiable in the hands of a teacher or baby-sitter than of their own mother.

ROUTINES

Any routine, once it has got under way, tends to go fairly smoothly at this age, but transitions from one situation to another can cause difficulty now as they did earlier at two and a half.

Toileting as a rule gives little difficulty. Children of this age may express their typically increased tension by urinating frequently, but most can handle this routine by themselves except that they may like to tell the teacher that they are going to the bathroom, and may like to report to her after they have been.

Milk-and-cracker time usually proceeds without too much difficulty, and may become increasingly lively as children's notion of what constitutes a social conversation becomes increasingly elaborate.

Story time, too, becomes more absorbing for all, as the children are increasingly interested in being read to and also show a growing attention span for this activity. As earlier, it is important for the teacher to hold up her book so that all can see and to speak loudly and clearly enough so that all can hear. It is important that she begin with an appealing book and fairly soon in the story hold up an attractive picture. At this age most children do not need books of their own but are able to sit and listen to the teacher.

Story interest now has expanded considerably beyond home and everyday routines. Now the child likes to hear about carpenters, painters, postmen, taxi men, and astronauts.

The world of fantasy, too, becomes more distinctly appealing as the child moves on toward four. With the customary interest in imaginary companions, anthropomorphized animals are especially popular. Books like *Curious George* or any other of the many books in which animals perform in human ways are much enjoyed. Children also like stories that feature aggression and wickedness and violent disaster. They seem to enjoy the fact that the security of the storybook people is threatened while they themselves remain personally secure.

Music time is also very much enjoyed now by most. They are especially pleased by extremes of volume—exaggeratedly loud or very soft music. They like having a "theme" for the music period, such as a visit to a toy shop and singing about all the things they see in the shop; or pretending they are on a picnic and singing about the different picnic activities. Children at this age are not quite as spontaneous about offering their own words to a tune or their own dramatic motions, but one does see a good beginning of spontaneous self-expression.

TRANSITIONS

Transitions tend to present a difficulty for almost any preschooler at almost any age, but they are especially difficult at two and a half and three and a half years of age. Once a child is *in* almost any situation, he or she tends to do rather well, but he may balk at practically any transition. And since he is not only more mature, but also more guileful and even more determined to have his own way than he was at two and a half, great skill and subtlety are needed on the part of the teacher to steer him from one activity to the next.

A three-and-a-half-year-old may balk with a strong "No, I don't want to," or with argument, or even with tears and wailing, when even some rather simple and usual move is suggested. Sometimes a teacher can take the child by surprise and override his objections by such a word as "Scat" when there is balking.

Or the teacher may outwit the child in more sophisticated and ever-changing ways. Just because something works one day does not mean that it will work the next day.

One of the best methods is to distract the child from the transition at hand by talking of something else, perhaps something that has been read in a story, as "Do you remember . . . ?" Children are also extremely vulnerable to compliments about their appearance and good behavior. Thus a compliment may smooth over a needed transition.

Occasionally a teacher may need to revert to sheer physical handling.

TEACHER AND VERBAL TECHNIQUES

Even more than six months earlier, this is a sociable "me, too" age. A skillful teacher can put to good advantage the fact that children like to imitate. Since they imitate the bad as well as the good, it is important to emphasize the "right" way to do things rather than commenting on things that may be being done "wrong." At this age a group may ring with the phrase "Me, too," so that once you get a leader going in the direction you prefer, others are more than likely to fall into line.

There is, at three and a half, a strong tendency for any group to become overexcited and rowdy, probably because of the marked tensions felt by individual children at this age. Thus a fairly well planned activity, as pasting, crayoning, painting, rather than free play, may be best, at least for a substantial part of the time.

Or a teacher can help calm a group by whispering to them, thus getting their cooperation in being quiet. Actually either extreme, a soft whisper or a rather loud command, may work better in getting attention than a normal speaking voice.

Teachers need to be forewarned that this is an age where group activity can steadily mount until things go all to pieces, as with a group block structure when the whole thing is suddenly demolished and blocks go flying hither and yon. The perceptive teacher will recognize this potential danger and will be able to hold the behavior this side of going to pieces by sending a more obstreperous member on an errand or shifting play to a new locale. In these situations one can sense and predict the wildness that will soon appear at four years of age.

Since any behavior tends to become exaggerated at this age, the timing of techniques is important to prevent excessive exuberance or negativism. As a rule it is important to step in quickly.

The element of surprise can be a timely motivator or distractor. "Do you know what?" is a question that interrupts a child's actions or thoughts and makes him receptive to whatever it is that the teacher is about to say. The idea of something new and exciting can be introduced by using the words "surprise," "new," "different."

Also, as mentioned earlier, compliments and praise can interrupt and distract a child from undesirable behavior and motivate him in a desired direction. One can hardly overuse such comments as "I like you," "You're my friend."

Most children are highly and imaginatively verbal at this age. A teacher can utilize this talkativeness to encourage desirable or interesting behavior. She may, for instance, repeat one child's conversation to another, may point out some attractive activity of some one child, or may make a suggestion as to further embellishment of imaginative play.

Since children of this age often call themselves by some name other than their own, a teacher can sometimes motivate them to desired behavior by using this other name: "And now Mickey Mouse does so-and-so" or "Now Kitten can do so-and-so."

CHILD-CHILD

There is much less quarreling between child and child at this age than earlier but much more ganging up of any two or three to exclude some other child. This seems to be the way that friendships are formed and cemented—by ganging up against somebody else. Thus one hears a great deal of "We don't want her"; "You can't come in"; "We don't want to play with you."

An important teacher task for this age, therefore, is to help encourage children to include the excluded other. Among the more effective techniques for doing this are the following:

1. Giving a choice: "Do you want her to bring you some bread or some butter?"
2. Singing something like "She can come in, she can come in."
3. Stretching out the child's horizon with a new word or idea: "She could be your guest."
4. Giving the new child a specific role to play by saying: "But he is the milkman." "She's your grandmother coming to visit." "He's the puppy, playing on the floor."
5. The teacher joining the group and bringing the excluded child with her.

Though such skilled intervention can often be effective, a teacher should avoid spending too much time seeing to it that an excluded child is included. She might, instead, start some other interesting activity with that child as a focus, including other children in this new group rather than trying to infiltrate the old.

Three-and-a-half-year-olds, with their customary individual tensions, may get into quite squabbly group tangles rather than solving every problem that involves demanding and commanding each other. If it comes to actual hitting, pushing, and shouting, a teacher should quickly terminate the situation and start something else, perhaps some more structured group situation in another part of the playroom. As a group, children of this age tend to become more animated toward the end of a week. This is not necessarily an improvement, as children tend to become *excessively* high-spirited. The last day or days of a week may thus not be as good a time to introduce a new game or a new song as earlier in the week. Behavior is often more individual on Mondays, but at this age that makes the group easier for the teacher to manage.

CULTURAL AND CREATIVE ACTIVITIES

BOOKS

1. Increasing interest span in listening to stories.
2. Can be held longer when stories are read to small groups.
3. Continued enjoyment of familiar experiences with repetition and more detail.
4. Likes information about nature, transportation, etc., woven into story form, as *Beachcomber Bobbie* and *Four Airplanes.*
5. Likes imaginative stories based on real people and real animals, as *Caps for Sale.*
6. Enjoyment of riddles and guessing, such as *The Noisy Book.*
7. Enjoys widening of horizon through information books, as *Sails, Wheels and Wings.*
8. Makes relevant comments during stories, especially about materials or experiences at home.
9. Some insist on stories being retold and reread word for word without changes.
10. Likes to look at books and may "read" to others or explain pictures.

MUSIC

1. Many can reproduce whole songs, though generally not on pitch.
2. Beginning to match simple tones.
3. Less inhibition in joining group singing.
4. Can recognize several melodies.
5. Experimenting with musical instruments.
6. Simple explanations concerning songs and instruments delight them and encourage interest.
7. Marked individual differences in interest and ability to listen to music.
8. Enjoys a diversity of musical experiences.
9. Most members of the group participate in a variety of rhythms.
10. Watchers will often participate when approached through another child, or through dramatizing.
11. Children gallop, jump, walk, and run in fairly good time to music.
12. Enjoys dressing up in costumes for rhythms.

PAINTING

1. Strokes are more varied and rhythmical.
2. Beginnings of design are emerging.
3. Often child covers whole page with one color, or with blocks of various colors.
4. Sometimes names finished product, but seldom any recognizable resemblance.
5. May be stimulated by watching an older, talented child paint, or by observing more advanced paintings of other children.
6. Joy and pride in product; exclaims, "Look what I made!"
7. Works with more concentration and precision.
8. Dislikes sharing paper with others.

FINGER PAINTING

1. Experimenting with finger movements as well as whole-hand movements.
2. Some feeling for design.

CRAYONS
1. Demands a variety of colors.
2. Enters representative stage earlier with crayons than with paint.

CLAY
1. Enjoyment of manipulating with hands, patting, making holes with fingers, and squeezing.
2. Beginning of form: making flat, round "cakes" and balls. Rolls long, narrow strips, etc.
3. Some naming of product, with general approximation in shape.
4. Makes products for others outside school, especially mother, but often forgets to take them home.

SAND
1. Makes cakes, pies, roads, tunnels, etc.
2. Combines with other materials, such as pegs, stones, shells, toy cars.

BLOCKS
1. Likes a diversity of shapes and sizes.
2. Order and balance in building.
3. Combining with toy cars, trains, etc.
4. Often names what he is making.
5. Enjoys the process of construction more than playing with finished product.

POSSESSIONS
1. Enjoys new clothes and likes to exhibit them to others, especially to teacher.
2. Beginning to share toys; less hoarding.
3. Brings possessions to school to share with others, books, for instance.

4. May enjoy exhibiting possessions, then forgets about them for the morning. Generally brings different things every day.
5. Dislikes having others wear his clothes.
6. Likes to have pennies to put in the bank. Knows that money is used in making purchases but has no idea of how much. Play money may be very satisfactory as a substitute.

HOLIDAYS AND FESTIVALS

1. Birthday—The moment the cake arrives, the child is three. He enjoys a small party of two or three friends. Best time for this is still mealtime.
2. Christmas—Interest in Santa Claus. Much interested in his own presents. Cannot keep secret the presents he is giving others.
3. Valentine's Day—Likes sending valentines to others and making a personal mark (as a scribble or the first letter of his name) on the back. Often brings valentines to school to show to other children.
4. Easter—Interest in Easter bunny and eggs.
5. Halloween—Delighted with jack-o'-lantern, which is the whole meaning of Halloween to him. Likes watching adult make jack-o'-lantern and gives some help.
6. Thanksgiving—The whole meaning of Thanksgiving is the turkey, which he knows about beforehand. However, he also enjoys the party aspect of this holiday, including guests or a trip to visit relatives.
7. Religion—Greater interest in going to Sunday school. Also enjoys the quietness of church or synagogue. May enjoy saying short prayers.

EXCURSIONS

1. Enjoys excursions to airport, railroad station, fire station, harbor, zoo, or farm.
2. Fascinated watching men at work, as carpenter, painter, mechanic. Likes to watch steam shovel, cement mixer in operation.
3. Interested in planning visits, as an afternoon with another child or lunch with grandmother.
4. Enjoys everyday excursions as going to market.

5. Definitely has a destination in mind and enjoys talking about it beforehand.

STORYTELLING AND IMAGINATIVE PLAY

That the relationship with mother may seem difficult to both the child and the adult is suggested by the fact that this is the peak period for having mothers presented in stories as playing a negative role. Forty-four percent of girls and half the boys we tested tell stories in which the mother is disciplining, deserting, hurting, punching, or ignoring the child. At this age, as later at four and a half, a quarter of the boys but none of the girls see their mother as a passive victim of aggression. It is an interesting comment on our culture that so far as the father's role is concerned, all girls at this age see fathers as positive and friendly, whereas one-third of boys see him in some disciplinary, punishing, or hurting role.

"Girl," "Mummy," or some animal are the chief characters in spontaneous stories by girls; "boys," "Daddy," or some animal, in stories by boys.

Three and a half years of age is the high point, in many, for play with imaginary companions. Some have only one such companion and play with him only now and then. With others, the entire daytime life of the child (and of the family) may be pervaded. One child may have several imaginary animal companions and several different human companions, and may himself play the role of an animal and/or another person, as well as personalize objects.

At this age the child's imaginary life often has a more definite pattern than earlier, and is bound up more intimately with his own activities. The imaginary companion may need a place at the table, may sleep in or under the child's bed, may go for a ride in the family car. The child is often very demanding about the rights of his imaginary companion—no one can sit in the companion's chair, for instance —and is very solicitous about teaching him many things. Rigid demands for the companion's rights are added to rigid demands for the child's own rights and often complicate daily living.

The companion is most often related to the child's home life. It is only rarely that he is brought to nursery school, though he may come as far as the schoolroom door. If he is brought into the room, this may well be an indication of a difficult adjustment which the child is handling through this imaginative means. The same is true of the child who takes on the role of an animal. This role is much stronger at home, and may exercise such complete domination that the hand becomes a paw, the speech turns into animal noises, the tongue becomes a lapping instrument when it is time to drink. The child may respond only when addressed as "Kitten" or "Doggy." This imaginative shift of personality is more likely to be carried into the nursery school than is the imaginary companion.

Any of these imaginative outlets should be respected by the parent, and utilized though not exploited. Though not all children experience imaginary companions, they do appear strongly in perfectly normal children and should not be considered an indication of loneliness or a sign that anything is wrong with the child.

With a fuller experience and more maturity, the child may shift his imaginary impersonations into group play by becoming the mother, fireman, truckdriver, doctor. Imagination is also expressed in dramatic play with blocks, housekeeping materials, art materials. Usually at this age children use real toy trucks and other implements. They pretend coming to call; go through daily domestic routines; play roles of others by dressing up. A child may pretend to tell time with an imaginary wrist watch. He may spontaneously tell imaginative stories that give good clues as to the child's sense of self and interests.

TELEVISION WATCHING*

Perhaps three-quarters of the three- and three-and-a-half-year-olds observed by us do watch television. Those who do not, for the most part, just do not have a TV set at home.

---

* Television viewing is included with other cultural and creative activities though it chiefly occurs at home.

Nearly half still accept their parents' ideas as to what programs they should watch and how long they should view. Others either decide for themselves (in extremely permissive households) or make a fuss, argue, and tease to watch more often or for longer periods than parents think they should.

Most parents who do permit television viewing feel that it does add to the child's life. Programs watched most are "New Zoo Review," "Sesame Street," "Lassie," "Mr. Rogers," "Captain Kangaroo," and "The Flintstones."

TIME AND SPACE

Expressions indicating past, present, and future time are now used in spontaneous conversation to an equal extent. Past and future tenses are used accurately. There are also many rather complicated expressions of duration, such as: "for a long time," "for years," "a whole week," "in the meantime." Or such phrases as "Two things at once." Also there come in many different new ways of expressing sequence.

There is not so much an increase in the number of time words used at this age as in the refinements of use. The child says, "It's almost time," "a nice long time." He expresses habitual action, as "On Fridays." With increasing complexity of time expressions comes a confusion characteristic of forty-two months. The child frequently refers to future happenings as in the past. Thus: "I'm not going to take a nap yesterday." Ability to answer questions about time is not much greater than at three years.

Increased interest in new dimensions in space is expressed by the use of such words as "next to," "under," and "between." "Go" (meaning "belong") and "find" express interest in appropriate places for objects. Interest in comparative size is indicated by "littlest," "bigger," "larger." "Way down," "way off," "way far" express expanding but also exact interest in location. In answering questions, the three-and-a-half-year-old actually uses fewer different words than the three-year-old; in spontaneous vocalization, a few more. He can now put a ball "on," "under," and "in back of" a chair. "In," "on," "to," "home," and "up in" are space words used most frequently.

Four Years

BEHAVIOR

The typical four-year-old is a highly social individual. In school he is, much of the time, talking to and playing with his contemporaries. Relatively little time is spent alone and even when alone the child may be talking to his imaginary companion or companions. Even when working creatively with paints or clay he tends to be highly aware of those around him.

Not only does the child spend little time alone; his attention to the teacher is much, much less than at earlier ages. He still talks to her on occasion. Thus he may give information: "Our Margie has a brand-new washing machine." "He [the janitor] never gets in the corners." "I told you—a pencil is a simple thing." "I don't mind. I don't mind anything 'cept when Mummy washes my hair." Or he may ask questions or ask for help. He may tell of his own abilities: "I can write." "I can count." "I can swing by my knees." And in typical four-year-old fashion he loves to boast. This may be about his own abilities—"I'm awful strong. I can even box"—or may be about his possessions: "I have some blocks at home much bigger than these."

As capable as he is socially, he may still ask for help against other children: "They won't let me come in." And, engagingly, he may tell his teacher how much he likes her: "You know, I often think of you. I'll call you up sometime. You could come to my house." Four may at times be very confidential and charming with her, whispering confidences, giving information, playing imaginatively, or just chatting.

There can be considerable interchange with the teacher on occasion, but many children may go through a whole morning without referring to her. And once teachers have arranged the possibility for activities, children often carry on almost without help. To many four-year-olds, it is the other children who *make* school. Interchange and cooperative and coordinated activities are the order of the day.

Four-year-old play is so active, so ever-changing, so imaginative, so speedy, and so constantly demanding of something new, exciting, and different to do that sometimes the teacher is hard put to provide the change and variety demanded.

In their dealings with each other, children of this age show a delightful maturity and often a good deal of consideration. There is now less talk about ownership. Children often ask permission to use toys and other objects: "Pretty soon will you let me use that red?" "May I please have my iron?" Or they may *ask* to have a turn: "It's my turn now. O.K.?" There is much use of the magic word "let's": "Let's play with this." Or a child may instruct another as to the role to be played: "You're a cemetery. Lie down."

Imaginative house play can now be carried on over longish periods, involving many children. Or they may play at being on a farm, running a store, sailing a boat. Such cooperative play on a single project might last as long as fifteen or twenty minutes, with children giving and accepting suggestions: "I'll be the conductor. You be the engineer." Children often initiate this kind of play without help or suggestion from the teacher. (Her role may be more to set up the room and materials in such a way as to encourage children's use of their own imagination.)

With girls there may be more talk than action, but cooperative play among boys may involve considerable use of real objects, such as blocks, and may turn into good construction projects with much gruff, masculine talk and admonition. Boys, especially, like to call each other by false, masculine-sounding names, as "Bill," "Joe," "Mike." Children of both sexes like to dress up.

There are many strong expressions of friendship: "playmate," "friend." There is some flirtation, and jealousy may be openly and strongly expressed if a friend pays too much attention to some third person.

Children boast not only to the teacher but also to each other: "I'm bigger than you are." "I have better ones at home than this." This is a very strong age for silly language and children can become very silly indeed: "Ready weady? Steady weady?" "My mother's gone goo goo." "Oh wee hee, you can't catch me." "Oh wee hee, I can too, you old poky." (Children also love silly humor in books, as *I Want to Paint My Bathroom Blue*.) Many like to make fun of others but usually are unable to accept humor directed against themselves.

Excluding commands can still be very strong: "Get outta here"; and a new type of verbalization expressed especially by girls is a cold rebuff of some other child: "That's only blocks" (when the child has pretended the blocks were bread). There is even criticism of some physical feature: "Richard, you have big ears." But many are so busy and active that they show less interest than earlier in excluding others. Also at this age there seems to be more emphasis on the positive—which children they *do* like—than on the negative—which ones they *don't* like. They seem able to include friends without necessarily excluding enemies.

Thus at this age, even more than just earlier, there is very little isolated play, only occasional twosomes, and very little play near or with the teacher. To a large extent the children play in highly integrated, self-directed, and lasting groups of three, four, or more children, carrying out cooperative and often highly imaginative doctor play, housekeeping play, and construction play.

TECHNIQUES

PHYSICAL ENVIRONMENT

Environmental restrictions such as shut doors or gates do not hold the child of four years. He responds better to verbal restrictions. The boundaries of a playground can be set verbally: "As far as the tree"; "as far as the gate." Or he can be told to run ahead to the corner and then wait. A feeling of responsibility can be built up in the child. He seems to enjoy knowing what the "rules" are, and will even enforce them. Four may, however, forget rules when led on by gang spirit.

At this age it is particularly desirable to provide nature experiences, such as an opportunity to plant a garden or to care for (caged) animals.

A large room can be effectively divided by means of rugs or some similar device that sets up boundaries without creating actual barriers. This holds the children informally to spheres of interest.

ADJUSTMENT

When adjustment problems occur at this age, they do not result from difficulty at leaving the mother, but rather from the child's preferring interests outside of school and not wanting to come to school. Preferred activities may be playing at home with older children or indulging in some particular passion of the moment.

Since children are more sophisticated at this age than earlier, it is important that the child be greeted on arrival in a manner that takes his individuality into consideration. Generalized greetings are not good now. Most like a warm, personal greeting and some special comment about what they are wearing, who brought them to school, what they are going to do. They enjoy being given some specific job to do at once, perhaps helping with pets or preparing materials.

Children who have some trouble entering the group may be helped by letting them bring something from home that they plan to show or to share with the group. If there is difficulty in releasing parents, they can he helped with such suggestions as "We'll say good-bye and then look out the window and wave."

ROUTINES

Toileting. Routines such as washing, dressing and undressing, midmorning rest go even more smoothly and independently at four than at three. The same is true of toileting, though this routine needs more supervision at this age than formerly because of the extremes of curiosity and reticence displayed by certain children. Some need teacher help in maintaining their privacy from others who are displaying extreme curiosity and silliness in regard to these functions.

But for most, toileting is quite casual and very few problems exist. The first day of school, the teacher shows the toilets to the children and tells them they can use them at any time and that they can go by themselves. Or that if they want a teacher to go with them she will. Thus children may go whenever they wish, but just before rest time all go to the bathroom to wash hands, and can use the toilet if they wish. And a final reminder is given before heavy outdoor clothing is put on at the end of the morning.

Milk and Crackers. Fours enjoy this routine, and conversation now is really lively. One thread of conversation may last for a whole period. Children like to save places for friends. Now most can abide by the rule "One cracker at a time," though the total number of crackers per child is not usually limited. Most can wipe their mouth and throw their cup and napkin away.

Dressing. All children can now help with dressing to a certain degree, and some can dress themselves entirely. If the teacher can put the snow pants on the floor, correctly oriented, this may be all the help the children need. Praise for the one who is independent often gets the others to imitate. Four-year-olds usually need a lot of space when getting dressed. It often works to put clothes in piles around the playroom, and encourage each child to dress near his own pile. They may need special help with drawstrings, zippers, rubbers, or gloves.

Midmorning Rest. This is readily accepted and for the first ten to fifteen minutes may hold up better with music or reading.

Books. Four-year-olds enjoy a long period looking at books and listening to them being read. Some children at four will listen as long as the teacher will read. It is not unusual for children to sit in rapt attention while five or six books are read, for a period as long as forty-five minutes. Since Four is an out-of-bounds age, it is not too surprising to find that the four-year-old has a voracious appetite for the dramatic, and no situation seems bizarre enough to overtax the active imagination of the fantastic, fanciful four-year-old. Children at this age also like books that experiment with words as well as with ideas. They like words flowing in alliterative abundance, words with magical chants, words with extremes of sound effects. They especially love silly humor.

Fours enjoy complexity of event and horror, executions, and miraculous rescues from destruction. Whereas the two-year-old demanded a single picture to a page, the four-year-old delights in a diversity of tiny detail.

Music. Children at this age are also able to enjoy a longer, richer listening experience with music than ever before. Sometimes they respond actively, sometimes passively. They like to express themselves in music, to make music themselves. They like to make up songs. They also like to manipulate materials—scarves, ropes, balls—and relate them to musical expression. They enjoy listening to or experimenting with such instruments as the guitar, recorder, drum, violin.

TRANSITIONS

At the earlier ages transitions from one activity to the next are best accomplished by shifting the group to another room. At this age, however, the same type of transition may be accomplished within the room by adding new materials.

Since this is an age of "tricks," new acquirements such as hopping or skipping can be utilized as activators. For example, "Let's skip to the bathroom."

Their awakening interest in numbers can also be used as an activating technique, as "One for the money, two for the show." "Can you get your suit off before I count ten?" The clock can be utilized in connection with their recognition of numbers, as "When the big hand gets on twelve you may get up."

Transitions are usually easy for four-year-olds because they like a schedule, and they also like to do what the rest of the group is doing. Any balking tends to be an individual problem and can be handled individually. A well-planned schedule fits what the children would naturally like to do, with rest after active times, and active and interesting periods following rest. For the most part, transitions do not present the problem here that they did at earlier ages.

When it comes time to leave, most are glad to see their parents and are quite willing to go. Delays are mostly to show off some product or accomplishment. Those who are slow to leave can often be motivated by appeal to their spirit of competition: "See if you can beat me to the gate."

TEACHER

The need for adult techniques is dropping out considerably at this age. What previously was in the realm of adult techniques is now being used spontaneously by the children and is under voluntary control rather than being superimposed.

It is easier to think preventively with the four-year-old by planning situations in advance with him so that he can work them out himself. Since he is characterized by extremes of activity and inhibition, handling him should be a mixture of holding to the dotted line and yet giving him the freedom he needs.

The teacher may stimulate play at four largely with equipment, and her best techniques may now be applied before the day starts, in planning the day's program and in arranging the room. Most four-year-olds like group work and planned activities, and can best adjust to other children when the play is flexibly organized. Thus the teacher needs to set up in advance centers of play for small groups —doll corner, block corner—and plan that highly noisy and aggressive play will not interfere with quiet play. The four-year-old has a notion of what is proper and is not likely to tolerate cars in the doll corner, as would a younger child.

The teacher should arrange several areas where different kinds of play are encouraged by the equipment: dolls and housekeeping materials in the doll corner; an area provided with good constructive materials, as wood that can be hammered and sawed, blocks, clay, paint—and a box of costumes in another area.

The appearance of free choice can be given if the teacher is working on a material, thereby arousing the child's interest. Sometimes the same material or equipment can be used in different ways on succeeding days, and plans for this should be made in advance. However, Four thrives on variety, and the teacher should anticipate this. With good planning, activities can be kept on a higher level than if the morning starts with free play.

Four-year-olds love projects—making murals, pasting, coloring—and enjoy long periods engaged in such activities.

The activity of four-year-olds will often deteriorate through silliness if not controlled. The adult can sense when play is about to fall apart and can bring in interesting new ideas or elaborate the play. A teacher of four-year-olds needs a wealth of information at her fingertips.

Isolation is an even more effective measure at four than at three because of the stronger social drive. The child accepts isolation best if he is given something to do and is made to feel that he is being isolated because he is tired or not getting on well with the other children rather than because he is being bad. Since this technique is resorted to when the child's behavior is already very low, any suggestion of a punishing attitude would only lower his behavior further. Being isolated from the group or having a privilege removed is serious enough without further punishment. The child organizes his behavior if told that he may look at a book and that the teacher will be back in a few minutes.

At this age the concept "It's the rule" (that no one brings mice or guns to school, or goes out of the yard) will often be accepted without question. The teacher must be careful not to overuse this expression in small, temporary situations. Do not say, "It's the rule that you have to give him that toy." The expression "It isn't fair" can also be useful.

Special silly words are effective. A child may respond better to "Don't be a goober" (any silly or inappropriate word) than to the instruction "Don't push."

Although positive suggestions tend to work better than negative, Fours can respond well to the negative: "Never, never, never!" or "We don't throw stones because people might get hurt."

Fours love exaggeration and verbal silliness, and a teacher can often use these effectively.

VERBAL

Key words used by the adult for three-and-a-halfs, such as "different," "surprise," "guess," etc., are now in the verbal equipment of the child and are used spontaneously, but he still responds to adult use of them. His use of language is so adequate that he does not respond as markedly to key words as earlier. The general *manner* of handling is more important—i.e., he responds to a man-to-man attitude in conversation and management.

The four-year-old demands reasons with "Why?" and "How?" and frequently can be answered by turning a question back to him. Whispering is still as effective as at three and a half.

Children of this age enjoy new, different, and big words. They use and like exaggeration: "as high as the sky"; "in a hundred years." This exaggeration often leads to the telling of "tall stories," which should be enjoyed momentarily by adult and child and then should be brought into perspective by pointing out the difference between real and imaginary.

HUMOR

Their silly language, such as "mitsy, witsy, bitsy," "goofy, woofy, spoofy," can be enjoyed by both adults and children through reading such nursery rhymes as Edward Lear's *A Nonsense Alphabet*. If it becomes excessive it can often be controlled by writing down and reading back to the child what he has said.

OTHER CHILDREN

The tendency (so marked at forty-two months) of two children to exclude any third from their activity persists and can be handled by the techniques already suggested. However, now the teacher may not need to suggest a special role for an excluded child. She may need merely to suggest that others include him in their play.

Most children of this age are gregarious and ready for activities but some do not join in easily. Thus the teacher may need to find a friend for those who need one. As earlier, she may make use of the word "friend." It is good to have on hand kinds of equipment that takes two to play, as a rocking boat, or a game of lotto. Pointing out similarities can stimulate friendship: "You have the same color hair." "You have the same kind of shoelaces." Or friendship can be stimulated by having two children carry a board or clean up the guinea pig cage. Play with dough and clay, where not too much conversation is needed, can help any solitary four-year-olds get acquainted with each other.

Tattling and disputes are fairly frequent and should be handled according to the demands of the situation or of the specific child involved. For instance, the teacher may ask, "What do you want me to do about it?" or "You can take care of that yourself." More serious reports should be commended with some such remark as "I'm glad you told me that the glass is broken. We can pick up the pieces so that no one will get hurt."

Praise and compliment, for appearance or activity, continues to be one of the most effective techniques for making things go smoothly. Frequent talks about expected good behavior from the child often produces good behavior. Or a teacher may say, "I bet he really appreciates the way you helped him." This statement may not only surprise and please both children but may help them cooperate.

Teachers can interpret other people's feelings, or give reasons why they do certain things. Or a teacher may suggest, "I think if you ask him nicely, he'll give you that toy."

If there is much quarreling or other difficulty, the teacher may change the physical setup the next day so as to avoid it. Right at the moment of trouble, some project, such as "moving" (changing the equipment around), may help. At this age children often can work out their own disagreements. If the teacher must intervene, sometimes just standing near does the trick. Sometimes reasoning works. Sometimes physical intervention—carrying a child away—is needed. Humor can be very useful. Or the teacher may fall back on "It's a rule." Or she may say, "I'll look at my watch and let you know when it's your turn."

Four-year-olds enjoy taking on a teacher or mother role in helping to initiate a shy child into group activities. They may do this spontaneously, whereas at three the suggestion usually came from the teacher.

GROUP ACTIVITY

Four is cooperative and imaginative. He can work for a goal such as making a building for dramatic play, instead of merely getting enjoyment from construction as the three-year-old does.

Four-year-olds are more apt to choose group play and to play better in groups than do younger children. Their activities need more careful planning. As discussed under teacher techniques, the teacher can advantageously give children an initial start by doing something that they can take over and elaborate, or by giving verbal suggestions for play. If they do not have this initial start, their own spontaneous play often begins at a much lower level with racing around and pushing each other. Usually both indoor and outdoor play need this initial start, which carries the play through in a constructive manner even though they shift from their original occupation. Four-year-old group behavior tends to change during the week. Children of this age actually improve in their behavior as they act more cohesively as a group in the progression of the week.

Fours usually start the fall quite easily as a group, most being anxious to go to school and excited to be there. Things generally go well for the first few months except for occasional days of boredom, when the teacher may feel she has little to offer. (New materials or rearrangement of the room or program may help when the group becomes bored.)

By spring there may occur a real testing of limits. Children may run out of the yard, urinate outdoors, indulge in other forbidden behaviors. They seem to be trying out the teacher and testing the firmness of the rules. At this time the teacher may need to introduce many new things—movies, trips, walks. An occasional overexuberant child may have to be given a short vacation from school. A teacher should not be discouraged at a spring turn for the worse in her group. Rather, she should consider it a sign that the group is ready for something new and challenging.

A suggested schedule for a four-year-old group is as follows:

Outdoor play	30–40 minutes
Music	10–30 minutes
Indoor free play	40 minutes

Rest
   Looking at books
   Listening to phonograph
   Talking, lying down
	15 minutes

Milk and crackers	5–15 minutes
Stories (children leave when they wish to)	10–30 minutes
Outdoor play	Until they go home

CULTURAL AND CREATIVE ACTIVITY

BOOKS

1. Much more control in listening to stories in larger groups over longer periods.

2. High interest in words, creating stories with silly language and play on words.
3. Enjoyment of nonsense rhymes, as in Edward Lear's *A Nonsense Alphabet*.
4. High interest in poetry, especially rhyming.
5. Delight in humorous stories, as *Junket Is Nice* or *I Want to Paint My Bathroom Blue*.
6. Enjoys exaggeration, as in *Millions of Cats*.
7. Interest in alphabet books, as *The Jingling ABC's*.
8. Interest in stories telling the function and growth of things, as *Mike Mulligan and His Steam Shovel* and *Tim Tadpole and the Great Bullfrog*.
9. Particularly enjoys information books answering his "Why?" about everything in the environment.
10. Awakening interest in religious books, as *The Christ Child*.

MUSIC

1. Increase in voice control, with more approximation to correct pitch and rhythm.
2. A few can sing entire songs correctly.
3. More responsive in group singing.
4. Enjoys taking turns at singing alone.
5. Can play simple singing games.
6. High interest in dramatizing songs.
7. Creates songs during play; often teases others on a variation of the minor third.
8. Likes to experiment with instruments, especially combinations of notes on the piano.
9. Enjoys identifying melodies.
10. Increased spontaneity in rhythms; likes to demonstrate different ways of interpreting music.

PAINTING

1. Holds brush in adult manner.
2. May work with precision for a long time on one painting.
3. Active imagination, with shifting of ideas as he paints.
4. Increase in verbal accompaniment explaining pictures.
5. Makes designs and crude letters.
6. Draws objects with few details.

7. Little size or space relationship—details most important to
   child are drawn largest.
8. Letters, people, etc., may be drawn horizontally, lying down.
9. Enjoys filling in outlines of objects he has drawn, frequently
   making them lose any representative character as interpreted
   by the adult.
10. Beginning of self-criticism.
11. Products have personal value to the child; he wants to take them
    home.

FINGER PAINTING

1. Continued experimentation with fingers, hands, and arms
   in rhythmical manner.
2. Some representation and naming.

CLAY

1. Large masses of clay used.
2. Increase in representation and imagination.
3. Enjoys painting products.
4. Wants products saved.

BLOCKS

1. Cooperation in building in small groups.
2. Extensive complicated structures combining many shapes of
   blocks in symmetrical manner.
3. Combines furniture and other equipment with structures, for
   dramatic play.
4. Enjoys finished product and frequently objects to demolishing it.
5. Little carry-over of interest to following day if structure is
   left standing.

POSSESSIONS

1. Beginning to possess his special contemporaries.
2. Showing off and bragging about possessions to others is
   common. "Mine's bigger than yours."
3. Is more apt to share possessions with special friends than
   with others.

4. Shows off new clothes.
5. Strong feeling for teddy bear. Treats him as a real person, talking to him as a companion and confidant.
6. Proud of big possessions, such as a large bed, about which he can boast.
7. Strong personal feeling for own products made in school; wants to take them home.
8. This is an age of barter and swapping of possessions.
9. May know what a penny or a nickel will buy and may save money to buy more expensive objects. Objects to parting with money.
10. Will help feed and care for pets under parents' direction, but not at all dependable about this.

HOLIDAYS AND FESTIVALS

1. Birthdays—Presents are important and he may have asked for special ones beforehand. "Holds birthdays over" others and talks all during the year about next birthday party and whom he will invite and whom exclude.
2. Christmas—There is a real interest in the story of Jesus, which is talked about and dramatized. Child asks for specific toys for Christmas and talks about them long after Christmas, bragging about size and amount of presents.
3. Valentine's Day—Likes making valentines to send to others. Has some idea that they are a token of friendship. Great interest in the number received.
4. Easter—Still believes in the Easter bunny and talks about things Easter bunny brought him. Still no conception of the meaning of Easter.
5. Halloween—Enjoys jack-o'-lantern and likes to help make his own and take it out in the evening.
6. Thanksgiving—Beginning to have some feeling for the meaning of this holiday. Interested in the story of the Pilgrims.
7. Religion—May sit through a small part of the church service, especially music, but should not be expected to remain through the entire service. Enjoys Sunday school and may say prayers, which he may elaborate from the original. Marked interest in death, heaven, etc. Begins questioning as to the source of things: who made the sun, moon,

world. The common answer, "God," either settles the topic without his finding out what he wanted to know, or may lead to the asking of ludicrous questions about God.

EXCURSIONS

1. Excursions are now a good outlet for out-of-bounds behavior. The child enjoys running ahead of the adult but will wait at crossings.
2. Interested in all kinds of transportation and enjoys talking about trips on a train or airplane. Not only likes to look at things but is interested in how they work.
3. Can go on a short excursion by himself if it doesn't involve crossing the street.
4. Enjoys nature trips.
5. Interested in planning and carrying out picnics and trips to the beach.
6. Continuing interest in the excursions enjoyed at three.

STORYTELLING

Children at four, if we can judge from their spontaneous stories, are creatures of considerable violence. Three-quarters of the stories told by children of both sexes deal with some kind of violent action. Children of both sexes relish telling tales of breaking, disaster, death, and illness. Only 40 percent of girls and 8 percent of boys discuss some kind, gentle, or friendly theme. This is by far the low point for gentleness in little boys.

Girls talk mostly about "Mummy" or some other adult or about animals. Boys talk about "boys," about some adult outside the family, or about animals. Over a third of the girls at this age see their mother as disapproving, disciplining, punishing, or hurting. No boys see her in unfriendly roles. They all picture her as friendly, providing, sympathizing, or protecting. We must conclude that conflict with the mother is stronger by far in girls than in boys at this time of life.

Girls see their fathers as friendly, sympathetic people. No boys mention their father, in any role whatsoever. As at other ages, girls describe mostly social activity or social scene; boys talk mostly about themselves.

Children of both sexes are now spreading out from home, their worlds are enlarging. Nearly half of our four-year-olds tell stories laid in somewhat distant places, other countries, the sea, sky, woods, water. Humor still occurs in only a small percentage of stories and consists now chiefly of describing impossible or unlikely activities: "The boat climbed on a rock." "A house punched itself." "He ate up hisself."

Children at four and a half are still extremely violent, if we can judge from the spontaneous stories they tell. Although this is a low point for violence in girls, it is a high point for violence in boys. The leading kind of violence in girls is that people or animals die, are killed, or are eaten up. Boys describe things smashed, pushed, or crashed into; people or animals dead, killed, or eaten up. Only one-third of each sex tell kind or friendly tales.

Leading characters in stories of girls, as at most ages, are "girls," "mummies," or some kind of animal. Boys talk mostly about "boys," some adult other than parents, or animals.

Girls see their mothers as chiefly friendly (20 percent), sympathizing (20 percent), or hurting (20 percent). Boys see their mothers as either nurturing (29 percent) or as passive victims of aggression (29 percent). Girls at this age see their fathers as chiefly playing negative roles, and a quarter of the girls see him as passive or a victim. The same number of boys see him in this role, but the larger number of boys (half) see their fathers as sympathizing with them or protecting them.

As at four, children of both sexes are spreading their interests far beyond the home. Most stories are laid in distant places. The realism of earlier ages has now given way solidly to fantasy; over half the stories told involve fantasy or imagination.

Humor, though not conspicuous, is present in silly rhyming, in exaggeration, or in describing ridiculous or impossible actions: "David's mother pulled off my nose."

IMAGINATIVE PLAY

As for imaginative play, the realism of the earliest ages has now given way to good use of fantasy and imagination. Many children play with imaginary companions, as described at three and a half, who may be an extremely strong, much enjoyed, and dominating interest in the child's daily life. But by four and a half years, play with imaginary companions begins to occupy less time and attention. The child makes less effort to dominate his family with his companions; may no longer require that they save a seat at the table or a place in the family car for his imaginary friend. Those who do still have their imaginary companion may not talk about him as much to others as they did earlier. As before, if the companion persists, he is usually left at home when the child goes to nursery school.

TELEVISION

Nearly all four-year-olds watch television unless, of course, there is no set in the household. Girls as a rule accept parents' ideas of what and when to watch. Boys are more likely to object, demanding more television time than parents think advisable.

Most parents do admit that although it may create some problems, television-viewing does add to the child's life since it keeps him quiet and entertained; many, however, feel that it should be limited or it becomes too engrossing. Some object because they feel that it is a passive activity; others complain that it gives a distorted view of life.

Programs watched most at this age include, in order of popularity: cartoons, "Lassie," "The Brady Bunch," "Captain Kangaroo," "I Love Lucy," "The Flintstones," and "Sesame Street."

TIME AND SPACE

Past, present, and future all continue to be used freely and about equally. Many new time words or expressions are added at this age. The word "month" is particularly used in different contexts. Also such broad time concepts as "next winter" and "last summer" are used accurately. By now the child seems to have a reasonably clear understanding of when events of the day take place in relation to each other.

The space verbalization of the child of this age includes most of the words used before plus a few new ones. The use of expansive words characteristic of the out-of-bounds tendencies of the four-year-old is outstanding. Some of these words have been used before but are especially prominent now. Thus "on top of," "far away," "out in," "down to," "way up," "way up there," "way far," "out," "way off" are popular. A new dimension is suggested in the use of the word "behind." The child can now tell both on what street and in what city he lives. He can put a ball "on," "under," "in front of," and "in back of" a chair. "In," "on," "up in," "at," and "down" are the space words used most frequently.

CHAPTER 24

ADAPTATION TO INDIVIDUAL DIFFERENCES

Individualized Attendance

Ideally, attendance in nursery school should be determined by the maturity of the child, his disposition and interest, and the motives of his parents. The amount and times of attendance should be, so far as practical, adjusted to the optimal needs of the individual child. Just as in the field of feeding the best practice is now based to some degree on self-demand and self-regulation, so attendance in the nursery school should *when possible* be determined by similar considerations.

By self-demand we mean here the capacity of the child to enjoy and to benefit by attendance. Experience has shown that with increasing age the amount of advantageous attendance tends to increase, with respect to both the length of the session and the number of times per week.

In times long past, when we included eighteen-monthers among our nursery students, we permitted them to attend school for one hour a week. Twenty-one-monthers came for two hours twice a week. Two-, two-and-a-half-, and three-year-olds attended, as a rule, for two and a half hours three times a week. Three-and-a-half- and four-year-olds came to school for two and a half hours five times a week.

However, this attendance plan was extremely flexible. If a child appeared to be unduly fatigued by any one plan, the amount of his school attendance was reduced. If it was felt that he would benefit by additional time in school, this was arranged for. Another possible change was not only in the amount of time spent in school but also in the group in which a child was placed. An extremely mature and rambunctious three-year-old might be moved up into a group of older children. An extremely immature and fragile four-year-old might be moved into a group of children younger than himself.

Things have changed considerably in recent years. We ourselves no longer offer a school opportunity to the very young girl or boy. But we stick to our notion of a flexible attendance program and, at least for the three-year-olds, alternate-day attendance.

Both practical and theoretical considerations have dictated the present attendance schedules. To begin with, although we have always to some extent prided ourselves on our ability to "adjust" even rather reluctant children to the nursery school situation, we have at the same time come to realize that added maturity on the part of the child would diminish the amount of adjustment difficulty experienced. That is, though it is quite possible to solve adjustment problems, we found that if we waited till children were a bit older to start with, these problems often simply did not arise.

Even more important in influencing our policies has been our own increased appreciation of the importance of having each and every boy and girl behaviorally ready for the school situation into which we place him, whether it be nursery school, kindergarten, elementary school, or grades beyond.

We have, through publications, workshops, and work in the schools themselves, strongly emphasized our belief that behavior age rather than chronological age should determine readiness for starting school and for subsequent promotion. Admittedly, the flexible atmosphere of a good nursery school can go much farther than can later school situations in adapting to individual immaturity. However, if our basic principle that each child should be behaviorally ready for the school situation in which we place him is valid, it should be applied even at the nursery school level.

More than that, if we are to encourage parents of immature five-year-olds not to enter their children in kindergarten but to wait an extra year, we can help make this course easier for them by taking care not to push a child through nursery school any faster than his behavior maturity would warrant.

For these reasons, we have come to pay strong attention to the behavior age of each child who enrolls in our guidance nursery and, as our theoretical policy dictates, to consider behavior age as well as chronological age in determining group placement of every child.

It is even hoped that possibly, in time to come, preschool teachers can be taught to administer a short developmental or behavior examination to help in the decision about a child's readiness for kindergarten. More needs to be known not only about a child's rate of growth but also about his individuality and how he adjusts to a group situation.

A teacher could be the key person in arriving at kindergarten-readiness decisions, always, of course, working with the mother and hopefully under the guidance of someone trained in developmental examining. It is our hope that eventually all children will have a developmental and a visual appraisal before starting kindergarten. Too often a child enters kindergarten without the school's knowing what he is like, what kind of past he has experienced, or whether he is actually ready. A preventive program is sorely needed.

Adaptation to Personality Differences

A nursery school teacher, presumably interested in and alert to individual differences, will nevertheless need to make many decisions about and many moves in relation to most children *before* she has had time to come to know them fully. Some general theoretical understanding of personality differences can be of great help to her in her initial contacts with any new group of children as well as in subsequent work with them.

If she is one who finds helpful Sheldon's classifications of human beings as being of primarily endomorphic, mesomorphic, or ectomorphic physiques (as described on pages 33 to 34), the following suggestions may prove useful.

The *endomorphic* child, soft and spherical in shape and tending to be relaxed and sociable by temperament, usually presents less of a problem in school than do children in whom either of the other two physical components predominates. Good-natured and cheerful, the plump little endomorph often asks nothing better than to follow along cozily where a more dominant friend may lead. The true endomorph is a born follower and should not be pushed into taking the lead.

The endomorph likes people and likes to have them like him. Whatever the role somebody else might plan for him, the endomorphic child is usually glad to fit in and play the way others want him to.

Interested in food, and liking to do what is expected of him, the endomorph often is one of the easiest children to guide through midmorning milk and crackers and other domestic routines. Warm and friendly, very responsive to personal approaches, endomorphic children, though they may cry easily, also laugh easily and are easily comforted by close physical contact. A teacher can take them on her lap, as a mother would, and can express sympathy and friendliness. Or she can give them something to eat. Food is especially effective in solving the problems of the endomorph.

The endomorphic child above all loves comfort. If outdoor play is too uncomfortable because of dampness or cold, he will complain. But in general, endomorphy in the nursery school as elsewhere makes for comfortable, easygoing relations with other people in all phases of activity.

The typical *mesomorph*, big-boned, muscular, firm, noisy, and vigorous, loves exercise and activity, loves to dominate. In school as elsewhere he expresses himself through almost constant vigorous, noisy, energetic gross motor activity. He is almost constantly in motion, covers a great deal of ground, and cannot seem to keep his hands off anything. Because of his energy and roughness, the things he touches often break, the children and animals he touches are often hurt. It is difficult for him to sit still, or to obey orders or suggestions, to do things in the way someone else wishes.

A mesomorph, however, with his enthusiasm and energy, can add a great deal to a nursery school group provided there are not too many of his type in any one group and provided the teacher understands his personality and makes allowance and provision for the way in which he will inevitably behave.

First of all, she must recognize that the mesomorphic child finds it very hard to sit still for any long period of time. Thus she should provide many opportunities for active play and make few demands that he remain still.

She must recognize that a child of this physique tends to be very hard to handle. He questions authority; he tests the limits. A teacher must be consistently firm with him but must make some allowance for his exuberance, aggressiveness, and tendency to go out of bounds. She must realize that such children are insatiable touchers, handlers, and explorers but that their ever-active hands are not always skillful. What they touch is all too likely to be dropped, bent, or broken. Since this natural destructiveness is seldom intentional, a teacher should try not to penalize too severely. In fact she may have to "not see" much that such a child does. Otherwise she may find herself engaged in a constant series of head-on collisions. Rerouting, preplanning, substitutions, watchful supervision all aimed to prevent the worst disasters can be more effective in dealing with a child like this than a heavy-handed and direct frontal attack.

Fortunately, though very active, the mesomorph seldom falls and even when he does is not likely to hurt himself. But he may hurt others, who may need to be protected from his often overaggressive approaches. It is wise to recognize that, in playing with other children, mesomorphs must be leaders. They fill this role effectively. It is not necessary to allow everybody a turn at leading—some do not need or like to lead.

The mesomorph likes to be liked. Other children's approval is important to him. What the other children will think, or that he may be "bothering" some other child, can thus often be used in steering a mesomorph's behavior from nonacceptable to acceptable.

Out-of-door play is usually much enjoyed by the mesomorph and presents little problem—in fact he may be at his best out of doors. He may seem quite impervious to rain, cold, snow down his neck. On the Junglegym or other climbing apparatus, this type of child is an enthusiastic, active, and secure climber, nearly always knows what he is doing, has good control, and even if he tumbles seldom minds any but major physical hurts.

The thin, fragile, linear *ectomorphic* child, flat of chest and with long, slender, poorly muscled, or pipestem arms and legs, presents an altogether different picture and, for the teacher, altogether different problems. In fact a teacher will probably need more techniques, and will be more aware of the need for techniques, with him than with any other kind of child. Also, the techniques needed will be quite different in many ways from those used with others. With the mesomorph, the teacher will, to quite an extent, be using her techniques to subdue the child; with the ectomorph, she will be trying to bring him out and to get him to take part in group activities.

Most important, she must realize that the child of ectomorphic physique needs time to warm up—not just hours or days but possibly weeks. Until he does warm up he must be allowed to go his own quiet way. And even once he is warmed up, it is important not to expect too much exuberance. Often such a child prefers to associate with teachers, and must be encouraged, though slowly, to associate with other children.

Children of this type tend to be oversensitive, and thus care must be taken not to hurt their feelings. They dislike trying things unless they think they can do them well—thus much support and encouragement are needed. They are easily embarrassed if too much attention is turned their way; but since they are not quick to speak out and to demand a turn, they may get left out and then *that* hurts their feelings.

The ectomorphic child is extremely vulnerable in almost every respect; he is particularly vulnerable about misunderstandings. His total adjustment may break down because of some very minor things that have gone wrong. If in trouble, he may best be comforted through discussion and distraction on an intellectual level—he often refuses to be picked up or touched or be comforted in ordinary physical ways.

These children have to be helped and encouraged to any physical activity. They do not care much for climbing, running, fast riding, violent jumping, or sliding down from high places. They do not care much for outdoor play, and are at their best indoors when involved in purely imaginative activities—taking on different roles in domestic play or playing with imaginary friends or animals. They greatly enjoy gentle humor, as the use of funny words or amusing ideas in a story. They are enthusiastic about story time.

More than with other preschoolers, the ectomorph's belongings and the things he has made seem almost a part of him. He treasures his art or clay products; loves to bring little things from home and may carry a little china animal or tiny flower around with him throughout an entire school session.

It is important that a teacher recognize his sensitivity, his slowness to warm up, his limited sociability. It is important that she respect his need to watch and wait, often for quite a long time, before he enters into any group or social activity.

One further basic and important individual difference that must be respected, and one that prevails for children of all physical types, is the difference between boy behavior and girl behavior. Though some of the environmentally-minded insist that sex differences come about because society *expects* different things from boys than from girls, our own observation is that large and important sex differences show themselves early and continue late, and are not simply caused by our differential expectations.

Our findings in this matter are described in some detail in a companion volume—*The Guidance Nursery School*, by Pitcher and Ames. Suffice it to say here that girls in general appear to have a more personal and emotional orientation; boys a more objective and logical orientation.

The young girl, much more than the boy, includes *people* in her spontaneous drawings and in her spontaneous stories. Boys draw and talk about *things*. In nursery play, girls know people's names; boys do not. Girls in general are quieter and less aggressive than boys. Boys act; girls talk. Boys are focal; girls peripheral.

As children grow older, differences seem even stronger. By three and a half to four years of age, girls like to play with girls; boys like to play with boys and enjoy behaving in a masculine, aggressive way, swaggering around and calling each other what they consider to be very masculine names, as "Joe" or "Bill."

Boys seem to have more trouble in school than girls do. They show more of what we consider typical two-and-a-half-year-old difficulties, and at four years of age it is the boys who go farthest out of bounds. The teacher of a four-year-old group is quite aware of "the boys" and "the girls" and the differing behavior and interests of each.

EPILOGUE

This book has ended but the story has just begun. *Your* story is beginning because even on our final pages your boy or girl is only five years old and there are many interesting, exciting, and complicated years to follow. *Our* story has just begun because the field of child behavior is still very young. New and effective ways are constantly being developed not only for improving the organism (by better nutrition even before the baby is born) but also for improving our ways of dealing with the organism. Parents themselves are becoming increasingly well informed and skilled. Society is taking an increased interest and an increased responsibility in the welfare of children.

Even by the time your own child is grown and becomes a parent, things may be almost entirely different in many ways from what they are today. As Alvin Toffler points out in his stimulating book *Future Shock*, things are changing so fast today that we all need to be extremely fast and flexible in our thinking if we are to keep up. But so far as children are concerned, the patterned growth of behavior still underlies all that goes on, giving a basis of stability to all the changes.

Thus as we come to the end of this revision, we are stirred by the thought that children are actually pretty much the same as they were when described by us thirty years ago. It is the parents who are changing, and who have a capacity for further change. There has never been such an informed parent group as today. We are thinking especially of those parents who are active and articulate, and who know what they want for their children. The best of this group are working for love of children and there is no better safeguard from taking a wrong turn.

We find that today's parents are *giving* parents. They are willing and eager to give themselves to their children as fully as they are needed, especially during those early years from birth to six years of age. Since they do not wish to raise their children in isolation, many of these parents are reviving community spirit in all sorts of ways. An hour's exchange of caring for each other's infants or toddlers provides time for the mother's shopping, and an expanding experience for the child. Further organization on the part of parents of two-year-olds to provide one or two mornings of group activities for their children, with two mothers at a time supervising, satisfies the needs of the children and gives the other mothers some welcome relief. And best of all, a sharing of experiences with a parent group of six to eight couples meeting once a month, under the supervision of a leader or by themselves, can give parenthood new meaning. A sharing with other parents can often give just the direction needed. Furthermore, the growth of small community centers could be useful, especially if they were staffed with those who could ferret out the needs of the more isolated young parents and help them to organize and intercommunicate.

We are definitely coming into a new spirit of community help for the group as well as for the individual. Already much of the therapy provided by the child specialist for the child in trouble has moved from merely giving help to the individual child to family therapy or even to group therapy.

However, we do feel that the currently proposed almost universal day care centers may be taking a wrong turn. The very young child, under three years of age, still needs much from his home and mother. There will of course be some need for day care centers, as there has always been. But, we may ask, if a mother who works for financial reasons only had a chance to stay at home with her child and didn't have to go to work, would she accept this choice? William J. Shannon of the *New York Times* editorial board has suggested that public money might better be spent in subsidizing a mother to stay at home with her child or children than in providing day care centers for all.

We really need to get down to the business of developing a community with facilities for all to share. Britain could well be our guide. She already provides a good deal in a public way and soon will have nursery schools available for those three- and four-year-olds whose parents wish them to attend.

However, and especially at the earliest ages, it is important that such groups not become too large. Groups of children can steadily increase in size as children grow older but should not increase beyond fifteen or twenty children right through the elementary school years. Smaller groups produce better living, and also better learning. Size of group may be more important than all the fancy methods and innovative materials that are constantly being tried.

We have already mentioned the need of a child to be placed in school and allowed to progress at his maturational age. We need to make children feel comfortable in living and in moving at their own speed, at home and at school. This is why we have described in so much detail the kinds of behavior that we may expect at the successive infant and preschool ages.

It is not important that your child fit the behavior described as appropriate for his exact birthday age. That is not why we describe the ages. Rather, we describe them so that you can, if you wish, find your child's actual behavior level from among those that we portray. If your child is three by the calendar but two and a half by his behavior, that is where you will have to accept him. Then hopefully, you will be willing to expect of him only those things that a two-and-a-half-year-old can do and will use techniques suitable for the two-and-a-half-year-old.

Our age descriptions delineate the path and direction of development. They cannot predict the exact rate at which your individual child will grow. These descriptions are intended to give you comfort, not to make you uneasy. Do not misinterpret them in a way that will make you feel anxious that your child is not up to par. Every child is an individual and part of his individuality involves the way in which and the rate at which he will experience the stages of behavior described here.

One special area not discussed in this volume but one which we hope will receive increasing attention from all parents and child specialists is that of nutrition. We have discussed safeguards through breast-feeding. But are our older children receiving the needed nutrients, the minerals, the vitamins, as well as the calories they need? Are they getting their energy from "junk foods" or what Roger Williams calls "naked" calories derived from processed foods, especially carbohydrates and fats deprived of the essential nutrients necessary for cellular well-being and deprived of the texture that encourages chewing?

Our belief in and concern for individuality needs to extend to each person's nutritional needs. Fortunately each individual has a regulatory mechanism that safeguards his digestive system up to a point. But what if his cells and tissues are not adequately nourished? Some children may need from two to ten times as much of one nutrient as another. We need much more knowledge about these differences and how they can be satisfied.

The chemistry of the body is an all-important area about which nearly all of us—parent and professional alike—know far too little. We agree with Dr. Albert O. Rossi of New York, whose approach to child behavior problems is primarily biochemical. He affirms the hereditary basis of much unsatisfactory school and home behavior. Dr. Rossi maintains that childhood learning disabilities are related to steroid insufficiency, genetically ordained, and that "the only pathway to protein remedial therapy in all areas of learning disability rests on a chemotherapeutic foundation." He agrees with Dr. Gesell that "a child inherits the nexus of his personality structure and his biochemical idiosyncrasies. . . . Early experience may modulate a child's personality but only to a minor degree."

Rossi prophesies poetically that "What our laboratories are discovering in rat brains today, our educators will be applying to your grand-children tomorrow."

One especially important aspect of the child's body—and of that body in action—is the whole area of visual performance. Many children who are in trouble because of inadequate functioning could be helped by an improvement in their visual response. We ourselves hope to make a major contribution in this direction soon.

And since in our opinion so very much of a child's behavior and timing is genetically determined, perhaps the most important advice we could give to you as parents is: *Don't push.* Make all the opportunities and advantages you wish available to your boys and girls. But divest yourselves of the currently popular notion that you can, by anything you do, make your children smarter or more mature than they would have been if you had not pushed them. It is *not* all up to you.

The age-old quarrel between those who feel that heredity determines and those who believe and hope that environment decides will probably never be completely resolved. We personally agree with those who say that heredity deals the cards but environment plays them. You as a parent can indeed see to it that your child has every possible advantage, but you as a parent do not determine the level of his potentialities.

This book has dealt mostly with the individual child, but it has also discussed the child as he interacts with others. We need to know more about both—the child and his body, the child as he relates to others as a member of an expanding community. Before a further revision is in order, we hope to know much more than we now do about both.

APPENDICES

APPENDIX A

Suggested Toys, Play Materials, and Equipment

Improvised and casual materials such as clothespins, discarded containers, firm cloth, clean short lengths of rope, and similar materials are often superior to more elaborate manufactured toys. Toys should of course be clean, and should be of such shape, size, and material that they cannot do harm to eyes, ears, nose, or throat!

BIRTH TO THREE MONTHS

Bright dangling objects
Bright piece of cloth to hang on wall over crib
Ring rattle—bright-colored plastic rings on one larger ring
Silver dumbbell rattle
Rubber squeaking toy
Mobile

THREE TO NINE MONTHS

Tot seat—can be used in home or car
Cradle Gym
Rubber blocks with bells inside
Teething beads
Water ball—heavy plastic with floating objects inside

SIX TO TWELVE MONTHS

High chair
Babee Tenda—seat suspended in the middle of a table (in place of a
  high chair: no tipping; convertible into table)
Spoon and cup
Playpen

NINE TO TWELVE MONTHS

Rubber blocks—good for biting
Square or round block stacks—colorful blocks fitted on large peg
Wooden plates, graduated sizes in primary colors with ball to fit
  on top
Box or basket with large clothespins
Small ball—encourages locomotion
Water toys
Wrist bells

TWELVE TO EIGHTEEN MONTHS

Stroller
Kiddie car—low enough so that child has whole foot on ground
Chair horse on wheels—satisfies child's pushing desire and holds
  child's weight
Cart—to fill and pull
Pull toy—as caterpillar of various colors
Push toy—a small cart with long handle
Sweeping sets with broom and mop
Balls
Blocks—small and bright-colored
Boxes—simple ones to open and close
Nest of circular plastic cups—to fit and take apart, fill and dump
Color cone—bright-colored rings of graduated size to fit over disk

Water toys

Woolly or soft cloth animals—eyes should be painted or embroidered, not buttons attached with sharp points

Cloth dolls and stuffed animals

Books—cloth and heavy cardboard with familiar objects and bright colors

EIGHTEEN MONTHS

Stairs

Chair swing

Rocking horse

Push cart

Pull toy—peg wagon, small cart, animal

Chest of drawers—child's size, easily manipulated

Large ball

Hammer and peg toy

Blocks—colored and small (about two-inch cubes)

Color cone—graduated wooden rings on peg

Pots and pans with covers

Pocketbook

Soft cloth and woolly animals

Wrist bells

Music box

TWENTY-FOUR MONTHS

Boards—for walking up inclines, bouncing, etc. (with cleats on end)

Climbing apparatus with platform easily accessible

Slide—attached to climbing apparatus or steps

Rocking boat

Kiddie car

Cars and trucks

Interlocking trains

Light hollow blocks
Small colored blocks—cylinders, cubes, etc.
Peg boards with large pegs in variety of colors
Jolly Jumper—bouncing seat
Pail and shovel
Baskets
Doll—soft and washable
Doll carriage
Doll bed—large and sturdy enough for child to get in
Dishes—nonbreakable
Iron
Cloth squares of bright colors—for doll covers, tablecloths, etc.
Telephone
Crayons—large size

THIRTY MONTHS

Large packing boxes
Toy logs
Boards for building, carrying, hauling, and walking
Large hollow blocks
Tricycle
Wheelbarrow
Fire truck, steam shovel, dump truck large enough for child to sit
   on
Large wooden beads and string with long metal tip
Screw toys
Clay
Finger paint
Soap bubble pipes
Large paintbrushes for "painting" with water

THIRTY-SIX MONTHS

Climbing apparatus with boards for different platform levels

Sawhorses and boards—for seesaw, bridges, etc.

Large hollow blocks with boards

Kegs

Tricycle

Transportation toys—wagon, train, dump truck, etc.

Solid blocks with unit and multiples of unit, cylinders, quarter circles, triangles, etc.

Simple wooden puzzles with few pieces

Object lotto—a matching game

Soap bubble pipes

Dolls

Doll equipment—bed, carriage, covers

Housekeeping equipment—stove, dishes, broom, clotheslines, clothespins, iron

Crystal climber

Legos—a fitting game

Fiddlesticks

Costume box—with hats, gloves, cloth, pocketbooks, etc.

Blunt scissors

Colored paper

Easel, easel paper, watercolor paint, brushes, at least one-half inch wide

Finger paint

Clay

Mounted pictures of nature, transportation, etc.

FORTY-EIGHT MONTHS

Climbing equipment—Junglegym

Trapeze and rings

Seesaw

Garden tools

Workbench with adult-size hammer, saw, nails, etc.

Blocks—large hollow and small unit

Wooden picture puzzles

Lotto matching games

Tinker Toys

Families of dolls and teddy bears (do not buy oversophisticated
dolls at this age or any other)

Doll clothes with large buttons and buttonholes

Housekeeping equipment

Materials for playing store

Nurses' and doctors' kits

Costume box

Chalkboard and chalk

Whiteboard and crayons

Blunt scissors—sturdy and fairly large

Paste and colored paper

Paint

Clay

Finger paint

Wide variety of nature items

Jump rope

EQUIPMENT SUITABLE THROUGHOUT
THE PRESCHOOL YEARS

Clay

Crayons—large size

Easel

Easel paper—unprinted newspaper satisfactory

Brushes—long handle with brush at least one-half inch wide for
paint

Wider brush with short handle better for "painting" with water

Paint—powder paint mixed with water. Ingredients should be
harmless and nonstaining

Musical instruments—as wrist bells, drums, dinner gong, xylo-
phone, music box

Nature specimens—as fish, turtles, salamanders, snails, birds,
plants, animals

Climbing apparatus—as Junglegym, Tower Gym, ladders, and
   boxes
Small and large boards in combination with climbing apparatus
   increase its usefulness
Packing boxes—large and sturdy enough for a child to climb on
Slide
Boards for balancing and sliding—with cleat on each end to hold
   securely
Bouncing board—suggested proportions 1" × 15" × 13' ash board
Boards and sawhorse—for seesaw, inclines, etc.
Small boards—for building, hauling, etc., suggested size ¾" ×
   6" × 36"
Hollow blocks—suggested size 6" × 12" × 12", and 6" × 12" × 24".
   Building possibilities increased when combined with small boards
Toy logs
Kegs
Sandbox
Sand toys: spoon, sugar scoop, pail, cans, sifter
Pail and shovel
Swing—better home than school equipment
Wheelbarrow
Wagon
Train, dump truck, steam shovel, etc., large enough for child to
   ride on
Small airplanes, automobiles, trucks, boats, and trains
Baskets and boxes
Nests of boxes or cans
Boxes of spools, small blocks, etc.
Rope and string
Animals
Dolls—rubber preferable for bathing purposes
Doll clothing—with large buttons and buttonholes
Doll carriage
Doll bed—sturdy enough and large enough for child to get in
Covers, mattress, pillow

Chest of drawers, cupboard
Suitcases, chest
Table and chair—child's size
Stove
Dishes and cooking utensils
Telephone
Broom, dustpan, mop, dustcloth
Laundry tub, ironing board, iron, adult-size clothespins
Bright-colored squares of cloth—for doll covers, table covers, laundry, costumes, etc.
Costume box—pocketbooks, hats, gloves, scarves, jewelry, curtains, various lengths of cloth, etc.

APPENDIX B

Books for Children

Our thanks are due to Barbara Steinau and Judy Silverman, director and head teacher of the Gesell Guidance Nursery School, for help in compiling this list.

Children's books go out of print very rapidly. If any of the books listed is not available from the publisher try the public library.

FIFTEEN MONTHS TO TWO YEARS

Aliki. *Hush Little Baby*. Englewood Cliffs, N.J.: Prentice-Hall, 1968.

Bright, Robert. *My Red Umbrella*. New York: William Morrow, 1968.

Brown, Margaret Wise. *The Diggers*. New York: Harper, 1960.

Davis, Daphne. *The Baby Animal Book*. New York: Golden Press.

Kruglovsky, P. *The Very Little Boy*. Garden City, L.I.: Doubleday.

——. *The Very Little Girl*. Garden City, L.I.: Doubleday, 1953.

Kunhardt, Dorothy. *Pat the Bunny*. New York: Simon & Schuster, 1962.

Lenski, Lois. *Little Baby Ann*. New York: Walck.

Marino, Dorothy. *Good-bye Thunderstorm*. Philadelphia: Lippincott, 1958.

Martin, Mary Steichen. *The First Picture Book*. New York: Harcourt, Brace, 1930.

Miller, Edna. *Mousekin's ABC*. Englewood Cliffs, N.J.: Prentice-Hall, 1973.

Reich, Hanns. *Baby Animals and Their Mothers*. New York: Hill & Wang, 1965.

Simon, Norma. *What Do I Say?* New York: Whitman, 1967.

———. *What Do the Animals Say?* New York: Young Scott, 1968.

Wildsmith, Brian. *Brian Wildsmith's ABC*. New York: Watts, 1963.

Wright, Blanche. *The Real Mother Goose*. Chicago: Rand McNally, 1966.

TWO TO THREE YEARS

Flack, Marjorie. *Angus and the Ducks*. Garden City, L.I.: Doubleday, 1939.

———. *Ask Mr. Bear*. New York: Macmillan, 1958.

Hurd, Clement. *Bumble Bugs and Elephants*. New York: William R. Scott.

Kraus, Robert. *Goodnight Richard Rabbit*. New York: Springfellow.

Lenski, Lois. *Animals for Me*. New York: Walck, 1941.

———. *The Little Family*. Garden City, L.I.: Doubleday Doran, 1932.

Steiner, Charlotte. *My Slippers Are Red*. New York: Knopf, 1957.

TWO TO FIVE YEARS

Brown, Margaret Wise. *The Little Fireman*. New York: William R. Scott, 1952.

———. *Goodnight Moon*. New York: Harper, 1947.

Krauss, Ruth. *The Carrot Seed*. New York: Harper, 1945.

Langstaff, Nancy. *A Tiny Baby for You*. New York: Harcourt Brace Jovanovich, 1955.

Lenski, Lois. *The Little Auto*. New York: Walck, 1934.

Moore, Clement Clarke. *The Night Before Christmas*. New York: Grosset & Dunlap.

Nakano, Hirotaka. *Elephant Blue*. Indianapolis: Bobbs-Merrill, 1970.

Skaar, Grace. *What Do Animals Say?* New York: Young Scott, 1968.

Tenggren, Gustav. *The Tenggren Mother Goose*. Boston: Little, Brown, 1956.

THREE TO FIVE YEARS

Adam, Barbara. *The Big, Big Box*. Garden City, L.I.: Doubleday.

Brown, Margaret Wise. *The Important Book*. New York: Harper, 1949.

———. *The Noisy Book*. New York: Harper, 1939.

———. *The Country Noisy Book*. New York: Harper, 1940.

———. *The Indoor Noisy Book*. New York: Harper, 1942.

———. *The Seashore Noisy Book*. New York: Harper, 1941.

———. *The Runaway Bunny*. New York: Harper, 1942.

Geis, Darlene. *Dinny, Big Little Dinosaur*. New York: Wonder Books.

Guilfoile, Elizabeth. *Nobody Listens to Andrew*. Chicago: Follett, 1962.

Keats, Ezra Jack. *Whistle for Willie*. New York: Viking, 1964.

McGovern, Ann. *Too Much Noise*. Boston: Houghton Mifflin, 1967.

Moffet, Martha. *A Flower Pot Is Not a Hat*. New York: Dutton, 1972.

Piper, Watty. *The Little Engine That Could*. New York: Platt & Munk, 1930.

Schlein, Miriam. *Fast Is Not a Ladybug*. New York: William R. Scott, 1953.

———. *Heavy Is a Hippopotamus*. New York: William R. Scott, 1954.

Seuss, Dr. *And to Think That I Saw It on Mulberry Street*. New York: Vanguard, 1937.

———. *The Cat in the Hat*. New York: Random House, 1957.

Tudor, Tasha. *Pumpkin Moonshine*. New York: Walck, 1962.

Udry, Janice. *A Tree Is Nice*. New York: Harper, 1956.

Wright, Ethel. *Saturday Walk*. New York: William R. Scott, 1954.

Zolotow, Charlotte. *Do You Know What I'll Do?* New York: Harper, 1958.

———. *William's Doll*. New York: Harper & Row, 1972.

THREE TO SIX YEARS

Bennett, Rainey. *The Secret Hiding Place*. New York: World, 1960.

Brown, Margaret Wise. *Shhhh Bang*. New York: Harper, 1943.

Buckley, Helen. *Grandfather and I*. New York: Lothrop, Lee & Shepard, 1959.

——. *Grandmother and I*. New York: Lothrop, Lee & Shepard, 1965.

——. *My Sister and I*. New York: Lothrop, Lee & Shepard, 1963.

Cook, Bernadine. *The Little Fish That Got Away*. New York: Scholastic Book Services, 1959.

Duvoisin, Roger. *The Rain Puddle*. New York: Lothrop, Lee & Shepard, 1965.

——. *The Crocodile in the Tree*. New York: Knopf, 1973.

Eastman, P. D. *Are You My Mother?* New York: Random House, 1960.

Ets, Marie Hall. *Just Me*. New York: Viking, 1965.

——. *Play with Me*. New York: Viking, 1955.

Flack, Marjorie. *The Story About Ping*. New York: Viking, 1933.

——. *Tim Tadpole and the Great Bullfrog*. Garden City, L.I.: Doubleday, 1934.

Ga'g, Wanda. *Millions of Cats*. New York: Coward-McCann, 1928.

Heide, Florence, and Van Clief, Sylvia. *That's What Friends Are For*. New York: Scholastic Book Services, 1968.

Hoban, Russell. *Bedtime for Frances*. New York: Harper, 1960.

Keats, Ezra Jack. *Peter's Chair*. New York: Harper, 1967.

——. *The Snowy Day* (and others in this series). New York: Viking, 1962.

Kessler, Ethel. *Do Baby Bears Sit on Chairs?* Garden City, L.I.: Doubleday.

——, and Kessler, Leonard. *The Big Red Bus*. Garden City, L.I.: Doubleday, 1964.

——. *The Day Daddy Stayed Home*. Garden City, L.I.: Doubleday, 1971.

Klein, Leonore. *Mud, Mud, Mud*. New York: Knopf, 1962.

Klein, Norma. *Girls Can Be Anything*. New York: Dutton, 1973.

Krasilovsky, Phyllis. *The Man Who Didn't Wash His Dishes*. Garden City, L.I.: Doubleday, 1950.

Krauss, Ruth. *The Backward Day*. New York: Harper, 1950.

——. *The Growing Story*. New York: Harper, 1947.

——. *Happy Day*. New York: Harper, 1949.

Langstaff, Nancy. *A Tiny Baby for You*. New York: Harcourt Brace Jovanovich, 1955.

Lear, Edward. *A Nonsense Alphabet*. Garden City, L.I.: Doubleday, 1962.

Lionni, Leo. *Little Blue and Little Yellow*. New York: Astor-Honor, 1959.

——. *Swimmy*. New York: Pantheon, 1963.

Lobel, Arnold. *A Zoo for Mister Muster*. New York: Harper, 1962.

McCloskey, Robert. *Blueberries for Sale*. New York: Viking, 1948.

——. *Make Way for Ducklings*. New York, Viking, 1941.

Meredith, Brenda. *First Counting and First ABC*. New York: Walck.

Minarik, Else. *Little Bear*. New York: Harper & Row, 1957.

Parsons, Ellen. *Rainy Day Together*. New York: Harper, 1971.

Rey, H. A. *Curious George* (and others in this series). Boston: Houghton Mifflin, 1941.

Ringi, Kjell. *The Sun and the Cloud*. New York: Harper, 1971.

Schick, Eleanor. *A Surprise in the Forest*. New York: Harper, 1964.

Skorpen, Liesel Moak. *Outside My Window*. New York: Harper, 1968.

Slobodkina, Esphyr. *Caps for Sale*. New York: William R. Scott, 1947.

Thompson, Blanche. *All the Silver Pennies*. New York: Macmillan, 1967.

Tippet, James. *I Go A-Traveling*. New York: Harper, 1929.

Villarejo, Mary. *Fuzzy the Tiger*. New York: Knopf, 1962.

Williams, Margery. *The Velveteen Rabbit*. Garden City, L.I.: Doubleday, 1958.

Zion, Gene. *Really Spring*. New York: Harper, 1956.

Zolotow, Charlotte. *The Three Funny Friends.* New York: Harper, 1961.

FOUR TO SIX YEARS

Brenner, Barbara. *Barto Takes the Subway.* New York: Knopf, 1961.

Brown, Margaret Wise. *Three Little Animals.* New York: Harper, 1956.

Duvoisin, Roger. *Our Veronica Goes to Petunia Farm.* New York: Knopf/Pantheon, 1973.

Flack, Marjorie. *The Restless Robin.* Boston: Houghton Mifflin, 1937.

Grollman, Earla. *Talking About Death.* Boston: Beacon Press, 1970.

Hample, Stoo. *The Silly Book.* New York: Harper, 1950.

Krauss, Ruth. *I Want to Paint My Bathroom Blue.* New York: Harper, 1956.

———. *Somebody Else's Nut Tree.* New York: Harper, 1958.

Kunhardt, Dorothy. *Junket Is Nice.* Boston: Houghton Mifflin, 1934.

Kuskin, Karla. *All Sizes of Noises.* New York: Harper, 1962.

Leaf, Munro. *Ferdinand.* New York: Viking, 1962.

Lionni, Leo. *The Biggest House in the World.* New York: Knopf/Pantheon, 1973.

Merriam, Eve. *Boys and Girls: Girls and Boys.* New York: Holt, Rinehart and Winston, 1972.

Milne, A. A. *The Christopher Robin Book of Verse.* New York: Dutton, 1967.

———. *Now We Are Six.* New York: Dutton, 1961.

———. *When We Were Very Young.* New York: Dutton, 1961.

Nôdset, Joan L. *Go Away Dog.* New York: Harper, 1963.

Ray, Wade. *A Train to Spain.* New York: Knopf, 1963.

Ringi, Kjell. *The Magic Stick.* New York: Harper, 1968.

Zolotow, Charlotte. *The Hating Book.* New York: Harper, 1969.

———. *Hold My Hand.* New York: Harper & Row, 1973.

FOUR TO SEVEN YEARS

Burton, Virginia Lee. *Mike Mulligan and His Steam Shovel*. Boston: Houghton Mifflin.

Darrow, Whitney, Jr. *I'm Glad I'm a Boy: I'm Glad I'm a Girl*. New York: Simon & Schuster, 1970.

Duvoisin, Roger. *Day and Night*. New York: Knopf, 1960.

———. *Jasmine*. New York: Knopf, 1973.

Ets, Marie Hall. *Gilberto and the Wind*. New York: Viking, 1963.

Fassler, Joan. *Don't Worry Dear*. New York: Behavioral Publications.

French, Viona. *King Tree*. New York: Walck, 1973.

Guilfoile, Elizabeth. *Have You Seen My Brother?* Chicago: Follett, 1962.

Johnson, Crockett. *Harold and the Purple Crayon*. New York: Harper, 1955.

Klein, Leonore. *Silly Sam*. New York: Scholastic Book Services, 1971.

Lionni, Leo. *The Greentail Mouse*. New York: Pantheon, 1973.

Moore, Lilian. *Little Raccoon and the Outside World*. New York: McGraw-Hill, 1965.

Nôdset, Joan L. *Who Took the Farmer's Hat?* New York: Harper, 1963.

Preston, Edna Mitchell. *The Temper Tantrum Book*. New York: Viking, 1969.

Seuss, Dr. *The Foot Book*. New York: Random House, 1968.

———. *Green Eggs and Ham*. New York: Random House, 1960.

———. *Horton Hatches the Egg*. New York: Random House, 1940.

Showers, Paul. *Your Skin and Mine*. New York: Crowell, 1962.

FOUR TO EIGHT YEARS

Aitchison, Janet. *The Pirate's Tale*. New York: Harper, 1971.

Benton, Robert. *Don't Ever Wish for a Seven-Foot Bear.* New York: Knopf, 1972.

Berger, Terry. *I Have Feelings.* New York: Behavioral Publications.

Brownstone, Cecily. *All Kinds of Mothers.* New York: David McKay, 1969.

Heilbroner, Joan. *The Happy Birthday Present.* New York: Harper, 1961.

Hoban, Russell. *Bread and Jam for Frances.* New York: Harper, 1964.

McCloskey, Robert. *One Morning in Maine.* New York: Viking, 1952.

Minarik, Else Holmelund. *Little Bear.* New York: Harper, 1957.

Parsons, Ellen. *Rainy Day Together.* New York: Harper, 1971.

Rodgers, Mary. *The Rotten Book.* New York: Harper, 1969.

Sendak, Maurice. *Where the Wild Things Are.* New York: Harper, 1963.

Seuss, Dr. *The Cat in the Hat.* New York: Random House, 1957.

Ungerer, Tomi. *The Beast of Monsieur Racine.* New York: Farrar, Strauss & Giroux, 1971.

———. *Crictor.* New York: Harper, 1958.

Ward, Lynd. *The Biggest Bear.* Boston: Houghton Mifflin, 1952.

Withers, Carl. *Painting the Moon.* New York: Dutton, 1970.

Zion, Gene. *Harry, the Dirty Dog.* New York: Harper, 1956.

———. *No Roses for Harry.* New York: Harper, 1959.

———. *The Plant Sitter.* New York: Harper, 1959.

Zolotow, Charlotte. *Big Sister and Little Sister.* New York: Harper, 1966.

———. *The Quarreling Book.* New York: Harper, 1963.

———. *The Sky Was Blue.* New York: Harper, 1963.

———. *Someday.* New York: Harper, 1965.

FIVE TO SEVEN YEARS

Crews, Donald. *We Read: A to Z.* New York: Harper, 1967.

Delessert, Etienne. *How the Mouse Was Hit on the Head by a Stone*

and So Discovered the World. Garden City, L.I.: Doubleday, 1971.
Lionni, Leo. *The Alphabet Tree.* New York: Pantheon, 1968.
———. *Frederick.* New York: Pantheon, 1967.
Raskin, Ellen. *Spectacles.* New York: Atheneum, 1968.
Zolotow, Charlotte. *A Father Like That.* New York: Harper & Row, 1971.

FIVE TO TEN YEARS

Grayson, Marion. *Let's Do Fingerplays.* New York: Robert Luce, 1962.
Kuskin, Karla. *Any Me I Want to Be.* New York: Harper & Row.
Post, Henry, and McTwigan, Michael. *Clay Play: Learning Games for Children.* Englewood Cliffs, N.J.: Prentice-Hall, 1973.
Silverstein, Shel. *The Giving Tree.* New York: Harper, 1964.

ALL AGES

Le Gallienne, Eva. *Andersen's The Nightingale.* New York: Harper, 1965.
White, E. B. *Charlotte's Web.* New York: Harper & Row.
———. *Stuart Little.* New York: Harper & Row.
———. *The Trumpet of the Swan.* New York: Harper & Row, 1970.

APPENDIX C

Selected Readings

Aldrich, C. Anderson, and Aldrich, Mary H. *Babies Are Human Beings*. New York: Macmillan, 1938.

Ames, Louise B. The sense of self of nursery school children as manifested by their verbal behavior. *J. Genet. Psychol.* 81 (1952): 193–232.

———. Children's Stories. *Genet. Psychol. Monog.* 74 (1966): 337–96.

———. *Is Your Child in the Wrong Grade?* New York: Harper & Row, 1966.

———. *Child Care and Development*. Philadelphia: Lippincott, 1970.

Ames, Louise B., and Chase, Joan A. *Don't Push Your Preschooler*. New York: Harper & Row, 1974.

Ames, Louise B., and Ilg, Frances L. The developmental point of view with special reference to the principle of reciprocal neuromotor interweaving. *J. Genet. Psychol.* 105 (1964): 195–209.

———. *Parents Ask*. Syndicated daily newspaper column. New York: Publishers Hall Syndicate, 1950–.

Ames, Louise B., and Learned, Janet. Imaginary companions and related phenomena. *J. Genet. Psychol.* 69 (1947): 147–67.

Augenstein, Leroy. *Come, Let Us Play God*. New York: Harper & Row, 1969.

Beck, Helen. *Don't Push Me, I'm No Computer*. New York: McGraw-Hill, 1973.

Berson, Minnie P. *Kindergarten: Your Child's Big Step*. New York: Dutton, 1959.

Bley, Edgar S. *Have Fun with Your Son*. New York: Sterling Press, 1954.

———. *Launching Your Preschooler: Ways to Help Your Child in His First Experiences*. New York: Sterling Press, 1955.

Bonham, Marilyn. *The Laughter and Tears of Children*. New York: Macmillan, 1968.

Brazleton, T. Berry. *Infants and Mothers*. New York: Delacorte Press, 1969.

Cannon, Walter. *The Wisdom of the Body*. New York: Norton, 1963.

Capa, Cornell, and Pines, Maya. *Retarded Children Can Be Helped*. New York: Channel, 1957.

Carl, Barbara, and Richard, Nancy. *School Readiness: One Piece of the Puzzle*. Peterborough, N.H.: New Hampshire School Readiness Project, 1972.

Chess, Stella; Thomas, Alexander, and Birch, Herbert G. *Your Child Is a Person*. New York: Viking, 1965.

Children's Bureau. *Infant Care*. Children's Bureau Publication no. 8, U.S. Government Printing Office.

———. *Prenatal Care*. Children's Bureau Publication no. 4, U.S. Government Printing Office.

Cleveland, Anne. *Parent from Zero to Ten*. New York: Simon & Schuster, 1958.

Coffin, Patricia. *1,2,3,4,5,6: How to Understand and Enjoy the Years That Count*. New York: Macmillan, 1972.

Collier, Herbert L. *The Psychology of Twins: A Practical Handbook for Parents*. Phoenix, Ariz.: Twins, 1972.

Cooper, Boyd. *Sex Without Tears*. Los Angeles: Charles Press, 1972.

Cross, Aleene A. *Enjoying Family Living*. Philadelphia: Lippincott, 1967.

Currah, Ann M. *Best Books for Children. A Catalogue of 4000 titles, 1967 edition*. New York: R. R. Bowker Co.

Cutts, Norma, and Moseley, Nicholas. *Better Home Discipline*. New York: Appleton, 1952.

——. *The Only Child*. New York: Putnam, 1954.

Despert, J. Louise. *Children of Divorce*. Garden City, N.Y.: Doubleday, 1953.

Dodson, Fitzhugh. *How to Parent*. Los Angeles: Nash, 1970.

——. *How to Father*. Los Angeles: Nash, 1974.

Doss, Carl, and Doss, Helen. *If You Adopt a Child*. New York: Holt, 1957.

Edwards, Vergene. *The Tired Adult's Guide to Backyard Fun with Kids*. New York: Crowell, 1957.

Eisenberg, Helen, and Eisenberg, Larry. *Family Fun at Home*. New York: Association Press, 1966.

Erikson, Eric. *Childhood and Society*. Rev. ed. New York: Norton, 1963.

Fass, Jerome. *A Primer for Parents. A Child Psychiatrist's Advice for Raising Emotionally Healthy Children*. New York: Trident Press, 1968.

Flanagan, Geraldine Lux. *The First Nine Months of Life*. New York: Simon & Schuster, 1962.

Foote, Franklin M. *Child Development Chart: From Birth Through Sixteen Years*. Hartford: Connecticut State Department of Health, 1967.

Forer, Lucille K. *Birth Order and Life Roles*. Springfield, Ill.: C. C. Thomas, 1969.

Fraiberg, Selma. *The Magic Years*. New York: Scribner's, 1959.

Gardner, Richard A. *The Boys and Girls Book About Divorce*. New York: Science House, 1970.

——. *Understanding Children*. New York: Aronson, 1973.

Gersh, Marvin J. *How to Raise Children at Home in Your Spare Time*. New York: Stein & Day, 1966.

Gesell, Arnold, and Amatruda, Catherine S. *Developmental Diagnosis*. New York: Haber, 1947.

Ginott, Haim. *Between Parent and Child*. New York: Macmillan, 1965.

Graham, Phyllis. *Care and Feeding of Twins*. New York: Harper & Row, 1955.

Grollman, Rabbi Earl A., ed. *Explaining Death to Children*. Boston: Beacon Press, 1969.

Gruenberg, Sidonie. *The Wonderful Story of How You Were Born*. New York: Hanover House, 1952.   ·

Guttmacher, Alan E. *Babies by Choice or by Chance*. Garden City, N.Y.: Doubleday, 1959.

Haire, Doris. *The Cultural Warping of Childbirth*. Milwaukee: International Childbirth Education Association, 1972.

Harms, Ernest. *Problems of Sleep and Dreams in Children*. New York: Pergamon Press, 1965.

Hartley, Ruth, and Goldenson, Robert. *The Complete Book of Children's Play*. New York: Crowell, 1957.

Hechinger, Fred M., ed. *Preschool Education Today*. New York: Doubleday, 1966.

Holmes, Carl A. *Letters to Tricia: A Pediatrician Writes to his Daughter*. Los Angeles: Sherbourne Press, 1966.

Holt, L. Emmett, Jr. *Good Housekeeping Book of Baby and Child Care*. New York: Appleton-Century-Crofts, 1957.

Hymes, James L., Jr. *The Child Under Six*. Englewood Cliffs, N.J.: Prentice-Hall, 1963.

Ilg, Frances L., and Ames, Louise B. *Child Behavior*. New York: Harper & Row, 1958.

——. *Parents Ask*. New York: Harper & Row, 1962.

——. *School Readiness*. New York: Harper & Row, 1964.

Kawin, Ethel. *The Wise Choice of Toys*. Chicago: University of Chicago Press, 1940.

Klein, Ted. *The Father's Book: A Common Sense Guide for Every Man Who Wants to Be a Better Father*. New York: Morrow, 1968.

Kraskin, Robert A. *You Can Improve Your Vision*. Garden City, N.Y.: Doubleday, 1968.

Laird, Donald A., and Laird, Eleanor C. *Sound Ways to Sound Sleep*. New York: McGraw-Hill, 1959.

La Leche League. *The Womanly Art of Breast Feeding*. Franklin Park, Ill.: La Leche League, 1963.

Levine, Milton I., and Seligmann, Jean H. *The Parents' Encyclopedia of Infancy, Childhood and Adolescence.* New York: Crowell, 1973.

Liley, H. M. (with Beth Day). *Modern Motherhood: Pregnancy, Childbirth and the Newborn Baby.* New York: Random House, 1969.

Lowndes, Marion. *A Manual for Baby-sitters.* Rev. ed. Boston: Little, Brown, 1961.

McIntire, Roger W. *For Love of Children.* Del Mar, Calif.: CRM Books, 1970.

McKay, Stella. *Your Child's Health from Birth to Adolescence.* Garden City, N.Y.: Doubleday, 1965.

Maynard, Fredelle. *Guiding Your Child to a More Creative Life.* Garden City, N.Y.: Doubleday, 1973.

Miles, Walter R. *Arnold Lucius Gesell. Vol. XXXVII of Biographical Memoirs,* Natl. Acad. Sci. New York: Columbia University Press, 1964.

Montague, Ashley. *Touching.* (Chapter III, on Breast-feeding). New York: Columbia University Press, 1971.

Moore, Mary Furlong. *The Baby Sitter's Guide.* New York: Crowell, 1953.

Moore, Raymond. "The Dangers of Early Schooling." *Harper's Magazine,* July 1972, pp. 58–62.

Moore, Sally Beth, and Richards, Phyllis. *Teaching in the Nursery School.* New York: Harper & Row, 1959.

Murray, Henry A. *Personality, Nature, Society and Culture.* New York: Knopf, 1953.

Offen, J. Allan. *Adventure to Motherhood: The Picture Story of Pregnancy and Childbirth.* New York: Simon & Schuster, 1964.

Patterson, Gerald R. *Families.* Champaign, Ill.: Research Press, 1971.

Pearlman, Ruth. *Feeding Your Baby the Safe and Healthy Way.* New York: Random House, 1971.

Pitcher, Evelyn G., and Ames, Louise B. *The Guidance Nursery School.* Rev. ed. New York: Harper & Row, 1974.

Pryor, Karen. *Nursing Your Baby.* New York: Harper & Row, 1963.

Pulaski, Mary Ann Spencer. *Understanding Piaget: An Introduction to Children's Cognitive Development*. New York: Harper & Row, 1971.

Richardson, Frank Howard. *The Nursing Mother*. Englewood Cliffs, N.J.: Prentice-Hall, 1953.

Rimland, Bernard. *Infantile Autism*. New York: Appleton-Century-Crofts, 1963.

Rondell, Florence, and Michaels, Ruth. *The Adopted Family*. New York: Crown, 1951.

Rossi, Albert O. "The Slow Learner." *New York State Journal of Medicine*, 68 (1968): 3123–28.

———. "Genetics of Higher Level Disorders." *J. Learning Disabilities*. 3 (1970): 387–90.

Sheldon, William H. *The Varieties of Temperament*. New York: Hafner, 1970.

Siegel, Ernest. *Helping the Brain Injured Child*. New York: Association for Brain Injured Children, 1961.

Skousen, W. Cleon. *So You Want to Raise a Son*. Garden City, N.Y.: Doubleday, 1962.

Smith, Lendon H. *The Children's Doctor*. Englewood Cliffs, N.J.: Prentice-Hall, 1969.

Smith, Robert Paul. *How to Grow Up in One Piece*. New York: Harper & Row, 1963.

Spock, Benjamin. *The Common Sense Book of Baby and Child Care*. New York: Duell, Sloan and Pearce, 1946.

Tanzer, Deborah, with Block, Jean Libman. *Why Natural Childbirth?* Garden City, N.Y.: Doubleday, 1972.

Thomson, Helen. *The Successful Stepparent*. New York: Harper & Row, 1966.

Toffler, Alvin. *Future Shock*. New York: Random House, 1970.

Wenar, Charles. *Personality Development from Infancy to Adulthood*. Boston: Houghton Mifflin, 1971.

Williams, Roger J. *Nutrition Against Disease*. New York: Pitman, 1971.

Wolff, Peter H. "Critical Periods in Human Cognitive Development." Chapter in *Annual Progress in Child Psychiatry and Child Devel-*

opment, 1971, ed. Chess and Thomas. New York: Brunner/Mazel, 1971.

Woodcock, Louise P. *Life and Ways of the Two Year Old.* New York: Dutton, 1941.

Wunderlich, Ray C. *Allergy, Brains & Children Coping.* St. Petersburg, Fla.: Johnny Reads Press, 1973.

Wylie, Evan McLeod. *The Nine Months.* New York: Grosset & Dunlap, 1971.

INDEX